WRITTEN DOCUMENTS IN THE WORKPLACE

STUDIES IN WRITING
Series Editor: **Gert Rijlaarsdam**

Recent titles in this series:

VAN WAES, LEIJTEN AND NEUWIRTH
Writing and Digital Media

SULLIVAN AND LINDGREN
Computer Key-Stroke Logging and Writing

HIDI AND BOSCOLO
Writing and Motivation

TORRANCE, VAN WAES AND GALBRAITH
Writing and Cognition

Related journals:

Learning and Instruction
Educational Research Review
Assessing Writing
Computers and Composition
Journal of Second Language Writing

WRITTEN DOCUMENTS IN THE WORKPLACE

EDITED BY

D. ALAMARGOT
Université de Poitiers, France

P. TERRIER
Université de Toulouse Le Mirail, France

J. -M. CELLIER
Université de Toulouse Le Mirail, France

Amsterdam • Boston • Heidelberg • London • New York • Oxford
Paris • San Diego • San Francisco • Singapore • Sydney • Tokyo

Elsevier
Linacre House, Jordan Hill, Oxford OX2 8DP, UK
Radarweg 29, PO Box 211, 1000 AE Amsterdam, The Netherlands

First edition 2007

Copyright © 2007 Elsevier Ltd. All rights reserved

No part of this publication may be reproduced, stored in a retrieval system
or transmitted in any form or by any means electronic, mechanical, photocopying,
recording or otherwise without the prior written permission of the publisher

Permissions may be sought directly from Elsevier's Science & Technology Rights
Department in Oxford, UK: phone (+44) (0) 1865 843830; fax (+44) (0) 1865 853333;
email: permissions@elsevier.com. Alternatively you can submit your request online by
visiting the Elsevier web site at http://www.elsevier.com/locate/permissions, and selecting
Obtaining permission to use Elsevier material

Notice
No responsibility is assumed by the publisher for any injury and/or damage to persons
or property as a matter of products liability, negligence or otherwise, or from any use
or operation of any methods, products, instructions or ideas contained in the material
herein. Because of rapid advances in the medical sciences, in particular, independent
verification of diagnoses and drug dosages should be made

British Library Cataloguing in Publication Data
A catalogue record for this book is available from the British Library

Library of Congress Cataloging-in-Publication Data
A catalog record for this book is available from the Library of Congress

ISBN: 978-0-080-47487-8

For information on all Elsevier publications
visit our website at books.elsevier.com

Printed and bound in The Netherlands

07 08 09 10 11 10 9 8 7 6 5 4 3 2 1

Working together to grow
libraries in developing countries

www.elsevier.com | www.bookaid.org | www.sabre.org

ELSEVIER   BOOK AID International   Sabre Foundation

Contents

Contributors vii
Long Abstract xi
Introduction: Written Documents in the Workplace xiii
        Jean-Marie Cellier, Patrice Terrier and Denis Alamargot

Section 1   **Defining Professional Documents** 1

Chapter 1   Linguistic Markers of Lexical and Textual Relations in
                 Technical Documents 3
                 Anne Condamines and Marie-Paule Péry-Woodley

Chapter 2   The Design, Understanding and Usage of Pictograms 17
                 *Charles Tijus, Javier Barcenilla, Brigitte Cambon de Lavalette and
                 Jean-Guy Meunier*

Chapter 3   Readability and Intelligibility of Procedural Texts: The Case of
                 Enumeration in Legal Texts 33
                 Céline Beaudet and Pamela Grant

Section 2   **Composing Documents** 47

Chapter 4   Considering Users and the Way They Use Procedural Texts:
                 Some Prerequisites for the Design of Appropriate Documents 49
                 Franck Ganier and Javier Barcenilla

Chapter 5   Highly Effective Writers and the Role of Reading: A Cognitive
                 Approach to Composing in Professional Contexts 61
                 Thomas Quinlan and Denis Alamargot

Chapter 6   Professional Editing: Emphasis on the Quality of a Text and
                 Its Communicative Effectiveness 75
                 Jocelyne Bisaillon

Chapter 7   Procedural Texts Written by Children 95
                 Eduardo Martí and Merce Garcia-Mila

Chapter 8   Developing an Online Writing Tutor to Improve Technical-Writing
                 Skills in Engineering and Science Students 107
                 *John R. Hayes, Diana M. Bajzek, Judy Brooks, Brenda Reyes,
                 Nicole Hallinen and Erwin R. Steinberg*

Chapter 9   The Implications of Blogs for Professional Writing: Speed, Reach, Engagement, and the Art of the Self in the Participatory Web 125
Doreen Starke-Meyerring

Chapter 10   The Production of Work Instructions in an Industrial Workplace: The Impact of a Functional Writer's Work Context on the Outcome of His Activity 139
Véronique Barret, Isabelle Clerc and Sylvie Montreuil

Section 3   **Understanding Documents** 159

Chapter 11   Situation Models and Their Role in Comprehension: The Need to Study Their Internal Structure 161
Isabelle Tapiero and José Otero

Chapter 12   The Effects of Interaction with the Device and Text Structure on the Mental Representations Derived from the Procedure 177
Patrice Terrier, Virginia Diehl and Julie Lemarié

Chapter 13   Comprehension Processes in Translation 193
Pedro Macizo and Maria Teresa Bajo

Chapter 14   How Reading Strategies Affect the Comprehension of Texts in Hypertext Systems 205
R. Ignacio Madrid and José J. Cañas

Chapter 15   Task-Guidance Systems and Procedure Context: Enabling Procedures to Enhance Worker Performance 217
Jennifer Ockerman

Chapter 16   Animated Documentation: A Way of Comprehending Complex Procedural Tasks? 231
Richard K. Lowe

Chapter 17   The Impact of Cognitively Based Design of Expository Multimedia 243
N. Hari Narayanan

References 261
Author Index 297
Subject Index 309

Contributors

Denis Alamargot
Laboratoire LMDC—Langage, Mémoire, & Développement Cognitif,
CNRS—Université de Poitiers, France

Teresa Bajo
University of Granada, Spain

Diana M. Bajzek
Carnegie Mellon University, Pittsburgh, PA, USA

Javier Barcenilla
ETIC—Equipe Transdisciplinaire sur l'Interaction et la Cognition,
EA 3947—Laboratoire de Psychologie de Lorraine, LABPSYLOR,
Université Paul Verlaine, Metz, France

Véronique Barret
Groupe Rédiger—Centre interdisciplinaire de recherches sur les activités langagières
(CIRAL), Groupe interdisciplinaire de recherche sur l'organisation et la santé au travail
(GIROST) chaire en gestion de la santé et de la sécurité du travail, Université Laval,
Québec, Canada

Céline Beaudet
Réseau canadien de recherches interdisciplinaires en rédactologie (RCRIR), Département
des lettres et communication, Université de Sherbrooke, Sherbrooke, Canada

Jocelyne Bisaillon
Centre interdisciplinaire de recherches sur les activités langagières (CIRAL),
Université Laval—Québec, Canada

Judy Brooks
Carnegie Mellon University, Pittsburgh, PA, USA

Brigitte Cambon de Lavalette
National Transport and Road Safety Research Institute, INRETS, France

José J. Cañas
University of Granada, Spain

Jean-Marie Cellier
Laboratoire Travail & Cognition—LTC, CNRS—Université de Toulouse Le Mirail, France

Isabelle Clerc
Groupe Rédiger—Centre interdisciplinaire de recherches sur les activités langagières (CIRAL), Department of Information and Communication, Université Laval, Québec, Canada

Anne Condamines
Université de Toulouse, CLLE-ERSS, Cognition Langue Langage Ergonomie-Equipe de Recherche en Syntaxe et Sémantique, CNRS, UTM, France

Virginia Diehl
Psychology Department, Western Illinois University, Macomb, IL, USA

Franck Ganier
Laboratoire d'Informatique des Systèmes Complexes (LISyC—EA 3883), Equipe SARA (Simulation—Apprentissage—Représentation—Action), Centre Européen de Réalité Virtuelle, Université de Bretagne Occidentale, Brest, France

Merce Garcia-Mila
School of Psychology, University of Barcelona, Spain

Pamela Grant
Canadian Network for Interdisciplinary Research on Rhetoric and Wrting (CNIRRW), Département des lettres et communication, Université de Sherbrooke, Sherbrooke, Canada

Nicole Hallinen
Carnegie Mellon University, Pittsburgh, PA, USA

John R. Hayes
Carnegie Mellon University, Pittsburgh, PA, USA

Julie Lemarié
Laboratoire Travail & Cognition—LTC, CNRS—Université de Toulouse Le Mirail, France

Richard K. Lowe
Curtin University, Perth WA, Australia

Pedro Macizo
University of Granada, Spain

R. Ignacio Madrid
University of Granada, Spain

Eduardo Martí
School of Psychology, University of Barcelona, Spain

Jean-Guy Meunier
University of Quebec in Montreal, Canada

Sylvie Montreuil
Group interdisciplinaire de recherche sur l'organisation et la santé au travail (GIROST), Chaire en gestion de la santé et de la sécurite du travail, Department of Industrial Relations, Université Laval, Québec, Canada

N. Hari Narayanan
Intelligent and Interactive Systems Research Group, Department of Computer Science and Software Engineering, Auburn University, Auburn, AL, USA

Jennifer Ockerman
Johns Hopkins University Applied Physics Laboratory, Laurel, MD, USA

José Otero
University of Alcala, Madrid, Spain

Marie-Paule Péry-Woodley
Université de Toulouse, CLLE-ERSS, Cognition Langue Langage Ergonomie-Equipe de Recherche en Syntaxe et Sémantique, UTM, CNRS, France.

Thomas Quinlan
Educational Testing Service, Princeton, New Jersey, USA

Brenda Reyes
Carnegie Mellon University, Pittsburgh, PA, USA

Doreen Starke-Meyerring
Centre for the Study and Teaching of Writing, McGill University, Montréal, Canada

Erwin R. Steinberg
Carnegie Mellon University, Pittsburgh, PA, USA

Isabelle Tapiero
Laboratoire EMC—Etude des Mécanismes Cognitifs, University of Lyon 2, France

Patrice Terrier
Laboratoire Travail & Cognition—LTC, CNRS—Université de Toulouse, France

Charles Tijus
Laboratoire Cognition & Usages, University of Paris 8, France

Long Abstract

With contributions from linguists, psychologists and ergonomists from various countries and continents, *Written Documents in the Workplace* seeks to bridge the gap between fundamental research into writing and reading and the issue of the efficiency of written communication in the workplace. The book is divided into three parts, the first of which provides a linguistic definition of professional documents, describing their different types and genres. This definition necessarily takes into account both the formal characteristics of these types of document (e.g. nature of linguistic units involved) and their functional goals (the way these linguistic units are used to fulfill the text's communicative aim). The second part focuses on the mental mechanisms involved in written production in the workplace. One of the aims of a professional writer is to compose a text that can be understood. Nevertheless, while it is vital to know something about the intended reader, there is more to it than that. Text composition involves specific processes and strategies that can be enhanced. One way of doing this is to give the writer suitable instructions, while another is to provide him/her with a suitable writing environment. This last aspect leads us to devote the third and final section to the comprehension of written documents in the workplace. Awareness of the strategies implemented by different readers (with more or less domain expertise) in order to understand technical and professional documents can enhance the latter's readability. Improvements in surface form and content structure are discussed and can be regarded as recommendations to professional writers.

Introduction: Written Documents in the Workplace

J.-M. Cellier, P. Terrier and D. Alamargot

Enhancing the Production and Comprehension of Written Documents

The quality of information transmission would appear to be a determining factor for both private companies and public services. In this context, the increasing use of computers and digital tools seems to have led to an increase in the number of written documents used to communicate or store information. One of the major issues in the workplace is the ability to produce relevant and effective documents as efficiently as possible. Aeronautics companies are frequently quoted as a typical example, as it is said that the documents relating to the airbus fill a space the size of an aircraft.

The term "professional documents" covers everything from instructions and guidelines to recipes and directions for use. These documents are characterized by the diversity of their contents (instructions, documentation, administrative files, etc.), the variety of their format (paper, digital) and their communicative goals (transmission or storage of information). Broadly speaking, the purpose of this type of text is to help people understand or perform a task (describing how to assemble parts or use a technical device, analyzing a technical problem, setting out new rules, justifying a decision, explaining a reform, etc.).

The technical (reliability of device), legal (causes of accidents, liability) and financial (consequences of misuse) impacts of professional documents have frequently been underlined (Veyrac, 2001; Virbel, 1999). And yet, as Heurley (1994, p. 6) has pointed out, these types of text are often inefficient, are very seldom studied and even more seldom taught.

It is tempting to assume that the professionals at whom most technical documents are aimed possess sufficiently homogeneous and expert knowledge to be able to understand them properly. However, many studies (e.g. Brangier, Barcenilla, & Eberhart, 2000; De Brito, 2000; Frantz, 1993; Park & Jung, 2003) have highlighted the difficulty of using technical documents properly, especially work (or safety) instructions. We can point to several causes: (1) the instructions may have been poorly drafted and their semantic and linguistic characteristics may make it impossible to construct a valid representation (Heurley & Ganier, 2002); (2) the user-reader does not possess the linguistic and/or referential skills needed to decode the text and grasp its meaning; and (3) the instructions are followed in an inappropriate context, thereby preventing the reader from making full use of the information contained in the written texts.

Although, as suggested above, most users (or readers) of technical documents are professionals, in the case of administrative documents, they may also include a broader range of people. Most of the time, they are written by people who are not text production specialists, and aimed at professionals or users who do not always possess the knowledge needed to grasp the meaning of the text. For all these reasons, professional writing can be a source of problems and numerous observations attest to the fact that poor comprehension of a crucial instruction can lead to serious dysfunctions or accidents. The best way of identifying the

Cellier, J.-M., Terrier, P. & Alamargot, D. (2007). Introduction: Written documents in the workplace. In G. Rijlaarsdam (Series Ed.) and D. Alamargot, P. Terrier, & J.-M. Cellier (Vol. Eds.), Studies in Writing, Vol. 21, Written Documents in the Workplace, xi–xviii.

causes of these difficulties in using or producing technical documents properly is to analyze the processes of production and comprehension, and the ways in which written documents are used in the workplace (Alamargot et al., 2005).

The Written Document in the Workplace: A Muldimensional Object

We can only improve the production and understanding of written documents in the workplace once we have actually defined them. However, these types of document have seldom been studied by researchers, even though they are extremely diverse and can have important social consequences. What, for instance, do a Post-It and an expert's report, a set of specifications and a memo, or a brochure and a traveler have in common? In the course of archiving the literature produced by French textile firms, Cottereau, Daviet, and Thévenot (1989) identified two main types of document: internal documents (rules and regulations, sets of procedures, etc.) and those intended for people outside the firm (customers and suppliers). Although this distinction between the company's internal and external targets is useful for making an initial classification, it is a crude one, and more fine-grained distinctions can be made, especially for in-house documents. For example, we can distinguish between private documents (for the writer's personal use) and ones intended for more or less public consumption. Another important dimension is the degree of formality and predetermination (e.g. forms).

The variety of a document's potential objectives is a heavy constraint for the writer, as the workplace is a far from neutral writing context. Issues of power and hierarchy constitute social constraints that modulate cognitive production processes, with the result that some documents serve chiefly to protect their authors against any future liability.

The diversity of readers targeted by this written communication is another constraint. Linguistic skills are unevenly spread within an organization. This is true not only of the writers but also the users of documents. It is not uncommon to find employees who are either illiterate or have very poor reading skills. The co-existence of workers who are poorly educated and have different mother tongues is another aggravating factor for document production.

In documents intended for personal use (notebooks, Post-Its, etc.), the writer and user are one and the same and there are relatively few writing constraints. If a document has to address a large number of potential users however, the writer must juggle with the diversity of their linguistic and technical skills as well as with their social position within the organization. Here, the constraints on the writing process are far greater. In this situation, Boutet and Gardin (2001) have found that language is used in three dimensions. (i) An instrumental dimension, where it serves as a vector for conveying information and orders. Instructions for use are a good illustration of this instrumental dimension. (ii) A cognitive dimension, where the very act of writing forces the writer to marshal his or her knowledge so that it can be communicated more effectively, and to find arguments that can be presented in a reasoned manner. Since the study by Hayes and Flower (1980), this is without doubt the dimension that has received the most attention from researchers. Cellier (2005), for instance, found that the simple fact of drafting instructions for major construction work in the field of rail transport enabled the writer to anticipate some of the problems potentially posed by the scheme. (iii) A social dimension, in which writing in the workplace always takes place within a hierarchical context.

Both the form and the content will vary according to whether the writer is producing a text for his or her subordinates, peers or superiors.

Documents may be produced by writers having different characteristics. For Beaudet (1998), a useful distinction can be made between the functional writer, drafting documents as part of a job that involves many other (and more important) duties, and the professional writer, whose sole duty is to produce documents. Although functional writers generally have the skills required to perform these tasks, more often than not they will have received little training in text production. Professional writers, on the other hand, who have received specialist training in writing, will probably not have such a fluent command of the field they have to write about. Unfortunately for the designers of writing aids, research into the constraints faced by these two types of writers is still in its infancy.

Another factor contributing to the complexity of research in the production, understanding and use of documents in the workplace is the sheer number of functions fulfilled by these documents (e.g. a personal memo such as a Post-It, the terms and conditions of a contract or a legal document such as a police report). Each of these functions is a constraint which affects not only the production of the document but also its understanding by the addressee. We can identify three such functions: informative (knowledge), injunctive (order) and legal (evidence). (i) The *Knowledge* function is probably the most frequent one, characterizing memos, minutes, travelers and schedules. These documents are designed for immediate use or, in some cases, for storage (e.g. the minutes of a meeting). (ii) The *Order* function is typically in documents such as instructions and directions for use. Although they are extremely common, little actual use is made of these procedural documents (Wright, 1981; Silver & Wogalter, 1991). This under use has prompted research, which is cited in this handbook. However, although researchers have investigated the use and understanding of procedural texts, they have tended to neglect the processes involved in their writing. (iii) Lastly, the *Evidence* aspect is the core function of documents such as contracts, police reports, etc. These are generally drawn up by lawyers, and their composition has to comply with a large number of constraints that affect their understanding by people with no legal training.

In reality, the picture is obviously more complex; while some documents exemplify a single function, others fulfill two or even three different ones. A ship's log, for instance, which records everything that happens on board, is primarily a source of information for the ship owner. In the event of a dispute or a problem however, it takes on a legal function. Similarly, the records of a hospital patient are intended to communicate information (Boucheix & Coiron, 2005; Grosjean & Lacoste, 1999; Lacoste, 2001), but may subsequently be used as evidence if there is an incident. Then again, in many procedural texts, the instructions are accompanied by information that is not at all relevant to performing the task in question. This is the case of many computer manuals. The instances in which all three functions are combined are somewhat rare, although Cellier (2005) came across this configuration in a study of written instructions. The injunctive component formed the bulk of the contents, but there was also some general information (reminders of the respective roles of each operator) and some legal information (references to rules and regulations). Indeed, the main function ascribed to them by potential users was one of legal protection. As indicated earlier, the document served, above all, to protect those responsible for drafting it.

We have already referred to the social context in which documents are produced and used. Putting a signature to a document is not a neutral act, as it binds the author. It also gives the addressee a means of gauging the document's importance prior to reading it, by indicating the relevance of the source. A signature, be it the name or the title of the writer, ensures the document's traceability, although this traceability may be relatively limited, given that many documents are merely reworkings of the previous ones. It is rare for someone to draft an entire document from scratch, without referring to any other documents, and the most common situation is that of someone revising a document written by someone else. This is a particular example of the revision process described by Hayes and Flower (1980). The introduction and subsequent massive spread of information technology has resulted in the coexistence of paper and electronic documents. This coexistence was certainly not foreseen by the promoters of office automation, who promised us "paperless offices". The availability of an electronic document almost always results in a paper copy, the one exception being e-mails, especially if they are short. Electronics has also brought with it new forms of writing, using new communication tools. With the advent of Web 2.0, forums, blogs and wikis have given companies new means of expressing and storing information, not only in terms of the form and content of this information but also and above all in terms of the speed with which it can be disseminated and shared.

The last factor we discuss in relation to written documents in the workplace is their life span. The ephemeral life of a Post-It or a daily work schedule is in sharp contrast with that of documents intended for storage (minutes of board meetings, legal documents, etc.). Between these two extremes, there is a large volume of documents with variable life spans, and their classification for storage purposes is left to the user's discretion. Given the difficulty of gauging the useful life of a document, there is a general tendency to overestimate it, thereby wasting valuable storage space. To gain an idea of this wastage, in the first forty years of its existence, the National Center for Space Studies (CNES) in Toulouse (France) accumulated technical records occupying more than three kilometers of shelving. With such a proliferation of documents in the workplace, finding relevant information is like looking for a needle in a haystack.

We end this short introduction to the field of written documents in the workplace by stressing two points:

1. First of all, these documents are primarily about action, as they are drafted with a view to performing some sort of action. This sets them apart from other texts, such as narratives. The constraints that affect their production, understanding and use differ from those of narrative texts. They are judged not on their literary merits but on their ability to support some form of work.
2. Second, these documents have a major social impact. They may affect the safety of people or equipment. They may have an impact on a company's business activities. Writers and readers may be held liable for any dysfunctions resulting from flaws in a document's composition or its subsequent misuse.

These two points clearly underline the need to identify the constraints impinging on the drafting and use of documents if we are to assist writers and users more effectively. The purpose of this handbook is therefore to give its readers a few scientific pointers to the problem of constraints on writers and users, and by so doing help them to design more effective supports and training programs for the workplace.

Overview of the Book

Featuring contributions from linguists, psychologists and ergonomists from various countries and continents, this multidisciplinary handbook brings together different skills and approaches with the aim of providing an initial answer to the question of how the production and comprehension of written documents in the workplace can be improved.

To achieve this goal, the handbook is divided into three parts:

- Section 1—"Defining Professional Documents"—deals with linguistic and pragmatic aspects.
- Section 2—"Composing Documents"—provides an overview of the knowledge required for the teaching and development of writing skills.
- Section 3—"Understanding Documents"—examines the reader's perspective, memory representations and the effect of new technologies on comprehension.

The aim of Section 1 ("Defining Professional Documents") is to characterize professional documents by providing an operational definition of their linguistic and pragmatic characteristics. In the first chapter, Anne Condamines and Marie-Paule Péry-Woodley ("Linguistic Markers of Semantic and Textual Relations in Technical Documents") propose a number of linguistic "handles" on the description of technical documents, at a lexical level (terminology) and a textual level (discourse coherence). Examples are given of how these insights can be put to good use in the production and management of documents, especially in the area of document engineering. The second chapter tackles pictograms—an aspect of linguistics that is still relatively unfamiliar and rarely studied in the workplace, even though they are extremely common in everyday life (road signs, computer interface, alarm signals, etc.). Charles Tijus, Javier Barcenilla, Brigitte Cambon de Lavalette and Jean-Guy Meunier ("The Design, Understanding and Usage of Pictograms") review research into the effects of pictograms, covering theoretical and experimental research conducted by linguists, psychologists and cognitive ergonomists into the design and validation, comprehension and use of pictograms. The last chapter in this section tackles the question of the efficiency and relevance of professional documents. Céline Beaudet and Pamela Grant ("Readability and Intelligibility of Procedural Texts: The Case of Enumeration in Legal Texts") investigate how configurational markers contribute to readability and intelligibility, before going on to explore the role of vertically configured enumeration in legal texts.

Entitled "Composing documents", Section 2 provides an overview of the cognitive processes involved in the composition of technical documents and presents ways of improving the efficiency of these processes. It ends with two examples in the professional context. The first three chapters provide complementary descriptions of the editorial processes and knowledge needed to compose technical documents. Franck Ganier and Javier Barcenilla ("Considering Users and the Way They Use Procedural Texts: Some Prerequisites for the Design of Appropriate Documents") focus on the relationship between the comprehension and production of procedural documents. Their aim is to show that a better understanding of (i) the relationship between the user, the procedural document and the equipment to be operated, and (ii) the problems that may arise during use, can help us to design more appropriate procedural documents. In the second chapter, Tom Quinlan and Denis Alamargot ("Highly Effective Writers and the Role of Reading: A Cognitive Approach to Composing in Professional Contexts") look at the role of source document reading during writing. As effective writing in the workplace requires skills for processing information, they explore the cognitive processes underlying writing expertise, focusing on the central role of reading. They show that while critical reading can enable the writer to adopt a sophisticated approach to writing, it may also create additional opportunities for conflict between cognitive processes.

Understanding the role of reading during/for writing raises questions about text revision. In the following chapter, Jocelyne Bisaillon ("Professional Editing: Emphasis on the Quality of a Text and its Communicative Effectiveness") discusses the work of professional editors and their self-set objectives for improving both the quality of a text and its effectiveness from the communicational standpoint. Editors must bear the future readers in mind when they are working on a document, to ensure that the final version is comprehensible to them—a crucial factor for the teaching of editing.

The issue of teaching and developing expertise in professional writers is explored in greater depth in the subsequent three chapters. The chapter by Edouardo Marti and Merce Garcia-Mila ("Procedural Texts Written by Children") deals with the main difficulties faced by children when they explore procedural texts, working on the assumption that these can provide important guidelines for the professional training of novice technical writers, helping them to understand the difficulties they may encounter in writing procedural documents in the workplace. The development of expertise raises the question of assistance and training programs, which can be offered to writers in order to improve their performances. It is from this perspective that John R. Hayes, Diana M. Bajzek, Judy Brooks, Brenda Reyes, Nicole Hallinen and Erwin R. Steinberg ("Developing an Online Writing Tutor to Improve Technical Writing Skills in Engineering and Science Students") present the basic theoretical and technical components of an online writing tutor providing students with instruction, practice and feedback in a variety of basic writing and graphic skills.

The final two chapters show how written texts can be concretely produced within private companies or institutions. Doreen Starke-Meyerring ("The Impact of Blogs on Professional Writing: Speed, Reach, Engagement, and the Art of the Self in Web 2.0") examines blogs as a growing and contested space for professional writing, analyzes the critical disruptive shift in workplace writing they represent and concludes with possible directions for reconsidering writing in the workplace. For their part, Véronique Barret, Isabelle Clerc and Sylvie Montreuil ("The Production of Work Instructions in an Industrial Workplace: The Impact of a Functional Writer's Work Context on the Outcome of His Activity") examine the work context of functional (non-expert) writers and demonstrate that in order to obtain a more accurate understanding of their operating constraints, their activity must be viewed within a broader framework. This premise is illustrated by the activities of a functional writer who was observed in a company located in Quebec, Canada.

Section 3 ("Understanding Documents") examines how comprehension processes can be influenced by task orientation or reading strategies. It also provides a set of principles for the practitioner based on the current use of new technologies and the study of comprehension (wearable computers, animation, hypertext and hypermedia). As procedures are used in almost all work domains to guide and define activities, a number of chapters deal with procedural texts or tasks (assembly, inspection, etc.). However, comprehension processes are also examined in the context of professional translation and scientific texts.

The literature on text comprehension is based on the assumption that there are two main components of the memory representation derived from reading a text: the textbase and the situation model. The first component—the propositional information contained in the text itself (textbase)—is the primary contributor to tests such as text recall. The second component is the situation described by the text, merging text propositions with inferences and information derived from the reader's background knowledge (situation model). The situation model is regarded as the primary contributor to tests that go beyond recall of the propositional content of the text. But what is the structure of a situation model? The introductory chapter by Isabelle Tapiero and José Otero ("Situation Models and Their Role in Comprehension: The Need to Study Their Internal Structure") deals with the different types of formalisms that have been used to describe meaning. In particular, it sets out to give a more fine-grained definition of how theories of knowledge (symbolic and analogical) account for the internal structure of situation models in discourse comprehension.

A shared feature of the next three chapters is that they discuss whether task orientation can influence the nature of comprehension processes, causing differences in performances on measures that tap into different levels of representations or influencing the order of these processes. In the case of procedural instructions, Does the distinction between situation model and textbase map onto a distinction between memory for instructions and memory for procedure as tested by later task performance? The chapter by Patrice Terrier, Virginia Diehl and Julie Lemarié ("The Effects of Interaction with the Device and Text Structure on the Mental Representations Derived from the Procedure") reviews the effects of enactment of a procedure and text structure variables on memory and task performance. Measures of textbase and situational representations were not always dissociated; in fact, they were sometimes positively correlated. Text structure variables appeared to affect the memory for the parts of the text that were highlighted. The reading objective is also considered in the chapter by Pedro Macizo and Maria Teresa Bajo ("Comprehension Processes in Translation") on the basis of a non-procedural text. The authors describe the varieties of translation and the main theoretical perspectives in this area. Afterwards, they examine lexical, sentence and discourse processes along with the role of working memory in reading and translation tasks. Can the strategies used by someone selectively reading a hypertext influence the textbase or the situation model? The chapter by Ignacio Madrid and Jose J. Canas ("How Reading Strategies Affect the Comprehension of Texts in Hypertext Systems") show that hypertext readers have to develop a particular strategy in order to determine which information they will read and in which order they will access it. A series of studies is presented, exploring the strategies that readers use and how these strategies influence text comprehension.

New technologies such as hypertext may have either a positive or a negative effect on comprehension processes. The three subsequent chapters address this issue and also highlight operational principles for the practitioner. Can technology be used to help operators follow procedures? The chapter by Jennifer Ockerman ("Task-Guidance Systems and Procedure Context: Enabling Procedures to Enhance Worker Performance"), showing that procedures are widely used in many industries to provide for safety and consistency in task completion, provides a brief background on the use of procedures, a description of task guidance systems and an explanation of procedure context, including results of some empirical investigations into their efficacy. In the case of a complex system, the depiction of the procedural task can be supplemented by animations, but do animations positively or negatively affect comprehension processes in procedural tasks? The chapter by Richard K. Lowe ("Animated Documentation: A way of Comprehending Complex Procedural Tasks?") explains the manner in which acquiring an understanding of how complex dynamic systems operate can be very challenging. Computer-based documentation allows operational processes to be represented explicitly via animated depictions rather than implicitly via static graphics. The author examines potential strengths and limitations of animated explanations, and then discusses research-based suggestions for improving their design. In the concluding chapter, which also deals with the presentation of complex systems, N. Hari Narayanan ("The Impact of Cognitively based Design of Expository Multimedia") focuses on cognitive principles for the design of technical documents that explain causal and dynamic systems. Design guidelines, derived from a cognitive model, are provided and illustrated with examples to show how to create effective multimedia documents that will help the reader build accurate mental models.

SECTION 1:
DEFINING PROFESSIONAL DOCUMENTS

Chapter 1

Linguistic Markers of Lexical and Textual Relations in Technical Documents

Anne Condamines and Marie-Paule Péry-Woodley

We provide a number of linguistic "handles" for the description of technical documents. Such insights into the "inner workings" of texts may be harnessed in various ways in the production and management of technical documents; we show some applications in document engineering, more specifically in systems designed to facilitate access to information. Our focus is on surface markers, i.e. observable text features identified through corpus analysis, which signal relations between lexical items such as may be used in building terminologies (such as generic/specific, see Section 1), or relations between text segments involved in discourse coherence (such as theme, or rhetorical relations, see Section 2). We insist on the relevance of the notion of genre when working with technical documents, and on the genre-dependent nature of our linguistic markers.

Our objective in this chapter is to provide a number of precise, theoretically motivated and descriptively relevant "handles" for the linguistic analysis of lexical and organisational aspects of technical documents. By "handles" we mean observable text features that can be associated with specific functions in the document—whether marking semantic relations between lexical items (Section 1) or signalling discourse organisation (Section 2).

Though concerned with two distinct types of semantics, the two sections share a number of methodological options: they focus on studies concerned with the precise analysis of linguistic realisations (surface forms) in attested texts (as opposed to made-up or experimental texts); a starting hypothesis for both is that the markers they are attempting to circumscribe are likely to be sensitive to genre, and that generalisations cannot safely extend beyond the genres that have actually been described.

Written Documents In The Workplace
Copyright © 2007 by Elsevier Ltd.
All rights of reproduction in any form reserved.
ISBN: 978-0-080-47487-8

Condamines, A. & Péry-Woodley, M.-P. (2007). Linguistic markers of lexical and textual relations in technical documents. In G. Rijlaarsdam (Series Ed.) and D. Alamargot, P. Terrier, & J.-M. Cellier (Vol. Eds.), Studies in Writing, Vol. 21, Written Documents in the Workplace, 3–16.

1 Using Linguistic Markers to Build Terminologies for the Management of Technical Documents

1.1 The Problem

The first section explains how terminologies can be used for documentation engineering.

1.1.1 Documentation management Documentation management has become an important issue for companies where each manufactured product is accompanied by numerous documents necessary to build, maintain and market the product.

For example, it is often stated that the documentation for an aircraft would fill the aircraft or that the documentation for a space project amounts to 150,000 pages of paper.

This situation is somewhat contradictory. On the one hand, we have technical objects that are highly sophisticated and considered to be extremely reliable, and on the other hand we have documents written in natural language with all the inherent difficulties that implies: ambiguity, polysemy etc. One possibility to limit these difficulties is to try to standardise document authoring, and this is sometimes mandatory in fields such as aeronautics (AECMA norms), the goal being to establish rules in order to guide technical writers in aeronautics (http://www.aecma.org/Publications.htm).

The most common norms concern terminologies. Most of the time terminologies are built by experts in a given field who decide to establish definitions within this field. For this purpose, terminologists meet writers' needs when they build thesauri, and some firms have tried to define their own thesaurus (e.g. the Nasa's thesaurus which contains 13,000 words, 9000 acronyms and 10,000 definitions).

In spite of the interest in these standards, it is clear that they are not much used. Sometimes, writers do not even know that they exist. One of the main problems is that these standards are established by official bodies with the aim of covering an entire field. However, the proposed terms do not always correspond to the ones actually used by a particular company.

Some years ago, the problem of documentation management took on a new perspective when it was examined by knowledge engineers. This has led to major changes with regard to the problems of terminology.

1.1.2 Terminologies and knowledge engineering During the last 15 years, there has been a significant evolution in artificial intelligence. The important point concerned the need to consider that it is not possible to build tools to take the place of humans reasoning but only tools to help humans in their reasoning. Then the development of knowledge engineering began. The most important element in this new perspective was the distinction between knowledge systems on the one hand and reasoning systems on the other (Clancey, 1993).

Initially built on the basis of interviews with experts in a given field, these knowledge-based systems are now very often built on the basis of document analysis; this new perspective is particularly relevant for documentation management as these systems can also be used for this purpose.

The knowledge module uses a form of representation called *ontology*, which presents clear similarities with terminologies as it is made up of nodes linked by relations, both labelled by lexical elements. But ontologies are different in an important respect: they must be formalised in order to be integrated into reasoning systems (Gruber, 1991). An ontology may be defined as: "a description (like a formal specification of a program) of the concepts and relationships that can exist for an agent or a community of agents" (Gruber, 1993).

With the possibilities of Natural Language Processing (NLP), it then became possible to envisage the design of tools adapted to the reality of language use within a specific firm's documentation in order to build terminologies or ontologies. In return, these terminologies can be integrated into tools devoted to document management.

Many NLP tools have been designed with the purpose of helping to create terminologies or ontologies from texts. All these new perspectives have boosted classical documentation and terminology, and given birth to new kinds of studies.

1.1.3 Development of a textual terminology

The first terminologist's theory (Eugen Wüster's) was based on the idea that it is fundamental to standardise terminologies in order to allow good communication between speakers in a given field (Cabré, 1999; Rey, 1995; Sager, 1990). It is easy to understand the idea underlying such a point of view: Standardisation can be seen as the only way to guarantee transparent communication between humans in a field. But this point of view does not consider the reality of language, which is always evolving.

In the early 1990s, several interdisciplinary teams identified the relationships between the aims of terminology and knowledge engineering, and a joint reflection process was initiated (Skuce & Meyer, 1991).

One of the main consequences of this new goal was that terminology and documentation came to be regarded as important activities in companies and, as a consequence, were forced to re-examine their own methods and their situation among other disciplines.

In terminology, a new field appeared that examined how it is possible to build terminologies from texts: textual terminology (Pearson, 1998).

With such an evolution, terminology has come into the spotlight as a linguistic issue, or more precisely, a corpus linguistics issue. A major point in corpus linguistic studies is to take into account variations in use, and to identify regularities among these variations in order to build a system that can explain them. Textual terminology has a very similar goal: taking into account real documents in order to create a system of terms, i.e. a representation of the contents of these documents in a relational form (terms linked by semantic relations).

This process must take into account how the terminology will be used. There may be variations in the construction of a relational representation according to the aim of the project. Therefore, building a terminology from a corpus presupposes an interpretation process.

The linguist's role consists in explaining how it is possible to construct a terminology, more precisely to describe on which linguistic elements this construction can be performed.

Building a terminology from texts (or an ontology, as, during the first step at least, the perspectives are very similar) requires the identification of terms and of the relations between them. Different ways of identifying terms have been developed, both from linguistic and NLP viewpoints (Cabré, Estopa, & Vivaldi, 2000); but, in this paper, we prefer to focus on the problem of the identification of relations between terms.

From a linguistic point of view, it is really interesting to examine how it is possible to identify relations between terms, especially through the use of relation patterns. These relation patterns constitute a kind of handle. Meyer (2001, p. 290) considers that there are three kinds of conceptual relation patterns (named "knowledge patterns" by Meyer): lexical patterns (involving one or more specific lexical items), grammatical patterns and paralinguistic patterns (they include punctuation, as well as various elements of the general structure of a text). The author stresses that these patterns are "complex in their nature, and in the way they can be realized in text": they are sometimes unpredictable, polysemic and/or domain dependent. In the next part, we are going to describe the role of these patterns in the identification of conceptual relations in texts.

1.2 The Role of Patterns in the Identification of Relations Between Terms

Before the development of textual terminology, linguists had already identified lexico-syntactic elements "expressing" semantic relations such as [all N1 except N2] for hyperonymy (generic/specific relation) (e.g. on the basis of *all flowers except roses* we can say that roses (specific) are a kind of flower (generic)). This was the case for Cruse who named these elements "diagnostic frames" (Cruse, 1986) or Lyons who named them "formulae" (Lyons, 1977). The study of these patterns has been developed over the past 15 years, specifically to design tools (Hearst, 1992). It is also very interesting to explore this field from a linguistic point of view both because it can constitute a way to understand how variations may be taken into account in corpus linguistic methodologies and because it may help to improve NLP tools.

In this case, the problem is to explain why relation patterns do not appear in all texts and/or in the same way. In other words, it is necessary to understand how the nature of a corpus can play a role within the conceptual relation/pattern pair. This point is really important in order to improve information spotting specifically in an NLP perspective. Concerning technical documentation, it is important to evaluate whether a specific pattern may be present considering the nature of this text (or set of texts).

Three kinds of dependences between corpus and patterns have been identified (Condamines, 2002).

1.2.1 Weak dependence Some patterns seem to appear in any text. This is the case for some hyperonymic (generic/specific relation, see above) or meronymic (part-of relation) patterns such as:

[N1 comprises N2, (N3) and N4] as in:

> [1] *The house comprises a living-room and two bedrooms* (*living-room* and *bedroom* are parts of *house*).

These patterns are the ones generally proposed spontaneously and used in NLP tools. Even if the relation/pattern seems very strong, some difficulties should be noted with these patterns. First of all, these patterns may be polysemic. For example *comme* (as) in French may be associated either with a hyperonymic relation or a comparison relation.

Another difficulty (and this is the case with all patterns) is that it may be difficult to determine whether the speaker using conceptual relation patterns is expressing his/her own point of view or if he/she is presenting the point of view of a group of speakers. In the perspective of terminology construction, only the second case needs to be modelled because such models must be acceptable and reusable within collective tasks.

Finally, despite their strong link with a relation these patterns do not always appear because the relations are not always used within texts. This may be surprising, as general relations such as hyperonymy (generic/specific) and meronymy (part-of) are considered very significant for structuring a field. Nevertheless this case was found in a corpus from Matra Marconi Space, built from specifications in the field of satellite simulations. There were no classical patterns of hyperonymy (such as the one presented above) because hyperonymy was not expressed. In this highly specialised field, experts do not need to explain concepts; they use them under the assumption that they will be understood by the readers. So concepts are never defined, i.e. never situated in relation with other concepts.

What can be retained from such an experience is that the corpus must be built according to the goal of the study. To build terminologies and in particular identify semantic relations, it is important to explore texts written by experts for less expert readers; in other words, texts with some kind of didactic intention.

1.2.2 Complete dependence In some corpora, some unpredictable structures play the role of patterns for some relations. It would be impossible to propose them spontaneously (Meyer, 2001). We found such a structure in a corpus from EDF (*Electricité de France*) concerning specifications and the writing of documents in computer science (Condamines & Rebeyrolle, 2001). In this corpus, written by several experts but with the same purpose, the pattern for the relation of condition was:

[(phase, stage) or nominalisation + (when, as soon as) + passive V]

> [2] *La phase d'intégration du composant peut commencer lorsque l'ensemble des éléments logiciels ont été codés.*
> *The component integration phase can begin when all the software elements have been coded.*

This example should be understood as:
Software elements must have been coded for the component integration phase to begin.
Therefore, the relation expressed is a condition relation and the pattern was very productive as for each of its 11 occurrences, the condition relation was present.

These patterns are very difficult to identify and only a fine-grained analysis will bring them to light.

1.2.3 Dependence in terms of text genre Sometimes, regularities of expression are not specific to a particular corpus but rather to a corpus to the extent that it is "representative" of other corpora with identical extra-linguistic and linguistic characteristics, i.e. when it is possible to identify the text genre to which the corpus belongs. This notion of genre is very ancient (Aristotle proposed to distinguish three kinds of genre: lyrical, epic and dramatic). In the middle of the 20th century, this notion was reactivated by two movements: one was a Russian movement which anchored this approach in a dialogical point of view (Todorov, 1984) and the second was an American movement, within sociolinguistics, which considered that text genre was the only way to take into account both situational and language regularities (Firth, 1969).

This notion of genre is used within corpus linguistics, which has a fundamental need to organise corpora in order to try to explain variations (Bahtia, 1993; Swales, 1990). But this notion of text genre is not easy to determine because its relevance may vary according to the element under study.

Concerning relation patterns, text genre is very often relevant but it does not affect all patterns in the same way.

Let us examine two examples of patterns. The first one concerns the preposition *chez*. In some cases, this preposition occurs in sentences where a meronymic relation can be identified:

> [3] *Chez les colobinés, le nez fait saillie sur la lèvre supérieure.*
> With the colobines, the nose juts out over the upper lip (there is a meronymic (part-of) relation between *nose* and *colobines*).

This phenomenon appears in particular in some specific texts: those that belong to natural science (only biology and zoology excluding geology) and are didactic (e.g. encyclopaedic articles relating to the natural sciences). This means that in texts belonging to such text genres, the probability for sentences with *chez* to be interpreted as a meronymic relation is high.

Beyond this quantitative aspect, it is interesting to study different examples containing this preposition to understand how the meronymic interpretation is possible. The point is that this preposition introduces a referent (either at the beginning, the middle or the end of the sentence) and in didactic natural science texts, what is said about this referent (animal or plant) concerns very often their anatomy or composition. Quantitative results show that anatomical information is more present than other kinds of information (habitat, feeding, reproduction etc.), around 50% of the occurrences. So it is not really the case that *chez* is a pattern for the meronymic relation: it does not intrinsically contain this sense. But, from a computational point of view, *chez* may be used to identify structures where a meronymic relation occurs in didactic texts of natural science. This case is very interesting because it shows that the linguistic and computational points of view are not always equivalent.

Another pattern has been studied with the same hypothesis concerning genre. It is the nominal anaphora. It is well known that in some cases, there is a generic (or hyperonymic) relation between a noun in anaphoric position and its antecedent (Cornish, 1986):

> [4] *Contrôle de la complétude des modifications effectuées. Cette activité est du ressort du Responsable Développement.* (*activité est un générique pour contrôle*).
> Completeness *check* for the modifications made. This *activity* is the responsibility of the Development Manager. (*activity* is a generic of *check*).

However, the relation may also be of another nature; for example, the anaphoric noun may be a synonym or a nominalised form of a verb (This guide proposes [...] this proposition).

The intuitive hypothesis was that this hyperonymic relation could be very frequent in specialised handbooks since it is commonly assumed that relations within specialised fields are extremely stable.

We studied nominal anaphora in three specialised handbooks and compared these results with texts belonging to other text genres (literary and journalistic). The results did not confirm the hypothesis. The frequency of hyperonymic relations in the handbooks compared with other genres was not very significant except for one of the technical handbooks. In the other four texts, the hyperonymic relation appears only between 15 and 30% of all occurrences. It is therefore not possible to consider that nominal anaphora can constitute a pattern for the hyperonymic relation in handbooks; the initial hypothesis was not confirmed. Nevertheless, fine-grained analysis shows that there are differences between technical handbooks and other texts. Several characteristics allow us to say that anaphoric nouns in handbooks are more often classifiers than in texts of another genre. This means that these nouns may be considered as the top nodes (generics) of possible classes. Thus, even if the nominal anaphora cannot be considered as a hyperonymic pattern, it can be considered as a hyperonym marker: it is not the relation itself that is identified, but only one element of this relation, hyperonym (specific). So, it would therefore be necessary to use other patterns in order to identify specific terms corresponding to generic terms identified by the anaphora pattern.

These two examples show that genre may be relevant for the description of relation patterns but it is very difficult to determine in what cases it will be relevant. Only large-scale studies of real corpora would make it possible to predict usage.

There are a growing number of studies attempting to understand how genre can be used to determine and anticipate variations within texts, especially in texts from restricted fields (Trosborg, 2000). For documentation engineering, it is clear that this notion could also be relevant. Even though variation is likely to be less in such specialised contexts, the different genres and the dividing lines between them are not easy to determine and this will probably constitute an important issue in coming years.

2 Three Levels of Text Organisation in Technical Documents: Models and Markers

We now turn from relations between lexical items to relations at the level of the text or document. A defining characteristic of texts is that they form a whole, and they show connectedness. Hence the importance of the notion of *coherence* in text and discourse linguistics. Coherence is most usefully seen as a mental phenomenon, rather than an inherent property of the text. To quote Sanders and Spooren: "Language users establish coherence by relating the different information units in the text" (2001, p. 7). "Relating information" is what discourse is about, whether one looks at production or comprehension.[1] A number of

---

[1] See Madrid and Cañas, this volume, on cognitive tasks involved in text comprehension and in the construction of a coherent interpretation in the specific case of hypertext.

hypotheses have been put forward—elaborated to a lesser or greater extent into models—which can be seen as different, often complementary, and take on the complex notion of coherence. For the textual analyst concerned with practical issues of communicative efficiency, they provide the necessary theoretical foundations to interpret and integrate observational data. A strong hypothesis here is that variations in wording, the presence or absence of certain "markers"—lexico-grammatical or visual—have an impact on meaning, i.e. they are used as signals in the construction of the interpretation model.

As a presentational device, this section on the textual organisation of documents is structured in terms of levels of granularity, from the proposition to the whole document. At the finest level, we will look at how contextual and co-textual factors can influence wording and word order in the proposition or sentence (*information structure*). At the next level, the focus will be on relations of connection between these basic units (*rhetorical structure*), before moving on to envisaging the document more globally, and also as a visual object (*document structure or text architecture*).

The descriptive studies presented below mostly concern technical documents, as the specific realisations are sensitive to parameters of genre; the models referred to, however, may have been developed with little reference to genre.[2]

2.1 Information Structure and Information Packaging

The notion of *information structure* belongs at the fine granularity level, despite the potentially deceptive, apparently all-encompassing term. The more expressive denomination "information *packaging*" was coined by Chafe (1976) to refer to the effects of a combination of factors—mostly to do with prior knowledge and cognitive state—which have a major role in shaping utterances: "The kind of phenomena at issue here (…) have to do primarily with how the message is sent and only secondarily with the message itself, just as the packaging of toothpaste can affect sales in partial independence of the quality of the toothpaste inside" (Chafe, 1976, p. 28). Chafe's intuition has been elaborated upon over time, and several parameters have been distinguished, amongst which are *aboutness*—whether a particular referent or entity is what the sentence is about; *givenness*—whether it is already present in the discourse; *activation*—whether it is the hearer's current focus of consciousness. These parameters influence linguistic choices in ways that differ from language to language, affecting stress, word order and syntactic choices. For instance, different configurations of these parameters lay behind the contrast between "The pipes are RUSTY" and "The PIPES are rusty"[3] corresponding respectively to the questions: "What about the pipes? In what condition are they?" (the entity referred to by "the pipes" is given in the question) and "Why does the water from the tap come out brown?" (the entity "the pipes" is new). Another example is the contrasting placement of a circumstantial adjunct: "Tomorrow, John is leaving" vs. "John is leaving tomorrow", adequate responses respectively to "What's

---

[2]This distinction between descriptive and theoretical studies is clearly an over-simplification, however, as some descriptive studies of technical documents have the potential to lead to the elaboration or revision of models of text organisation (e.g. Thompson, 1985).

[3]Examples from Gomez-González (2001), with capitals indicating stress. Note that in some languages, such as French, this contrast is likely to be realised syntactically.

happening tomorrow" and "When is John leaving?" The question–answer minimal pairs are of course a somewhat contrived device for introducing context; what must be stressed is that "Tomorrow, John is leaving" in answer to the second question, though syntactically correct, is seriously flawed from a discourse point of view. Another angle on this is to look at the choice of referring expression (e.g. pronoun vs. definite expression) as a signal given to the reader as to the degree of mental accessibility of a piece of (given) information: for instance the use of the pronoun "he" or "she" implies a highly accessible referent, whereas a definite expression ("June's friend") indicates a relatively low degree of accessibility. For a detailed account of information structure, see Lambrecht (1994); of the notions of theme and topic, Gomez-González (2001); and of accessibility theory, Ariel (2001).

Importantly for workplace communication, therefore, writers (and speakers) have a choice of different linguistic realisations for the same propositional content, and must at every step shape their utterances in accordance with the current assumptions about the readers' (or hearers') cognitive state at this point in the discourse, as well as with their discourse intentions. In turn, the specific shape of the utterance works as a set of signals, or instructions, to the reader. In a ground-breaking article, Grosz and Sidner (1986) propose a model for relating "attentional state" and speakers' intentions in a task-oriented dialogue. They look at how entities come in and out of focus, and how processing decisions at a local level are constrained by the textual form of an expression, as determination (e.g. definite or indefinite) or syntactic function (e.g. subject or object) make it a more or less likely candidate for attentional focus. This study opened the way for an important dynamic model relating discourse intentions and attentional states (changes in focus of attention): Centering Theory (cf. Walker, Joshi, & Prince, 1998).

The relations of specific "packagings" to particular configurations of information and cognitive parameters are of obvious interest to linguists and applied linguists (Davison, 1984; Foley & Van Valin, 1985; Fries, 1995; Gundel, Hedberg, & Zacharski, 1993; Prince, 1981; Virtanen, 1992a, *inter alia*). In the wake of Clark and Haviland's (1977) "given-new contract", a number of psycholinguistic studies have shown the negative impact on comprehension of text disrespectful of information structure, for instance violating the given (information) before new (information) principle. On the basis of these linguistic and psycholinguistic studies, the information structure approach is clearly highly relevant to the study of the production and comprehension of professional documents.

A number of linguistic devices are associated with information packaging choices, as they allow a reshuffling of elements away from the canonical word order: passivation, clefting, topicalisation and differential positioning of adjuncts. Though they affect the ordering of elements within the sentence, they reflect contextual constraints, where pragmatics touches on syntax, and they can play a role in the development of larger textual units. With regard to technical and more specifically procedural texts, a particular question concerns the ordering of action pairs when an instruction is given in relation to a purpose, as in the following examples borrowed from Delin, Hartley and Scott (1996):

[5] a. *In order to turn on the light, flick the switch.*
b. *Flick the switch in order to turn on the light.*

Thompson suggests a strong functional contrast between these two positions: whereas final purpose clauses (as in [5] b.) have a purely local role, merely stating the purpose for which the action named in the main clause is undertaken, initial purpose clauses (as in [5] a.) "guide the reader's attention [...] by naming a problem which arises from expectations created by the text or inferences from it, to which the following material, often consisting of many sentences, provides a solution" (1985, p. 67). A series of initial purpose clauses, each extending their scope over a number of instructions, can structure a passage, reflecting a particular text-building strategy (cf. Péry-Woodley, 2001; Virtanen, 1992a, 1992b). Delin et al. (1996) propose a framework for the contrastive analysis of such choices (in English and French instructional texts) based on the semantic relations of *generation* and *enablement* (cf. Goldman, 1970).[4] This text-organising role observed in the case of purpose clauses placed in initial position also applies to other detached adjuncts, such as time or place adjuncts (e.g. "for the first thirty minutes"), or praxeologic adjuncts (e.g. "in biochemistry"), a behaviour which has been studied under the term of *discourse framing* (Charolles, 1997; Charolles, Le Draoulec, Péry-Woodley, & Sarda, 2005; Péry-Woodley, 2005).

It already appears quite clearly that the level of granularity we started with, the sentence, cannot possibly be seen as self-contained, as many aspects of linguistic realisation at sentence level are constrained by higher levels of textual organisation, and in turn influence interpretation so far, and the expectations upon which further interpretation will proceed. The relations between propositions (purpose clause and main clause) just considered provide a transition with the next level of granularity as they can apply between sentences as well as within sentences.

2.2 Rhetorical Structure: Connecting Text Spans in a Meaningful Way

Coherence relations, discourse relations, rhetorical relations—different terms are used in different models for the meaning relations which connect text segments (such as cause–consequence, problem–solution). In the previous section, we looked at purpose clauses with respect to their position in the sentence, and the role this position confers on them, a role which may extend over a wider text segment. Such subordinate clauses, whichever position they occupy, are one possible way of materialising in text a semantic or rhetorical relation between segments—here a purpose relation between two propositions. In [5], the relation is made explicit via a particular syntactic construction, but authors agree that relations may be realised in diverse ways, including implicitly. In [6] below, an extract from a software manual, the appearance of the dialog box (second sentence) is likely to be interpreted as resulting form the action instructed in the first sentence:

[6] *From the Project menu, choose Components. The Components dialog box appears.*

Yet there is no cue to a relation between these text contents beyond mere juxtaposition, which iconically suggests temporal succession. The level of explicitness of relations is

---

[4]See also Di Eugenio (1998) for a formal computational approach to the representation of actions in instructional texts.

linked to writer's assumptions about the reader (e.g. regarding competence level) and the situation (e.g. greater necessity to guide the reader through explicit use of markers in highly technical or risky situations).

There are a number of models and a wealth of studies of discourse relations, with a general consensus on their vital importance in the comprehension process (see Bateman and Rondhuis (1997) for a review covering several models). Among these, Rhetorical Structure Theory (RST, Mann & Thompson, 1988, 1992)[5] has over the years become a sort of reference model, widely known and used in different communities (descriptive, computational and psycho-linguistics). RST posits a basic asymmetry between the members of most relations: thus in [5] the purpose ("to turn on the light") is seen as a *satellite* in relation to the action instructed, the *nucleus* ("flick the switch"), an asymmetry conveyed in this example through syntactic status (subordinate vs. main). RST relations apply recursively, with text spans resulting from the application of a relation entering into further relations and so on; at the highest level of representation, if a text lends itself to a coherent reading, it should be possible to represent it by a single overarching relation. This combination of recursive span construction and asymmetrical informational status of satellite and nucleus can be exploited to select informationally richer text spans (see Marcu (2001) for an implementation in an automatic summarisation system).

In short, discourse relations are seen by most authors as serving a twofold text building role: they connect segments via semantic and/or rhetorical links, and they create a hierarchy of segments, some appearing as subordinate to others. The importance of these functions for efficient technical writing is clear. A number of specific studies of discourse relations in instructional and explanatory texts have been conducted, mostly with a view to computational applications such as automatic text generation (Grote, 1999; Scott, Delin, & Hartley, 1998; Vander Linden & Martin, 1995). A major problem for automatic generation is the variability in the markers used to express relations, which is equally a problem for human text production and comprehension. Much research in descriptive and computational linguistics has focused on identifying cues associated to particular discourse relations (Knott & Sanders, 1998; Redeker, 1991 *inter alia*), while psycholinguistic studies have researched the impact of their presence or absence on comprehension (Degand, Lefèvre, & Bestgen, 1999; Sanders & Noordman, 2000; Townsend, 1997), or taken the RST account of relations as a tool for studying the writing process (Torrance & Bouayad-Agha, 2001).

2.3 Document Structure: The Linguistic Nature of Layout

The most immediately obvious form of document organisation is its visual—graphical— structure: a long document is typically organised in chapters and sections—headed by titles or headings—then in paragraphs and *text-sentences* (Nunberg, 1990), within which various further *textual objects* (Virbel, 1989) stand out through contrasting disposition (e.g. indentation) or typography (e.g. bold face). Luc and Virbel (2001) stress that a graphical token cannot be devoid of visual properties—shape, size, colour—and must be interpreted spatially in relation to other tokens; these properties cannot be envisaged as a simple

---

[5]Much information can also be obtained from the RST website: http://www.sfu.ca/rst/index.html.

coding of an already constituted message, they have to be seen as playing a part in the realisation of the writer's intentions. Though layout issues have generally been overlooked in linguistic approaches to discourse, a number of authors have been keen to study the specific potentialities of written language linked to its visual realisation: Nunberg (1990) analyses punctuation as manifesting a coherent linguistic subsystem (*text-grammar*) coexisting with what he calls the system of *lexical grammar*; a distinction picked up and extended by Power, Scott, and Bouayad-Agha (2003) in their study of *document structure* in patient information leaflets. Virbel calls *text architecture* the text structures which are realised via the physical page layout (see Luc and Virbel (2001) for a synthetic presentation of the "Model of Text Architecture"). These authors (along with Delin, Bateman, & Allen, 2002), though they may differ over several points, agree on some fundamental principles and points of interest:

a) They stress the need to distinguish between the concrete realisation of the graphical form of text (typography, punctuation, disposition) and an abstract structure, diversely called *document structure* (Power et al.), *text architecture* (Virbel), *layout structure* (Delin et al.); this abstract structure interacts with choices in wording, and is therefore an aspect of the linguistic realisation of discourse acts.
b) They focus on the interaction between this abstract document structure and rhetorical structure (propositional meanings and their semantico-pragmatic relations). Both Luc and Virbel (2001) and Power et al. (2003) show that the two structures are distinct and not necessarily isomorphic. They both address the problem for RST, whose representations are based on relations between text spans (document structure, architecture) when in fact the relations are between text meanings.

Studies of the impact of layout on written text comprehension are of obvious relevance in the workplace context (on instructional texts, cf. Garcia-Debanc, 2001). A number of recent studies approach document structure in its interaction with other discourse structures: Bouayad-Agha, Scott, and Power (2001) look at the impact of layout on the interpretation of referring expressions; Luc, Mojahid, Virbel, Garcia-Debanc, and Péry-Woodley (1999) focus on a structure of particular interest in this perspective: enumeration. The signalling of enumeration can be placed on a continuum from purely discursive (linear form with lexical markers—e.g. "first..., second...") to purely visual (vertical disposition with indentation and bullet points). Linguistic and psycholinguistic studies of enumerations have turned them into a sort of test case for a view of rhetorical and document structure as separate, interacting, types of structure (Luc et al., 1999; Luc, Mojahid, Péry-Woodley, & Virbel, 2000; Power et al., 2003; Garcia-Debanc & Grandaty, 2001). It seems important to take further the understanding of a structure which appears to be a fundamental way of organising text, and is a major device in new document forms (cf. homepages of most websites).

3 Technical Documents in the Workplace: From Linguistic Analysis to Document Engineering

We have presented approaches to the analysis of different linguistic aspects of documents that strike us as being essential keys for the study of their production and comprehension in the workplace. These approaches typically focus on surface features that, in a particular genre, may signal a semantic or textual function. Two types of descriptive "handles" have been described.

Section 1 looked at surface patterns signalling lexical/conceptual relations, i.e. linguistic features (lexical or grammatical) that can be used in order to identify semantic relations such as generic/specific, part of, is cause of, etc. Our focus has been the link between these patterns and the nature of the corpus: the fact that the probability of occurrence of a pattern, as well as its interpretation, are corpus-dependent. In order to describe and explain these variations, we call upon the notion of text genre, which allows us to take into account both extra-linguistic and linguistic features. Variations in extra-linguistic parameters lead to variations in wording. Text genre thus constitutes a way of anchoring linguistic phenomena in sociological contexts and of taking into account the reality of linguistic usage. We also saw that the degree of genre dependence is highly variable, with some patterns totally genre dependent and others applying across genres.

In Section 2, we also looked at markers and relations, but this time our focus was text structure rather than relations between lexical items or concepts. Accordingly, the markers considered included visual features of documents (typography, disposition) as well as lexico-grammatical expressions. There is a clear cognitive dimension to the research presented, concerned as it is with the textual basis for the construction of an interpretation by readers. We considered three interrelated aspects of text structure which may be seen as vital for comprehension, and therefore have to be carefully "encoded" by the writer: *information packaging*—given vs. new information, theme vs. rheme; *relations between text segments*—what is said in segment B is meant to be understood e.g. as the consequence/result of what is said in segment A; and finally *text architecture* as the abstract structure underlying the graphical realisation of documents.

These linguistic studies take on particular relevance in the current technological context, with the spread of digitised documents leading to the development of new modes of production, access and management of documents in work situations. These mostly have to do with information overload and the need to access selected information efficiently. We propose to give a brief overview of some applications in language and document engineering where the identification of linguistic markers is important: information retrieval, information extraction and automatic summarization.

The term "information retrieval" refers to a process that aims to identify, in a textual database, documents corresponding to a query. In order to reduce silence, the search may be extended to other semantically linked key words. For query extension, information retrieval systems may use linguistic resources constructed on a semantic basis, i.e. terms and conceptual relations; these resources may be elaborated using patterns such as the ones presented in this chapter.

In the case of information extraction, the goal is to determine which text elements correspond to categories of information that have been identified as relevant for the domain. For example, in the case of dispatches, the system has to identify what happened, where, when, why and so on. The linguistic approach is to characterise linguistic structures corresponding to these categories of information in order to retrieve this information as reliably as possible. Obviously, descriptions are guided by the fact that linguistics regularities appear according to text genre. The markers described in this chapter belong to such regularities: they take into account lexical and grammatical elements but also their place in the discourse.

Automatic summarization, or document synthesis, aims to produce a shortened version of a document while retaining the most important points of the text. Given current technological limitations—no computer can "understand" a document—most systems rely on extraction techniques, i.e. the selection of "key" text segments that are extracted and assembled to form the summary. The selection is based on a composite score, with a major lexical statistics component, to which are then applied various weightings. This weighting stage is where markers of the type described in Section 2 may be called upon, as for instance so-called "cue phrases" which signal segments with a specific rhetorical function (e.g. *"In summary"*, *"In conclusion"*, see *inter alia* Mani (2001); Minel (2003) for a recent account). Marcu (2001) proposes a method to identify discourse units on the basis of connectives and punctuation, in order to produce a complete rhetorical tree according to RST (cf. above), which can then be pruned of some of its satellites to retain the "most important" information. Other approaches use the rhetorical conventions of certain genres (e.g. scientific papers) to help the user find "zones" of text with a particular function in the argument (Teufel & Moens, 1999).

This last mention introduces a new agent in document synthesis: the document user. Initially, most approaches tended to take for granted that there were objectively "more important" text segments. New systems are now designed to take into account the user's aim in consulting a document. Various levels of interactivity are introduced, which blur the boundaries between applications: information extraction can be seen as a form of summarisation where the user determines in advance what information is wanted from the text base. Question–answering systems constitute a totally user-centred form of consultation, which takes no account of writer's purpose. Document browsing systems may be seen as both text- and user-sensitive: they are interactive systems designed to help readers find, in a long document or in a series of documents, segments which are relevant with respect to a query (Minel, 2003; Bilhaut, Charnois, Enjalbert & Mathet, 2003). They use various discourse markers (e.g. frame introducers), together with other techniques, and aim to provide sophisticated display functions, so as to overcome the disadvantages of on-screen reading.

This brief overview has focused on systems designed to help users access relevant information in documents or document bases. Considerable research is also being devoted to the development of aids for the production of technical documents, with concerns ranging from terminological coherence to document normalisation, and also calling upon analyses of textual markers. We have tried to show that linguistic studies of markers of semantic relations within texts have a twofold relevance to the theme of this book: they form the basis of linguistic resources used in document engineering systems, and they can lead to insights into fundamental issues in the production and understanding of written documents in the workplace.

Chapter 2

The Design, Understanding and Usage of Pictograms

Charles Tijus, Javier Barcenilla, Brigitte Cambon de Lavalette and Jean-Guy Meunier

This review of research on the pictogram effect covers theoretical and experimental studies from linguistics, psychology and cognitive ergonomics on the design and validation, comprehension and usage of pictograms. Pictograms form part of our daily lives through their use in medication, transport, computers, etc., because they indicate—in iconic form — places, directions, actions or constraints on actions in either the real world (a town, a road, etc.) or virtual space (computer desktop, Internet, etc.). This chapter is essentially a review of research on the pictogram effect, which can be summed up as follows: a pictogram is better than a label, and recognizing an image is easier than reading text (Norman, 1990). This review covers theoretical and experimental studies from linguistics, psychology and cognitive ergonomics on the design and validation, comprehension and usage of pictograms. Among the various methods, an emphasis is placed on classification and the creation of pictogram taxonomies as tools for homogenization and design.

This chapter summarizes the results of studies investigating how to use pictograms to convey safety information in the workplace, as well as some new insights into how to study the effects of the iconic nature of pictogram information. Here we are talking about *signaletics*, which we define as being the *science of signalization*, which is to say the study of external representations of object meanings, of object properties, and of mandatory, warning and prohibitive statements for categories of objects and users in more or less well-defined situations (Tijus, Chêne, Jadot, Leproux, Poitrenaud, & Richard, 2001).

After a short section defining what a pictogram is, this chapter is composed of four main sections. The first section describes empirical data reported in specialized domains publications (related to the use of pictograms in public information, pharmaceutics, road signs and the workplace), when assessing the role of pictograms in conveying recommended modes of behavior. The second section concerns the theoretical contributions of semiotics, of cognitive psychology for pictogram readability and understanding, and of the contextual categorization approach, a theory that accounts for the contextual effects involved in the understanding of pictograms. The third section describes the methodology, some examples and some outcomes from studies on the creation of taxonomies and ontologies of pictograms for evaluation and design. This provides a basis for understanding how a signaletic system can more or less help to solve the problem of iconic external representation of categories of objects, as well as of actions, which are two cognitive entities that, on their own, cannot be entirely captured by an image. The final section provides recommendations for the ergonomic conception of pictograms, in order to improve the readability and understanding of pictograms used to convey user safety information in the workplace.

1 Common Definitions and Uses of Pictograms

A pictogram is a stylized figurative drawing that is used to convey information of an analogical or figurative nature directly to indicate an object or to express an idea. Pictograms can fulfill many functions. They are used to replace written indications and instructions expressing regulatory, mandatory, warning and prohibitory information, when that information must be processed quickly (e.g. road traffic signs), when users speak different languages (i.e. non-natives), have limited linguistic ability (e.g. people with low levels of literacy or little education) or have visual problems (e.g. older people), and especially when there is a legal obligation to inform and for the user to comply with the information, mainly for safety purposes (e.g. use of dangerous materials at work). A pictograms needs to capture users' attention (users' need to *see* the pictogram), to improve users' comprehension of warnings (users' need to *attend to* it), and it also needs to increase their awareness of risk, generally by serving as an "instantaneous memorandum" of a risk (Otsubo, 1988).

There are a number of recognized advantages of pictograms in the literature (see the CACP report, 2000, for a summary). First of all, they have the potential to be interpreted more accurately and more quickly than words. Thus, they can serve as "instant reminders" of a hazard or an established message. They improve understanding of warnings for those with visual or literacy difficulties. They can make warnings more noticeable or "attention grabbing", and they can improve their legibility. Pictograms or brief textual information are suitable when users undertake familiar or routine tasks (although this does not apply for novel or highly complex tasks). In addition, pictograms are more easily processed at a distance compared to textual information, although a distinction should be made between abstract symbols and more explicit icons.

However, there are also a number of disadvantages to relying on pictograms. First, very few pictograms are universally understood; therefore, depending on their use, they may not be interpreted correctly by all groups of consumers and across all cultures. Next, it always takes many years for any pictogram to reach maximum effectiveness. There is also the potential for significant confusion (interpreting the opposite or often inappropriate meaning), which can create an additional safety hazard.

2 Understanding Pictograms

In order to be adopted, a pictogram must reach a certain level of effectiveness, especially when the information to be conveyed concerns safety. The method of testing the comprehension and effectiveness of pictograms used in ISO 9186 (Public Information Signs) relies on judges choosing from a number of response categories: correct understanding of the symbol is certain; correct understanding of the symbol is likely; correct understanding of the symbol is fairly likely; the meaning conveyed is the opposite to that intended; incorrect response given; "don't know" response given; no response given. According to the ISO standard, a symbol is accepted if 67% of the users understand it in an unquestionable way or almost (ISO 9186-1989). In the United States, the pictogram must be understood by 85% of the users in order to be standardized (ANSI Z535, 1987).

Although the effectiveness of pictograms relies on characteristics such as color (Christ & Corso, 1982), shape (Arend, Muthig, & Wandmacher, 1987) and visual complexity (Byrne, 1993), all of which have been widely studied, the main difficulty in processing the iconic information represented in pictograms relates to its meaningfulness. One of the main causes of difficulty in interpreting iconic signs relates to the fact that natural language signs use "text" or sequences of sentences in order to aid interpretation of a given word. For example the word "BANK" cannot be interpreted if used alone. In order to interpret it, one must apply a "context". This "context" can be the "context of use". The only equivalent tool pictograms have to realize the same functions seems to be their "context" of use, which allows some type of categorization. For example, an arrow at the corner of a street is not the same as an arrow on the edge of a bottle cap.

Much of the empirical data on pictogram comprehension are to be found in specialized domain literature. Many studies have investigated the legibility of pictograms used to convey information to people about their orientation in public space, use of pharmaceutics products, road safety and organization of the workplace.

2.1 Public Information

Not only do poorly designed pictograms with complex content cause problems for people with limited literacy skills, but also basic pictograms can be problematic for literate readers. For instance, when computing the first response made by each participant for each basic pictogram, Cross (1994) found that the highest "first word label" score was only 46%; for instance, when shown a drawing of a comb, only 46% of participants gave this as their first response. Davies, Haines, Norris, and Wilson (1998) set out to investigate the role of 13 product-related pictograms in conveying consumer safety information. In general, the pictograms were found to be poorly understood. In fact, it appears to be very difficult to design highly representative symbols, requiring no learning, to convey public information such as consumer information, warnings or information in public places. For instance, Zwaga and Easterby (1984) considered the issue of designing symbols to be used for the purpose of public information. When participants were shown an entire set of 29 pictograms for use in a railway station and asked to find the required target, the authors found that only one symbol was identified by almost all (99%) of the sample population of 400. In addition, it has been noted that the chances of two users choosing the same name for a picture is less than 18%.

Furthermore, many studies have shown that even after testing and redesign, public information pictograms did not reach optimal levels of comprehension (Wogalter, Wolff, Magurno, & Kohake, 1994).

Moreover, with regard to understanding, Zwaga and Easterby (1984) reported that familiarity with a sign improved its comprehension. On the subject of the noticeability of public information warnings, Otsubo (1988) reported that the type of label (words only, pictogram only or words and pictogram) did not significantly affect whether participants noticed, comprehended or remembered the warning. However, 12–50% of the participants complied with the warning labels as opposed to 0% in the control group, with the highest level of compliance found for the "words plus pictogram" type warning label on the product perceived as most dangerous. Participants tended to read warnings only when they perceived the product to be dangerous, unfamiliar or in need of a warning. In general, making warning pictograms more explicit and more severe increases consumers' intentions to act cautiously.

Thatcher, Mahlangu, and Zimmerman (2006) designed an icon set involving illiterate people and evaluated three public prototype interfaces: icon-only, text-only and text-and-icon interface. Comparisons were made between these three interfaces, and a functionally illiterate group and a comparison literate group. Results suggested that within each group there were few significant differences based on the type of interface, although there were significant differences between the groups. Significant differences in the literate group were primarily due to prior exposure to interfaces, whereas significant differences in the illiterate group were primarily due to icon comprehensibility.

2.2 Pictograms in Pharmaceutics

Pictograms are also common in patient information leaflets for medicinal products. Pictograms in these leaflets are intended to provide full and comprehensible information because patients' ability to understand information about medication is crucial to both patient safety and drug effectiveness.

Pictograms are of benefit to the comprehension and recall of prescription instructions, and participants who are given "natural language plus pictogram" labels understand information better than participants with only "natural language labels" (Dowse & Ehlers, 1998, 2003). However, some research has not supported the hypothesis that pictograms are beneficial for the acquisition and comprehension of information. In order to evaluate the effects of pictograms in patient information leaflets, Bernardini, Ambrogi, Peroli, Tiraltri, and Fardella (2000) interviewed 1004 patients in pharmacies and reported that participants usually read the patient information leaflet but they neither understood it easily nor found the required information readily. However, most participants (74.3%) considered the use of symbols helpful in finding the required information. They analyzed to what extent five symbols could be used for each of five topics, and found consistent responses for "side effects", "pediatric use", "use in pregnancy" and "dosage", but not for "therapeutic indications" and "contraindications".

Such discrepancies may not be related to education, but to familiarity and context. Dowse and Ehlers (2003) collected demographic data together with information on literacy skills for participants asked to interpret 46 pictograms. Results showed misinterpretation across all educational groups. Knapp, Raynor, Jebar, and Price (2005), who examined the effects of repeated presentation of pictograms on understandability, found great variability in the rate of correct interpretation (8–90%) and that only three of the ten different instruction and warning pictograms were understood by at least 85% of the population. After providing their interpretation, participants were informed of the correct meaning and then the experimental trials were repeated a week later. Results showed that participants performed significantly better at the second presentation of pictograms.

In a series of experiments, Barcenilla and Tijus (2002) analyzed the responses of 134 participants to the question "What does it mean?" for 14 medicinal pictograms. The average correct response rate was 39%. This rate increased to 65% when a scenario introducing the pictogram was provided.

2.3 Road Signs

Drivers encounter many signs on the road. Road sign design includes the use of colour, shape, symbols and icons. For instance, warning signs are made up of a white triangle, a red border and black graphics, usually an icon of the hazard. They are standardized across Europe, and road sign knowledge is tested as part of the driving test. They are supposed to help drivers deal with road network dangers and driving regulations, to ensure quick recognition and to indicate the category of action to be undertaken. According to Allen, Lunenfeld, and Alexander (1971), drivers need information in case they are unsure of their perception of a situation; in this situation, road signs are useful for problem solving and the task in hand. For example, Dubois, Fleury, and Mazet (1987) have shown that drivers have different representations of the different types of road they drive along (such as rural roads, town streets, city ring roads, etc.), and that they look out for information according to these representations. Do drivers perceive visual information when it is not within the context of the task they are performing? It is probable that information not meeting task requirements is not as well processed as information that responds directly. With reference to speed signs, for example, Triggs and Harris (1982) found that traffic signs tended to generate a very low braking response rate in drivers. For instance, the signs "Traffic Hazard Ahead" and "Road Plant Ahead" caused only about 3% and 4% of drivers respectively to respond. The rate was slightly higher at 6% for the sign "Roadworks Ahead". The response rate for a "Speed Check Ahead" sign was statistically significantly higher. The investigators found that reaction time depended on the ease with which one signal could be distinguished from other possible signals. For example, one can distinguish between highway signs differing in shape faster than those varying in verbal message alone.

Surprising, driving skill and experience do not appear to mean increased levels of performance on tests of road sign knowledge and understanding. It is often reported that road users' knowledge of road signs is generally rather poor, and this presents an unquestionable source of danger. In France, an investigation concluded that 97.75% of drivers would need to retake their driving test if they were subjected to a full road sign test; only a third of drivers could recognize signs indicating "Give Way" (Averous, 1975). More recent results corroborate these poor performances (Al-Madani & Al-Janahi, 2002). Similarly, according to Borowski, Shinar, and Parmet (2005), experienced drivers pay less attention to road signs located in unexpected places. They found that, under simulation conditions, drivers experienced difficulties in identifying traffic signs when their location did not conform to expectations; the authors felt this was because drivers have a well-learned pre-determined schema for scanning the roadway.

With reference to driving experience, Tijus, Barcenilla, Cambon de Lavalette, Lambinet, and Lacaste (2005) compared the understanding of road signs by novices and expert drivers in isolation or in the context of a real road situation. The main results showed that, unlike novices, experts failed on the "What does it mean?" question when road signs were displayed in isolation but responded successfully to the "What to do?" question. In short, they found that driving experience does not improve people's understanding of the meaning of road signs. Furthermore, the number of years' experience is inversely correlated with the level of understanding of the intended meaning: the more one drives, the less one is able to provide the intended meaning of road signs. A result that was interpreted as being a proceduralization effect (Anderson, 1982): the "what to do" acquisition builds compiled driving actions that no longer require the "what does it mean" representation and verbal mediation drops out.

2.4 Pictograms at Work

As in studies mentioned above, Wilkinson, Cary, Barr, and Reynolds (1997) reported that pesticide users found it significantly easier to obtain information from labels containing text only than from labels with added pictograms. Moreover, labels with pictograms were associated with a significant increase in the proportion of users taking correct safety precautions when storing the pesticides, but not when mixing or applying them. Thus, it appears difficult for pictograms to be use to demonstrate a procedure. Adding pictograms to labels did not significantly alter perceptions of the danger of the pesticide to the user either. Although pictograms did enhance the accessibility of safety information on the labels, some users found them to be confusing.

In the workplace, pictograms are being used more and more frequently in computer applications, rather than written instructions or drop-down lists. Here again, we know that the use of icons is improving usage; however, the effect of icon use on individuals' performance levels for a particular system are to a large extent unknown. Two opposing arguments have been presented. The first states that icons make sense because they have a single unambiguous meaning, while the second position describes the use of icon as metaphor, for instance the use of the scissors icon for "cut" in the text edit function. McDougall (2001) employed either concrete, abstract or arbitrary icon sets in a computer-based problem-solving task and found that knowledge structures do depend on the nature of graphic information but do not rely as much on the use of visual metaphor. In addition, although most measures were sensitive to initial differences between icon sets, only some measures were sensitive to the long-term differences that remained after users had gained experience with the icon set.

Computers also offer the possibility of animating pictograms. An experiment was conducted by Bodner (1994) to measure differences in identification of static and animated buttons. Twelve subjects were given both static and animated keys, and asked to identify the function of each key. Subjects were able to choose the function of animated keys (83%) more often than that of static ones (68%). The results indicate that animation is useful in helping users identify a key's function. Because animation could be also an effective means of portraying complex processes evolving over time, Baecker, Small, and Mander (1991) investigated the use of animated icons to improve comprehension of functions. They found that all users understood the icon's function after seeing the animation, but they also noted that some users did, in fact, make misinterpretations. They also reported that there is the added danger that too much animation can be a distraction.

3 Theoretical Basis for Understanding Pictograms

The way that humans process iconic information is a complex issue. Although pictograms hold certain advantages related to image processing, research has revealed a number of difficulties and problems related to the interpretation of intended meanings. First of all, although drawings can be used effectively to represent static objects, there are limitations to their use in representing events and actions in which objects are modified. Since pictograms need to incorporate the shapes of specific objects, there are limitations to the use of drawings to represent categories of objects, especially the kind of superordinate categories that group objects of different shapes. For example, the pictogram "No Smoking" which shows a cigarette also applies to cigars and pipes. Another difficulty arises from the symbolic nature and polysemy of pictograms (Olson, 1970). A drawing of a car in a pictogram could refer to the car itself, to driving, or to vigilance, as is the case with medicinal pictograms, etc. Thus, one cannot expect an isomorphism between the pictogram and its meaning (Kolers, 1969). The meaning of a pictogram has to be inferred through a process of interpretation constructed from both the task in hand, knowledge and context.

As underlined by Horton (1994), the interpretation of a pictogram depends on multiple subjective and visual factors. However, the science of signaletics might find some basis in cognitive, semiotic and linguistic approaches.

3.1 A Cognitive Approach to Pictograms

Vezin (1984) has provided a number of arguments promoting the pictogram as a powerful tool for the cognitive system: (i) the pictogram reduces mnemonic load and thus allows cognitive saving; (ii) its descriptive nature provides high quality pictorial representation which facilitates memorization; and (iii) since it can be used to represent a category, it can provide broad information exceeding the specific items it portrays.

The pictogram also benefits from the efficiency of visual imagery. (i) Identification is more precise from a single glance, at a greater distance and at a greater speed than with words (Collins & Lerner, 1982; Lehto, 1992): an image is processed in parallel and therefore more quickly than words, which require serial processing. (ii) Higher resistance to cognitive interference (King, 1975; Santa, 1977): an image, memorized and recalled as a single unit, would resist interference better than a text made up of several parts. (iii) Images are perceived better in suboptimal conditions (Ells & Dewar, 1979) (iv) A pictogram can also be better stored in memory due to dual encoding, that is both visual and symbolic (Paivio, 1986); this engenders a deeper level of processing and greater consolidation in memory. For instance, Haber and Myers (1982), who were interested in the storage of pictograms in memory, found that recognition accuracy was greatest for pictograms and poorest for words. Although participants were able to disregard shape within pictograms, they were most accurate when presented with the same shapes as those used in the original trials. But across all conditions, participants were most accurate when forced to recall both the shape and the content. These and other results were taken to be mildly supportive of a dual encoding hypothesis.

However, for McDougall (2001), an image's cognitive effect needs to be distinguished from its relationship with function. The author argues that semantic distance between the visual representation and the action to be applied to the object, rather than concreteness, and should be the main determinant of comprehensibility and performance. Although representations of real-world items, through icons, may help users in their initial encounters with pictograms, forming strong systematic relationships between icons and functions should be more important. Thus, the problem at hand would be how to measure the semantic distance between icon and function, particularly for prescription information of pictograms in pharmaceutics.

3.2 A Cognitive Approach Based on Contextual Categorization

Pictograms, being symbols, are polysemic. For example, a trash can with a cross on it could mean "do not throw away", "do not empty trash in this area", "pick out household waste" and so on. In fact, the difficulty here is to link image with information. When interpreting danger signs, users not only have to infer the action required of them, linking both the action with the specific danger, but also need to infer which objects are involved in the action. For example, the round road sign showing two cars, where the left one appears in red, means, "*overtaking prohibited*". But does it also mean that a motorcycle or a van can undertake?

In fact, context helps to disambiguate a pictogram's intended meaning. For instance, Hameen-Anttila, Kemppainen, Enlund, Bush, and Marja (2004) tested whether children of 11 and 13 years could understand pictograms developed by the United States Pharmacopoeia. Every second child was given a leaflet with plain text and the others received the same text accompanied by pictograms. Most of the children understood the meanings of the pictograms correctly, the percentage of correct explanations varying from 30 to 99%, according to the pictogram used. Even well understood pictograms did not help the children understand the leaflet information. This study shows that the context in which pictograms are tested makes a difference to their comprehension. Testing plain pictograms without incorporating them within their real context (e.g. in a patient information leaflet) may overestimate their usefulness in leaflet information.

In order to evaluate to what extent context can aid understanding of the meaning of pictograms, Tijus et al. (2005) tested 167 participants' comprehension of a pictogram presented either in isolation or fixed to a box of medicine. The experimental design aimed to vary the level of information provided by the context (pictogram alone, pictogram with text, pictogram with complete packaging, pictogram with complete packaging with user instructions given by the doctor to the patient) in which the pictogram was presented. The results showed that the context in which a pictogram is perceived and used can lead to it being interpreted more accurately; context improved comprehension of the pictogram in an incremental way, starting with the least optimal situation (a pictogram alone: 33%) to the optimal, where contextual facilitation is maximal (a pictogram with complete packaging, label and user instructions, 91%).

Thus, contextualization appears to contribute significantly to the understanding of pictograms by providing a support for interpretation and reducing polysemy. That is why some authors (for instance, Wolff & Wogalter, 1998) recommend presenting the pictogram in the environment in which it will eventually be seen.

The role of context may be explained by contextual categorization (Tijus, 2001), an approach consistent with the theory of perceptual learning proposed by Gibson (1969). Perceptual learning is a process by which one becomes increasingly attuned to optical information specifying properties of the environment and thus becomes increasingly capable of differentiating similar stimuli (Gibson, 1966). According to Gibson "what is learned can be described as the detection of properties, patterns and distinctive features" (1969, pg. 77). Contextual categorization is a theory of information processing which advocates that all objects are seen in the context of other objects, through the construction of a hierarchical, *ad hoc* network of categories. It follows that objects are simultaneously put in relation and differentiated. The whole situation in which a user sees a pictogram can be modeled using contextual categorization in order to discover what she/he will infer to be the meaning of the pictogram.

3.3 A Semiotic and Linguistic Approach

Natural language and iconic signs do have one thing in common: they both use atomic and complex signs to construct sentences. Hence they both can convey information, that is, they both can have a propositional meaning of any type (assertion, orders, etc.). But what really differentiates one from another is that iconic signs cannot easily be used to build "texts", that is sequences of sentences expressing narration, argumentation, demonstration, conversation, etc… which is one of the important functions of natural language.

It seems difficult to accept that symbolic and iconic languages are both semiotic systems. Many researchers suppose that icons and graphic signs have a unique coded meaning, unlike words, which they recognize as symbols (one word, different meanings); this is because icons are analogues of what they represent or indicate and graphic signs are used to express a unique meaning (one sign, one meaning). Thus, the "cow" icon (see Figure 1a) means "cows", and a red triangle means "danger", whilst a red circle means "prohibited"; therefore a cow on a red triangle would mean "danger: cows" (Figure 1b), whilst a cow on a red circle would mean "cows prohibited" (Figure 1c).

Unlike authors who advocate that iconic languages belong to the analogical mode of external representation, like visual signs and representations such as pictures, semioticians analyze pictograms as modes of representation (or signs) having structure (syntax), meaning (semantics) and usage (pragmatics). Like any other type of language, iconic languages possess a grammatical structure. They are not generated haphazardly and are not meaningless. For Meunier (1998), it is not their semantics that renders them so easy to use, but, as we shall discover, their functional structure. This author shows how a particular type of grammar — algebraic or categorical grammar — is heuristic in modeling the compositional structure of iconic languages: iconic languages (i) operate through material carriers; (ii) have distinctive properties, or features, which become the basic constituents of the structure; (iii) are organized according to categories, operations and rules; (iv) therefore are open to systematic interpretation. For Meunier, features performing an identical functional role make up a category. We recognize a category SHAPE because the features it is composed of can have a color superimposed on them. In other words, the features of the SHAPE class belong to a category, not because they resemble geometric figures and respond to an intuitive perception, but because they are the only features that may be colored according to the features of the COLORS

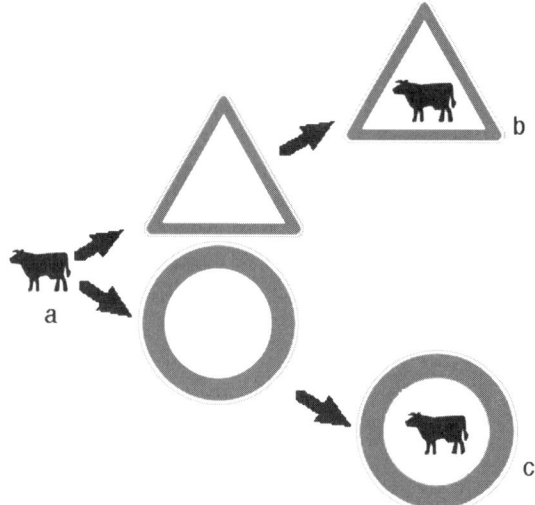

Figure 1: The making of a road sign.

category. In contrast, COLORS form a category because of the common possible operation of applying them to a figure (an inverse relation to superposition). It is because of their categorical structure that many semiotic systems are often so easy to learn.

However, iconic languages are not complete languages. A road sign is not a logical proposition that drivers can choose to adopt or ignore in their decision-making (Droste, 1976). As symbolic languages, pictograms are halfway between being rule-governed systems and being *ad hoc* solutions to communication and expression problems. Languages will often accept very *ad hoc* configurations. For example, natural language is full of idiomatic expressions; the same applies to iconic languages and notations (Meunier, 1998).

Figure 1 represents the construction of a road sign: the "cow icon" (which stands for any cattle) combined with (b) a red bordered triangle would mean that there is a danger *because* of the eventual presence of cattle on the road; with (c) a red bordered circle, it would mean that this route is prohibited *to* cattle. Note that (b) could be "danger for cows" and (c) could be "prohibited due to cows". Similarly, note that Figure 1b means "danger *because of* cows", not "danger *for* cows", and Figure 1c means "cows prohibited", not "prohibited *because of* cows". Road signs do not provide the nature of the relationship between different components: the whole of the icon is more than the sum of its parts (Harmon & Julesz, 1973; Szlichcinski, 1980). Given that object category (commonalities of possible instances) and action (at least two states of an event) cannot be pictured in static visual images, at issue here is the problem of icon polysemy or "multi-meaning icons". In linguistics, the word "polysemy" is used to describe how many words can have multiple meanings. Thus, the word "fence" can mean an enclosure, a receiver of stolen goods, to engage in swordplay or to screen off. The actual meaning within a sentence is determined by the context. The same concept can apply to pictograms (Figure 2).

Figure 2: Icons in road signs are of a symbolic nature. The "do not overtake" road sign on the right applies to all kinds of vehicles, including trucks. The left hand "do not overtake" sign is only for trucks.

Figure 3: From left to right: a figurative, an abstract and an arbitrary pictogram.

4 Typological of Pictograms for Evaluation and Design

4.1 Creating Pictogram Taxonomies

A possible approach to the study of pictograms is to construct taxonomies, or hierarchical typologies, by differentiating classes and subclasses of pictograms. For many researchers (Edworthy & Adams, 1996), three types of pictogram exist: figurative, abstract and arbitrary (Figure 3).

The figurative pictogram is made up of a direct representation of the object. It is supposed to evoke without ambiguity the object or the situation represented (e.g. a flame to indicate a flammable product). The abstract pictogram comprises only certain aspects of the concept to evoke it in its totality (e.g. a curved line to indicate a turn). Lastly, the arbitrary pictogram bears no resemblance to physical reality (e.g. the symbol used to indicate "radioactive"). Rogers (1989) has provided a more refined description of figurative pictograms, classifying them as either (i) similar images (e.g. landslides), (ii) typical examples or the use of specimens to represent categories (e.g. a book to represent a library) or (iii) symbolic icons, when an image is used to represent a higher level of abstraction than the image itself (e.g. a broken wine glass to show fragility). Similarly, in terms of the way the meaning is expressed, Barcenilla and Tijus (2002) distinguish figurative pictograms as being either (i) metonymic, when one element indicates the whole (e.g. a book for library, a knife and the fork for restaurant), (ii) metaphoric, when another object is used to express an intended meaning (e.g. a bomb for a computer bug) or (iii) categorical, when a pictogram indicates a category (e.g. a car for both cars and trucks).

There are other dimensions such as meticulousness (the degree of detail in object drawings), dimensionality (portraying an object's depth in only two dimensions: with shading, nuances of colors and perspective) and functionality (using drawing to represent a function: for writing, one can show a pencil in isolation or a pencil with drawn lines coming from it). However, a major dimension concerns meaning and classifying pictograms according to categories based on semantic content. According to Easterby and Hakiel (1981), security instructions conveyed by pictograms have three functions: (i) to describe a situation: the image identifies the risk, (ii) to prescribe an action: the image describes the action to be carried out, and (iii) to prohibit an action: the image shows the prohibited action. Tijus et al. (2001) showed that pictogram semantics can be described according to a limited set of basic categories organized hierarchically, right from the portrayal of an object ("this is X", a sign saying "Eiffel Tower"), to the representation of procedures ("how to use X", for example the representation of how to purchase a travel pass from a ticket machine), or to the use of functional objects ("how to use Y on X", for example "how to use the travel pass in the transport system"). These hierarchical levels have an inclusive relationship: one cannot say, "X is in this direction" without saying at the same time "this is X" (what you will find will be X). One cannot say "how to get to X" without indicating "the direction that X is in".

The creation of taxonomy for a given set of pictograms can be useful in increasing users' ability to learn them. Tijus et al. (2001) used pictograms relating to danger in the workplace (Figure 4) in order to study participants' ability to learn pictograms presented taxonomically. In an initial learning phase, 40 participants were exposed to the above ten signs warning of potential dangers in the workplace together with their written labels for ten minutes before carrying out a distraction task. Then, in a second phase, they were presented with the danger pictograms without their labels and had to give the corresponding meanings; this learning test was repeated three days later. The group of participants that had been presented with the pictograms within a taxonomy tree (as in Figure 4-right) performed significantly better than the group that was shown the pictograms at random (as in Figure 4-left), (67% vs. 49%).

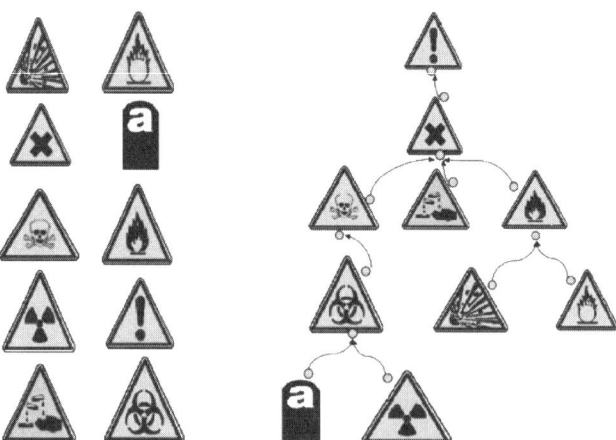

Figure 4: Ten danger pictograms displayed at random (left panel) or in a general-to-specific taxonomy tree (right panel) — 1: General danger; 1.1: Harmful materials or irritants; 1.1.1: Poison; 1.1.2: Corrosive; 1.1.3: Flammable; 1.1.1.1: Biohazard; 1.1.3.1: Explosive; 1.1.3.2: Flammable gases; 1.1.1.1.1: Asbestos; 1.1.1.1.2: Radiation.

There was a significantly higher rate of correct responses after the first learning phase than in the second learning phase three days later (66% vs. 50), and performance after three days was less diminished for the taxonomic group (12% less vs. 21% less).

The creation of pictogram taxonomies makes it possible to illustrate how a signaletic system can solve the problem of representing classes and types of actions to perform. In terms of training, the beginner's task is to learn the categorical organization of pictograms and to understand the basic meanings of actions in intension (What does "to copy" mean vs. "to duplicate", when applied to a computer file?) as well as in extension (To which objects does the "copy" function need to be applied?).

4.2 Creating Pictogram Ontologies

In addition to taxonomies (classes and subclasses of pictograms), it is possible to construct pictogram ontologies or hierarchical organizations of knowledge based on the components of pictograms. In order to carry out such ontologies, it is necessary to break up pictograms into their components and to compile an inventory of all the basic elements used to create pictograms. As an example, Tijus et al. (2005) used the property tree framework (Poitrenaud, 1995) to describe an entire set of 300 road signs in an attempt to capture the internal structure of the road signs (Figure 5). From a semantic point of view, each sign could be described in terms of one property tree. Four types of properties were identified: (i) surface properties corresponding to the shape and color of the sign, (ii) the label indicating the sign's function, (iii) the category of action involved (information, danger, prohibition, obligation), and (iv) the object to which the action is to be applied.

The creation of ontologies can fulfil many goals. They can facilitate an evaluation of how closely pictogram properties correspond to information and prescribed action; they enable us to investigate whether a single category of target objects or actions, corresponds to one category of shapes, colors, or icons. Bromberg, Tijus, Georget, Jadot, Leproux, and Poitrenaud (2002) have used the construction of ontologies as a means for producing a harmonized signage system that could be used in railway systems across Europe.

5 Conclusion: Ergonomic Recommendations for Conception of Pictograms

A pictogram is better than a label, and recognizing an image is easier than reading text (Norman, 1990). Thus, pictograms are used in a number of situations in which verbal messages are not possible or adequate. Interpreting the meanings of pictograms is part of everyday life, both at home and in town, and also in the workplace in the case of special safety precautions. However, the user's perspective is not always taken into account when pictograms are conceived and implemented. Moreover, many studies reveal poor levels of user understanding of pictogram content. Ultimately a pictogram's effectiveness should be measured primarily in terms of people's ability to understand it.

A number of recommendations for pictogram conception have been proposed: (i) there must be appropriate levels of complexity and detail to maximize visibility and comprehension; a good pictogram should contain little detail and should be easily distinguishable; excessive

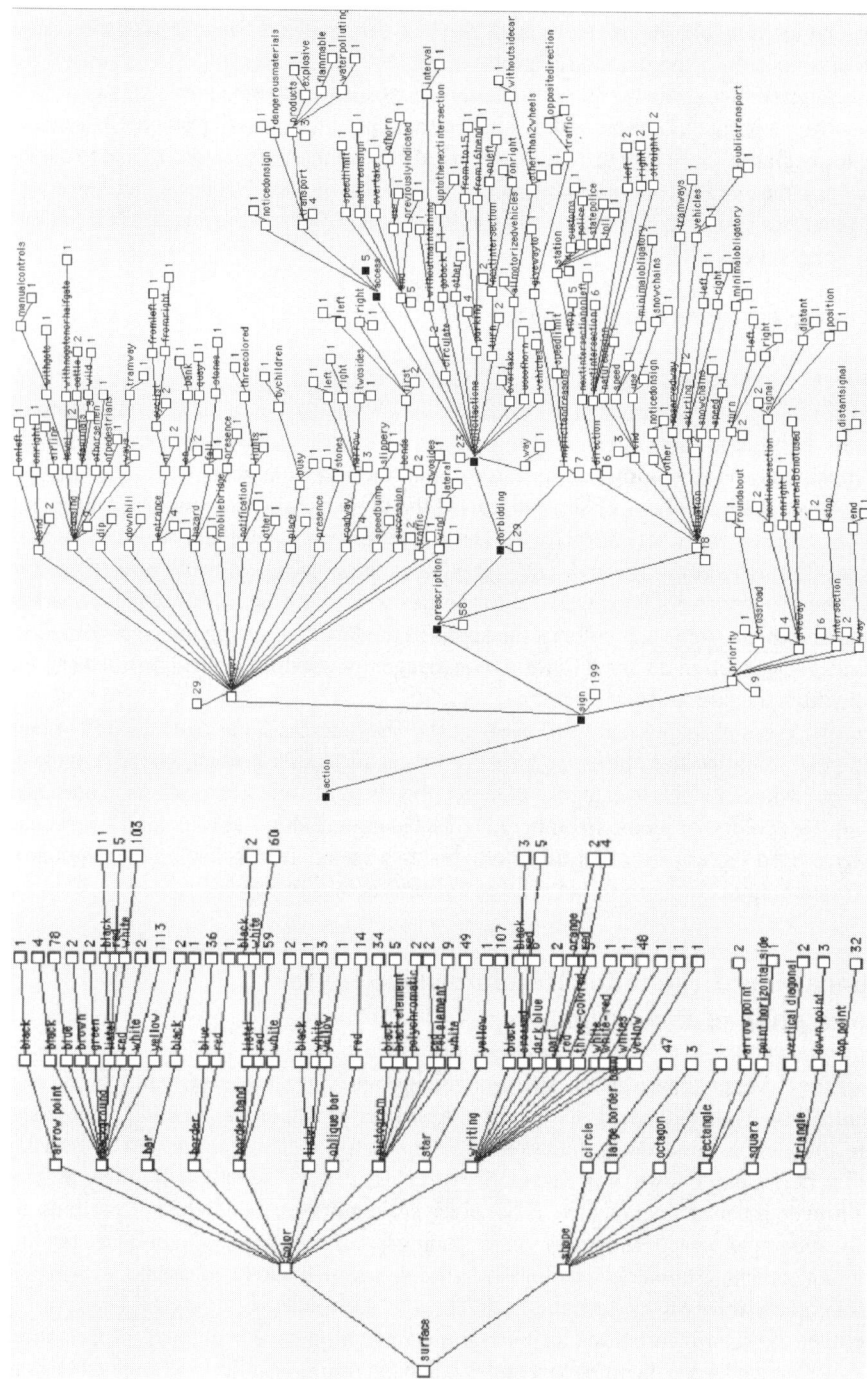

Figure 5: The taxonomy of action properties for a subset of 199 road signs relating to danger, prescription and priority.

representations of reality should not be used; objects should not be drawn merely with contours; shading and nuances of color should not be used with thin or flat objects; 3D representations should be used for objects with several dimensions; (ii) uniformity: new symbol designs must be consistent with existing pictograms which are well understood; (iii) discriminability: an effective symbol must be easily distinguishable compared with others; (iii) legibility: the size of elements and their separators, the levels of contrast between elements, and also content familiarity facilitate legibility and comprehension; (iv) lastly, note that an appropriate level of complexity and detail will depend on how the pictogram is to be used. It is advisable to adopt a sequential design approach (component by component): start with a basic shape with few details and add additional details one by one until an optimal level of comprehension is obtained (Wogalter et al., 1994).

Pelegrina and Gallifa (1994) and Beltran and Auque (1993) recommend that typicality effects should be considered and familiar and typical images used in the contents of pictograms, given that user understanding does not depend on the number of features nor on concreteness but mainly on familiarity. In addition, given the poor levels of understanding associated with some pictograms, certain authors recommend displaying pictograms in conjunction with verbal information in order to ensure the correct message is communicated.

When assessing pictogram effectiveness, Wolff and Wogalter (1998) recommend presenting the pictogram in the environment in which it will eventually be seen. This environment forms part of the context, the task at hand being another part. Context is a support for interpreting a pictogram's meaning. Context helps to reduce a pictogram's polysemy. Studies have demonstrated that increasing the level of contextual information tends to eliminate a certain number of errors, such as those due to activating typical schemas, or selecting the wrong function, or when there is a misunderstanding as to what is actually represented in the pictogram. For instance, when a pictogram on sun cream packaging showing a sun with a cross on it is interpreted as "do not leave the sun cream in the sun", while the correct meaning is "once cream applied, do not expose skin to the sun". Context helps to disambiguate the message expressed in the pictogram.

Recommendations also have been made regarding learning. Pictograms that are not immediately recognized may be learned rapidly, after which the role of the pictogram is to stimulate recall of that information. Thus the ultimate success of a pictogram would depend on trainees' ability to learn it carefully. One recommendation for optimal learning is to use taxonomies to enable trainees to differentiate between pictograms, and to use ontologies in order for trainees to differentiate between the meanings of pictogram components.

All these recommendations can be achieved through the collaboration of sector specialists, designers, ergonomists and psychologists.

Chapter 3

Readability and Intelligibility of Procedural Texts: The Case of Enumeration in Legal Texts

Céline Beaudet and Pamela Grant

This article explores how configurational markers contribute to the readability and intelligibility of procedural texts. More specifically, it examines the role of the textual configuration of enumerations in legal writing. The authors situate legal writing as a distinct form of procedural writing governed by certain constraints. They observe that enumeration is a dominant procedure in the thematization of legislative texts and pose their research question: In a legal text, does readability cumulate through the vertical configuration of a series of elements? Studying any type of metatextual operation from the perspective of readability involves investigating the relation between readability and textual intelligibility. The question is thus treated here by examining the language and discourse operations that interact within the text, that account for the signalling of textual organization, and that influence the clarity of the text.

1 Introduction

Readability and intelligibility are of primary concern to legal drafters, who must formulate legal texts so as to reflect the intention and the spirit of the legislator as clearly and accurately as possible. This paper will examine one of the many factors that contribute to the readability and intelligibility of procedural writing: the configuration of enumerations.[1] Specifically, we will explore the following question: In a legal text, do enumerations presented in vertical configuration make a text more readable and more intelligible?

---

[1]Céline Beaudet began this research in December 2000, when she was a French language consultant to the Legislative Services Branch of the Department of Justice Canada. The authors thank Philippe Hallée, from the Legislative Services Branch, for his help with this research project.

Written Documents In The Workplace
Copyright © 2007 by Elsevier Ltd.
All rights of reproduction in any form reserved.
ISBN: 978-0-080-47487-8

Beaudet, C., & Grant, P. (2007). Readability and intelligibility of procedural texts: The case of enumeration in legal texts. In G. Rijlaarsdam (Series Ed.) and D. Alamargot, P. Terrier, & J.-M. Cellier (Vol. Eds.), Studies in Writing, Vol. 21, Written Documents in the Workplace, 33–46.

We will address this question by first giving an overview of the language and discourse operations that interact within a text to signal textual organization, and then by exploring the relationship between readability and intelligibility and between cohesion and coherence. The role of enumeration in legal texts will then be investigated within this framework.

2 Configurational Markers

In legal drafting, the addition of properties, parts, or actions is a most common method of developing topics and clarifying thematic concepts. Ideally, the drafter can marry form and content through the use of enumeration, with the segmenting, sequencing, and clustering of constitutive parts reflecting the organization of ideas.

The configuration of enumerations is of particular concern. Enumerations may be listed in random order or in prioritized order. When the order is random, the absence of intrinsic order can make it difficult for the reader to understand the full meaning of the enumerations. Seriation procedures (Adam & Revaz, 1989) can facilitate comprehension by providing marks of interpretive instruction (Charolles, 1988) and thus act as navigational aids.

To clarify an enumeration, the writer can use a set of configurational markers (Charolles, 1994), also called markers of linear integration (Turcot & Coltier, 1988), to inform the reader about both the ordering of the segments and the unit of discourse to which they belong. Thus, linear or temporal connectives such as "first," "next," and "finally" have a dual function: they inform the reader about the intrinsic order of the discursive segments introduced by these terms, and they give a sense of unity, reflecting the fact that together these segments form a whole.

3 Architectural Predicates

More specifically, these markers of configuration or of linear integration signal the sequencing, segmentation, and clustering of the constituent parts of a descriptive expansion. They signal textual organization and are therefore considered to be architectural predicates by Péry-Woodley (2001) and Condamines and Péry-Woodley (this volume). According to Péry-Woodley, architectural predicates include lexical marks—all of the expressions that signal textual organization—as well as non-lexical marks, such as punctuation, layout (for example, vertical configuration of a list), typography, and numbering. Based on the work of Virbel (1985) and Pascual (1991), Péry-Woodley confers linguistic status on all marks that signal textual architecture, whether they be lexico-syntactic or visual. As she explains, these marks have the same function: they are textual acts, that is, "discursive acts of textual construction, calling upon metalinguistic performatives whose performativity is directed towards the text itself" (2001, p. 30). [our translation]

Visual layout procedures include the use of white space to separate blocks of text, the indentation of blocks of text, the use of headings and sub-headings, the use of bold or upper-case characters, and the vertical listing of items in an enumeration. Such procedures are, by inference, erased textual acts, with the same functional value as the lexico-syntactic performatives (enumeration, division, combination, etc.) of which they are the trace. The use of vertical enumeration is an implicit textual act, a signaller of textual architecture and, as such, an architectural predicate. Thus vertical configuration of enumeration is one of the metatextual procedures that can enhance the readability of a text.

4 Textual Organization and Textual Meaning

All procedures that signal the logical organization of a text affect the meaning of the text, and this is why legal drafters are concerned with the use of configurational markers. The clarity of a text is influenced by various parameters: linguistic (related to the lexicon), textual (related to the discourse), metatextual (related to the spatial configuration of the text), and communicational (related to the communicative situation and the status of the partners in the exchange). Textual meaning results from, among other things, the interaction of various linguistic and discursive operations; these operations can be identified and described, their dynamic interaction can be analysed, and the writer can use them consciously to improve the clarity of a text (Beaudet, 2000, 2005; Labasse, 1999).

Constructing meaning is a complex activity. In our opinion it is not possible to examine the effect of an operation (in this case, the configuration of an enumeration) that produces meaning without considering the context in which it occurs; the metatextual procedure must be contextualized within the general problematic of textual clarity.

5 Procedural Texts and Language Acts

A legal text is a type of procedural text—a text whose reading leads to action. The pragmatic effect of procedural writing, or of instructional-prescriptive writing (Adam, 2001), is the measure of its readability and intelligibility. This type of writing is a language act undertaken by a discourse community. Swales (1990) cites the explanation of the term "discourse community" as given by Bruce Herzberg in a 1986 paper presented at the CCC Convention in New Orleans:

> Use of the term "discourse community" testifies to the increasingly common assumption that discourse operates within conventions defined by communities, be they academic disciplines or social groups. The pedagogies associated with writing across the curriculum and academic English now use the notion of "discourse community" to signify a cluster of ideas: that language use in a group is a form of social behaviour, that discourse is a means of maintaining and extending the group's knowledge and of initiating new members into the group, and that discourse is epistemic or constitutive of the group's knowledge. (Herzberg cited in Swales, 1990, p. 21)

In the legal text we are examining, the discourse community is the legal community, made up of all those actors who play a role in the conception, formulation, and interpretation of laws. The drafting of laws has a dual purpose: to inform the public and its various communities of interest about the rights and obligations that result from the law, and also to persuade the community of legal specialists, and indirectly the rest of the population, that the legislative decisions it has reached are valid and legitimate.

Readability and intelligibility cannot be dissociated in the context of professional writing. An intelligible text is not just easy to read; it is easy to understand. Préfontaine and Lecavalier (1996) distinguish the two concepts as follows:

> Readability and intelligibility are concepts that are often confused. Frequent use of the former term has conferred upon it a generic status that encompasses all other related concepts. For us, intelligibility encompasses the components of readability and extends beyond, for we take into consideration the macrostructural elements of the text. (1996, pp. 99–100) [our translation]

It is important to distinguish between readability and intelligibility, for the two concepts do not always go hand in hand. Articles in popular magazines, for example, favour readability over intelligibility, for they are intended to entertain rather than to inform. This is not the case for laws and regulations: the effectiveness of legal discourse depends on its intelligibility. First, it must not give rise to contestation, and second, it must guide, frame, mark out, standardize, authorize, prohibit, and regulate actions and transactions in society in such a way as to actualize the individual rights and obligations provided for by the law. The legal text therefore is performative, a language act, which both states and accomplishes what it states at the same time (Searle, 1969). In order to be enforceable, a law must first be formulated and drafted. In order to be respected, it must first be understood.

The intelligibility of a legal text is not an absolute quality and cannot be explored without being contextualized, for intelligibility depends on the set of operations used to clarify the meaning of the discourse in a specific situation. Therefore the question of the readability of enumerations in law, and of their intelligibility (these objectives being considered indissociable), must be examined differently according to whether we adopt the perspective of the legal specialist or of the non-specialist, that is, of the average citizen. An online document of the Faculty of Law at the University of Geneva (*La spécificité de la communication législative*: webdroit.unige.ch/cours/formel/communication_legislative.htm) reads as follows:

> The legislator is caught between two contradictory obligations: to adopt an increasingly precise and technical language to protect freedom and security; and to adopt a language that is comprehensible to most readers. This dual constraint is difficult to overcome. Attempts to democratize legal language have proven futile. They can even be dangerous. In essence, laws are made by legal specialists for legal specialists, who have the delicate mission of ensuring the interface between the specialized language of the law and the everyday language of those subject to the law. [our translation]

The following analysis takes into account this dual concern.

6   Readability and Vertical Enumeration

The vertical listing of enumerations is one of the procedures that signal textual organization and thereby contribute to the cohesion of the text at the level of the superstructure. Vertical enumeration reveals the subdivisions of thematic content, the organization of the constitutive chunks of the text, and the logic that links them together. It also contributes to the text's intelligibility: the cohesive markers act as navigational aids and thus help to create meaning.

Cohesion is dependent on cohesive markers, which are defined as signals of thematic progression and continuity in the text. (Charaudeau & Maingueneau, 2002). The set of cohesive markers distributed throughout a text creates a network and serves to indicate the relationships between the different elements in a sentence (relationships regulated by syntax and grammar) and the different sentences within a text (sequential logic), thereby conferring a certain continuity or homogeneity to the discourse (Charolles, 1994; Condamines & Péry-Woodley, this volume).

These cohesive markers include the standardized order of words in the sentence; the respect for rules of agreement; the use of connecting expressions; the use of anaphora, renominalization, and synonyms; and the use of configurational markers and architectural predicates. Together, these cohesive markers can be seen as textualization procedures that "consist in the creation of isotopic series which contribute to establishing thematic coherence. Fundamentally linked to the linearity of the text, they explain to the reader the major hierarchical, logical, and/or temporal articulations of the text" (Bronckart, 1996, p. 123). [our translation]

Cohesive markers inform the reader about the superstructure of the text and its logical organization. Vertical layout serves as an architectural predicate: it provides visual information about the logical connection which underlies the segmentation and grouping together of concepts—in other words, about the correlation between chunks of text. The enumeration may be descriptive, explanatory, or argumentative; however, this distinction is not revealed by the spatial layout of the constitutive elements. Rather, other strategies must be used to reveal logical relationships. The link between the elements may be specified by the use of lexico-syntactic markers, such as connecting expressions, conjunctions, adverbs, and other indicators of organization, by statements of transition, or by the explicit hierarchization of elements.

7   A Tool of Textual Cohesion

The vertical layout of an enumeration plays a role similar to the paragraph, in that it visually conveys meaning about the articulations of a text, and as such is a tool of textual cohesion. It reflects the packaging of the constituent parts of the text and the logic that unites them. It does not simply give information about the textual cohesion of the text; it helps to create it.

Vertical enumeration can be accompanied by related typographical techniques, such as bullets, dashes, asterisks, or other marks of configuration, such as lettering or numbering. (Lettering and numbering are more frequently used when enumerations are listed in prioritized order and are particularly useful for reference purposes). The use of prioritized ordering guides the reader by presenting the information as a sequential unit as well as showing its hierarchical position in the whole.[2] Adam asserts that the use of such procedures is characteristic of the procedural genre:

> The designs of the "family" of texts under consideration share one characteristic: "vi-readability", that is, very strong typographic segmentation and the very systematic exploitation of typographic layout: the use of varied and often coloured characters, frequent alphanumeric marks and/or paragraphs which are more or less marked (by round, square, black or coloured bullets) [...] These procedures are characteristic of all forms of didactic discourse (the visuo-texts of Jacques Anis, 1997) and can also be found in the hyper-structures which the print media use, increasingly frequently, to draw the reader's eye and encourage fast reading. (2001, pp. 25–26) [our translation]

The use of vertical enumeration must also take into account the limited capacity of the reader's memory to retain information presented in an additive structure. According to Clerc (2000), a reader can have difficulty recalling more than five elements listed in a series. Thus enumerations can both foster and detract from textual readability and intelligibility; this has been confirmed by studies carried out in cognitive psychology over the past ten years on the limited capacity of working memory and its effects on comprehension, particularly comprehension of technical and specialized texts (Alamargot, Terrier, & Cellier, 2005; Coirier, Gaonac'h, & Passerault, 1996; Fayol, 2002b; Levy & Ransdell, 1996). On the one hand, the separating of elements visually facilitates reading: smaller units are easier to read. On the other hand, the fragmentation of an informative passage that constitutes a whole diminishes its intelligibility.

8 Discontinuous Readability or Continuous Readability?

Vertical layout is also a stylistic procedure that gives prominence to part of a text; the discontinuous division of type in a textual space draws attention to itself and sets its content apart. By emphasising specific parts, the use of vertical enumeration thus increases the discontinuous readability of the document, that is, the ease with which the document can be consulted in order to extract a specific piece of information. The use of vertical enumeration facilitates the reading of each individual part. However, it diminishes the prominence of the overview. Consequently, horizontal layout of an enumeration, wherein items in the enumeration are presented in continuous linear form, enhances its explanatory value. From this point of view, horizontal enumeration is a superior cohesive marker for the continuous readability of the text, measurable during an attentive reading in which the reader seeks to

---

[2]The merits of vertical enumeration are described in the following: *Écrire pour être lu, Présentez les énumérations verticalement*, from the Conseil supérieur de la langue française, Ministère de la communauté française de Belgique (1998, pp. 67–68); and Michel Leys's "Comment améliorer la lisibilité des textes administratifs," from *Administration publique* 1 (1988, pp. 47–60).

clearly understand the overall meaning of a text, rather than to extract one part. Horizontal enumeration gives the paragraph its value as a metatextual cohesive marker; the paragraph brings together elements closely linked by meaning, and identifies discursive developments that are considered important.

The decision to use vertical enumeration therefore depends on the dominant intention of the writer: Does the writer of a document seek to improve the text's discontinuous readability, or its continuous readability? The use of multiple enumerative structures in a text detracts from its overall intelligibility: the text remains superficially easy to read, but more difficult to understand as a whole. Enumeration, whether vertical or not, creates an effect of fragmentation that leaves the reader unable to foresee what will come next. According to Arcand and Bourbeau (1995), "the enumerative structure obstructs anticipation, for it is often difficult to predict when the enumeration will end" (p. 251). [our translation] These authors emphasize the importance of signalling the end of the enumeration by using, for example, the conjunction "and" between the final two elements, instead of a comma or semicolon, which has less informative value.

Use of multiple vertical enumerations has another disadvantage: the overuse or repetition of the same structure is tedious and decreases the reader's attention and interest. Vertical presentations are effective precisely because they break with the normal order of presentation; this emphatic effect is lost when vertical presentation dominates the page.

9   Intelligibility and Vertical Enumeration

Enumeration is a discursive strategy, a form of logical organization that bestows meaning upon the elements that compose it. Its effects on readability cannot be considered separately from its effects on intelligibility.

Enumeration depersonalizes discourse and erases the writer: it places emphasis on results, which are often designated by abstract nouns. Enumerations give the impression that they reflect objective, factual reality rather than that they result from a process of analysis and selection undertaken by specific actors in a specific time and space, with a particular goal. The process through which they are constructed is erased. By erasing the process, the writer gives the list the value of truth. The value of enumerations in prescriptive texts is thus clear: the text is less likely to invite possible contestation because the analytical links between the parts are not specified and therefore do not invite scrutiny. Furthermore, the apparent absence of the agent that produced these lists creates the impression of an objective, neutral vision of reality. In other words, the discourse seems to be a direct reflection of reality rather than a creation of human agents. This tendency to present a situation as a depersonalized reflection of objective reality can be observed in administrative discourse. Richard Mitchell (1979), for example, describes how administrative writing often evokes "an imagined world in which responsible agency is hardly ever visible" (p. 15), and in which events are brought about "by the very nature of the universe" (p. 52). Similarly, in legal texts, logical links between ideas are sometimes intentionally left inexplicit (Fernbach, 1990, p. 34).

In this sense, enumeration attains its goal: it asserts as legitimate the point of view of the discourse community that produces the text and thus favours its persuasive aims.

On the other hand, it poses a problem of intelligibility for the reader. Measures of clarification must therefore be considered, which will improve the coherence and not just the cohesion of the text.

The coherence of a text is based on the underlying principle of referential continuity. Christian Vanderdorpe (1999) writes: "[F]or a text to be coherent, all elements evoked in a text must have a relationship of pertinence with the central theme, and possible disparities between different points of view will be smoothed out through the use of connectives and transitions." (p. 38) [our translation] Thus a text is coherent when its constitutive parts refer to the same subject, developed or thematized with a shared intention, and wherein the identity of the writer and his or her reader are stabilized. Some writing strategies increase textual coherence by specifying implied relationships between parts. Charolles asserts this point of view:

> The recognition of what makes a discourse coherent implies not only the interpretation of whatever cohesive marks it may contain, but also, and much more fundamentally, the use of inferential operations, and in particular bridging inferences, which rely jointly on the discourse content, the situation in which it is communicated, and the background knowledge of the subjects. (1994, p. 133) [our translation]

In other words, some cohesive markers reflect textual organization and "packaging." Others may signal: (1) the passage from one idea to another; (2) logical links between ideas and their significance in relationship to the overall meaning of the text; and (3) consideration of the communicative situation of the reader. To these markers we can add:

- any procedure that indicates the hierarchy of ideas: marks of linear integration (opening of a series, links between elements, conclusion of a series) and explanatory, summarizing, and anticipatory markers which situate each part of the text with respect to the general thematic progression;
- any procedure that clarifies the enunciative voices;
- any popularization strategy, such as providing definitions, explanations, or examples, that is designed to translate the concerns of the discourse community producing the text into language that is accessible to a non-specialist community.

Coherent markers will be used more frequently in texts with high conceptual density, no matter who the intended readership may be.

10 Emergence of the Intelligibility of an Enumeration in Legal Text

The segmentation of a text has meaning only to the extent that the resulting subdivisions contribute to the general meaning of the text (the packaging function). Enumerations are common in legal texts: they give form to the definitions whose expansions may be both explanatory and descriptive. Lists of inclusions and exclusions and of circumstances, for example, are forms of descriptive expansion. However, every right, obligation, or prohibition must be clarified before the constitutive parts of each are listed. In other words, in order for an enumeration to be intelligible, the statement that introduces it, that precedes and presents the enumeration, must allow the reader to anticipate the content that follows.

Lists are generally of two types: the introduced list, which provides a more formal, separate introduction to the enumeration, and the continuing list, in which the enumeration is a natural continuation of the sentence. Michael Jordan distinguishes between the two types:

> ... those that formally introduce the elements of the list with a statement that could be a complete sentence, called "introduced lists"; and those for which the elements of the list are essential grammatical complements of the introductory words, called "continuing lists." (2001, p. 15)

An introduced list provides the writer with the opportunity to represent the general idea that underlies the enumeration by explicitly formulating an introduction using a hypernym or superordinate expression. The content of continuing lists is signalled more implicitly. In either case, if the general idea that underlies the enumeration is to be clearly represented, the wording that precedes the enumeration should have predictive and informative value.

11 Cohesion in Enumerations: Some Examples from a Legal Text

Whenever possible, the legal drafter should ensure that an introductory statement is used to allow the reader to anticipate and interpret the items in the enumeration that follows. Our analysis of the intelligibility of vertical enumerations included studying a draft version of the Canadian Employment Insurance Act,[3] which is the source of the following examples. In the following introduced list, the predictive value of the expression "the following rights" enhances the intelligibility of the enumeration:

> Section 50 (3)
> A claimant is not disqualified from receiving benefits if, in order to take advantage of the opportunity to obtain employment, the claimant would have lost any of the following rights:
> (a) to join or not join an association, organization or union of workers;
> (b) to continue to be a member and observe the lawful rules of an association, organization or union of workers.

It is also important to clarify the relationship between the items, and specifically, to indicate whether their connection is conjunctive or disjunctive (Jordan, 2001). This distinction is

---

[3] The examples given in this article have been taken from an unpublished draft of the Employment Insurance Act of November 28, 2003. We thank the Legislative Services Branch and Lynn Douglas of the Department of Justice Canada for providing us with material for reflection and analysis.

usually made by the use of the conjunctions "and" or "or" after the penultimate item in a list; however, it is preferable to also signal in the introductory statement whether the items are cumulative (conjunctive connection) or exclusive (disjunctive connection). In the following example of a continuing list, the word "both" in the introductory statement signals that the list that follows is conjunctive:

> Section 24 (2)
> A claimant may request that a claim for benefits be backdated to an earlier date. The claim is backdated to the earlier date if the claimant shows both that
> (a) they met the conditions referred to in paragraphs 5(1)(a) and (b) on the earlier date; and
> (b) there was good cause why they did not apply for benefits before.

Similarly, in the following excerpt, the word "either" in the introductory statement indicates that the list that follows is disjunctive:

> Section 23 (1)
> A claimant must submit an initial claim for benefits either
> (a) to the office of the Commission that serves the area of the claimant's residence; or
> (b) to any other place indicated in the regulations or, if there are none, by the Commission.

Cohesion is created by the judicious use of cohesive markers. Pronominal reference and sentence structure, for example, must support and reveal the underlying relationship between parts of a sentence. Pronominal reference can become increasingly problematic in legal texts in which the pronoun "they" is used as a gender-neutral pronoun to refer to a singular antecedent. This practice is becoming increasingly frequent in the drafting of Canadian federal and provincial legislation as a means of ensuring gender-neutral language, although some legal drafters are more comfortable with it than are others. Granted, such use avoids the cumbersome alternative "he or she" and the politically incorrect inclusive use of the masculine form "he." But this use of a plural pronoun to refer to a singular antecedent should be avoided where it could detract from the clarity of the text, particularly when other cohesive markers are absent or are themselves open to various interpretations. This situation can be seen in the following example:

> Section 32 (1)
> A claimant is eligible for sickness benefits if they are unable to work because they are sick, injured or in quarantine, as described in the regulations, and would have been available for work if not for the sickness, injury or quarantine.

In this example, the potential for confusion is compounded by the following factors: the text preceding the pronoun "they" contains another plural noun ("benefits") which could be retrieved as a potential (albeit illogical) antecedent for "they"; the proximity of the contrasting singular and plural forms of the verb "to be" ("is eligible" and "are unable") highlights the shift from singular to plural; and the presence of a compound verb structure ("are unable…" and "would have been available…") requires a close reading of the sentence in order for the subject of the second verb to be retrieved.

We suggest the following revision that uses vertical enumeration, repetition of the antecedent, and parallel wording to enhance intelligibility and to make the text more easily understandable on first reading:

> A claimant is eligible for sickness benefits if:
> (a) the claimant is unable to work because of sickness, injury or quarantine, as described in the regulations, and
> (b) the claimant would have been available for work if not for the sickness, injury, or quarantine.

Similarly, when the singular antecedent is mentioned in the introductory statement and the plural pronoun is used the vertical list, repetition of the antecedent in the enumeration can increase readability. In the following text, readability would be improved by replacing the pronoun "they (refuse)" with a repetition of the noun, "the claimant (refuses)":

> 38 (3): A claimant is considered to have voluntarily left an employment on the day on which any of the following occurs:
> (a) the loss of employment occurs, if they refuse an employment offered as an alternative to an expected loss of employment;
> (b) the employment was supposed to resume, if they refuse to resume an employment;
> (c) the work, undertaking or business is transferred, if they refuse to continue in an employment after the employer's work, undertaking or business is transferred to another employer.

12 Expression of Logical Links in Legal Text

Establishing links between the sections of a statute entails demanding analytical work. The various sections of a statute are not composed of the same number or type of distinct conceptual categories. It is up to the writer to signal these conceptual categories in introductory statements that clarify the various encompassing categories, and summarize the subsequent developments. Each element may specify a circumstance that restricts the scope of the statute, and may be accompanied by further enumerations when a circumstance itself encompasses several constituents. In the absence of clear logical links and connectives, the text will be difficult to read, no matter what layout is used.

Interminable lists are not meaningful: the drafter should avoid the "CNN effect" in which the world is seen as a seemingly endless series of separate facts, like a series of railway cars, without specification of relationships of cause, effect, opposition, or analogy. In the selected examples of Canadian statutes that we have studied, it is not unusual to find lists of up to 12 elements that refer back to one statement. When the situation allows, the writer should clearly identify the link between the introductory statement and the list, as well as the links between the items in the enumeration.

13 Other Markers with Analytical Function

Legal texts often combine linear and tabular layout of text, thus requiring the reader to combine two modes of reading. Vanderdorpe explains these two concepts:

> Linearity describes a series of elements which follow one another in an intangible or pre-established order. [...] This concept contrasts with that of tabularity, which indicates that readers are able to access visual data in the order that they choose, by identifying at the outset the sections that are of interest to them, just as, when reading a table, the eye can focus on any part, in an order determined by the reader. (1999, p. 41) [our translation]

To situate the reader in the overall text and to help him or her combine linear reading and tabular reading, in addition to statements of transition, summary, or anticipation, the writer can use other configurational markers and architectural predicates that favour an analytical rather than a fragmented segmentation of the text, such as:

- a summary of the parts, given at the outset or accessible at any time by a hyperlink if the text is online;
- decimal enumeration that indicates the analytical links between the subdivisions of the text;
- headings and subheadings, in the margin or in the body of the text, which reflect progression from one idea to another and from one category to another;
- overall typography and layout that transmit and amplify the role of linguistic markers of textual configuration.

This concern for textual clarity may result in a longer final text, and may require more time in the drafting of the text.

14 Genre Restraints and Situational Restraints

Interest in the intelligibility of a text requires that the conditions that surround the act of reading be examined. The coherence of the text is in part linked to the acceptability of the text within the genre in question. The text appears even more coherent to the extent that its organization and content conform to the standards of the genre. The text of a law belongs to the genre of legal writing, of the instructional-prescriptive type, and its primary user is the legal specialist. In the text of a law, it would be inconsequential to define each of the specialized terms used, and it would be dangerous to illustrate abstract concepts with concrete examples taken from real-life cases. It would be senseless to strip the text of the language that belongs to the legal world: this language of speciality is a tool of precision, shared by the members of the legal discourse community.

Sir Ernest Gowers (1973) famously described the special nature of legal writing as follows:

> Acts of Parliament, statutory rules and other legal instruments have a special purpose, to which their language has to be specially adapted. The legal draftsman… has to ensure to the best of his ability that what he says will be found to mean precisely what he intended, even after it has been subjected to detailed and possible hostile scrutiny by acute legal minds. For this purpose he has to be constantly aware, not only of the natural meaning which his words convey to the ordinary reader, but also of the special meaning which they have acquired by legal convention and by previous decisions of the Courts. Legal drafting must therefore be unambiguous, precise, comprehensive and largely conventional. (1973, p. 8)

For these reasons, it seems to us that the intelligibility of the text of a law must be approached first from the point of view of the legal discourse community, the producer and primary reader of this type of text. As a consequence, revision in order to make such texts more readable and more intelligible can be undertaken only with the presumption that the reader is a legal specialist. This is not to say that the legal text should be obscure; however, the clarity of a legal text is restricted by the restraints of the genre, which express the obligations of the community from which it emanates. Moreover, every statute is part of the complex network of legal discourse, and a comprehensive understanding will depend on the knowledge of other legislation, civil and criminal law, and concepts fundamental to justice and the legal system.

Nevertheless, the texts of laws can be made more readable by the deliberate inclusion of material designed to facilitate their reading. The draft of the Employment Insurance Act that we studied includes guidelines and aids designed for the reader. The Act begins with a Guide on how to use the act and an introductory "Overview." It includes "readers' aids" (which the Act specifies "have no legal effect"), which are strategically placed throughout the text and included summaries, notes, and examples. Such means significantly increase the readability of a statute.

To reach a broad community of readers, the legal community often undertakes another form of writing: that of popularization, a discursive activity that aims first and foremost to explain rather than to prescribe. Changes of genre are required: the text of a law is replaced by brochures, booklets, posters, or Internet sites, to name only a few popularized forms. In such cases, the writer can use definitions, explanations, analogies, and examples to contextualize the law in the life of the reader. The content of the legal discourse is necessarily modified: the popularized version contains a selection of facts, chosen as pertinent to the reader's comprehension of issues at hand.

15 Conclusion

In conclusion, the readability of a textualization procedure cannot be measured in the absolute, separate from the constraints that characterize the intelligibility of the text, or separate from the communicative context in which the text occurs. To write more readable texts, the legal drafter must understand the context and purpose of the communicative situation and must consider the interrelation between textual clarification procedures and the text's overall meaning. As Ken Hyland (2005: p. 23) points out: "The meaning of a text depends on the integration of its component elements, both propositional and metadiscoursal, and these do not work independently of each other. Metadiscourse is an essential part of any text and contributes to the ways it is understood and acted upon; it is not a separate and separable set of stylistic devices that can either be included or not without affecting how a text is presented and read. These two texts indicate that while a re-textualization may have recognizably similar content, the fact it is written for a different genre, purpose and audience means it will have different meanings, not least because of the metadiscourse it contains."

Configurational markers and architectural predicates play their role fully in a text only when all considerations relating to coherence and intelligibility have been addressed. Coherence is the fundamental property of an intelligible text, and cohesion cannot substitute for it. The writer may take advantage of the typographical features and other procedures of visual text layout that have become accessible to everyone through information technology (Adam, 2000). But first, the writer must grapple with the broader issues of language, meaning, and complex communicative situations.

The research question that this article has tried to answer—whether vertical enumeration contributes to the readability of a legal text—is one aspect of a more general concern that all workplace writers face: how to improve the clarity, readability and intelligibility of written texts. Research in the field of writing studies reveals that there is no easy answer. The meaning of a text cannot be addressed in isolation, separate from the communicative context or from those who produce and read the text. Clarity does not result from the application of a set of standardized rules. Writers who are looking for simple guidelines that can be followed in all situations are bound to be disappointed, for there is no simple formula, no "one size fits all" strategy, when it comes to matters of written communication.

SECTION 2:
COMPOSING DOCUMENTS

Chapter 4

Considering Users and the Way They Use Procedural Texts: Some Prerequisites for the Design of Appropriate Documents

Franck Ganier and Javier Barcenilla

> *In spite of the prominence of procedural documents in the workplace and in our daily life, research as well as our own experience as consumers generally shows that in some cases a poor design of the documents may be responsible for mistakes, failures, or for the misuse of equipments or consumer goods. This chapter proposes to outline the major factors implied in the use and the processing of procedural documents. These factors can be linked to the user (his/her cognitive resources and prior knowledge), to the equipment to operate (its affordances, constraints on its use, etc.), and to the document itself (its role, its content, the information layout). The analysis then focuses on the situations in which the user/document/equipment interaction can be problematic. At the end of the chapter, a production/revision procedure is suggested to enable the creation of more efficient documents suiting the users' needs more appropriately.*

1 Introduction

Laboratory or field research results together with the experience of our everyday use of diverse pieces of equipment (car wash stations, softwares, video-recorders, ready-made meals, DIY furniture kits, etc.) show that the use (or the no-use!) of procedural documents may at times lead to failures. These failures can be different in their nature. In some cases, when linked to the reader's difficulties in understanding the document, they could only imply a rereading. In other cases, when related to the application of the information, they can lead to the damaging of the equipment. Most of the time, these failures are due to the fact that the documents do not correspond to the users' needs; whereas, in general, technical writers feel that they have applied the principles of technical writing. The idea supported in this chapter is that the design of documents matching the users' needs depends not only on the knowledge of the

---

Written Documents In The Workplace
Copyright © 2007 by Elsevier Ltd.
All rights of reproduction in any form reserved.
ISBN: 978-0-080-47487-8

Ganier, F. & Barcenilla, J. (2007). Considering users and the way they use procedural texts: Some prerequisites for the design of appropriate documents. In G. Rijlaarsdam (Series Ed.) and D. Alamargot, P. Terrier, & J.-M. Cellier (Vol. Eds.), Studies in Writing, Vol. 21, Written Documents in the Workplace, 49–60.

user's characteristics and of technical writing principles, but also, and most importantly, on the knowledge of the user's functioning when interacting with the document and the equipment to operate (or either assemble or handle), all these actions being performed in a specific context with its own variables. In this light, the aim of this chapter is to relate studies emphasising the different connections in the user/document/equipment interaction with those emphasising the user's difficulties in this interaction. Thus, this chapter summarises research conducted on the use of procedural documents. The first part focuses on each of the factors present in the interaction, whereas the second part studies the interaction itself. This synthesis is aimed to have a better understanding of the difficulties faced by people using this type of document. It also aims to explain the reasons for these difficulties, which may be due to either the user, the document, the equipment, or their interaction. That way, some recommendations will be proposed concerning the design of procedural documents, which aim to reduce those problems. At the end of the chapter, a production/revision procedure is proposed to enable the creation of more efficient documents suiting the users' needs more appropriately.

2 The Use of Procedural Documents: An Interweaving of Four Dimensions

Many authors have agreed that the use of information provided by procedural documents is a complex activity occurring in a multiple informational context (Ganier, 2004; Ganier, Gombert, & Fayol, 2000; Guthrie, Bennett, & Weber, 1991; Heurley, 1994; Marcus, Cooper, & Sweller, 1996; Wright, 1999). In such a situation, the users must process information coming from (a) the instructions (a text, a recording, a static or dynamic image, a movie); (b) the equipment that must be handled (a software, a DIY furniture kit, etc.); and (c) their own skills (his/her ability to read and/or understand text or image, to turn verbs into actions; his/her experience with similar equipment, etc.). Moreover, in some cases, the use of the document can be heavily hampered by the context (time pressure, risky situations, technical hitches, etc.). In order to have a better understanding of the interaction between the user, the document, and the equipment involved in the processing of procedural documents, it is necessary to look first at the main elements involved in this relationship and at their most salient features (Figure 1).

2.1 The User

When designing procedural documents, technical writers have to keep in mind that there is not one unique user but a wide range of users. For a variety of reasons, these are likely to face different kinds of problems. Identifying the main factors affecting the use of procedural documents has enabled researchers to get a better understanding of some of the difficulties that occur when using procedural documents and to suggest some solutions capable of resolving these difficulties. These factors include the user's age, working memory capacity, prior knowledge, and reading skills.

2.1.1 The user's age The use of procedural documents can be affected by the user's age or, to be more precise, by psychological and cognitive factors related to the individual's

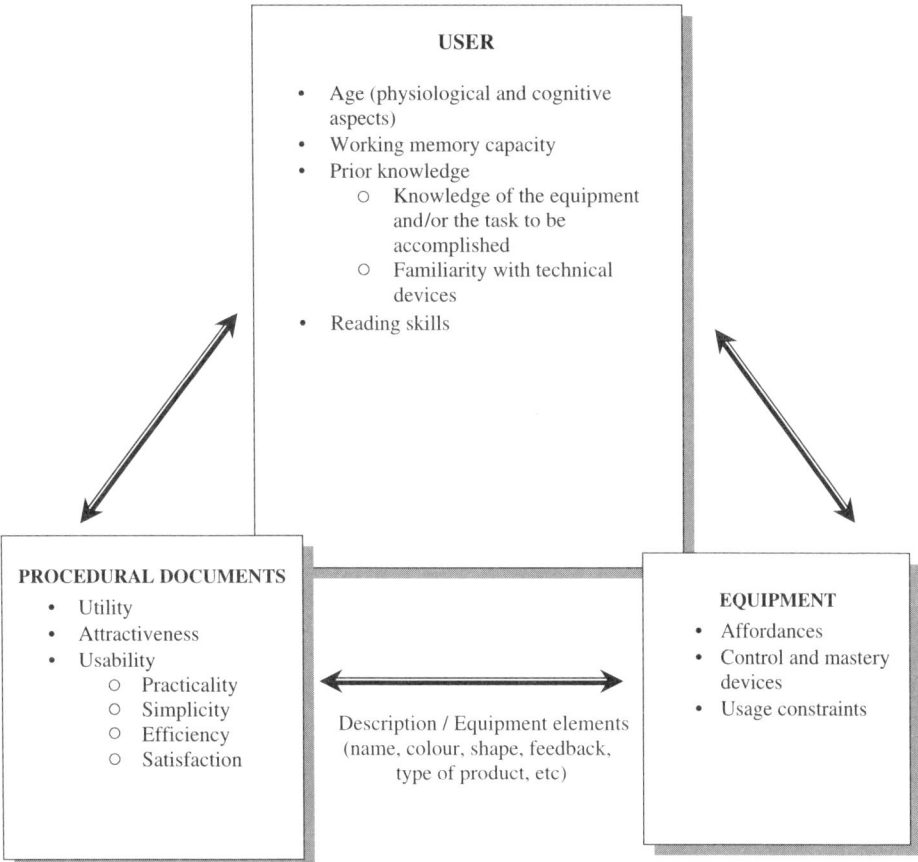

Figure 1: The user/equipment/procedural document interaction.

development. With regard to physiological factors, declines in the user's visual perception and motor capacity, due to the ageing process, are of key importance. As for cognitive factors, changes in working memory capacity (with a span increasing from childhood to adulthood and decreasing then), prior knowledge, and reading skills play a very important part in the processing of procedural documents (see Salthouse, 1991; Schaie, 1994; Van Hees, 1996).

Much has been written about the deterioration in visual perception. For instance, Kline and Scialfa (1997) state that the ageing process affects visual capacities, including sensitivity to contrast and colour discrimination. Most of the time procedural documents (e.g. medication instructions) are written in such small characters that a large part of the population is unable to use them (e.g. people with a relatively severe visual impairment, such as the elderly; Barcenilla, 2005). Van Hees (1996) and Kline and Scialfa (1997) suggest that, in order to take the decline of the user's capacities into consideration in the design of procedural documents, more attention should be paid to:

- the size of the font, with the "x" character ranging in height from 6 to 9 mm;
- the contrast between the text and its background;

- not using some colour combinations, such as green and blue or green and red, or not using pastel colours; and
- the detail given in illustrations, which should be limited.

As far as motor capacity is concerned, studies have generally highlighted a decline in grip strength and in motor coordination, as well as in the accuracy of movements (Haigh, 1993; Kallman, Plato, & Tobin, 1991). This means, for instance, that the elderly are likely to experience some usability problems when trying simultaneously to keep the document open while handling the equipment (Van Hees, 1996). These kinds of problems can be easily extended to those encountered by users who have disabilities. That way, Van der Geest (2006) proposes to run usability studies with people who are elderly or have disabilities.

Regarding cognitive factors, changes, as one gets older, in both working memory capacity (Babcock & Salthouse, 1990) and reading comprehension capacity must be taken into consideration. This point will be further investigated later in this chapter.

2.1.2 Working memory capacity   A lot of studies have shown that working memory plays a key role in the processing of information presented in procedural documents (Ganier, 2004). It has been proved that the user's capacity to process information has a major impact on the success or failure of the use of these documents. For instance, in an experiment ran by Engle, Carullo, and Collins (1991), children aged 7, 9, and 12 were given instructions with variable levels of difficulty. The results showed that, whatever the age, the complexity of the information had a greater impact on children with a limited working memory span than on children with a wider working memory span. Thus, working memory appears to be an essential element in the process of understanding instructions. Nevertheless, processing instructions seems to induce a heavy cognitive workload (for a description of the processes involved, see Ganier, 2004). Indeed, locating the relevant items of equipment and executing appropriate actions require the user to store in his/her working memory the information he/she has collected from the instructions. This means that processing written instructions demands important resources and imposes a heavy workload on working memory. Therefore, observational data by Vermersch (1985) and Duggan and Payne (2001) about switching between the instructions and the equipment can be considered as a strategy aimed at reducing cognitive demands on working memory. To facilitate the user's switching behaviour and to reduce the cognitive load implied in the localisation and memorisation of instructions, Frase (1981) suggests opting for a different layout and proposes that the instructions should be presented in the form of numbered lists and not paragraphs.

2.1.3 Prior knowledge   Prior knowledge can have an influence on the use or the non-use of instructions. The influence of prior knowledge does not depend on the user's age but seems to be related to other factors such as familiarity with the product (Wright, Creighton, & Threllfall, 1982), the existence or lack of prior knowledge about the equipment or the task to be performed (Celuch, Lust, & Showers, 1992), and the relative familiarity with technical systems (Amerine & Bilmes, 1988; Hegarty & Just, 1993). For Richard (1990, 1994), lack of familiarity with the domain provides an explanation for the difficulty in understanding instructions. He observes that inexperienced users, with little or no experience of the domain or the task to be performed, face more problems in understanding procedural documents than more experienced users. For this author, these problems are linked to the fact that procedural instructions are often ambiguous and not very detailed. Whereas experts can easily make inferences to solve these ambiguities (thanks to their knowledge of the domain), inexperienced users, with no sufficient knowledge, can neither understand what is implicit nor solve the ambiguities.

2.1.4 Reading skills Many studies were conducted in the 1990s in France on reading and comprehension difficulties among poorly educated people. Part of this work aimed to study these people's difficulties when using texts describing procedures to be implemented both in daily life (Richard et al., 1993) and in the workplace (Barcenilla & Brangier, 1998). Various problems faced by this population group were thus revealed. Thus, the main problems were:

- Problems measuring and calculating because of a lack of expertise in even simple logical and mathematical operations (Mariné, 1992; Patel, Branch, & Arocha, 2002; Richard et al., 1993; Riondet, 1992).
- Problems working out a procedure and putting it into practice in specific cases and deriving it from general instructions (Richard et al., 1993).
- Difficulties planning the task from all the information given on specification sheets (Barcenilla & Brangier, 1998; Higelé, 1992).
- Misunderstanding due to the documents' conceptual organisation and their layout, which does not fit with the usual visual progression of the reading process (Richard et al., 1993).
- Misunderstanding technical words (Barcenilla & Brangier, 1998).

This research work leads to a series of recommendations such as:

- Getting rid of calculations when possible and, among other solutions, presenting information spatially (e.g. on a graph) to enable the user to work out the relationship between the information and the related numerical data more directly (Boucheix, 2003).
- Illustrating the information contained in procedural instructions with examples (LeFevre & Dixon, 1986; Catrambone, 1995).
- Offering a time- and space-related layout that emphasises the temporal succession of events and the explicit causal relations.
- Using typographic techniques to prioritise information and to emphasise the main piece of information.
- Simplifying terminology and syntactic structure or using symbols and drawings instead of text.

2.1.5 Conclusion An initial barrier to the usability of procedural documents has been determined. It concerns the users' inherent characteristics, which, most of the time, combine with other factors separately studied in this part. For instance, for the elderly, a decline in working memory capacity can modify understanding (linked to inferences making) and create significant discrepancies in their results when compared with those of young adults. Thus the elderly would be more likely to face comprehension problems than young adults, as processing instructions require to make inferences (e.g. in the domain of medical prescriptions; Diehl, Willis, & Schaie, 1995). In such cases, the improvement of instructions aims to produce—if possible—a document which is more appropriate to the users' physical, physiological, or psychological features (by taking into account certain characteristics related to the ageing process, memory, or level of knowledge). Thus, well-designed instructions suiting the targeted public could reduce usability problems. This means, for instance, providing the elderly with clues to understanding such as images (Morrell, Park, & Poon, 1990); with lists and subheadings for the layout (Morrow & Leirer, 1999); with a description of equipment feedback to user actions (Van Hees, 1996), etc.

2.2 The Document

What is typical of procedural documents is the fact that their purpose is to enable people to perform a task. As such, they can be considered either as guides for carrying out some actions, or as forms of external memory. When considered the former, their purpose is to enable users who have never used the product before—and who do not know any other similar products—to handle the equipment appropriately. When considered the latter, instructions are available in the document, which should be workable for occasional users (Sticht, 1977). This has different consequences. First, the document has to be useful. Many examples of incidents or accidents reported by research studies state "non-usage of the instructions" or "ignoring the procedure", which reminds us of the usefulness of this type of document (Degani & Wiener, 1994; Silver & Wogalter, 1991; Veyrac, Cellier, & Bertrand, 1997). Furthermore, the way procedural documents are being used must be efficient. Regarding this last point, two usability features can be differentiated. These are the "material usability" and the "cognitive usability" of the document suggested by Veyrac et al. (1997). Considering the notion of "material usability", these authors have noted that in a working environment, it is not always possible to read these documents. Their reading can be hampered by time and space constraints, by the (sometimes prohibitive) weight of the document, and by the task to be carried out. The cognitive use of the document concerns the activities emerging from the interaction between the user, the document, and the equipment to operate. A user having to perform a new task must first locate the needed information in the document. When located, he/she has to read and understand the instructions in order to be able to carry out efficiently what was understood. Thus, the document should be devised so as to facilitate these activities. Consequently, the size and content of the document as well as the way the information is presented must simplify as much as possible manipulating the document while using the equipment, as well as seeking, reading, understanding, and application of the instructions. And still, in addition to the difficulties related to user characteristics or the context of use (e.g. car compartments, semi-darkness…), some problems can result from the inappropriateness of documents for adequate equipment usage. For example, in some cases, the instructions are located on the tool itself whereas it would be more appropriate to dissociate them from the tool, in order to facilitate reading and handling activities. Sometimes also, the information contained in the document does not correspond to the product features or the user's mother tongue. The usability of the document is generally accountable for its usage. Schriver (1997) has noted that only 41% of people needing to solve computer problems use printed or electronic documents (technical manuals, online help). This confirms Kern's (1985) and Sticht's (1985) results and their points that users do not use procedural documents spontaneously either because they feel they do not need them, either because the document is not available or because it is too cumbersome, or because they consider the information displayed in these documents as badly designed. Thus it is necessary to create documents that present such criteria as practicality, simplicity, efficiency, and even attractiveness. If more practical, these documents can be read/used without hampering operation of the equipment; if more simple, they allow a great variety of users to read and understand them; if more efficient, they not only contribute to a progressive discovery of how to operate the equipment, but also enable the user to get to the information more rapidly; if more attractive, they appeal to a great number of users.

2.3 The Equipment

The equipment used can be relatively complex. It can be anything (e.g. consumables, professional materials, pieces of equipment, a machine, large fittings, etc.) upon which the user performs actions described in the procedural document, or performs assembly operations (for industrial products on assembly lines, for DIY kits, for models, etc.), transformation operations (cooking a meal), or other operations such as playing a game, filling in a form, etc. The equipment itself can provide some information to the reader. In this case, researchers in the field of technical system usability generally follow two strategies. These are the presentation of usage constraints, and the selection of natural conformity between the user's motor behaviour and the results' display (any operation with the equipment must result in a result which is visible to the user). A third, more recent strategy, deals with the selection of "proper" affordances during the conception of the device (Norman, 1990). In this case, the user can take the object's visible features as sources of information. For instance, the shape of a control can provide some information about how to handle it. Norman (1990) considers that when a piece of equipment offers some affordances, the potential actions performed on it should be inferred without using any instruction leaflet or illustration. To illustrate this point, he shows some examples of non-affordant configurations and that they require additional verbal information in order to be understandable and to be performed appropriately by the user. Thus, affordances should be designed so as to facilitate the interaction between the user and the equipment and to allow him/her to achieve rapidly the best performance level possible. Nevertheless, it is not possible to explain all the equipment's working processes: affordances can be lacking and, consequently, fail to describe the object's function and operation. Indeed, new technical systems offer increasingly greater functionality improvements that can be executed automatically, which prevents the user from mastering his action on the equipment. Thus, good product usability seems to result from a compromise between didactics and technology: information not provided by the equipment must be provided by procedural documents and vice versa.

2.4 The Context of Use

Some authors (Newell & Gregor, 2001; Vanderheiden, 2000) suggested that a healthy individual could end up in a situation similar to that of a disabled person performing tasks in "exceptional environments" (driving or working at night, poor visibility) or in poor working conditions with spatial constraints and specific movements that prevent the user from consulting instructions, or with time constraints that hinder the use of instructions. Depending on the context of use, the technical writer must consider the following aspects in order to make the use of a procedural document possible:

- its material aspects: its size, weight, material, its page positioning, the nature of the medium (paper vs. electronic document), the type of binding…;

- its durability, which determines the availability (or unavailability) of the document at a certain period in time: its opacity, its resistance, the quality of its paper, and its storage conditions;
- the conditions for which and in which the document will be used (immediate vs. delayed execution of described actions; time pressures or not; etc.), which can be helpful in determining the information layout (e.g. Veyrac et al., 1997, who recommended the use of diagrams for problems solving related to train driving).

3 Procedural Documents: Problems in Usage

In a great number of situations, using procedural documents appears to be an additional task that can come into conflict with the task in progress. Some of the factors likely to provoke these conflicts when using procedural documents have been identified. For instance, these difficulties can emerge when documents are processed by poorly educated individuals with reading difficulties (Barcenilla, 2005; Fayol, 1992), or by individuals unfamiliar with technical systems (Amerine & Bilmes, 1988; Hegarty & Just, 1993), even if these same individuals have otherwise appropriate reading and comprehension skills. Moreover, a lack of prior knowledge about the device or the task to be performed (Celuch, Lust, & Showers, 1992) or a low working memory span (Engle et al., 1991) can also result in some problems. Finally, a poor analysis of the task to be performed can also create (and this happens frequently) difficulties locating and matching the information; anxiety about technical documents must also be taken into consideration (disregarding them or using them only in cases of emergency); and finally environmental and organisational factors which prevent people from using technical documents (e.g. at work). On top of these general skills and features come some specifically related to the interaction between the user, the document, and the equipment to be handled. It seems interesting to study the various types of usage and the problems arising from these situations. Different types of explanations can account for the inefficiency of procedural documents. This can result from the fact that the instructions were disregarded, or because one particular instruction was disregarded and/or not properly performed, or because of a discrepancy in the instructions.

3.1 When Instructions are Disregarded

It appears that disregarding instructions seems to be a very commonplace behaviour. Studies carried out over the last twenty years show that, frequently, users make exploratory trials and do not read the available documents (Barcenilla, 1993; Richard, 1990). Such behaviour happens when, for instance, users think they can reach their goals without reading the instructions (because they consider that they know how to use the equipment or that they can guess it), when instructions are swamped by a mass of related information (advertisements, food energy values, translations of the instructions in various languages, etc.), or when users have already had an unsuccessful experience with procedural documents (Kern, 1985). Generally speaking, users are ready to use some items of equipment or a product provided that it can be done easily (Wogalter, Allison, & McKenna, 1989). If they think they know how the equipment works, or if they think they can guess its operation, then, they disregard the instructions and start using the product straight away (Carroll & Mack, 1984). By analogy, users can test procedures they already know and then work out new ones. In such situations, their actions imply some feedback from the equipment, which enables the user to know if it is working properly. Thus, with an action-related learning process, the user can discover not only what it is possible to do but also what it is impossible to do, thanks to his/her mistakes (Richard, 1990). The danger linked to this learning process is that mistakes, which are sometimes useful for the user and his/her learning process, can also be prejudicial to the equipment. Tijus, Poitrenaud, and Richard (1996) have shown that, in the medium term, mistakes and failures have sometimes serious consequences: (a) they lead to a wariness about the operation of the equipment on the user's part, (b) they prevent the user from using all the possible functions provided by the equipment (users content themselves with what they know even if the result is not satisfactory), and (c) they lead to the user abandoning the equipment.

3.2 When Actions are not Performed or are Improperly Performed

Certain studies have shown that, in many cases, users process instructions partially, i.e. they read them without carrying out the actions, or they read them but improperly carry out the actions. Wogalter et al. (1989) noted that the execution cost—even if reduced—plays a key part. They described an experiment where students had to handle supposedly dangerous products, and showed that 72% of the students observed the safety instructions and wore a mask and gloves when these protective items were stored in the room where they were. Only 20% of the students used them when they had to go and get them in the room next door. In another situation, Brangier and Barcenilla (2001) showed that social pressure could have some impact on the performance of protective actions such as using instructions. They took the example of the wearing of individual protective items in a furniture factory. The proportion of staff who freely underwent a submission procedure (and who got involved freely, publicly, and without payment in a programme for safety procedure training at work) and who wore protective gear was greater (65% of participants) than the proportion of staff who was not the target of social manipulations (in this case, only 20% of staff wore their protective gear).

Furthermore, it has been noted that even people with reading and comprehension skills, which are well adapted to certain domains, can face difficulties when using technical equipment. These problems emerge essentially when they are confronted with the product and its specifications. There are various types of problem (Barcenilla, 2005):

- Problems linked with locating the part of information relevant for the task in progress (see Ockerman, this volume). The information can be divided into several sources (between the various documents provided with the product, between the printed manual and the online help for software, for instance).
- Problems linked with the way instructions are expressed, in a non-discursive form, with only sets of initials and codes.
- Problems linked with the discrepancy between equipment operation and the user's prior expectations and knowledge.
- Problems linked with the equipment's lack of affordances (i.e. it does not guide the user in his/her actions) and lack of properly marked use constraints; or to the lack of feedback provided the user.

- Problems linked with the user's incapacity to work out the procedure in progress either because information is incomplete, or because different steps in the procedure are unclear, or because technical terms are not understood.

3.3 When there is a Discrepancy Between Instructions and Equipment

Lacks in the processing of procedural instructions could be due to a discrepancy between these instructions and the equipment. Kern (1985), Helyar (1992), and Ganier and Heurley (2003) identified several causes of discrepancy when

- instructions are partial: users make more mistakes and need more time to perform the assembly task when instructions are incomplete;
- the size of the document is inappropriate;
- no coherence between the equipment and the instructions: the instructions allude to a yellow button whereas the actual button on the device is green;
- the order in which the information is given does not match the way the equipment is used;
- the content of the information is inappropriate (the information does not match the equipment model), or is not updated, or vague, or incomplete.

Helyar (1992) lists about a hundred legal actions taken between 1945 and 1992 involving American firms that had provided information not corresponding to the products they had marketed. The instructions were considered incomplete or incorrect to guarantee safe use of the products to which they referred. In this period, no existing standard was relevant to the format and design of instructions for use or safety signs on products. In the 1990s, an effort was made to provide standards in the domain of the design of instructions for use. Thus, safety label standardisation in the United States dates largely to the creation of the ANSI's Z535.4 standard in 1991. Concerning instructions for use standardisation, ISO/IEC published a guide in 1995 (the ISO/IEC's Guide 37) in order to establish principles and detailed recommendations for their design and formulation. However, the development of documents corresponding to users' needs is far to be as easy as it looks.

4 The Development of Documents Corresponding to Users' Needs

The problems faced by users arise from the interweaving of different factors associated with the users' personal characteristics, the document's features, and the context in which the equipment is used. When designing a procedural document, those factors must be taken into consideration, together with the various minor tasks the user needs to perform: (a) handling the document when performing the task; (b) reading it thoroughly to locate the relevant information (i.e. defining clearly his/her objective; reading more information than actually need, etc.); (c) understanding different types of information (declarative vs. procedural information, for instance) presented in different forms (e.g. text vs. image) and (d) performing the action (planning the action, monitoring the activity, comparing the result to the initial goal or the expected result, etc.). The areas where technical writers can intervene in order to make adjustments likely to facilitate the actions are: (a) the size of the document (appropriate dimensions can facilitate the handling of the document and the equipment, and it can also reduce the cognitive load linked to the user's switches between the instructions and the equipment); (b) its structure (the information layout) and the signposting of its organisation (e.g. using headings); (c) its content (compatibility between the document, the public, and the described product) and more precisely the combination of different layouts to present the instructions (e.g. combining verbal and pictorial instructions lead to better results); and (d) the structure of the instructions (when the syntax used for the instructions corresponds to the user's potential reasoning, better implementation results are obtained) and headings (they can enable users to elaborate a mental representation of the ultimate goal of the instructions and to check what they are doing) (Barcenilla, 2005; Barcenilla & Brangier, 1998, 2000; Ganier, 2002a, 2004; Heurley, 1994).

Matching up documents with their users requires more than just information about the average user's information processing. It is necessary also to consider the users' characteristics and interpersonal differences. Smillie (1985) and Schmalhofer and Glavanov (1986) suggest, as a first step in the adaptation of the document to the users' characteristics, that it is important to identify the users being targeted with the equipment and to determine the impact of prior knowledge when accomplishing the task. Then, the skills required to perform the task, the domain knowledge, and the reading capacities necessary to perform the task should be taken into consideration. In fact, according to these authors, a description of the features relevant for this type of interaction should be carried out for each category of user. This is virtually impossible when the document takes the form of a leaflet and when the equipment is intended for a large group and a variety of users. Nevertheless, switching from a leaflet-type of document to a computerised one seems to be a promising breakthrough. Doane, Sohn, McNamara, and Adams (2000) showed that it was possible to match some technical documentation for the UNIX programming language to the needs of users with different levels of expertise by creating a knowledge database integrating each user's level of prior knowledge. According to this research, in the long term, it will be possible to think in terms of individualised users and not in terms of average or prototypal users, which will enable the development of more accurate specification sheets.

5 Conclusion: Toward a Creation Process Combining Feedforward and Feedback Approaches

A procedural document can be used in several ways (it can be thoroughly read before or when performing the task, it can be read after having spotted a problem, etc.). Moreover, its objectives are numerous (to assemble something, to operate something, to fix something, to solve a problem, etc.), and its users belong to different generations (children, adults, elderly people). Furthermore, the users' prior knowledge may vary (inexperienced, intermediate, or expert). Therefore, procedural documents should not be considered as intended for the "general public" but for a targeted public with special needs. Thus, it is essential to match the document to the users' various profiles, which is a real challenge for technical writers.

When creating a usable procedural document, it is necessary to aim at meeting the users' needs at work or using a device for the first time. According to Kern (1985), this goal cannot be reached without taking into consideration the users' performance. In order to improve the usability of procedural documents (i.e. their adequacy in terms of users' needs), it is necessary for technical writers to integrate the way users process the information (i.e. how they interact with procedural documents) and to think about the effects the information layout has on the mental processes and behavioural patterns involved in this interaction. Therefore, implementing a new approach to the conception/correction relationship would be one possible solution. This could mean combining two complementary approaches: a feedforward approach together with a feedback approach. The former approach would mean supplying technical writers with scientifically tested recommendations that would have been worked out from behavioural studies, computer-assisted simulations, and from theoretical models of the user's cognitive functioning (Heurley & Ganier, 2002). For example, research carried out by Anderson (1996), Poitrenaud, Richard, Tijus, and Leproux (1992) and Ganier (2002a) have shown that procedural instructions drawn up in accordance with this approach and then tested on real users turn out to be more efficient than "regular" procedural instructions. The feedforward approach would enable technical writers to go beyond their intuitive approach and to work out a first draft of the document by being aware of the potential effects of their design choices on future users and by enabling them to anticipate their potential behaviour. This first draft would be completed by a feedback approach. Some authors (Allwood & Kalen, 1997; Ganier, 2002b; Hartley, 1995; McClelland, 1995) consider that the mere implementation of suggestions cannot always ensure the efficiency of such documents, therefore they emphasise the importance of controlling a document's usability, i.e. its suitability for the user. Others (Swaney, Janik, Bond, & Hayes, 1991) have shown that even good editing techniques can turn out to be inefficient if users are ignored. In a series of experiments they used conventional editing techniques to improve the understandability of various technical documents (e.g., giving revisers a passage and telling them to revise it in such a way as to improve performance on recall protocols, recognition, factual or inference tests, etc.) and showed significant improvements only for cases where users protocols were used. Because procedural documents are created in order to be put into action, they naturally lead to the accomplishment of actions. These actions (performed according to the information in the document) provide objective, perceptive evidence likely to inform the technical writer about the use of the document and its results. This characteristic, which turns procedural documents into especially appropriate tools, means that the effects of the feedback approach should be taken into account when revising the document (Ganier 2002b; Heurley & Ganier, 2002). In the long run such reasoning can turn out to be useful for the creation of appropriate documents as well as for the training of technical writers. To meet this goal, an emphasis should be placed on the study of the processes made by users, for whom the device and the accompanying documents are created (Ganier, 2002a). Thus, when creating a technical document, or when assessing its usability, it is necessary to integrate an approach focused on the user, who is too often disregarded, just when he/she should be at the very core of the design process.

Chapter 5

Highly Effective Writers and the Role of Reading: A Cognitive Approach to Composing in Professional Contexts

Thomas Quinlan and Denis Alamargot

In the workplace, effective writing requires skills for processing information. In this chapter, we explore the cognitive processes underlying writing expertise, focusing upon the central role of reading. Skilled writers often reread sections of their text, which raises the question of how reading might contribute to planning, translating, and reviewing. Reading the developing text can represent a flexible and powerful strategy for generating content, by facilitating the activation of information in long-term memory (LTM). When composing from sources, reading strategies may be directed toward evaluating and selecting information in source documents. Not surprisingly, a writer's ability to comprehend a source text determines his or her ability to integrate information from it. Revising also depends upon reading strategies. While critical reading can enable the writer to adopt a sophisticated approach to writing (i.e., knowledge transforming), it may also create new opportunities for conflict between cognitive processes. To a large extent, effective writing in the workplace becomes a matter of coordinating specific reading strategies for the purposes of writing.

1 Introduction

Imagine a chief financial officer pouring over financial reports and market surveys, as she writes her statement for a quarterly report; or a sales representative reading an email from his manager, and carefully wording his response; or a stockbroker reading numerous industry reports, to synthesize advice for his clients. Although handling information has long characterized work in professional settings, professionals today contend with an ever-increasing flow of information. In today's workplace, the Internet delivers a flood of information to one's desk. (One often hears, "My inbox is totally out of control!") The easy accessibility

Written Documents In The Workplace
Copyright © 2007 by Elsevier Ltd.
All rights of reproduction in any form reserved.
ISBN: 978-0-080-47487-8

Quinlan, T. & Alamargot, D. (2007). Highly effective writers and the role of reading: A cognitive approach to composing in professional contexts. In G. Rijlaarsdam (Series Ed.) and D. Alamargot, P. Terrier, & J.-M. Cellier (Vol. Eds.), Studies in Writing, Vol. 21, Written Documents in the Workplace, 61–74.

of reports published on websites puts new demands on one's abilities to summarize and synthesize information. How do professionals handle this information when writing in the workplace?

The United States National Adult Literacy Survey defined "literacy" as the ability to use "printed and written information to function in society, to achieve one's goals, and to develop one's knowledge and potential" (Kaestle, Campbell, Finn, Johnson, & Mikulecky, 2001, p. 2). In today's workplace, literacy clearly takes on a particularly intense meaning. Professionals must be able to comprehend information from written text; they must also be able to communicate that information to others. Thus, professionals need strong skills for comprehending, summarizing, evaluating, organizing, and synthesizing information. In the workplace, writing well requires highly efficient skills in processing information, most especially fluent reading comprehension. In this chapter, we explore the cognitive processes of writing expertise, focusing especially upon the ability to read critically.

2 Reading in Current Models of Writing

Researchers have tended to view skilled writing in terms of achieving goals through solving problems (Bereiter & Scardamalia, 1987; Flower & Hayes, 1980; Hayes & Flower, 1980). With goals for informing and moving particular readers, the writer must find appropriate information and decide how to present it. Information may be in the mind of the writer or in external sources. The writer's job requires finding and selecting information, then integrating that information into the text under construction, which itself becomes a new, developing source of information (Alamargot, Chanquoy, & Chuy, 2005). Thus, the writer continually interacts with source materials (e.g., reports, magazine articles, email message, etc.), as well as his or her own text. The act of writing yields the developing text, while reading contributes to text production at many levels. Writers use reading in a variety of ways to accomplish their writing goals.

Influential models of writing suggest that reading plays an important role in the problem solving of skilled writers. In their original model, Hayes and Flower (1980) described competent writing in terms of three processes: planning (which generates and organizes content), translating (which convert ideas into words, transcribing words into text), and reviewing (i.e., involving reading and editing). Within reviewing, reading would facilitate reflective evaluation for the purposes of improving the quality of the text. Reading serves to bring language into working memory (WM), so that it can be evaluated by the editing process, the function of which is to detect errors. Hayes and Flower (1980) recognized that the developing text was "a very important part of the task environment because writers refer to it repeatedly during the process of composition" (p. 12).

In subsequent research, Hayes and his colleagues found evidence for an extensive involvement of reading in skilled writing. In Kaufer, Hayes, and Flower (1986), expert and competent adult writers engaged in some initial planning, and then handwrote essays on the topic "My Job." During writing, they also thought aloud. Analysis of the protocols revealed that sentence composing proceeded in a characteristic way, with the writer proposing and evaluating sentence parts, with approximately 75% of the proposed words being included in the final sentence. Writers would often ask themselves a question, such as "What do I want to say?" or "What do I mean?" Of these formulating episodes, 66% involved local reading, as the writer reread the sentence currently under construction. Much less than often, i.e., 8% of formulating episodes, writers would read globally. When interpreting these results, we must consider the possibility that thinking aloud may have altered writing processes (Janssen, Van Waes, & Van den Bergh, 1996), such as by increasing formulating time in pauses, and recognizing how the small sample size (12 adults) may limit generalizability. Still, the results of this study suggest that skilled writers do much reading while composing sentences.

Interpreting their results, Kaufer et al. (1986) proposed that sentence composing involves two distinct processes, "selecting a meaning to be expressed and selecting a surface form in which to express the meaning" (p. 138). They concluded that rereading the previous sentence may facilitate the latter process (i.e., translating). However, in the analysis of the protocol data, one cannot exclude the possibility that reading served other functions, such as retrieving content from long-term memory (LTM), rehearsing sentence phrasing, or evaluating the previously written phrase. The results of this study and others (e.g., Hayes, Flower, Schriver, Stratman, & Carey, 1987; Wallace et al., 1996) led Hayes (1996) to revise some of his earlier ideas (i.e., Hayes & Flower, 1980), to see reading comprehension as a major component of skilled writing.

3 Reading in Knowledge Transforming

Bereiter and Scardamalia (1987) also suggest that reading is essential to skilled writing. The authors propose that skilled writers often problematize a writing task adopting a strategy they called "knowledge transforming." Expert writers often develop elaborate goals, especially rhetorical goals, which require sophisticated problem solving. In contrast, novice writers typically take a simpler, "natural" approach to composing. In adopting a "knowledge telling" approach, content is generated through association, with one idea prompting the next. Whereas the inefficient skills of novices may restrict them to a knowledge-telling approach, skilled writers can move freely between knowledge telling and knowledge transforming.

Bereiter and Scardamalia (1987) assume that knowledge transforming involves a restructuring of knowledge in the mind of the writer. When the existing structure of knowledge in the writer's mind proves inadequate for solving a certain problems, it must be restructured with the forging of new connections between ideas. Problem solving moves between two spaces, for developing "What do I mean?" (i.e., the content space) and "What do I say?" (i.e., the rhetorical space). Thus, Bereiter and Scardamalia (1987) claimed that "the distinctive capabilities of the knowledge-transforming model lie in formulating and solving problems and doing so in ways that allow a two-way interaction between continuously developing knowledge and continuously developing text" (p. 12). At some level, a dynamic interaction like this surely depends upon reading? Reading provides opportunities for defining and solving rhetorical problems—alas, infinite opportunities. And to the extent that knowledge transforming is revising intensive, reading is indispensable.

Bereiter and Scardamalia (1987) fail to explicate the role of reading in knowledge transforming. However, in "Literate Expertise" (Scardamalia & Bereiter, 1991), they draw an important comparison between expert writing (i.e., knowledge transforming) and expert reading. They argue that expertise in both reading and writing involves an interaction, i.e., a "dialectical process," between one's knowledge of a domain and a text. Domain knowledge contributes to both text production and text comprehension, the processes of which may serve to restructure domain knowledge. In a knowledge-transforming approach to writing, this dialectical process occurs in the manner described above. For a model of expert reading, they refer to Van Dijk and Kintsch's (1983) model, in which comprehension involves building mental representations, specifically, a text base and a situation model (see Tapiero & Otero, this volume). In normal reading (not during writing), the text base reflects elements and relations derived most directly from the text, and represents its propositional content. The integration of the text base with knowledge from LTM results in a situation model. "In the dialectical process the situation model is used as the basis for inferences necessary in constructing the text base, and the comprehension of text propositions in turn modifies the situation model" (Scardamalia & Bereiter, 1991, p. 176). Although they describe expert literacy—both writing and reading—in terms of this same knowledge/text interaction, the authors fail to take the next step, to explain how reading expertise transfers to expert writing.

However, Van Dijk and Kintsch (1983) provide the most useful framework for beginning to think about a model of reading-during-writing. The authors hold that a complete model of discourse processing should also explain discourse production. Thus, they specify how the representational structure-building strategies, which underlie reading comprehension, might also be utilized for the purposes of writing and speaking. Initially, the macro-planning strategy constructs a plan, which includes elements from the writers' knowledge and pragmatic elements (relating to the intended audience, goals, and the communicative context). Under the guidance of the plan, the macro-structural strategy constructs a macrostructure reflecting the (likely partial) global text, by retrieving propositions from long-term or episodic memory. The micro-structural strategy executes the macrostructure, retrieving and ordering additional propositions, in order to produce the text base. This text base consists of the semantic content of the text, which is then translated by the local coherence strategy into the surface form of a linguistic representation. Dansac and Alamargot (1999) argue that these strategies compare to processes in the Hayes and Flower (1980) model.

According to the Van Dijk and Kintsch (1983) model, writing is to some extent a "reading process." Some have argued that writing processes cannot be simply reading processes operating in reverse (Read, 1981; Rubin, 1980). However, if building representational structures serve both comprehension and production, it should not matter if those structures are specified via analysis or synthesis (Van Dijk & Kintsch, 1983, p. 16). We know that the knowledge and strategies of reading and writing are highly interrelated (Shanahan, 1984; Shanahan & Lomax, 1986, 1988). For example, a skilled reader may monitor his own comprehension, and use the same strategy for evaluating text during writing (Hacker, 1994). To a great extent, knowledge transforming can be seen as leveraging the strategies of reading comprehension for the purposes of defining and solving the problems of writing.

4 Reading for Writing and Memory

4.1 Demands upon Working Memory

Knowledge transforming involves solving sophisticated problems, which makes it considerably more cognitively demanding than knowledge telling. Writing has been compared to a switchboard operator juggling phone calls (Flower & Hayes, 1980) and an underpowered computer running too many programs (Torrance & Galbraith, 2005). The individual processes of planning, revising, and translating have all shown to be cognitively effortful (Piolat, Roussey, Olive, & Farioli, 1996). Accordingly, WM capacity has been closely linked to processes for reading, such as comprehension (Just & Carpenter, 1992; Turner & Engle, 1989), as well as writing, such as translating fluency (McCutchen, Covill, Hoyne, & Mildes, 1994). WM describes a limited capacity system, by which information is temporarily maintained and manipulated (Baddeley, 1986; Baddeley & Hitch, 1974). Because of its limited capacity, writing requires managing the demands of WM, such as by using strategies for allocating resources and automating graphomotor processes (McCutchen, 1996). Knowledge telling represents an economical strategy, which enables the writer to operate within the capacities of WM; in contrast, knowledge transforming is a costly strategy that can lead to overloading WM resources.

In some cases, reading can compete for limited cognitive resources. Inefficient reading processes can draw cognitive resources away from other writing processes. Consequently, we might expect weak readers to do minimal reading-during-writing, as a strategy for allocating cognitive resources. However, as reading skills improve and encoding processes become increasingly encapsulated (or automatized), reading will require minimal resources (Stanovich, 1990). At this point, a writer may start leveraging reading skills for planning and evaluating, to interact more dynamically with the developing text.

While the ability to read during writing may enable the writer to adopt a more sophisticated approach to writing (i.e., knowledge transforming), this ability also creates new opportunities for conflict between processes. During composing, reading can evoke other processes, such as planning (to cue retrieval of information from memory or to help organize one's), translating (to rehearse the wording to a sentence), editing (to detecting errors), or reviewing (to evaluate written text against one's goals). A major influence upon shifts between processes is the writer's goals, which fall into two meta-categories, produce-text or evaluate-text. According to Elbow (1981), "Writing calls on two skills that are so different that they usually conflict with each other: creating and criticizing. …It is true that these opposite mental processes can go on at the same time" (p. 7). Reading can promote this create/criticize conflict. Consider the following series of events: Pausing to compose his next sentence, a writer reads a prior sentence in order to spark ideas—but is suddenly struck by its awkward wording. Does he stop to revise immediately or continue composing? This commonplace scenario illustrates a competition not so much for processing capacity, but attentional resources. The cognitive system can handle a certain amount of multitasking. For example, for writers with fluent reading and typing skills, minor typographical errors may be detected and corrected on the fly, with barely a break in composing. However, when evaluating gives rise to difficult revising problems with a myriad of possible solutions (e.g., Largy, 2001), criticizing may interrupt creating. Seemingly, writers must develop strategies that allow them to maximize the benefits of reading, while minimizing its disruptive effects.

4.2 Retrieving Content from LTM

Reading can also cooperate with other writing processes. Moment to moment, writers must find something to write. Writing effectively depends upon having flexible access to context-relevant information in order to produce and comprehend texts. In writing research, there has been considerable discussion about how information is retrieved from LTM, whether via automatic or controlled processes (Galbraith & Torrance, 1999). Early theories of skilled writing (e.g., Bereiter & Scardamalia, 1987; Hayes & Flower, 1980) assume that knowledge is stored via a semantic network, in which ideas are interconnected in various ways (Anderson, 1983; Collins & Loftus, 1975). In Hayes and Flower's (1980) model, generating (a subcomponent of planning) is responsible for retrieving relevant information from LTM. Retrieval is automatic. Information about the topic and/or the audience serves as an initial memory probe, which is then elaborated, as each retrieved item serves as additional probes in an associative chain. Simlarly Bereiter and Scardamalia (1987) see automatic activation underlying a knowledge-telling approach. However, the authors hold that for knowledge transformation depends upon strategic retrieval. In knowledge transforming, problem solving includes analysis of the rhetorical issues, as well as topic and task issues, which results in multiple memory probes of LTM. Then retrieved content is evaluated and selected, *a priori*, according to the writer's goals (Alamargot & Chanquoy, 2001). Thus, influential models of writing differ in their accounts of how retrieval happens in skilled writing.

In proposing his knowledge-constituting model, Galbraith (1999) provides an alternative account, in which writing expertise relies upon automatic activation (rather than controlled retrieval). In contrasting knowledge constituting with knowledge transforming, he argues that complex problem solving alone cannot fully account for the experiences of professional writers. In describing their own writing experiences, professional writers often use the word "discovery," since novel ideas often emerging spontaneously through process of writing. The knowledge-constituting model provides a cognitive framework for explaining this experience of discovery. In contrast to the semantic network (described above), Galbraith assumes that knowledge is stored implicitly, as sub-conceptual units within a distributed network (Hinton, McClelland, & Rumelhart, 1990). Patterns of activation result from input constraints and the strength of fixed connections between nodes in the network. Accordingly, different ideas can emerge as a result of different patterns of global activation. Less a direct challenge to knowledge transforming (Bereiter & Scardamalia, 1987), the knowledge constituting model serves as a corrective to the either/or view that expert writing relies solely upon sophisticate problem solving, with a controlled retrieval of information from LTM.[1] (We return to this topic of discovery in the final section.)

---

[1] The knowledge-constituting and knowledge-transforming models compare to the Augustan literary notions of wit and judgment, respectively. Poets have long been aware of the inherent conflict between creativity and criticism, the two essential dimensions of writing expertise: "For wit and judgment often are at strife,/Though meant for each other's aid, like man and wife." Excerpted from Alexander Pope's (1758) "An Essay on Criticism."

How might reading facilitate planning? When pausing to plan their next sentence, skilled writers often reread sections of their text (Breetvelt, Van den Bergh, & Rijlaarsdam, 1996; Kaufer et al., 1986). These observations raise the question of how reading might facilitate retrieval, for planning and/or translating. Bereiter and Scardamalia (1987) recognized that reading a previously written sentence could serve to cue activation, which they characterized as a simplistic strategy consistent with knowledge telling. In contrast, Hayes (1996) concluded that local reading may represent a mature strategy, as evidenced by the adult writers' observations in Kaufer et al. (1986). Different modes of reading might facilitate retrieval in various ways. Reading may be goal directed for the retrieval of specific, context-relevant information. Or, scanning the developing text could activate information, from which goal-relevant products are selected. As a part of either automatic or controlled processes, reading for generating could provide a flexible mechanism accessing information from LTM.

Under certain circumstances, reading for content retrieval could be quite powerful. Within the WM system, limitations in capacity force a trade-off between storage and processing (Baddeley, 1986; Baddeley, Gathercole, & Papagno, 1998; Baddeley & Hitch, 1974). However, Ericsson and Kintsch (1995) argue that WM capacity does not account well for the extensive information processing demonstrated by expert performance. For example, they cite the ability of skilled readers to maintain access to large amounts of information— seemingly exceeding the limits of WM—in order to integrate new information from the current sentence into the previously read text. For Ericsson and Kintsch (1995), such performance is best explained by experts' ability "to use parts of their LTM as WM" (p. 219). According to the long-term working memory (LT-WM) model, LTM elements activated in WM serve as retrieval structures for quickly linking to other relevant LTM elements. Thus, an LT-WM includes elements active in WM, as well as those additional LTM elements connected by retrieval structures. LT-WM may be viewed as the emergent property of a highly efficient cognitive system. Highly fluent reading encoding processes are fast and draw little cognitive load; while stable, well-practiced knowledge can be readily activated. When automatized low-level processes (such as encoding during reading) operate in conjunction with highly developed domain knowledge, the efficiencies gained result in fast links between WM and LTM.

Ericsson and Kintsch (1995) propose that LT-WM explains expert performance in many domains (e.g., chess). Writing researchers have applied the theoretical framework of LT-WM to explain skilled writing (Kellogg, 2001; McCutchen, 2000). McCutchen (2000) proposes that "fluent encoding processes and rich knowledge bases enable skilled writers to move beyond the limits of ST-WM and capitalize on the resources of LT-WM" (p. 15). For support, she points to the beneficial effects of domain knowledge in both reading (Peskin, 1998; Spilich, Vesonder, Chiesi, & Voss, 1979; Voss, Vesonder, & Spilich, 1980) and writing (Caccamise, 1987; DeGroff, 1987; McCutchen, 1986; Voss et al., 1980). In a study by Voss et al. (1980), college students, grouped according to their knowledge of baseball, were asked to compose texts about the game. Two weeks later participants were asked to recall the contents of those texts. Baseball experts also demonstrated a superior ability to recall aspects of the texts (i.e., flow of action and change of game states). Also, relative to baseball novices, experts produced texts that were longer, more detailed, and better structured. In Kellogg's (1987) study, secondary response times were significantly shorter for high-knowledge participants, across planning, translating, and reviewing; suggesting that highly developed and structured domain knowledge reduces cognitive effort during composing. These beneficial effects of domain knowledge on writing tend to support the notion that skillful writers, composing in a familiar domain, gain access to LT-WM.

How might LT-WM operate during writing? McCutchen (2000) provides a general explanation of the relevance of LT-WM to writing expertise, without committing to an underlying mechanism. We propose that one way by which skilled writers gain access to LT-WM is via reading the developing text. Although reading and writing share important underlying processes (e.g., linguistic processes, WM, and sometimes LT-WM), they also differ in important ways. Generally, comprehending a text involves analysis, whereas producing a text requires synthesis. In reading, encoding the text provides a continual stream of prompts to activate relevant information in LTM. Encoding a sentence creates a mental representation of a text's local structure (a microstructure). With access to LT-WM, this microstructure can quickly connect to other relevant information in LTM, serving as a retrieval structure. Because encoding precedes knowledge access, it can serve to cue it.

By contrast, in writing, encoding follows knowledge access; so, it cannot serve to cue it. Encoding happens at the end of the cycle, following the macro-planning, macro-structural, and micro-structural strategies; that is, the writer types out a sentence only after he or she has established goals, generated and organized ideas, and put those ideas into words. Since, in writing, knowledge is accessed before the corresponding microstructure is constructed, the microstructure obviously cannot retroactively serve to retrieve that knowledge. However, one potentially rich source of retrieval cues is the developing text. Producing one phrase can facilitate the retrieval of information relevant to planning *the next phrase*. In conversation, an interlocutor's remarks can serve to activate knowledge in the mind of another. However, writers must struggle along without a conversational partner (Bereiter & Scardamalia, 1987). To compensate, writers may employ a conversation-like strategy to prompt their own writing, where writing one phrase serves to generate ideas relevant to the next. Bereiter and Scardamalia (1987) recognized the existence of this conversation-like strategy, which underlies the knowledge-telling approach. However, some conversations are much more sophisticated than others. With access to LT-WM, a strategy such as reading-for-retrieval could be quite powerful.

Reading the developing text may enable the writer to gain access to LT-WM. The sentences within a paragraph usually relate topically, with the paragraph topics sharing a common theme. Reading may cue retrieval in various ways. Reading in the vicinity of the point of inscription (local reading) might activate topic-relevant information, for the purposes elaborating a topic within a paragraph. In contrast, global reading may serve to activate both intra- and inter-topic information, to be used in generating and organizing ideas for starting a new paragraph. At major text junctures, writers tend to pause longer (Matsuhashi, 1981; Schilperoord, 1996), which may be partly due to local or global reading for planning. For the writer with rich domain knowledge and very fluent encoding, by which LT-WM becomes operative, reading the developing text can represent a flexible and powerful strategy for accessing knowledge.

Writers face the chronic problem of knowing what to write. Reading to cue retrieval represents a potentially powerful strategy for addressing this problem. Although reading for retrieval may have greater utility in some types of writing tasks than others, it seems particularly indispensable to composing from sources.

5 Reading When Composing from Sources

Samuel Johnson once said, "When a man writes from his own mind, he writes very rapidly. The greatest part of a writer's time is spent in reading, in order to write; a man will turn over half a library to make one book" (Boswell, 1948, p. 45). The 18th century poet and lexicographer captures the challenges of composing from sources, in which the writer labors to incorporate information into his or her own texts. Writers find information in all sorts of medium, both digital (e.g., email and websites) and hard copy (e.g., printed journals and reports). In some cases, writers may summarize, providing "a brief statement that represents the condensation of information" (Hidi & Anderson, 1986, p. 473). A good summary tends to reflect the macrostructure of a text. Although many reading studies have used written summaries to assess participants' comprehension, forming a summary may not be an inevitable result of comprehension (Brown & Day, 1983; Brown, Day, & Jones, 1983). Some writing tasks will require the writer to go beyond summarizing, to synthesize information, drawing connections across sources. When synthesizing, the writer must comprehend sources well enough to determine how the ideas represented may relate to his or her own ideas. In scholarly and professional writing, wherein much content comes from source documents, writers may often shift between summarizing and synthesizing.

When composing from sources, a writer's reading strategies follow from his or her writing goals. For example, if a writer reads and understands a particular market report, and then wants to summarize the findings in an email to a colleague, they could probably do so quite readily, without consulting the source. However, if the writer were writing a quarterly report to the board of directors, the need for detail and precision would compel to review the source document. In the latter case, the writer would probably not reread the whole document, but would probably scan it, in order to find and select certain key pieces of information. Bazerman (1985) observed physicists reading journals in their field. He found that these highly skilled professionals tended not to read in a thorough, systematic way; rather, they searched and scanned for specific information relevant to their current research projects. Thus, when composing from sources, reading strategies may be directed toward meeting the specific content and rhetorical goals of the writing task.

While task variables (such as audience, communicative purpose, and genre) can influence reading behavior when composing from sources, comprehension skills also play an important role. The degree to which a writer comprehends a source text determines his or her ability to integrate information from it. Reading research distinguishes between the ability to recognize a previously read sentence (recognition memory) and the ability to recollect the major propositions of a text (recall memory). In tests of recognition, complete retrieval is not required, which likely helps explain why people recognize much more than they recall. Further, recall decays rather quickly with time, while recognition remains durable (Bjork, 1975). The ability of a writer to recall what he has read "from his own mind" has great advantages: Content retrieval is fast and does not require consulting. In contrast, a recognition level of comprehension may be insufficient for composing a complete summary. However, recognition memory could help guide rereading, in a search for the relevant content. If the source document is at hand, the writer need only recognize that relevant information resides in a particular section of the document, and then can reread it. However, when a source document is unavailable, the writer may be forced to work around his or her own ignorance. During writing, recognition and recall can work together, with recognition prompting rereading, which reactivates mental structures of the text for the purposes of planning. For this reason, strong reading skills greatly benefit the writer, because good comprehension carries over directly into planning.

For tasks involving composing from sources, much research indicates that effective strategies for reading comprehension transfer to writing. In Hyona, Lorch, and Kaakinen (2002), adults (n = 48) read texts of approximately 1,200 words, during which the location and duration of their eye fixations were recorded. Fifteen minutes after reading, after an intervening task, participants wrote summaries without the benefit of consulting source texts. Clustering analysis revealed four distinct patterns of reading: slow linear, fast linear, nonselective, and topic structure. Participants in the topic structure group produced the most accurate summaries. These results suggest that effective reading strategies, such as using text structure (i.e., topic headings), may benefit summary writing by facilitating recall.

Effective reading strategies, such as using text structure, can also help writers identify important facts in source documents. (For a review of this research, see Alamargot et al., 2005). Good readers tend to use elements of text structure, as part of comprehending (Hyona et al., 2002; Nash, Schumacher, & Carlson, 1993; Spivey & King, 1989). When composing from sources, one particular challenge is selecting relevant information from source texts. After all, writers must necessarily exclude much of what they read. Spivey and King (1989) explored how undergraduate writers integrated content from three source documents into writing a synthesis. Relative to less-skilled readers, more-skilled readers succeeded in integrating more source content into their syntheses. More-skilled readers proved more able to select content of greater importance, on the basis of position in text hierarchy and repetition across sources. Brown et al. (1983) found that the ability to select relevant content develops with writing experience, with college and older high school students being more able than younger (5th and 7th grade) students.

Skill in reading comprehension serves not only content retrieval, but also content organizing. Nash et al. (1993) found that competent writers (undergraduate students) used the structure of sources in writing compare/contrast essays, using the first-presented source as a model. Seemingly, there is no advantage to indiscriminately patterning one's own text after the organizational structure of a source. However, to the extent that published source texts tend to be well organized, structuring one's text after a source may be a sound strategy.

When composing from sources, reading strategies for comprehension can become writing strategies for planning. During reading, source information that becomes successfully encoded into LTM becomes content available for writing. Thus, one can argue that reading strategies benefiting comprehension will in turn benefit planning for writing. For example, highlighting or underlining a text during reading has shown to improve recall (Blanchard & Mikkelson, 1987; Gaonac'h & Passerault, 1990; Nist & Simpson, 1988). During writing, highlighted sections of the text can also speed the writer's search for relevant content. Similarly, taking notes during reading has shown to facilitate comprehension (Kobayashi, 2005). In this case, the notes themselves become planning tools for writing. As products of summarizing, notes gather the important points of a source text (in Kintschean terms, the propositions in the macrostructure), to which the writer may refer. In his case study of college students composing from sources, McGinley (1992) found that "writing notes served as an intermediate text that helped them to plan and organize their ideas and arguments" (p. 241).

One writing strategy involves taking notes on cards. By arranging the note cards in different configurations, the writer can easily evaluate different organizational schemes for a report or essay. A strategy that supports reading comprehension can directly benefit planning, because the same representation-building processes underlie both reading and writing.

6 Reading for Revising

Thus far, we have focused on reading for the purposes of planning, because this aspect has not been well developed in the research literature. Yet, reading obviously plays other roles in writing, most especially in revising. Revising is a key feature of skilled writing (Hayes, 1996; Hayes et al., 1987; Sommers, 1980). However, attempts to define and operationalize "revising" typically run into difficulties. Fitzgerald and Markham (1987) defined "revision" as "making any changes at any point in the writing process" (p. 4). If so, revising is pervasive in skilled writing. The composing of skilled writers in the study by Kaufer et al. (1986), in which sentences take shape in fits and starts, with stating and much rephrasing, certainly qualifies as revising. Lindgren and Sullivan (2006) have also observed that revising can happen anytime, and can involve changes either in the writer's mind or any level of the text. Accordingly, their taxonomy classifies revisions according to the location and nature of the revision. Internal revisions occur in the mind of the writer, and may be conceptual (pre-linguistic) or conceptual/form (pre-text) in nature. External revisions involve changes to language representations, which have been instantiated either partially (pre-contextual) or fully (contextual). Thus, an external-contextual revision would involve a change to the developing text. The authors acknowledge that some revisions lie "on the borderline between internal and external" (p. 40). So defined, revising appears indistinguishable from other writing processes, such as planning and formulating. Hayes and Flower (1983) explicate the difference between internal and external revision, by distinguishing between reviewing and revision. However, the question arises: Is revision is a writing process, in its own right, or rather an instance of managing other writing processes? (Olive & Piolat, 2002)

Yet, accomplished writers do revisit their texts. Why? Writers aim to inform, move, and/or entertain a reader. This becomes a complicated task, because the writer cannot fully determine how a reader will understand the text. Rather, reading is an interpretive act, with each reader bringing his or her own knowledge and beliefs into the interpretation. Texts often have multiple readers (such as an email posted to a wide audience). Thus, the writer must attempt to constrain a wide range of possible meanings. Writers can do many things to facilitate a certain "reading." The foremost advice from writing manuals is to write "clearly" (e.g., Strunk, 2000). Flower (1979) contrasts "reader-based prose," which anticipates the needs of the reader, with "writer-based prose." It follows that writers must become readers of their own texts in order to produce reader-based prose.

In the revising model of Hayes et al. (1987), reading facilitates comprehending, evaluating, and defining problems. Hayes (2004) sees revising as largely a function of reading comprehension. Identifying, diagnosing, and solving various types of problems calls for different types of analyses. For example, detecting various types of typographical error can involve processing various types of linguistic information, including orthographic, phonological, syntactic, and semantic (Levy, Newell, Snyder, & Timmins, 1986). The semantic level of a text presents some of the thorniest revising problems. The ability to critically read one's own text allows the writer to assess the difficulties his or her readers might encounter. Critical reading encompasses a host of strategies. Palinscar and Brown (1984) found that experienced readers employed six strategies in the course of comprehending a text: (a) understand the implicit/explicit purposes of reading, (b) activate relevant background knowledge, (c) allocate attention to major content, (d) evaluate content for internal consistency, (e) monitor ongoing comprehension, and (f) draw and test inference. All of these strategies can transfer to writing, being useful for producing reader-based prose.

As a reading strategy, comprehension monitoring involves assessing one's on-going understanding and recognizing comprehension failures (Markman, 1979). Studies of comprehension monitoring have typically examined readers' abilities to detect various kinds of errors introduced into texts. In his review of this research, Hacker (1994) concludes that comprehension monitoring has come "to be viewed as a multidimensional process consisting primarily of evaluation and regulation" (p. 162). The goal of reading is comprehension, whereas the goal of writing is producing text that is comprehensible to a reader. During reading, the ability to recognize comprehension failures can trigger compensatory strategies, such as rereading. Comprehension monitoring enables the writer to consider the needs of the reader, such as to detect potential locations of misunderstanding, then re-engage planning to define and solve the problem. By critically reading the developing text, the writer can evaluate the text against rhetorical goals, to assess how well the target reader will be moved and informed. When the writer sets elaborate rhetorical goals, critical reading enables the writer to evaluate the text against those goals. Thus, reading strategies, such as comprehension monitoring, may lie at the heart of a knowledge-transforming approach to writing.

Critical reading compounds the complexity of writing, perhaps explaining why writers often limit their revising to surface changes. Some writers may be unable to cope with the complexity of revising. First, some writers may be unable to read their own texts critically because of weak reading comprehension, whether due to inadequate decoding skills, language skills, and/or domain knowledge. Many people carry reading difficulties into adulthood. Although one factor can compensate for a weakness in another, to some extent, such a weakness could impair the writer's ability to identify problems in the text. Second, since reading is itself a complex activity, critical reading can be cognitively costly, even for strong readers. Since producing text and evaluating text both depend heavily upon common resources within WM, particularly the central executive (Kellogg, 1996), engaging both contemporaneously may result in overload. Hacker (1994) has suggested that comprehension monitoring may place considerable load upon cognitive resources, making it a difficulty strategy to execute. Comprehension monitoring is but one of several possible reading strategies one might adopt during revising.

In addition to the high cost, writers may fail to revise effectively because they hold inadequate revising schemas. Namely, writers may believe that revising pertains primarily to making surface changes. In a study by Wallace et al. (1996), entry-level writing students in two classrooms composed application letters for college. One class received brief (8-minute!) instruction in reading their own texts globally, while a control class received general writing instruction. All participants then revised their letters. The results showed that this 8-minute instruction significantly improved the quality of revising. The study was replicated with less-skilled freshman writers (as identified by low scores on the verbal section of the SAT). In Experiment 2, revising failed to improve students in either class. Collectively, these results suggest that a prompt to read globally can be effective for redirecting revising schemas, for writers with solid literacy skills. However, writers with weaker skills may have difficulty reading and addressing global issues in their text, perhaps due to a relative inability to coordinate reading with other writing processes.

In spite of the cognitive costs involved, some skilled writers do much revising at the point of inscription, because it affords opportunities for discovery. While "revising" typically refers to the external-contextual variety, writers also engage in internal reviewing. Several writing teachers and researchers have observed that the composing experiences of professional writers can often be best characterized as discovery (e.g., Britton, 1982; Elbow, 1973; Galbraith, 1999; Matsuhashi, 1987). In contrast to the writing models reviewed above, which emphasize how problem solving drives writing (i.e., top-down), a discovery approach assumes that important thinking happens as text is produced, through spontaneous invention (i.e., bottom-up). The skilled and expert writers in the study by Kaufer et al. (1986) appeared to proceed in a fashion resembling "discovery," as each sentence unfolded tentatively, with initial plans expanding considerably. The authors conclude that "Writing sentences can lead to more than just a change in the writing plan. It can also provide the occasion for writers to change their understanding of the topic" (Kaufer et al., 1986, p. 124). Thus, discovery is characterized by this internal reviewing (Murray, 1978). In this context of discovery, this internal reviewing appears at odds with dominant views of writing as either simple versus complex problem solving (e.g., knowledge telling or knowledge transforming).

By considering how reading may hinder or facilitate discovery, we move beyond what may be a false dichotomy between planning and revising. What appears at issue is the goal of reading, whether for discovery or evaluation. Britton (1982) argues that reading prompts discovery, through what he calls "shaping at the point of utterance." He asserts "Once a writer's words appear on the page, ... they act primarily as a stimulus to continuing—to further writing, that is—and not primarily as a stimulus to re-writing" (p. 30). According to Elbow (1981), discovery is at odds with criticism, which can hinder the spontaneity of invention. Elbow (1973; 1981) advocates separating creating and criticism by adopting a dual-draft approach, with the first draft devoted to discovery, writing freely and uncritically, with subsequent drafts reserved for critical revising. Accordingly, discovery may rely upon reading for generating, while holding evaluation in abeyance.

7 Conclusion

When writing in the workplace, professionals must develop strategies for accessing and evaluating information, which involves reading for various purposes. Achieving writing goals often requires the writer to read for different purposes. The writer must read his or her own text to evaluate it, in order to revise. In this way, reading the developing text enables the writer to adopt a sophisticated (knowledge transforming) approach to composing. Reading may also play an important role in generating new content. When composing from sources, professionals must comprehend information from text sources, such as reports and emails. Recalling and recognizing information from sources enables the writer to integrate that information into their own texts. To a large extent, effective writing in the workplace becomes a matter of developing reading processes and adapting them to the purposes of writing.

The importance of reading-during-writing holds practical implications. Fluent reading skills afford a host of advantages for accessing and evaluating information. Yet, inherent cognitive limitations impose limits on all writers, to some extent. Accordingly, writing effectively requires finding ways of either overcoming or compensating for those limitations. Developing fluency in a particular writing tool (whether handwriting, word processing, or speech recognition) can minimize interference due to transcription. A rich, well-structured knowledge of the writing topic can greatly benefit both planning and revising, validating the counsel of writing coaches, to write about what one knows best. When a writing task involves sources, reading strategies (such as note taking and highlighting) can transfer directly over into planning for writing. Understanding the different purposes of reading can increase writers' meta-cognitive awareness of their own writing processes, and so help them develop effective strategies for reading-during-writing.

Although early models of writing ascribed a rather marginal role to reading (Bereiter & Scardamalia, 1987; Hayes & Flower, 1980; Kellogg, 1996), some recent models now see reading as central to skilled writing (Hayes, 1996). At present, we still know relatively little about reading during writing. Investigating the processes of writing involves some big methodological challenges. Reading-during-writing is difficult to observe, and is bound up with other processes that are not yet well understood. For more than 20 years, think-aloud protocols have been used to investigate the processes of writing. Although such protocols can and have been used effectively, they have various limitations. To gain more fine-grained insights into writing processes, Janssen and his colleagues (Janssen et al., 1996) suggest combining think-aloud protocols with other methodologies, such as systems for keystroke logging and eye tracking. For many years, researchers have used eye-tracking systems to study reading (Rayner, 1998); however, only recently have researchers begun to overcome the technical difficulties involved in applying eye tracking to the study of writing (e.g., Alamargot, Chesnet, Dansac, & Ros, 2006; Andersson et al., 2006; Chesnet & Alamargot, 2005). These new methodologies promise new insights into the involvement of reading in writing.

Chapter 6

Professional Editing: Emphasis on the Quality of a Text and its Communicative Effectiveness

Jocelyne Bisaillon

In this chapter, I discuss professional editors' work and their self-set objectives for improving both the quality of a text and its effectiveness from the standpoint of communication. Editors must ensure, on the one hand, that the rules of language and form are respected—work usually ascribed to "copy editors"—and on the other hand, and more importantly in terms of defining the work specific to "professional editors," that the reader is taken into account—in short, that for this person, the final text is clear, comprehensible and easy to read. To achieve these particular ends, professional editors draw on a broad range of strategies. But what exactly defines such strategies? What particular difficulties do editors have to negotiate? And do new technologies have a role to play in their work? In this chapter, I will try to provide some answers to these and similar questions.

1 Introduction

Until recently, researchers have rarely focused their attention on the details of professional editing and revising, preferring to concentrate their efforts on understanding the self-revision process in the school context, as is confirmed by the latest book to present an overview of revision/editing research (Allal, Chanquoy, & Largy, 2004). Moreover, while the editing process in a professional context has occasionally been the object of some study, the subjects have generally been writing professionals such as authors or journalists who revised their own texts (Berkenkotter, 1983; Britton, Dusen, Gulgöz, & Glynn, 1989; Magee, 1995), and not professional editors who have been trained to revise, edit and proofread, and who spend their working days improving other people's texts. And yet, given their expertise, it is the professionals' work that should by all rights aid us in gaining a better understanding of editing, whether the text involved is one's own or another person's. Given the expertise of professionals, it is only natural that we should look to their work as an aid in better understanding the editing process, whether the text to be modified is one's own or someone else's.

In this chapter, I discuss the work of professional editors and their self-set objectives for improving both the quality of a text *per se* and its effectiveness, from the standpoint of communication. Editors must read texts from the point of view not only of evaluators but also of potential readers. How do these experts go about accomplishing such objectives? What factors influence their editing process? And do new technologies have a role to play in their work? In this chapter, I will to provide some answers to these and similar questions.

2 The Professional Editor's Task

Professional revision is a highly complex activity, as is suggested by the model of professional revision proposed by Laflamme (2007). The author takes up the factors defined by Hayes et al. (1987) in their model of self-revision, keeps certain of them that are shared by both types of revision, modifies them and adds others in order to describe the professional activity of editing. To take one example, while, in self-revision, determining the task is part of the revision process, this is not the case in professional revision, where the editor does not define the task but instead receives his instructions from the client.

2.1 Mandate

At the outset of a professional editing experience, a client (e.g., publisher, project manager, author, etc.) gives an editor an editing assignment. Often, the client quite simply asks the editor to "edit" the work, without specifying what she/he exactly means by this term. But, as Billingham (2002, p. 7) has noted in her book on the subject, "Editing means different things to different people." All too often, for this client, editing is viewed as merely a normative activity aimed at removing such errors of grammar and mechanics as may be encountered in the text (work which, in English, is often referred to loosely as copy editing). Nevertheless, while editing may be linguistic in nature, it may also be structural or stylistic, to mention only two of the main aspects. As is noted on the Website of the Editors' Association of Canada (2005):

> The editor's functions start when the writer declares the manuscript more or less complete and continue through to the point at which it is ready for publication, regardless of the medium. Editors perform many tasks along the way, including structural editing, stylistic editing, copy editing, markup/coding, and proofreading.

Thus, if the editor intends to satisfy the client's expectations concerning any and all required modifications, she/he must ask for specifics about his/her mandate. It does happen that the client specifies what she/he genuinely wants—for example, to simplify a text written by a specialist on a given subject so as to make it more comprehensible and readable for the lay reader.

To illustrate the various mandates involved, I will refer to the assignments of the six editors participating in the study conducted in the professional editors' revision process.[1] Four of the six editors were given the mandate of performing revision of a purely formal variety: i.e., mechanics and grammar (Editors 1, 2, 5 and 6). The other two were granted a broader mandate: rewriting texts so as to make them comprehensible for their target readership (Editor 3), and revising both form and content of a book (Editor 4).

We observed them in a real-life situation—namely, when they were working on a document that they had contracted to edit. We analyzed both the process and the product of editing. The process component was studied using protocol analysis based on retrospective verbalization. Since professional editors strive to do their work quickly and efficiently, it was our view that retrospective verbalization was the best way to approach the real-life situation. The products component was analyzed on the basis of our own taxonomy.

The texts to be revised were of various types: a land-use plan (Editor 1), a teacher's guide (Editor 2), magazine articles (Editor 3), a book (Editor 4), a report (Editor 5) and an ecology guide (Editor 6). All were revising texts that were intended for specific readerships (e.g., seniors, "cégep" students [in Québec, the cégep is roughly equivalent to the junior college of the U.S. and the other provinces of Canada], heritage enthusiasts), with the exception of Editor 4, who was revising a text intended for the general public.

2.2 Editors' Conceptions of the Editing Process: Accounting for the Target Reader

While the client's mandate represents the starting point of the editor's work, the conception or representation of editing and revising held by the editor plays a role in the approach that she/he adopts to his/her work. Indeed, it would be difficult to argue the contrary, as the results of our research showed that the four editors who had been asked to perform formal revision clearly did not limit their corrections to instances of straying from the rules. Moreover, as Hayes et al. (1987) noted, the job of revising is a reflection of an editor's conception of what revision means.

It is our view that there are essentially two main conceptions of revision: one having a normative focus and another having a communicational focus. In the "normative" conception, the editor's main concern is to bring the text in line with the linguistic rules—whether these apply to typography, spelling, grammar, vocabulary, syntax, spelling or punctuation. This conception generally coincides with that of the less proficient writers who, in the performance of their duties, concern themselves merely with the surface of the text, as was noted by Hacker, Plumb, Butterfield, Quathamer, and Heineken (1994, p. 66): "Most [student writers] make very few changes; instead, they change spelling, grammar, and punctuation [...]. They seem to see the goal of revision as proofreading."

In the "communicational" conception, the editor continues to be concerned about the formal quality of the text, yet also devotes his/her attention to the effectiveness of the text from the viewpoint of communication with the reader. This care or concern for the reader's needs is

---

[1]This research project was made possible through a grant from the Social Sciences and Humanities Research Council of Canada (SSHRC 2002–2005). Co-researchers on this project were Gilles Fortier and Clémence Préfontaine, both at the Université du Québec à Montréal.

of greatest importance in the case of procedural texts in which the reader is charged with accomplishing a task (Ganier, Heurley, & Barcenilla, this volume). As Ganier and Heurley (2005) wrote, the objective of the reader is not to learn—that is, to understand and retain information—but instead to perform a task correctly.

In the first conception, the emphasis is on the text and in the second, on the text–reader relationship. By simplifying, smoothing, rounding out or clarifying the text, the editor ensures that the reader expends the least effort in return for the greatest gains in terms of comprehension (see Sperber & Wilson, 1989). Taking the reader into consideration is one of the recommendations made to writers and editors (Anderson, 1991; Billingham, 2002), and is apparent among expert writers (Hayes et al., 1987; McCutchen & Kerr, 1997).

3 Work on the Text

Once the client's editing mandate has been established and the editor's own conception of editing has been defined, the editing work can begin in earnest. Or so it would seem, as mandate and conception are not always compatible. As our research on the revision process of professional revisers serves to show, the client's mandate coincided with the conception of editing held by four of the editors and failed to coincide in the case of the other two (see Table 1). Below, I will discuss at greater length how this compatibility/incompatibility had an impact on the modifications made by the editors to their texts.

What do editors change? To answer this question, authors of guidebooks for writers and editors involved in the practice of revision address the various qualities that a text must possess or, alternately, draw up a list of errors to be corrected. Billingham (2002) is a good example of the first case, addressing structural flow, linguistic flow, editing style and tone, accuracy, brevity and clarity of the text. Lachance (2006) instead points out certain errors that a text may contain such as forms of animism, archaisms, incorrect usage and poor grammar. Nonetheless, these authors do not provide a taxonomy serving to group together the various types of possible modifications. Thus, for the purposes of analyzing the work of editing, we developed our own taxonomy of the rationales given by the editors for their respective modifications (Bisaillon, in press). It consists of four main categories that correspond to the four main objectives pursued, consciously or unconsciously, by editors as they perform an evaluative reading of texts. It should be noted, however, that the objectives were a subject of concern to editors to varying degrees (see Table 1).

The first objective targeted by all of the participating editors, and which explains 50.7% of the modifications noted (i.e., 607 out of 1198), is compliance with the rules. In addition to the above-mentioned rules are those applying to usage in a particular context of use or readership, conventions governing genre and uniformity. In this instance, editors strive to rid the text of all errors.

The other three objectives are related to the concern for communication with the reader. Accordingly, 25% of modifications were made for the purpose of making the text more enjoyable or readable for the reader (second objective). To this end, the editor corrects inadequacies of style, tone or presentation; alleviates woodenness and dryness; and, as needed, deletes a word or group of words and removes pointless repetitions that unnecessarily lengthen a text and increase the difficulty of reading it. She/he may also modify the punctuation.

Table 1: An editor's work from the viewpoint of his/her mandate and his/her conception of editing.

Editor	Mandate N: normative C: communicational	Conception	Normative objective Compliance with rules (%)	Communicational objective		
				Clarity of wording (%)	Comprehensibility of text (%)	Readability (%)
2	N	N	69.7	5.3	7.8	17.3
6	N	N	45.8	0	27.1	27.1
3	C	C	31.3	18.7	26.1	23.9
4	C	C	33.3	14.7	14.3	35.7
1	N	C	56.9	8.8	10.2	21.2
5	N	C	67.2	4.2	9.2	19.3
Average			**50.7**	**8.6**	**15.8**	**25**

The third objective is to make the text more readily understandable for the reader (15.8% of modifications). To do so, the editor makes corrections to the content or to the organization of the text. She/he modifies an idea, corrects inaccurate information and brings coherence to the text or the title. She/he separates ideas that do not go with one another or, on the contrary, combines ideas that share affinities. She/he highlights a particular idea—the thrust of a paragraph or text, or, conversely, downplays information of secondary importance. Finally, she/he enhances the interrelationships between ideas, or carefully delineates the specific referents.

The last (fourth) objective is to make the wording clearer or tighter for the reader's benefit (8.6% of modifications). In this instance, the editor remedies weaknesses of vocabulary, including terminological inaccuracies and jargon, or rewords portions that are ambiguous, awkward or convoluted.

In their study of ten third-year students in the computer science program, Eklundh and Kollberg (2003) examined the goals pursued by the students whenever they made modifications to their texts. Some of these goals match up with the previously mentioned objectives or the means required to achieve them. In this instance, the students edited out of concern for uniformity and to remove repetitions, to make the text coherent and well structured, and to improve clarity. This finding leads me to believe that the objectives that we have identified among professional editors could be used to good effect by writers who edit their own texts.

I also noted that three of these professional editors' self-set objectives relate to taking the reader into consideration (communicational objectives), which seems to confirm Schriver's (1992a) statement that "Successful revision has been shown to depend on writer's ability to anticipate the needs of a reader and to identify ways to help clarify whole-text problems from the reader's perspective" (pp. 150–151). To illustrate the fundamental importance of the reader, in technical texts, Buehler (2003) noted that "If an electronics manual is to be used by men who are technically proficient but whose reading ability is at the eight-grade level, that manual is not going to be very useful unless it is prepared with that reading level in mind" (p. 462).

Table 1 examines the work that the editors performed on a text, from the viewpoint of their mandate and their conception of editing. The objectives were grouped together under normative or communicational objectives, thus enabling me to determine whether and to what extent congruence was achieved between the client's mandate, the editor's conception of his/her work and the modifications made to the text.

The first finding of note from the table is that even when the client's mandate is formal revision (mandate = N), all the editors do more than merely rid the target text of mechanical and grammatical errors. In other words, while reading the text, their attention is not focused exclusively on problems related to non-compliance with standard rules. Nevertheless, the editors given this mandate showed evidence of expending greater effort on such matters than did the editors who had received a "communicational" mandate (shadowed rows in the table). To wit, the first group based between 45.8% and 69.7% of their modifications on considerations of compliance with rules, whereas this same rationale accounted for approximately one-third of the modifications made by the second group. These editors accorded nearly the same importance to clarity of wording, although Editor 3 favored comprehensibility and Editor 4 readability.

While the mandate has an obvious impact on the work performed by the editor, this is less true of the editor's own conception of editing. Indeed, how is one to explain that all of the editors identified as receiving a normative mandate and having a normative conception of their work also made modifications for the purpose of facilitating the reader's comprehension? I believe that it is because all six of the professional editors think about the reader of the text as they revise—even if they do not say so explicitly during the interview—much in the way that expert writers do. However, other research will be required in order to validate this hypothesis.

The results for Editor 6 are, moreover, surprising. For it appears that his concern for comprehensibility is disproportionately high, considering that both his conception and mandate have a normative focus. His difficulty understanding the content of the text he had been assigned (ecological types) prompted him to modify it so as to grasp it and thus be in a position to aid others to comprehend it. If the text had been less difficult, no doubt he would have gone about his task differently. Having taking considerable time to understand the meaning of his text, this editor made only 40 modifications during the two hours of work during which he was observed, whereas the others made upwards of 275.

4 Physical Environment

The editor's physical environment is his/her workplace—that is, an office in the home or on an organization's premises or both. On his/her table, printed reference tools lie within easy reach. A computer and various related information sources are equally close to hand and are most often installed on the desktop. Professional editors have little time to waste and their office set-up must be functional.

Reference works and other helpful tools are also part of this environment. Some reference tools are common to all editors, while others are specific to each, owing to the contents of the text to be revised (e.g., specialty dictionaries), their training and education, or merely to different habits. Among the works that the editors in the study used regularly, I selected *Le Nouveau Petit Robert*, *Le grand dictionnaire terminologique*, an online dictionary operated by a Québec government agency and a useful bilingual resource for specialized vocabulary, and the *Multidictionnaire de la langue française*, a practical dictionary considered to be essential by editors in Québec, as it takes into consideration spoken French in Québec and attempts to provide answers to the thorny questions of norm. All regularly consult the Internet. Throughout the experiment sequence, *Le Petit Robert* was consulted 51 times, the *Multi* 26 times and the Web 24 times. However, it was surprising to note that the software versions of the printed works referred to above were used little if at all by the editors participating in our study, even by those who edit on screen. Previous versions of the document on which they were working (versions that they themselves had edited), were relied on as a source of answers by some of these editors.

During the two-hour observation period, with the exception of Editor 4, who used reference tools a mere nine times, the other editors used them on an average of 22 times, which works out to once every six minutes. The importance of having a functional workspace stands out all the more clearly as a result.

As reference tools did not provide all the answers to their questions, the editors call or write the authors for any remaining unanswered questions, which generally concern the terms or expressions specific to a given field or which involve a passage whose meaning is obscure for the editor.

5 Reading and Problem-Solving Strategies

Whatever the mandate accorded by the client, the type of text to be revised, or the experience of the editor, reading is always central to the latter's work process, just as it is for writers who edit their own texts (Hayes et al., 1987; Hayes, 1998). And much like writers who use reading in a variety of ways to accomplish their writing goals (Quinlan & Alamargot, this volume), editors use reading in a number of ways. However, just as the classroom context differs from the professional context, so too does the type of reading performed differ according to each setting. Thus, in contrast to a student, a professional editor will seldom have to read in order to understand grasp the job that she/he is given because his/her assignment is almost always given orally by the client. As concerns reading background texts (Hayes, 1998), the underlying objective is not to search for ideas but to validate the information contained in the text, if that indeed is a part of the mandate. It nevertheless remains that reading is fundamental in either editing context.

I observed that professional editors could employ four types of reading: reading to comprehend, reading to evaluate, reading to solve and reading to check.

5.1 Reading to Comprehend

It is highly unusual for an editor to read the entire text to be revised. How would reading a 200-page text before beginning to revise help him or her to be a better editor? If he or she wants to have an idea of the contents, he or she will instead skim the document or examine the table of contents, if there is one. However, if the text is quite short—a media release or a letter, for example—he or she will read all of it. This does not mean that the editor does not read the text to understand it before revising. In fact, most of the editors observed read the paragraph first in order to understand it before re-reading it to evaluate it. With the exception of Editor 2, who immediately *tackled* the text for the purpose of evaluating it, the other editors started in on their work by first reading a paragraph so as to grasp its meaning and only thereafter re-read it with a view to evaluating it. During the initial reading for comprehension, they inevitably corrected the spelling or punctuation errors that "leapt out at them." As Flower, Hayes, Carey, Schriver & Stratman (1986, p. 25) noted, "Some evaluation can occur simply as a side effect of reading." However, some editors skip this phase and begin with the evaluative reading.

Furthermore, none of the editors read a text from start to finish unless it was very short (e.g., press release). It is worth mentioning that Hayes et al. (1987, p. 197) noted that failure to read a text in its entirety before beginning a revision did not testify to poor editing habits but perhaps owed instead to solid familiarity with the task at stake—an observation that appears to be confirmed by the approach taken by the professional editors whom we observed.

5.2 Reading to Evaluate

Once an editor finished reading the paragraph to grasp its meaning, she/he read it a second time through in order to detect whatever could be improved in the text. During the evaluative reading phase, this professional attempted to take in all of the various types of problems at once: he sought out the elements of the text that were open to improvement because they did not comply with conventions of language, genre or text, or because, when compliance was not the problem, they were unsatisfactory in terms of the rules of maximum communicational effectiveness (or relevance of information, as defined in terms of "cognitive effects gained and processing effort expended" (Sperber & Wilson, 1989)).

With the exception of Editor 2, all the editors completed at least two evaluative readings.

However, if an editor was given a very long text (e.g., 400 pages) and a very short amount of time in which to edit it, she/he could well make do with performing only one evaluative reading. When both evaluative readings were of equal value, he devoted a bit more attention to text organization and interrelationships during the first reading, and to wording during the second.

5.3 *Reading to Solve or Re-Reading*

In addition to serving as a basis on which to detect problems, reading was also a strategy of problem solving that all the editors used in varying degrees. Re-reading signifies that she/he re-reads a sentence or paragraph because the meaning is not clear. To correct a textual unit, she/he must understand its meaning—a task she/he is unable to accomplish after only a single reading. In this case, we are no longer dealing with an evaluative reading to detect a problem, as the problem has already been detected. Instead, this type of reading is performed in order to help him/her to find the solution. For example, she/he re-reads when she/he is attempting to reformulate a phrase.

Compared with other problem-solving strategies, re-reading is little used. In our study of the editing process, it accounted for between slightly less than 10% of an editor's strategies (Editor 2) and 26% of them (Editor 4). It is worth recalling that in the first case, the editor was primarily concerned by compliance with rules whereas in the second, the editor was concerned with contents and the clarity of the wording, whence the value of re-reading.

Reading as problem-solving strategy ranks third among the strategies used. Below is the ranking of all strategies:

1st place: Immediate search for solution (44.2%)
   As soon as a problem has been detected, the editor immediately uses one of the tools at his/her disposal to find a solution.
2nd place: Reflection (31.8%)
   When confronted with a problem, the editor pauses to reflect before making a modification to the text.
3rd place: Re-reading (12.2%)
4th place: Postponing the solution or the search for a solution (10%)
   The editor decides to make no modification for the moment, or even to seek a solution in the near term. She/he will do so at some later time or will request the author to do so.
5th place: The tentative solution (1.8%)
   The editor hazards a tentative solution so as not to lose his/her thread or idea, but with the mental pledge to revise the wording later—which is effectively what she/he does more often than not.

It should also be noted that 57.2% of the problems detected by the editors were corrected without resorting to any problem-solving strategy. In such cases, the editors quickly solved the problems encountered. It would be worthwhile comparing these findings with the results obtained for writing students who revise their own texts or with the results for future editors. For the time being, however, I have no data on which to base a comparison, as Hayes et al. (1987) did not analyze problem-solving strategies in the same way, opting for a typology of five strategies, which are to: (1) ignore; (2) delay the effort to solve the problem; (3) search for more information to solve the problem; (4) rewrite and (5) revise.

5.4 Reading to Check the Text

Some editors, on finishing the revision of the text, will read through the entire text in order to make sure that they made the correct modifications and did not forget anything. The reading also enables them to see if the text flows—that is, if it reads well. It is rare, however, for an editor to take the time to re-read the entire text. When he or she checks his/her revisions, it is after a paragraph, because he or she made a lot of modifications.

It is thus true that reading is omnipresent throughout the editing process, serving to: understand a segment of the text, assess and solve a problem and, finally, validate his/her editing work.

6 Pace of Work and Quantity of Modifications

Experience, as well as the type of editing—whether involving considerable or little rewriting—has an influence on the pace of work. In a comparison of experienced versus less-experienced editors in our research, it is clear that the former edit a great many more words than the latter do. In cases where little rewriting had to be performed, the more experienced editors were able, in an hour's time, to revise 3320 and 4944 words (Editors 4 and 2), whereas the less experience edited 465, 1200 and 2475 words (Editors 6, 5 and 1, respectively). In the case of a text requiring considerable rewriting (Editor 3), it was possible to revise between 1200 and 1400 words. Thus, it is not surprising that clients seldom call on editors to rewrite copy, knowing that it will cost them considerably more money if they choose to have this type of work performed.

Not only did the more experienced editors edit a greater quantity of words than those having less experience, they also made more modifications to the text being edited. The participating editors having the most experience made 233, 272 and 277 modifications to the text (Editors 4, 2 and 3), whereas those having less experience made 46, 107 and 125 such modifications (Editors 6, 5 and 1). These results bear out the outcome of previous research projects comparing beginners and experts. Experience thus has an impact on both the quantity of text that is edited and on the quantity of the modifications made to the text.

7 Writing Operations and Target Units of Text

Upon examining the writing operations employed by the editors to improve their texts, it becomes clear that all of the editors, with the exception of Editor 5, used the four writing operations (Sommers, 1980) referred to as insertion (18.19%), deletion (21.11%), replacement (57.59%) and movement of pieces of text (3.11%). Among all of the editors, replacement was the most frequently used operation (41.30–62.50%) and movement of text pieces the least used (0–4.35%), with Editor 5 making no use of this operation at all. In terms of use, the percentages obtained for each of these operations do not appear to bear a relationship to the editor's conception of his/her work or of the mandate that she/he was given by the client. The editors who deleted the most are those who also had the most experience. It may be surmised that experience has given them the assurance required to delete one or more items of the author's text.

In a comparison of these results with findings from previous research projects, it is apparent that replacement is the predominant operation for all professional editors having considerable or little experience as well as among beginning or advanced student writers.

Table 2 shows that for all the editors, with the exception of Editor 3, these modifications primarily concerned a unit consisting of a single word. It is possible to make out a relationship between this editor's mandate and the units targeted by the modifications, as he was the only one of the six to have been granted a clear mandate to rewrite. It is thus to be expected that he should take the liberty of making as many multi-word modifications as he in fact did. Likewise, it is easy to explain how Editor 2 is associated with so many modifications (77.3%) involving a single word, as his mandate was defined in favor of bringing the text in line with the rules. In addition, in an interview he stated that he did not like to have to rewrite. He found standing in for the author to be a sensitive matter, and, he also claimed, he lost a considerable amount of time whenever he had to reword a text.

8 Word Processing in the Work Process of Experienced Editors

As Piolat (2007) has written, there has been insufficient research into the use of word processors by professional editors. Nonetheless, as the author demonstrated in her text, "word processing and software tools (typography, spelling and syntax correction software, dictionaries) are handy in the three major revision processes: comparing, *diagnosing* and changing the written product."

Table 2: Percentage of modifications in relationship to one-word unit and multi-word unit. $n = 1061$.

Editor/reviser	Mandate	Conception	One word only (%)	More than one word (%)
2	N	N	77.3	22.7
6	N	N	60.9	39.1
3	C	C	48	52
4	C	C	62.3	37.8
1	N	C	72	28
5	N	C	69.2	30.8

As word processing helps to simplify both writing and editing (Eklundh & Kollberg, 1996), particularly by reducing the laborious work involved in copying over various writing operations, one might think that editors view word processing as a necessary tool of the trade. That is not, however, what I observed among the professional editors whom I studied in this research project and whose use of word processing in the editing process can be classified according to one of the four ways:

(1) word processing is absent from the editing process;
(2) word processing is only drawn on at the end of the editing process as a polishing tool;
(3) word processing is a major component of the editing process as a tool to be used in rewording the text;
(4) word processing is the main support of the editing process.

Let us now examine these four approaches in detail.

8.1 Non-Integration of Word Processing into the Editing Process

Two experienced editors did not use word processing in their editing work at all: Editor 2, who had a normative mandate and conception of editing, and Editor 4, who had a communicational mandate and conception. Of the two, Editor 2 was the one who modified a single word most often (77.3%), a fact serving to explain why he did not really require the advantages to be had from word processing in terms of reworking the source text. Such was not the case, however, with Editor 4 who, on the other hand, worked at the multi-word level to a considerable extent (37.8%). It is likely that word processing does not figure among his work habits, as he has edited using hand corrections to paper since the beginning of his career and felt no need to change his methods now. Editor 4 is also the oldest of the six (approximately 65 years of age) and doubtless the one least interested in learning word processing.

8.2 Integration of Word Processing is Non-Essential: WP as a Tool for Polishing

Editors 1 and 6 used word processing at the end of the editing process. Even if they received a text in computer file format, they did not use a computer for revision purposes. Editor 1 did not like to "work on screen, because it's hard on the eyes and you can't see [the text] well" (interview). Piolat, Roussey, and Thunin, (1997, p. 567) noted, moreover, that according to some researchers, the on-screen detection of errors is slower and catches fewer errors.

Once the editing work had been completed, both of these editors entered their modifications into the computer file. As part of this process, they recopied the hand corrections, occasionally modifying those that no longer suited them while also inserting new ones. Whenever their work called for word processing, they used it to put the final touches to the document.

When Editor 6 was able to skip this step, as he was short of time, he left it up to the author to do the word processing. Finally, Editor 6 would only enter modifications on the computer file if the client requested him to do so. It cannot be said that word processing represents an essential step in these editors' editing processes, since the use of this tool is conditioned by external constraints.

8.3 Integration of Word Processing is Essential: WP as a Tool for Rewording

For Editor 3, the use of word processing for editing purposes was a step of equal importance to the hand corrections made on paper. He even made more modifications on screen (146) than on the paper printout (129). The first stage (hand corrections) served to familiarize him with the entire text and to detect whether there were any problems of structure or any cuts that needed to be made to the text. He called this stage the "spadework" stage. During the second stage, not only did he enter the hand corrections into the computer file, he also refined these corrections and made additional ones. Retracing the transformations occurring among a few sentences will serve to illustrate this editor's approach to work.

Example 1:

> **Original version of text:** *En effet, pour rendre les combles habitables, on eut tôt fait de percer des lucarnes pour assurer l'éclairage naturel, (rappelons-nous que l'électricité est une invention somme toute récente dans l'histoire de l'architecture) et permettre la ventilation de ces espaces qui servaient souvent pour dormir; d'ailleurs en anglais la lucarne s'appelle "dormer".*
>
> [To make garrets habitable, it was not long before roofs were fitted out with dormers as a means of providing natural lighting (it is worth recalling that electricity is, all in all, a recent invention in the history of architecture) and of ventilating these spaces often used for sleeping—whence the origin of the English word "dormer," from the French "dormir," meaning "to sleep."]
>
> **Version revised by hand:** *Pour assurer l'éclairage naturel et pour rendre les combles habitables, on a **très vite** percer* [sic] *des lucarnes. **En plus de permettre un meilleur éclairage, la lucarne rend l'espace mieux ventilé, ce qui favorise un sommeil plus quiet;** d'ailleurs en anglais la lucarne s'appelle dormer.* (The modifications made to the text from one version to the next appear in bold.)
>
> [In order to provide garrets with natural lighting and make them habitable, roofs were soon fitted out with dormers {"sic" in the French version refers to a grammar mistake}. **In addition to serving to improve lighting, dormers improved the ventilation of this space, thus affording greater tranquility for sleeping**—whence the origin of the English word "dormer," from the French "dormir," meaning "to sleep."]
>
> **Version revised on screen:** *Pour assurer l'éclairage naturel et pour rendre les combles habitables, on a très vite **percé** des lucarnes. En plus **d'apporter** un meilleur éclairage, **elles permettent une ventilation adéquate,** ce qui favorise un sommeil plus quiet. **D'ailleurs**, en anglais la lucarne s'appelle "dormer".*
>
> [In order to provide garrets with natural lighting and make them habitable, roofs were soon fitted out with dormers {the French grammar mistake is removed}. In addition to **improving** lighting, **they ensured decent ventilation**, thus affording greater tranquility for sleeping. Incidentally, the origin of the English word "dormer" is the French "dormir," meaning "to sleep."]

In the revision performed in the form of hand corrections, this editor grouped the objectives together, thereby successfully highlighting the relationship between an action (fitting out roofs with dormers) and the underlying objectives (providing natural lighting and making garrets habitable). He removed an idea that was un-germane to the topic of discussion (the statement appearing between parentheses) and he inserted wording in order to make clear the link between two ideas. At this stage, the editor's focus was not on rewording statements, for he perceived these modifications as being tentative or trial versions serving to "set down [his] idea." He knew that he would come back to them once he had begun to edit on screen.

Once he was into the on-screen stage, not only did he correct the grammatical error that had been previously left uncorrected, he also replaced an item of wording that he did not like. The resulting new version was more fluid, and avoided repeating the word "dormer." He also modified the punctuation so as to break up a very long sentence.

Example 2:

>**Original version of text:** *Elle servait aussi à donner plus d'espace utile et à se rapprocher du mur extérieur considérant la difficulté d'accéder debout aux côtés avec la pente prononcée des versants.*
>
>[They {the dormers} also served to increase the amount of useful space and to allow one to move closer to the outer walls, considering how it was otherwise difficult to reach them on account of the pronounced slope of each side of the roof.]
>
>**Version revised by hand:** *Elle servait aussi à donner plus d'espace et à se rapprocher du mur extérieur compte tenu de la pente prononcée des versants.*
>
>[They also served to create more space and to allow one to move closer to the outer walls, **given** the pronounced slope of each side of the roof.]
>
>**Version revised on screen:** *Autre avantage: la lucarne permet de se rapprocher du mur extérieur lorsque la pente du toit est prononcée, ce qui augmente l'espace d'occupation.*
>
>[**As an added advantage**, **dormers enabled** one to move closer to the outer walls **whenever the roof had** a pronounced pitch, **thus freeing up additional space for occupation**.]

As this editor made hand corrections to this text, he removed a word whose intended meaning was not clear (*useful*—for what?) and simplified the sentence by tightening a cumbersome, wordy clause (going from 9 words to 3 in the French [and from 12 words to 1 in the English translation]).

On screen, he reworded this sentence out of a concern for clarity, preserving only 8 of the 30 words contained in the original sentence in French (and 28 words of the 41 in the English translation). The first operation of simplification did not go far enough. When rewriting the text on screen, this editor took advantage of word processing, leaving the original sentence on screen and inserting his modifications next to it. "I decided to do my rewrite directly [on the computer]. At some later time, I'll erase what doesn't suit me," he said (interview statement 306). In the process of simplifying, he reorganized the ideas so as to bring out the relationship of cause and effect and thereby facilitate comprehension. He employed more specific terms that aid in visualizing the places being discussed: *useful* space thus became a space *for occupation* and the slope *of each side of the roof* became the slope *of the roof*. In addition, he inserted "As an added advantage" to enhance the rhythm—and the style—of the text: in the French original, the syntax was altered from the initial, conventional subject-verb-complement structure.

As the editor himself noted, hand corrections give him the opportunity to establish the caliber of the modifications to be made. The work that he performs on screen is an integral component of his editing process, as is illustrated by these modifications.

8.4 Word Processing: The Main Support of the Editing Process

For Editor 5, editing was performed on screen from beginning to end, since his mandate was to revise an electronic document. He was required to use the "track changes" mode featured on *Word*. But even when he is not given this type of mandate, he increasingly tends to revise directly on screen as a way of saving time. He much appreciates being able to use the *find* and *replace* functions, for example. As this editor did mainly formal editing work, the inconveniences that I examine below affected him to a lesser degree.

How is one to explain that four out of the six editors have not integrated word processing into their editing process? One of the reasons is undoubtedly the discomfort of reading on a screen, which displays only a portion of what is visible on a page of paper, and the fatigue that develops as a result. In addition, the screen detracts from the useful spatial coding of information that occurs during the comprehension phase (Piolat et al., 1997). As has been noted by Piolat et al. (1997, p. 567), "the characteristics of the computer and word processing software can make it difficult for writers to grasp the overall organization and flow of a text." It should also be mentioned, in order to detect errors of meaning, it takes a more attentive type of reading than is involved in flagging surface errors. This observation is confirmed by Editor 3, who performed his first reading on paper precisely for the purpose of gaining an overview of the text—something which he would have undoubtedly had difficulty achieving on screen. It is also confirmed by Editor 5, who used word processing from the very beginning of his revision work, as he modified these aspects of the text only to a very slight degree (9.2%), in contrast with Editor 3 (26.1%), and instead corrected non-compliance with rules to a much greater extent (67.2%).

In previous studies conducted among secondary and post-secondary students who revised on screen, their corrections were primarily of the surface variety. I do not agree, however, that they are the only type of corrections that can be made using word processing. Witness, for example, Editor 3: even though he felt the need to begin by making hand corrections, he took practically the same approach to his work as when he edited the computer file directly. In both cases, he modified the information, organization and form, with information-related modifications nevertheless becoming much more numerous whenever he worked on printed copy.

9 Implications for the Teaching of Editing

Based on the findings concerning editing by professional editors, and in light of my previous reflections on the teaching of editing (Bisaillon, 1991, 1992) and on the integration of word processing into this form of education (Bisaillon, 1997, 1999), I will now propose a number of avenues to be explored from the perspective of teaching of editing. I will ask myself how a teacher can guide students of writing or future professional editors to edit better—that is, to improve not only the formal quality of the text but also its communicational quality as well.

9.1 Trigger Reflection on Editing

I have noted the impact that is produced by a professional editor's conceptions of editing on the way that she/he goes about his/her work. Therefore, I believe that prior to telling students to edit or revise their texts, the teacher should prompt them to reflect on the nature of editing. In the case of self-editing, she/he should inform students of the role of editing in the activity of writing and explain that it begins the moment that one begins to devise a text (Bisaillon, 1991, p. 62). This is the moment to address the creative side of editing and not just its corrective side. With respect to professional editing, the teacher must guide future professional editors to adopt a conception of editing that accords room to concern for the reader. If this conception is not restricted to the correction of surface errors, the students will have to take a more global approach to editing. These are the results arrived at by Wallace et al. (1996), who noted that students who have an inadequate conception of editing (or an inadequate task schema) would be unable to edit well: "Deficiencies in revision may have their origin in inappropriate task schemas" (Wallace et al., 1996 p. 683). In their research, students who had been taught to take a more global view of the task of editing managed to make corrections to a text on both a spot and global basis.

9.2 Direct Editing Work

In addition to prompting students to reflect on the nature of editing, a teacher may, as students set out to edit and revise, direct them in their work. In my research on the teaching of editing strategies in a computer-based environment (Bisaillon, 1999), the teacher directs the editing work towards the content and organization of a text, first using pre-written texts and then the students' own texts. In the post-test, the students did a better job not only of editing the content and organization of their text but also of its form, even though no special attention had been dedicated to these aspects.

9.3 Keep the Reader and His/Her Needs in Mind When Editing

I have noted that professional editors are continually concerned about the target reader, which leads them to add or remove information and to modify certain words or statements. Students of writing or future professional editors must learn to generate a representation of the reader of their texts. They will find it difficult to take the reader into consideration if they have no idea who she/he is. There a number of questionnaires (e.g., Pfister & Petrik, 1980) available with which to flesh out notions of the reader's identity and which the teacher can draw on to help students to imagine him/her.

Once students have managed to devise a representation of the reader, how do they then go about accounting for the reader's needs when editing? In the psychological analysis of the reader proposed by Warren (1993), an editor must pose three questions prior to editing and then keep them in mind while working.

What does the reader need to know? is the first question an editor should ask him/herself. The answer will lead him/her to remove information that she/he deems to be of no value to the reader, or vice versa, to add missing information so that the reader will be able to understand the text more fully. Thus, an editor will delete excess information, saying "whether it is used or not, it's not important at this point in the text" (Editor 5; verbalization 78 (5; V. 78)) because it does not further anyone's understanding of the subject at hand. Elsewhere, she/he will add information "to explain who Fernande was" (5; V. 127), thereby making the statement clearer for the reader.

How can I help the reader to understand the text? is the second question. Here, the editor attends more to the form and organization of the text than to the content. This attention is worthwhile even if the reader is skilled. As one editor explained when replacing a technical word with a simpler word, "Even when you are dealing with an informed target readership, there still occurs what is referred to as 'noise' (interference) in the communication. Reading grinds to a halt because a particular word is so specialized that one is forced to scour one's memory in order to recall its meaning (3; V. 33). Another editor demonstrated the same concern when he justified an item of rewording when he stated that "people will understand it more easily" (5; V. 71).

What do I want the reader to do with what I am presenting him/her? is the last question. If the editor is working on a procedural text (e.g., set of instructions), she/he will ensure that an ordinary user/reader will properly understand all of the operations to be performed. Will she/he be able to install his/her printer or use the software? In texts in which the editor would like the reader to retain certain information, she/he will highlight it by moving it to a particular position in the text or even suggesting some form of typographical emphasis.

9.4 *Use Highly Focused Practice Exercises*

I have noted that professional editors detect all types of errors at the same time. They have developed this skill through experience. Such competency is entirely out of reach for a student who is learning to detect them. The teacher should consider preparing some highly focused exercises. In any one exercise, they will be required to work on accomplishing a given objective, but will have them start in by familiarizing themselves with the techniques associated with this objective. To make a text more readable or enjoyable, the teacher could, for example, ask students to remove any unnecessary repetitions. Next, she/he could ask them to remove any unnecessary words or groups of words. Thereafter, both methods could be combined in yet another exercise. Furthermore, as I have stated elsewhere (Bisaillon, 1992), detection can be developed progressively, with progression to occur in respect of text length, number of difficulties, variety of problems, etc. In the case of self-editing, students would first work on pre-constructed texts and then on their own texts.

9.5 *Proposing Detection Aids*

The teacher could propose detection aids for each of the objectives. She/he can suggest, as Moran (1997) has advised, that students read the text out loud (including using one's inner voice) in order to detect problems of style. Through this step, they will have an easier time of locating any potential weak points. If comprehension problems have arisen, the teacher could explain to the students why they are having so much difficulty uncovering these problems. As Lumbelli, Paoletti, and Frausin (1999 p. 144) explained, "subjects tend to monitor their own comprehension processes by comparing each single information item with their own previous knowledge rather than with information items within the text itself." Knowing this, the student should be able to ask him/herself if she/he is making a connection between two ideas expressed in the text or between an idea in the text and his/her personal knowledge.

10 Conclusion

In this chapter, I have seen that the professional editor's task is defined not only by the mandate given to him/her by a client but also by his/her conception of editing—a fact that explains why an editor who has been mandated to perform a formal revision also makes modifications that concern more than grammar and mechanics. Moreover, as an editor goes about revising, she/he always bears the reader in mind, however implicitly so. Out of a concern for the reader's needs, she/he will strive to make the text more readable and enjoyable, clearer and devoid of any undue wordiness. She/he will also make the text more comprehensible by making a more judicious selection and organization of the information it conveys. However, all such concerns will be shaped by the client's mandate to the editor.

An editor's task is a complex one, for she/he must read a text with a view not only to evaluate it but also to understand it. An editor must be attentive to the contents, structure and form of a text, all at the same time. Whenever she/he has doubts over the use of a given word or over the clarity of a particular item of wording, she/he will pause to reflect or seek out the answer to his/her question in or via a support tool. To facilitate this demanding job, she/he sets up a work environment that provides him with quick access to all his/her research tools. In itself, the use of support tools is a topic warranting further research. For example, what are the types of problems for which editors consult Internet? How effective are these tools? What kinds of problems appear to offer no solution?

I also saw that word processing is not relied on by all professional editors and that it is possible to integrate word processing into the editing process in a variety of ways. It would appear that in the case of an editor who is prone to reworking a text's contents and organization, it is preferable that she/he first produces a series of corrections on a printout. The physical conditions and limitations associated with a computer screen lend themselves poorly to achieving a grasp of the text as a whole and of its organization, and are not conducive to the spatial coding operations that occur during the comprehension phase. It is my belief, moreover, that even those editors who take a normative approach to editing and revising would benefit from using both hand corrections (on a printout) and word processing. That way, they may detect problems appearing on paper that otherwise escape notice on screen, and vice versa. For example, it is easier to correct errors of spacing on screen, where each space can be represented—and mentally registered—by a dot.

The best solution, in my view, consists in a combination of both mediums. There is a need to conduct further research into the use of word processing in professional editing. What kinds of uses do editors accustomed to revising with word processing software make of standard word processing functions (cut, paste, etc.), specific editing functions (find and replace, spell-checker, etc.), as well as editing process/mark-up functions (track changes, highlight, etc.)? How do they combine the use of word processing and hand corrections? Much remains to be discovered about the ways to improve the use of word processing alone, as well as of a word processing/hand correction combination. Piolat (2007) notes that the manner in which word processing and software tools "are used in real-time, the cognitive cost that they may entail, the modification of habitual procedures depending on the editor's degree of expertise, text characteristics (genre, length, technicality, target readership, support) and the nature of the task have not been sufficiently studied using the methods of cognitive psychology."

Although much has been written on the revision process in recent years, there is still a considerable quantity of objects begging further reflection. For example, if self-revision and professional revision are compared with each other, it is clear that whereas self-revision is a recursive process of creation, professional revision is, on the other hand, a linear or iterative process of improvement. While the writer who revises his/her own text often goes back to previously encountered portions of the text and moves from the revision sub-process to other sub-processes of writing (planning and drafting phases), a professional editor most often performs his/her work in order, step-by-step, line-by-line, until she/he reaches the end. She/he will go back to previous sections of the text when, for example, in correcting a problem, she/he realizes that she/he must also modify a textual unit encountered at least once before. It is iterative in the sense that the editor repeats his/her line-by-line evaluation at the level of a paragraph and even for the text as a whole. It would be worthwhile to devote further reflection on the differences between professional revision, which is a full-fledged process, and revision, a sub-process of writing. In such comparisons, the various ways in which reading procedures and processes are manifested could provide valuable clues.

Even at this time, the results of our research concerning the work process of professional editors suggest a number of avenues for further exploration with respect to the teaching of editing. However, where longer term or in-depth analysis is feasible, they could also be made to pay off even more handsomely in terms of benefits to teaching programs.

It is vital to dedicate further research to professional editing so as to end the general ignorance surrounding this craft and to garner for it the recognition that it deserves. Unfortunately, however, many clients have not yet recognized the value of communicational editing, opting instead to make do with eliminating only the most glaring errors. And yet, as has been shown in a number of research papers, revisions that are made with the reader in mind can prove decisive in terms of whether a text will be understood or misunderstood, interesting or dull—not to mention read or unread.

Chapter 7

Procedural Texts Written by Children

Eduardo Martí and Merce Garcia-Mila

The chapter analyses the characteristics of procedural knowledge, in order to explain its acquisition from a developmental point of view, and most important, to better understand how to manage procedural texts. This acquisition is explained in terms of the proceduralization in acquiring expertise at the performance level, on the one hand and representational redescription (Karmiloff-Smith, 1992) at the communication level, oral or written, on the other. The prior analysis flows toward the difficulties children encounter when they explore a procedural text, which are summarized as follows: the combination of linguistic and graphic modes of representation to deal with the temporal sequence of actions and to describe the spatial information of the device; the correct segmentation of the information following the main actions to be executed; the adaptation of the content of the text to the needs of the audience and, finally, the organization of the text in separate chunks of information (for example by means of numeration). These difficulties about children's productions can become important guidelines in the professional training of novice writers of technical documents since they may help to understand the difficulties they may encounter when they have to write procedural documents at their workplace.

A chapter on child development research may seem a little out-of-place in a book devoted to professional documents. Children are rarely asked to produce or interpret guidelines, recipes or instructions, except in play contexts (for instance, when they need to understand or explain the workings of a toy or an object in a science museum). Nevertheless, we believe that an analysis of their ability to produce procedural texts may shed light on the performance of adults in tasks of this kind, and thus help to improve the quality of written documents in the work place. This is so for two reasons. First, if we know how a skill develops, we will be better placed to understand the form it takes in adults; indeed, developmental analysis can broaden our understanding of the nature of a skill and help us to identify the main difficulties it has to overcome in order to reach its final, mature form. Second, data from research on children's production of procedural texts can be an important source of information for the design of instructional settings that help children and young adults to acquire expertise in writing procedural texts.

The chapter is structured in four sections. The first compares the main characteristics of procedural texts and other text types. The second presents a developmental analysis of the acquisition of procedural knowledge as opposed to other types of knowledge. In the third section we discuss research conducted on the development of procedural text production and comment on our own empirical data concerning the production of procedural texts by children. In the last section we discuss some of the issues raised in the developmental literature that are relevant to improving the production of written documents in the workplace.

1 Characteristics of Procedural Texts

The main purpose of professional documents is to help people to understand or carry out a task. Regardless of the type of text considered (guidelines, recipes, directions for use, etc.), the central feature of documents of this kind is the description of a procedure: a sequence of actions related to the accomplishment of a goal. Indeed, this is the main function of a procedural text (Ganier & Barcenilla, this volume). Like narrative texts, procedural texts are concerned with temporality; however, while the essence of narrative texts (i.e. a story) (Hudson & Shapiro, 1991) is to describe a sequence of events chronologically, the essence of procedural texts is to describe a sequence of actions in order. One of the main difficulties facing both genres is to adequately represent the temporal dimension using the formal features of writing. But procedural and narrative texts differ in other aspects. An important one is that procedural texts are directed to guide and regulate people's actions in order to reach a specific goal, whereas narrative texts describe chronological events but have no practical objective. Procedural texts need to describe the type of actions and their sequence very precisely, a restriction that is not imposed on narrative texts.

On the other hand, narrative texts are also often contrasted to informational texts (Chapman, 1995; Donovan, 2001; Freedman, 1993; Kamberelis, 1999; Tower, 2003). The latter are organized around a topic and aim to describe its features. Informational texts focus on the characteristics of the topic in question and do not need a temporal dimension. The difficulty, in this case, is to exhaustively and accurately represent the different aspects of the topic and to relate these aspects to each other in a coherent way. Procedural texts also require an accurate description of the actions involved. In this way, procedural texts are similar to informational texts and indeed share some common features with narrative and instructional texts. Like narrative texts, they have to integrate the temporal dimension involved in a sequence of actions. Like informational texts, they need to communicate the relevant aspects of the situation in great detail (in this case, the kind of action to be reproduced).

2 Developmental Issues in the Acquisition of Procedural Knowledge

The goal of this chapter is to understand how children set about the task of producing a procedural text, as a way to identify some of the difficulties in producing professional documents. To do so we must first analyse the cognitive processes involved in the acquisition of a procedure (an ordered sequence of actions). This analysis will then facilitate the understanding of the cognitive demands required to explain a procedure once it has been learned.

Procedural knowledge is normally introduced and defined by contrasting it with declarative knowledge. This distinction has been classically recognized by philosophers (Ryle, 1949) and cognitive scientists (Anderson, 1983). According to this distinction, procedural knowledge is knowing "how" (how to do things), while declarative knowledge is knowing "what" (possessing factual information). These two types of knowledge are learned in completely different ways. Procedures are best learned by combining modelling with instructions, provided orally by the instructor while performing the task (for example, a child learning to ride a bike with the help of her father). Also, a given procedure can be learned by simply reading the instructions in a text. In this case the action is ideally illustrated with diagrams and drawings (imagine the same father using a new device to pump up the tyres of the bike).

Although the issue of how procedural knowledge is mentally represented while it is being learned has not been completely resolved (Kintsch, 1991), there is a consensus that procedural knowledge starts out as declarative knowledge (Pressley & McCormick, 1995). Initially, a sequence of cognitive actions is expressed by the instructor and therefore represented by the learner declaratively, where the "how-to-do" consists of a verbal characterization of the procedure as a list of instructions whose order and sequence are essential for completing the task successfully. At the beginning, the action is carried out slowly and with a high cognitive cost (working memory/short-term memory). With time, execution of the entire sequence becomes smoother until it is no longer a sequence of declarative directions but a fluent process. The move from the declarative representation of a sequence of actions to a single procedure is known as proceduralization. With practice the sequence can then be executed automatically without the need to think of the steps in the sequence (Anderson, 1983).

Let us look at the details of the process in the example mentioned above. The first time a child tries to ride a bike, she must make sure that she understands each instructional message (or in the case of the father trying to learn how the pump works, he must understand each line of the instructions in the written text). Then one repeats these instructions either aloud or mentally in order to reproduce them in action. At this stage, and in either case, the learner needs to make a semantic and a referential analysis of the information, as suggested by Bovair and Kieras (1991) in their model of the acquisition of procedures from texts. They claim that for a procedure to be executed, the actual physical object referred to must also be identified in the environment (it is in this sense that the analysis becomes "referential"). At the start of the learning process, one continually dictates the instructions to oneself step-by-step while performing the actions. As the learning process goes on, there is less and less verbal self-cuing, until one can eventually perform the action without thinking about it, with the body moving automatically as the action is done. At this point, the short-term memory is not used at all because the control of the procedure is transferred to the motor system (Rumelhart & Norman, 1988). That is, once proceduralization occurs, the action is performed without retrieving the information consciously from memory. An important benefit of knowledge compilation is that much less conscious capacity is expended in carrying out a compiled action than in carrying out a sequence of productions.

What potential difficulties, then, may undermine the correct performance of the procedure? An important constraint is the cognitive demand associated to the fact that procedures are sequentially represented. A great deal of research has highlighted the developmental problems encountered by children when they have to deal with sequential information (Dean, Scherzer, & Chabaud, 1986; Kosslyn, Cave, Provost, & Von Gierke, 1988; Piaget & Inhelder, 1948). A different type of problem is the difficulty of retaining in the short-term memory everything that must be considered to recall declarative knowledge (Anderson, 1983). One sign of this problem is the omission of steps. Another closely associated problem is the learner's lack of sufficient working memory to execute the procedure while interpreting the information (Cariglia-Bull & Pressley, 1990). This is especially serious if the information is given in different representational formats such as drawings, labels, numbers, text and diagrams. It may also be that the learner does not understand how to perform the task, and her representation of the correct procedure may lead to the use of inappropriate actions. Finally, the lack of declarative knowledge needed for the procedure may be another reason for the failure to perform the task satisfactorily. Alternatively, children may have the appropriate declarative knowledge, but may not be able to organize it properly. In a comparison of experts and novices designed to assess the latter's difficulties in learning procedures, Zeitz and Spoher (1989) state that the organization of knowledge is a crucial step. In their description of expert subjects' organization of knowledge in the acquisition of procedural expertise, they claim that these subjects have a large body of well-structured domain knowledge that they organize hierarchically; they also have a large amount of proceduralized domain knowledge, and easily form an executable, functional-level representation of a device (a mental model). These authors disagree with Anderson's claim that the repeated application of knowledge aids the formation of procedures because, in their view, there is an added constraint: practice only results in the proceduralization of knowledge that has already been appropriately structured. Before efficient procedures can be formed, declarative knowledge must be well organized in an abstract and hierarchical manner, rather than as pieces of knowledge which are like "bunches of cards to be swapped" (Gitomer, 1984, cited in Zeitz & Spoher, 1989, p. 315).

Having analysed the cognitive processes and difficulties involved in the acquisition of a procedure, we can now turn to the cognitive demands required to explain a procedure once it has been learned. Under the premise that the two processes are symmetrical, we can better understand the latter by appealing to the former. A necessary condition for the child to be able to explain a procedure to another person, either orally or in writing, is "behavioural mastery" (Karmiloff-Smith, 1992). The process can be understood by rewinding the above description and reversing the sequence. The analysis, thus, starts with automatic performance, implicit and hard-to-attain conscious control, and goes backwards with respect to the above description, towards consciousness and explicitness. At the automatic stage, performance does not require attentional demands and knowledge is implicit and compiled. For the process to be made explicit and declarative, it needs to be translated into a set of instructions (as a set of propositions in the form of conditional statements) in a given sequence that can be easily followed by the reader, ideally with diagrams and drawings to facilitate understanding. In fact, in his pioneering studies of the grasp of consciousness, Piaget (1974a, 1974b) showed the difficulties children have in representing a sequence of actions by verbal descriptions. Piaget insisted that the conceptual level of knowledge (at which procedural information is represented) is very different from the practical level of knowledge (at which a set of ordered actions is executed). For example, to be able to explain to another person what needs to be done in order to be able to scratch one's back is not an easy task, although one may know how to scratch successfully: the first competence requires a complex process of explicit knowledge elaboration that is not a direct translation of the procedural knowledge.

This process is very well described by Karmiloff-Smith (1992) in her developmental analysis of problem solving. This author claims that development and learning take place in two complementary directions: "On the one hand, they involve the gradual process of proceduralization (i.e. rendering behavior more automatic and less accessible). On the other hand, they involve the gradual process of 'explicitation' and increasing accessibility (i.e. representing explicitly information that is implicit in the procedural representation sustaining the structure of behavior)" (p. 17). Karmiloff-Smith describes it as a move from implicit information embedded in an efficient problem-solving procedure to render the knowledge progressively more explicit. She illustrates the two directions contrasting the novices' performance—the initial conscious attention to particular steps, which gradually become proceduralized—with the experts' difficulty in the explicitation of the automatized procedure. The latter is very well illustrated in the following paragraph in which she describes her own performance (Karmiloff-Smith, 1992).

> I found that I had to "switch off" my consciousness to solve Rubik's Cube. In other words, I had to stop trying to analyze what I was doing until I could actually do it! In the early course of learning to solve the problem, I developed a sort of propioceptive solution which I could perform very rapidly but which I had much more difficulty repeating at a slower pace. My "knowledge" at that stage was embedded in the procedural representations sustaining the rapid execution. But I did not stop there. After reiterating a solution many times, I found that I started to recognize certain states of the cube and then knew whether or not I was on the path of my solution. But I still could not interrupt my solution and proceed from just any starting state. With more time still, I found that I could predict what the next few moves would be before actually executing them. Finally I came to a point where I could explain it to my daughter. (p. 17)

So it becomes clear that the first cognitive action that must take place in the explanation of proceduralized knowledge is the explicitation of such knowledge. This can be done, according to Karmiloff-Smith (1992) by a *representational redescription*, which attempts to account for the way in which children's representations become progressively more manipulable and flexible, for the emergence of conscious access to knowledge and theory building (p. 17). *Representational redescription* involves a sequence of recursive processes of redescriptions that yield four different degrees of explicitness. As we said, the process begins at the implicit level, where representations are in the form of procedures. Then with a redescription, they lose part of the procedurally encoded information and become partially explicit and partially manipulable, although they are still inaccessible to conscious reflection or to verbal report. With another redescription the representation gains another degree of explicitness allowing conscious access but remaining inaccessible to verbal report. Still another redescription of this representation will facilitate conscious access with verbal report, with knowledge that can be coded into a format close to the natural language. By means of iterative re-representations in different formats, knowledge becomes progressively more accessible and explicit, allowing reflexive processes upon it: "the mind can then exploit internally the information that it has already stored" (p. 15).

As mentioned above, and with the aim to make it simple, the main problem associated with the acquisition of a procedure is the transformation of an explicit representation expressed declaratively into one that is implicit and procedurally compiled. In contrast, the problem associated with the explanation of a procedure (in our case by means of a written text) arises from the explicitation, and thus the declarativization, of an implicit and compiled procedure. In both directions, the difficulties are similar: (1) the lack of properly organized declarative knowledge or simply, the lack of declarative knowledge to explain the action by means of semantic and referential connections; (2) the lack of conditional knowledge about procedures and proper ways to express it; (3) insufficient working memory to put in words the information while performing the action, and insufficient short-term memory to retain all the declarative information that must be considered to explain the action verbally; (4) an undeveloped ability to deal with sequential information. And we should add another developmental constraint: the lack of expertise in formats to represent dynamic information externally such as diagrams, schemas, drawings with labels and numbers, in addition to the restrictions associated with the mastery of writing. This limitation is specific to the task demand, that is, the production of a procedural text. Another limitation also specific to the task demand is the children's ability to adopt the perspective of the audience, and to make an analysis of the information the novice needs to perform the action (see Bisaillon, this volume who discusses the question of audience perspective with professional editors). All these difficulties are illustrated in the studies on developmental issues of procedural text production, which are the subject of the following section.

3 Children's Production of Procedural Texts

Procedural texts have received little attention in studies of the development of writing. In fact, this genre is seldom represented at all in the research on writing composition. Informational and narrative texts are the most frequent topics studied (Bamberg, 1997; Donovan, 2001; Freedman, 1993; Kamberelis, 1999; Pappas, 1993; Tower, 2003). Nonetheless, there are a few studies that contribute to understanding cognitive aspects related to the representation and writing of procedural information.

As mentioned above, Piaget showed how the grasp of consciousness transforms the information under consideration: some actions are forgotten, others are modified. But Piaget's research centred only on verbal descriptions and did not study how children translate a procedural information into a written representation. Some studies have addressed this issue (Bolger & Karmiloff-Smith, 1990; Kroll, 1986; Kroll & Lempers, 1981; Lee & Karmiloff-Smith, 1996; Lee, Karmiloff-Smith, Cameron, & Dodsworth, 1998; Wilkinson, Barnsley, Hanna, & Swan, 1980). They analyse how children of different ages write instructions related to a game in order to communicate the rules to another person. Wilkinson et al. (1980) analysed the texts produced by children aged 7, 10 and 13 years instructed to explain to others how to play a game. In this case, the game was chosen by a child. Young children (7-year-olds) succeeded in writing some of the actions of the game chronologically, though in most cases the sequence of actions produced was incomplete. This precocious competence in describing actions chronologically seems to be based on an early capacity to capture the temporal sequence of narrative discourse (Hudson & Shapiro, 1991), though with the cognitive constraint of representing sequential information in general, as noted above. It is important to note that language is a process displayed in time. For this reason, writing, like oral language, has an intrinsic temporal organization that probably helps children to represent a sequence of actions in order. It would be worth analysing whether this order is implicit or if it is introduced by children in their texts by means of temporal markers (first, second, after, then, etc.). This issue was not addressed in Wilkinson et al.'s study (1980). In fact, children chose the game themselves and, consequently, the amount of knowledge of the rules may have differed widely from one child to another.

In the studies of Kroll (1986), Bolger and Karmiloff-Smith (1990), Lee and Karmiloff-Smith (1996) and Lee et al. (1998), the amount of information about the rules of the game to be explained in writing was the same for all subjects. In Kroll's study, children and young adults from five school grades (fifth, seventh, ninth, eleventh and college) were asked to produce a text after viewing a tape in which an expert explained the rules of a game to another child. As in the study described above, young children introduced some specific actions of the game in their descriptions, but this information was not complete; they only rarely included the aim of the game and the material needed to play it. In contrast, the texts of older subjects (ninth, eleventh and college degrees) were complete and, more important, better organized. These older subjects applied certain strategies to organize the text in adequate chunks of information: they either introduced a list of pertinent actions or distinguished paragraphs to differentiate parts of the procedure.

In the other three studies each participant practised the game themselves until they were able to play it successfully, before communicating the rules to another person. In Bolger and Karmiloff-Smith's study (1990), a group of children between eight and ten solved a task (the Tower of Hanoi task or the Cannibals river-crossing problem) and, when able to complete it successfully on their own, were asked to write a text to enable another person to understand. In fact, they were specifically asked to "jot something down" to avoid any suggestion, and were left free to choose either written or graphic productions or a mixture of both. For some of the children, the text was addressed to a child of the same age (the peer condition), and for the others, to a 6-year-old child (the younger condition). The percentage of adequate solutions in the two conditions was very low (10%). The majority of solutions were either incomplete or impossible to follow. One of the major problems was the failure to include necessary spatial and temporal markers. Once more, young children's procedural texts were incomplete; the major problems were the ambiguity of the description of the actions (spatial aspects) and the indication of the exact order of the actions of the procedure (temporal aspects). One of the reasons for this poor performance may have been the difficulty of the tasks. In fact all children in this study needed some help from the experimenter to solve the task before the text production stage. In order to control for this, two other studies were designed with an easier task (the board puzzle), which 8- to 9-year-old and 10- to 11-year-old children performed without difficulty (Lee & Karmiloff-Smith, 1996; Lee et al., 1998). The goal of the puzzle (a board with five pieces) was to move the largest piece through the slot in the lower right-hand corner of the board by moving the other four pieces, one at a time, out of its path.

In Lee and Karmiloff-Smith's study (1996), the text adequacy of children's productions was much higher than in the previous study (Bolger & Karmiloff-Smith, 1990). But one important difficulty still remained: the representation of sequential information using writing or drawing. In the board puzzle, two kinds of information are relevant. The first (state representation) concerns the description of blocks and direction of movement. The second (transformation representation) concerns sequential information. The results are clear-cut: 77% of children at 8–9 years and 93% of 10- to 11-year-olds made adequate representation of states, but only 10% of 8- to 9-year-olds and 21% of 10- to 11-year-olds presented adequate sequential marking. It is interesting to analyse the notational medium used: linguistic, graphic or a combination of both. In general, the children who used the linguistic medium produced more adequate texts than the children who used the graphic medium. These results can be explained by the fact that the linguistic medium is useful to encode sequential information, but this encoding seems to remain implicit for the majority of children. In contrast, in most drawings, the adequacy of the representation was low, because the only way to represent sequential information with drawings is to mark it explicitly.

In the second study (Lee et al., 1998) the same task was addressed to a similar age population (8- to 9-year-olds and 10- to 11-year-olds, and also adults). The authors examined an important question in procedural texts: how children adapt their texts to the communicative needs of addressees of different ages. In fact, one of the difficulties of producing professional documents is to adapt the informational content to a novice audience. Is this sensitivity to audience present in children? Results show that most children of both age groups (8- to 9-year-olds and 10- to 11-year-olds) and also adults were aware of the difference in communicative competence between the younger addressee and the peer. But as age increased, children became more inclined to adopt the assumption that the younger addressee needed redundant information. Adults also preferred the redundant strategy for the younger addressee. As the authors explain, it is possible that both children and adults were aware that the younger addressee needed a simpler notation. However, it may be that younger children focused on the quantitative aspect of a text and considered a text with less information to be a simpler one, whereas older children and adults may have focused on the qualitative aspects of a text. A text with redundant information was in this case considered "simple" since it provided the addressee with multiple cues and assistance. These results not only show the early competence of children in adapting their procedural texts to the audience, but also show that this adaptation improves with age (see Bisaillon, this volume).

In order to check some of these results, we designed a study in which children of different ages and adults had to explain to another person how to make a call from a cell phone (Martí & Tantaros, 2005). Four age groups (eight, nine, ten and adults) participated in the study. The task included two phases. In the first one (execution phase), participants had to make a call using a cell phone to another cell phone located in the same room. The cell phone was switched on and participants were invited to explore it and try to make the call from it. The experimenter gave the information needed by the participants; in all cases, the PIN and the telephone number of the second cell phone were available on the table. Once participants succeeded in making the call (i.e. the second phone rang), they were invited to make the call by themselves, without any further help. This phase finished when participants could make the call on their own, without any help. In the second phase (notation phase) we asked participants to write down on a sheet of paper everything they believed necessary to inform a peer about how to make a call from the cell phone. We stressed the fact that the other person did not know to use a cell phone. We asked participants to repeat what they were asked to do, to make sure that they had understood the instruction. When participants finished their notations we asked them to explain the content of their message.

All participants, children and adults, successfully completed the procedure: that is, they all managed to make the call without any help in the second trial, except for one child who needed three trials. Therefore, we can conclude that knowing how to make a call on a cell phone is an easy task for children of these ages as well as for adults. In contrast, the production of a complete text was much more difficult, especially for children. This first result confirms the gap between the ability to execute a procedure and the ability to represent it notationally (using writing or drawing). The latter is much more difficult, for a number of reasons.

First, many of the children's notations were not complete. The mean number of pertinent actions included in the notations (out of a total of five) was quite low: 2.3 in the 8-year-old group; 2.7 in the 9-year-old group; 3.5 in the 10-year-old group; and 4.6 in the adult group.

Therefore, many children did not seem to be aware that an informative message has to include the complete sequence of actions. Interestingly, the actions most frequently omitted were "confirm the introduction of the PIN" and "press the button to call", which, as stated above, could be interpreted as the most automatized and therefore implicit information. These two actions are also special in the sense that they merely confirm a previous action (dialling the PIN and the telephone number) rather than adding something new. For this reason, we suppose, children had difficulty representing them explicitly as separate actions.

However, the content of the message is not the only aspect that matters for a message to be functional. The actions have to be represented in the right order. We classified the notations in three categories according to the degree of functionality: *low*, when they indicated a correct sequence that included up to two actions; *medium*, when they indicated a correct sequence that included three or four actions; and *high*, when they indicated the complete correct sequence of five actions. Only adults presented a high percentage of notations with a high level of functionality; in children, especially the 8- and 9-year-olds, the level of functionality was low.

So far, we have considered how the content of notations changes with age and have shown some of the most frequent difficulties that children face in trying to produce informative notations. But what formal properties do these notations have? To analyse this question, two dimensions were chosen: the "type" of notation used and the "format", that is, the organization of markers in the graphic space. Three categories of notations can be distinguished: (a) those that contain only a figurative representation (i.e. a drawing); (b) those that contain only writing; and (c) those that contain a combination of the two. Remember that the combination of writing and drawing is a very useful strategy in most notations related to technical devices because writing is well suited for representing sequential information and drawing for representing the spatial details of the object. Only adults presented a high proportion of combination of the two modes (around 80% of their notations). In contrast, few 8-year-old children produced combinations; in general this age group preferred only writing. Nine- and ten-year-old children presented approximately the same proportion of both types of notations (combined and written only). So the strategy to combine writing and drawing in order to issue functional instructions is not well established among children below ten.

The second dimension for analysing the formal properties of notations is "format", the organization of markers in the graphic space. Three distinct formats are identified: (a) *Text*, which refers to notations whose information is organised in a sequence. Sometimes, notations of this kind included pictorial information, but the important feature is that the markers are organized linearly. (b) *List*, notations that explicitly distinguish between the parts of the procedure and list one beneath the other in a sequential way. The important feature here is the introduction of different graphic devices (different sentences in different lines, space between lines, numbers of the components of the list) to emphasize the different components of the procedure. (c) *Nonsequential*, characterized by the absence of an explicit reading order of the components of the notation. All cases of notations that included a general drawing of the cell phone belong to this category, and others containing information that was not organized sequentially. The results are clear: the *List* format appeared in a high proportion only in adults; children seemed to prefer the *Text* format although 8-year-olds also produced a substantial proportion of *Nonsequential* notations. Indeed, *Text* is well suited to transmit the sequential information of a procedure although the sequential order of the components of the procedure remains implicit. The format *List* is cognitively more advanced in the sense that it implies an effort to distinguish the different components of the procedure explicitly and graphically (see Beaudet & Grant, this volume). This format is rarely used by children below ten (see Figure 1 for one example of each format).

Finally, our own data from another study (Garcia-Mila, Rojo, & Anderson, 2005) show the importance of the specific instruction in the task demands addressed to produce a procedural text. This study involved a scientific inquiry task lasting seven sessions, in which children, working individually, had to investigate the effect of given factors (i.e. light, fertilizer and seed) on plant growth. They had to manipulate the material in order to design experiments:

Figure 1: An example of the three formats of written instructions produced by children in the cellular task. From left to right: Text, List and Nonsequential.

for instance, filling pots with soil, adding plant seeds, using different types of fertilizer and exposing the plants to light of different intensities, and measuring the plants growth over several sessions. In the middle (fourth) and last (seventh) sessions, they were asked to write a report, with the explicit instruction that it should include a "Methods Section" explaining how they had done their experiments. There were 34 participants—11-year-old children attending a school in a middle-class urban environment in Barcelona. Two children did not include a method section in their reports, and among those who did, none reported any of the characteristics of procedural texts mentioned above. Their method section comprised a set of four or five lines of linear text using at most the gerund form of the verbs: *I did it by observing and measuring the plants*, mainly describing "what" they had done, rather than "how" they had done it. A few of them used temporal markers to indicate a very general sequence of actions normally related to the factors such as: "*First I planted a seed, then I put in the fertilizer and turned on the light, and then the following day, I measured the plant.*" Only two reports included specific actions in the design of the experiments and the material manipulation (i.e. *Add 8 drops of the fertilizer and then put the seed into the soil*). Perhaps the excessively general wording of the instructions—*Write a report containing a Method Section that should include information about how you did the work*—omitting the specific target—*write ... for another person to do the task*—led them to focus on the factors they had chosen to design the experiments (what) rather than on the procedure they had followed (how).

4 Concluding Remarks

The studies reviewed here underline the main difficulties that children face in writing procedural texts, and highlight the progress they make with age. Knowledge of these difficulties and how they are overcome them is useful information that should be taken into consideration when professional documents are analysed.

One of the main difficulties in producing procedural texts is to represent the temporal dimension of the procedure. Children tend to omit any indication of the exact chronological succession of the actions in their texts. The representation of dynamic information (sequence of actions) seems more difficult than the representation of static information (i.e. descriptions of the pieces of a device or the telephone number). One of the important decisions is to choose the mode of representation: linguistic or graphic. Each mode of representation has its own advantages and limitations. In general the linguistic mode is better suited since it permits coordination between the temporal order of the sequence of actions and language, since language is temporal in nature. Nevertheless, results of developmental studies show that this temporal dimension remains implicit in the texts of most young children. In contrast, the graphic mode is better suited for describing qualitative and spatial aspects of the components of the display rather than for describing actions and temporal aspects of the procedure. It is possible, as some research with adult populations has shown, that the combination of graphic and linguistic modes is a good strategy for producing more informative and complete technical documents (Ganier et al., 2000; Hegarty & Just, 1993; Mayer, 1993). As the cell phone study shows, only adults predominantly choose this strategy.

A second difficulty in producing procedural texts is the exact segmentation of the actions that comprise the procedure. When a procedure is executed, the sequence of actions is performed quickly and with little or no awareness of its different components. To transfer these actions to a representational level requires a grasp of consciousness of each component to make these different components explicit in the text. As developmental research shows, this process of explicitation is difficult for young children, who tend to choose the global description of the procedure. This aspect, which is related to the adequate segmentation of the components of the procedure, should receive special attention in the design of training programs for the production of professional documents (see Beaudet & Grant, this volume).

A third difficulty in producing procedural texts is adapting the content of the text to the needs of the audience. One of the important findings of research is that young children (as old as eight) are able to make changes in their texts depending on the knowledge they attribute to the audience, but this ability improves with age. In fact, one of the requirements of professional documents is their high degree of accuracy in order to allow a novice to reproduce the exact procedure smoothly and without difficulty (Fayol, 2002a). As we have seen in earlier studies, in spite of children's precocious ability to adapt their texts to their audience, the adaptation they make may not be appropriate. One of the reasons may be the degree of difficulty of the execution of the procedure. In the cell phone experiment, the fact that all children easily reproduced the actions needed to make a call may have made the awareness of the informational needs of the addressee more difficult. More studies are needed to test this hypothesis.

Finally, an important limitation of children when they are asked to produce a procedural text is poor organization of text. One important finding of the cell phone study is that adults' procedural texts are highly organized. Texts are organized in separate chunks of written information that corresponds to meaningful actions that need to be undertaken. This internal organization of texts is important because it can facilitate text interpretation (Ganier, 2002a). Comparatively, children's texts are less organized or, as other studies show, are organized linearly. In this sense, the mastery of writing allows children to adequately express (by use of connectors, temporal markers and punctuation) the sequence of information that is crucial in producing a correct procedural text.

This chapter has presented results from developmental studies concerning the production of procedural texts to identify the main difficulties children encounter when they write a procedural text, and also to see how these difficulties are progressively solved. It is clear that these difficulties cannot be directly applied to adults. Children's and adults' writing and communicative skills are not comparable; neither is the amount of conceptual knowledge related to the content of the information. However, we think that the developmental trends of the cognitive progress in children can be a source of information to better understand novices' obstacles when confronted with the same task. In this sense, the four difficulties indicated above about children's productions when they explore a procedural text can become important guidelines in the professional training of novice writers of technical documents: the combination of different modes of representation (linguistic and graphic) to deal with the temporal sequence of actions and to describe the spatial information of the device; the correct segmentation of the information following the main actions to be executed; the adaptation of the content of the text to the needs of the audience; and, finally, the organization of the text in separate chunks of information (for example by means of numeration of the different actions or by spatially separating and structuring the different parts of the text).

Chapter 8

Developing an Online Writing Tutor to Improve Technical-Writing Skills in Engineering and Science Students

John R. Hayes, Diana M. Bajzek, Judy Brooks, Brenda Reyes, Nicole Hallinen and Erwin R. Steinberg

Engineering and science students need instruction in basic technical-writing skills. Typically, engineering and science faculty are not trained to teach writing and often they do not have the time to do so. In addition, universities may be reluctant to provide financial resources for such instruction.

To help meet this need for basic technical-writing instruction, we have undertaken the development of the Carnegie Mellon Writing Tutor, an online, stand-alone tutor that provides students with instruction, practice, and feedback in a variety of basic writing and graphic skills.

Much, perhaps most, technical writing is done by engineers and scientists. For examples, journal articles and technical reports are almost always written by the researchers who have done the work. Unfortunately, a person with a university degree in engineering or science does not necessarily have good communication skills. Indeed, a survey of science faculty at Carnegie Mellon University (Young & Gordon, 1995) found the following:

1. Science faculty believes that slightly fewer than a third of all their students graduate with the writing abilities the faculty think are important.
2. Three of the abilities cited by all faculties as abilities students should acquire at the university level are: (1) the ability to write with grammatical correctness, (2) the ability to write clear and coherent sentences, and (3) the ability to organize paragraphs and sections logically. Faculty members feel that the percentage of their students who graduate with these abilities is unacceptably low. Because of the nature of these abilities, we would call the problems students seem to be having "problems of basic intelligibility." The issue,

in other words, is not of students not writing eloquently or creatively enough, but one of students simply not writing intelligible prose.

Ammer (1998) indicates that many science and engineering faculties are concerned with the quality of their students' writing. Indeed, ABET (Accrediting Board for Engineering and Technology), in its 2001–2002 criteria for accrediting engineering programs has specified, "Engineering programs must demonstrate that their graduates have an ability to communicate effectively."

It appears, then, that there is a need to provide basic technical-writing instruction for science and engineering students at the university level. Unfortunately, the resources needed to provide such instruction are scarce. On many campuses, writing centers are an important source of supplemental writing instruction. Griffin, Keller, Pandey, Pedersen, and Skinner (2006) have identified more than 1000 writing centers providing writing instruction at two- and four-year colleges in the U.S. (p. 1). However, *The College Board College Handbook* (2006) lists 3800 two- and four-year colleges in the U.S. It is clear that many, perhaps most, colleges do not have writing centers. Further, engineering and science faculty usually cannot make sufficient class time available to teach writing. Young and Gordon (1995) found that science professors do not have adequate time to integrate writing activities more fully into their courses. But even if time were available, many engineering and science faculty members would not feel comfortable teaching writing skills. As Pemberton (1995) notes, "successful, publishing academics do not think of themselves as writers, and consequently, doubt their own ability to comment on and respond effectively to student writing." Russell (1991) reports that lack of time and lack of inclination to teach writing have hindered the development of writing across the curriculum programs in many colleges (pp. 292–298).

Engineering and science students need better technical-writing skills but it is sometimes difficult to find resources to fill that need. Therefore, we undertook the development of the Carnegie Mellon Online Writing Tutor as a tool to help improve students' technical-writing skills without requiring faculty members to teach writing. Of course, as Albers (2005, p. 269) notes, technical writers need more skills than just the ability to write. For example, they may need skills in management, in information design, or in human factors. But they do need writing skills. That is our focus here.

Readers can access a current version of the tutor at http://telstar.ote.cmu.edu/writingtutor/.

1 Judgment Training

The core instructional concept underlying the tutor is judgment training. By judgment training, we mean instruction that is aimed at providing students with skills that allow them to evaluate the quality of their own texts and of texts written by others. Graves (1994) and Tierney, Carter, and Desai (1991) stress the importance of teaching students to evaluate their own writing. Hayes et al. (1987) found that freshman writers often failed to detect problems that were immediately evident to more advanced writers. For example, they observed that some freshman writers failed to find any fault in sentences such as "Many naïve women possess the assumption that it is necessary that they be superlative athletes in order to successfully be a member of a varsity team" and "In sports like fencing for a long time many of our varsity team members had no previous experience anyway." The problem was not inattentive reading. The freshman might read these sentences as many as eight times and still evaluate them as "good." Many of the freshmen appeared to be persistently insensitive to the problems in the text. Apparently, they were deficient in skills needed to evaluate text quality.

We believe that one of the most important causes of poor writing is the inability of writers to judge the quality of their own texts. If writers fail to perceive problems in their texts, they cannot take action to fix them. Further, if writers fail to see problems such as poor organization and wordiness in their texts, they may be unable to understand comments on their papers about these problems. When teachers write "wordy" and "awkward" on their papers, the comments will convey nothing to these students. The ability to evaluate texts is a crucial skill for writing and for learning to write. For this reason, we have adopted judgment training as our primary pedagogical principle.

There are many ways to implement judgment training in practice. We will comment on four judgment-training methods that have been evaluated for effectiveness (for a more detailed discussion, see Hayes, 2004):

1. Commenting on students' papers (commenting)
2. Familiarizing students with models of writing (models)
3. Teaching students to use evaluative scales (scales)
4. Providing students with reader feedback (reader feedback)

1.1 Commenting on Students' Papers

The familiar procedure in which composition teachers write comments on student's essays is an example of judgment training. The teacher's intention in commenting on text problems such as lack of organization or wordiness is to help their students recognize and fix such problems when they encounter them in later texts. The teacher's goal is to provide students with judgmental skills that they will take with them when they write or edit new texts.

Hillocks (1986, pp. 153–168) reviewed research on the effect on students' writing quality as a result of teachers commenting on students' final drafts and on their intermediate drafts. Hillocks concluded, "The available research suggests that teaching by written comments on compositions is generally ineffective" (p. 167).

1.2 Familiarizing Students with Models of Writing

With this method, students might be asked to read models of good writing, to read and identify features of good (and sometimes poor) writing, to attempt to imitate examples of good writing, or all three. Hillocks (1986) reported that the results of studies evaluating this method were mixed. Some studies showed gains but others did not.

1.3 Teaching Students to Use Evaluative Scales

A third judgmental training method involves teaching students to use evaluative scales. A study by Sager (1973) illustrates this procedure. Sager taught sixth-grade students to use scales focusing on four aspects of writing quality: vocabulary, elaboration, organization, and structure. Each scale had four values ranging from zero for the poorest quality to three for the best. A high score on vocabulary was given to essays that had a variety of new and interesting words rather than common ones. A high score on elaboration was given to essays that had an abundance of related ideas that flowed smoothly from one idea to the next. A high score on organization was given if ideas were arranged in a way that was interesting and easy to follow, and a high score on structure if the story could be read aloud with ease. For each scale, students learned what features earned a zero and what features earned one, two, or three.

In introducing each scale, the teacher led a discussion of the features that a specific composition did or did not have. Students then received extensive practice in rating compositions both by themselves and in small groups. Differences of opinions about ratings were discussed and an attempt was made to achieve consensus in the class. If the compositions did not receive a three, the students suggested improvements and made revisions. At first the students rated one component at a time, then two components, finally, all four.

Students in the control group studied the same four components of composition but followed the standard school curriculum. Both groups studied 45 minutes a day for five days a week for eight weeks. By comparing pre- and post-test essays, Sager found that the experimental group made significantly greater gains than the control group on all four aspects of writing quality, that is vocabulary, elaboration, organization, and structure.

Hillocks (1986) reviewed seven studies that taught evaluative scales and concluded, "As a group, these studies indicate rather clearly that engaging young writers actively in the use of criteria, applied to their own and others' writing, results not only in more effective revisions but in superior first drafts." That students' first drafts improved is important because it suggests that students are applying the criteria to their own text production.

1.4 Providing Students with Reader Feedback

In a procedure developed by Schriver (1992b) students were taught to evaluate the clarity of text by exposing them to reader feedback in the form of think-aloud protocols of readers trying to understand the texts. In a sequence of ten lessons, participants first read an unclear text and underlined those aspects of the text that they thought the intended readers would find unclear. Next, they read a think-aloud protocol of an intended reader attempting to understand that text. Finally, the participants were asked to revise their initial judgments of clarity on the basis of the protocol.

Shriver found that students who studied the ten lessons showed significant gains in predicting what readers would find unclear. The control group consisting of students exposed to the standard-writing curriculum including peer critiquing, role-playing, etc. showed no gain.

2 Comparing Judgment Training Methods

To help us design an effective tutor, we wanted to understand why some of these methods worked better than others to identify features that might be useful in the design of the tutor. To do this, we compared them by asking five questions about each method.

1. Does it decompose complex skills?
2. Does it promote active student participation?
3. Does it provide scaffolding for the student?
4. Does it provide clear, prompt feedback about student performance?
5. Does it provide sufficient practice?

We have chosen these questions, discussed in more detail below, to differentiate good and poor teaching procedures on the basis of the pedagogical literature.

2.1 Decompose Complex Skills

There is a controversy in the instructional literature about whether practicing the parts of a skill is an effective way to teach a complex skill. Gagne and Briggs (1974) emphasize its value but Brown, Collins, and Duguid (1989) emphasize its failures. Schneider (1985) cites data indicating that teaching part skills can, in fact, promote the acquisition of a complex skill.

We believe that many writing skills consist of relatively independent part skills. For example, basic writing skills such as punctuation can, and usually are decomposed into part-skills such as using commas or using hyphens, that are appropriately taught separately. Further, we believe that even relatively complex skill such as judging whether a text is appropriate for a general audience can benefit by practicing part-skills such as identifying undefined terms, identifying abstract language, and identifying the need for examples, each of which can be practiced separately.

Although teachers using either of the first two judgment-training methods, commenting and models, can or may decompose some skills for the reader, this is not the focus of either method. In contrast, the third judgment-training method, the scales method, makes explicit use of decomposition, breaking complex evaluations of text quality into simpler part evaluations. The reader feedback method does not use decomposition.

2.2 Promote Active Participation

Schneider (1985) emphasizes the importance of learners' active participation in the instructional process. He says, "Active participation is enhanced if subjects need to respond every few seconds …Without these [responses] subjects' observation becomes passive and there is little improvement with practice" (pp. 297–298). Constructivist learning theorists strongly agree that the student's active participation in learning is a critical factor determining the effectiveness of instruction. If students are not required to respond to the instructional materials, they may not give full attention to the learning task.

In the commenting and models methods, student engagement is typically sporadic. Students are heavily engaged when they are writing papers but may be only occasionally engaged during other parts of the instructional process. In contrast, students are continuously engaged in both the scales and reader feedback methods.

2.3 Provide Students with Scaffolding

Scaffolding, the process of providing support to students as they are acquiring a skill, is also widely recognized as an important aid to instruction (Farnham-Diggory, 1992, p. 571; Collins, Brown, & Newman, 1989, p. 23).

Of the four methods, the scales method provided the greatest opportunity for scaffolding both from the teacher and from the student's peers. Both the commenting and the models method provided opportunity for scaffolding by the teacher. Only method four, the reader feedback method, did not provide scaffolding.

2.4 Provide Clear, Prompt Feedback

One of the most reliable results in the literature on learning is that quick feedback promotes learning. Of course, that feedback must be sufficiently clear that the student can understand it. As their third principle in the design of computer based tutors, Anderson, Boyle, Farrell, and Reiser (1984) recommend that immediate feedback be provided for errors.

In the comments method, feedback is typically delayed. Often, students receive comments days or weeks after they have written their papers. Further, the comments may not be clear. For example, when reading a marginal comment, the student may not understand what specific feature of the text is being referred to. In addition, if students are not already able to judge whether their texts are awkward or not, they may not know what their teachers are referring to when they write "awkward" in the margin. To the extent that feedback in the models method is given by writing comments on papers, the models method would suffer the same feedback problems as the comment method. In both the scales and reader feedback methods, feedback is rapid and specific.

2.5 Provide Sufficient Practice

Schneider (1985) recommends that many practice trials be provided in skill training. With the comment and models methods, teachers may have relatively few opportunities to comment on any particular text problem for each student during the course of a semester. If a student receives five or ten comments on organization or wordiness over the course of a semester that may not be enough to make a difference in the student's writing. Both the scales and reader feedback methods provide students with substantial amounts of practice. Results (Hillocks, 1986; Schriver, 1992b) indicate that the amount of practice was sufficient to yield significant improvements.

Results of the comparison, summarized in Table 1, indicate that the features most clearly differentiating the more successful from the less successful methods were providing active participation, quick feedback, and sufficient practice. These three features appear to be the most important to incorporate into the tutor. The other features, although they do not differentiate more effective from less effective methods, may still contribute to the effectiveness of methods that incorporate them. In particular, we believe, as we have argued above, that decomposing complex writing skills into simpler skills can be an effective strategy for teaching the kinds of skills we plan to address with the tutor.

Table 1: Properties of the four judgment-training methods.

	Comment	Models	Scales	Reader feedback
Decompose?	No	No	Yes	No
Active participation?	No	No	Yes	Yes
Scaffolding?	Yes	Yes	Yes	No
Quick feedback?	No	No	Yes	Yes
Sufficient practice?	No	No	Yes	Yes
Effective?	No	?	Yes	Yes

In addition to these five features, we plan to include a sixth feature to address a problem we discovered in our early formative assessments of the writing tutor. We found that many engineering students did not believe that writing skills are important for their careers. Therefore, the introduction to each module explains why the topic of that module is important for engineering and science professionals. It will also explain clearly what skills the student can expect to acquire as a result of studying the module.

3 The Tutor

In its final form, the tutor will consist of independent instructional modules, accessible in any order, each focused on specific writing topics that have been identified by engineering and science faculty members as important for their students or by writing centers as common student-writing problems. At present, we anticipate that the tutor will include modules designed to teach the following skills:

- Addressing a general audience
- Providing adequate thesis statements
- Punctuating accurately
- Writing in active voice
- Providing logical organization
- Writing clearly
- Revising
- Formatting for clarity
- Improving charts and graphs
- Using articles appropriately
- Avoiding wordiness
- Citing sources and avoiding plagiarism

The first four modules on the list have been completed and three more are under construction. Additional modules can be added as the need for them is identified. We plan to conduct a survey of those who teach writing to engineering and science students to identify the final list of technical-writing skills that the tutor will teach.

Each tutor module will consist of two parts, an instructional section and a practice section. The *instructional section* will introduce the writing topic and present the basic principles and strategies for carrying out the module's writing tasks. It will include embedded mini exercises to provide interactivity and feedback. In modules not yet constructed, the choice of principles and strategies will be based on available research. For example, the revision module will make use of strategies shown by Wallace and Hayes (1991) and by Wallace et al. (1996) to produce improved revision. The clarity module will use strategies that Schriver (1992b) developed and tested—strategies that significantly improve writers' abilities to identify text that will confuse readers.

In the *practice section*, the student will be asked to apply the rules and principles presented in the instructional section to a sequence of exercises. In these exercises, they will read a text and evaluate it for its adherence to the principles outlined in the instructional section. Then, as feedback, they will be shown how an expert writer responded to the same exercise.

4 A Typical Module: Addressing a General Audience

The audience module is designed to address a common writing problem that occurs when technically sophisticated writers attempt to address general or non-technical audiences. The problem is that technically sophisticated writers often overestimate what general audiences know. The result is that the audience may be confused by unfamiliar terms and concepts, and may have no idea why the topic is important.

Instructional section. The section starts by discussing the professional importance of addressing a general audience, pointing out that on the job a scientist or engineer typically has to communicate with many people who are not specialists in their field: bosses, clients, and possibly coworkers on multidisciplinary teams.

Then the module introduces five principles for writing clearly to general audiences:

1. Define unfamiliar terms
2. Clarify abstract language
3. Use concrete examples and common sense analogies
4. Catch the reader's interest early
5. Explain why the topic is important

Each principle is explained and illustrated. Figure 1 shows some of the material explaining and illustrating the principle "Provide concrete examples."

After each principle is illustrated, the student is asked to answer a few questions relevant to the principle. For example, after students read the material in Figure 1, they are asked to decide whether or not several sample sentences would profit from concrete examples (see Figure 2). These questions are designed to promote students' active participation and to provide them with confirmation of their understanding of the principles.

After each decision, the student receives immediate feedback in the form shown in Figure 2.

Online Tutor to Improve Technical-Writing   115

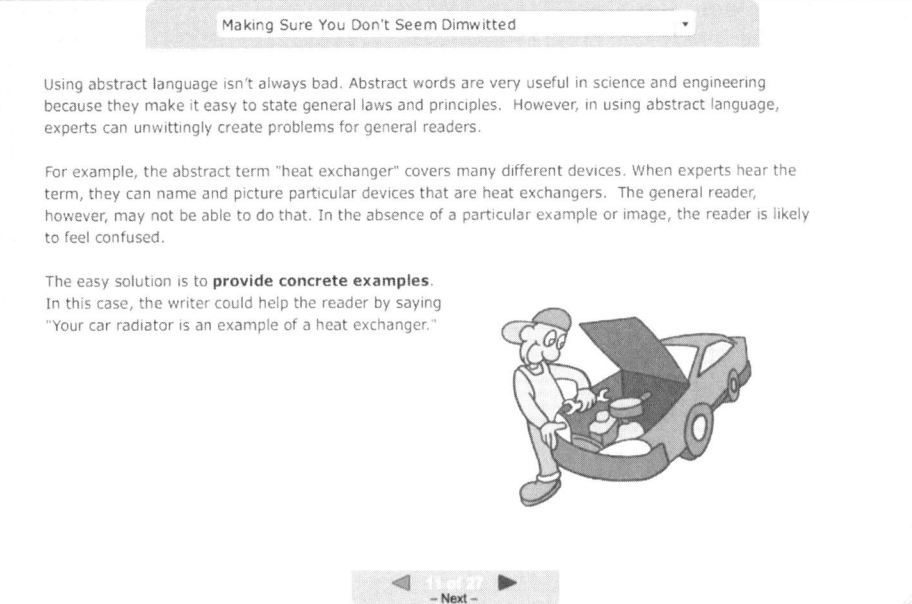

Figure 1: A screen that illustrates the principle, "Provide concrete examples."

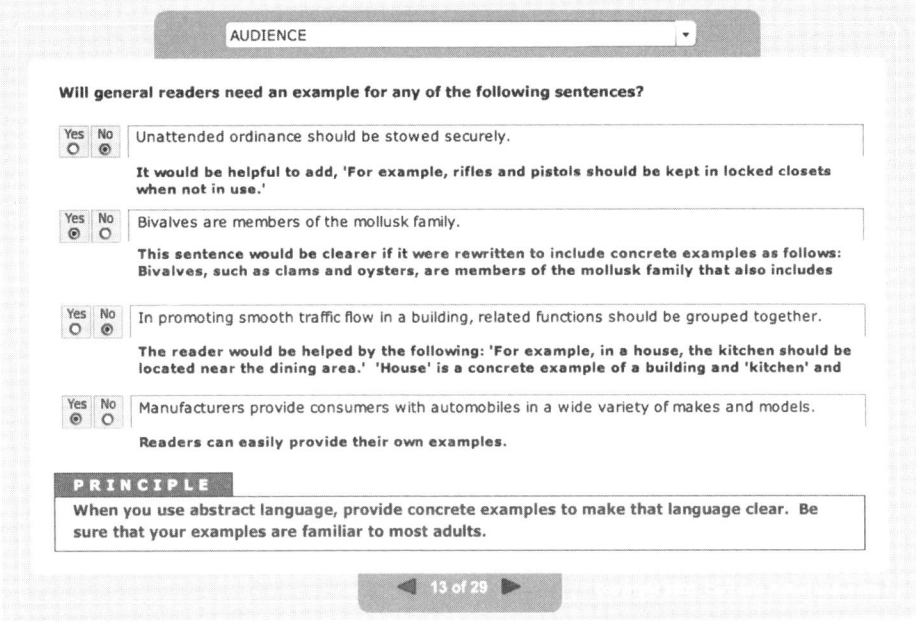

Figure 2: An exercise designed to promote the student's active participation in learning the principle "Provide concrete examples."

5 Early Lessons Learned From Assessment

By assessing the initial versions of the first two modules, we learned two important lessons.

5.1 Lesson One

At first, we had designed the tutor modules to mirror the scales method as described in Sager's (1973) study. For example, in the first version of the audience module the exercises in the practice section required students to rate a set of texts on six scales that had been introduced earlier in the instructional section. Students chose a value from one to four on each scale and then received feedback about the accuracy of their judgments.

Generally, participants found the exercises dull and repetitive. The reason, we believe, is that they were asked to answer six very similar questions about each text. Further, many found the prescriptive feedback annoying and overly precise. (For example, they might ask "Why was a quality rating of 2 definitely wrong and a quality rating of 3 definitely correct?") Although Sager's method worked for sixth graders, it did not seem well adapted to college students.

In response to the students' critiques, we completely reorganized the practice section: we abandoned the strategy of asking students to answer a fixed set of questions about each text. Instead, we adopted a three-step pattern for each exercise.

- The first step (see Figure 3) was to present a text on the left and to ask the student to check off the major problems with the text on the right. Most texts had one or two major problems.

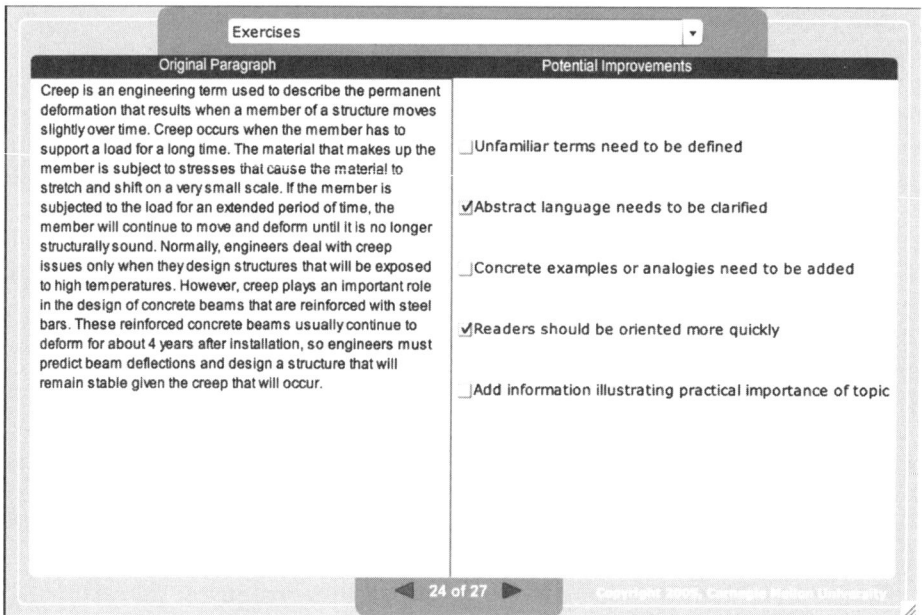

Figure 3: Students are shown a text written by a student and asked to evaluate the text's problems.

- The second step was to show another two-page spread (see Figure 4). The left-hand page presented the original text with annotations by an expert writer listing major problems with the text. The right-hand page presented the expert's revision of the original text with annotations by the expert explaining why the changes were made. This procedure allowed us to provide feedback as a suggestion about what might be done and to avoid telling students that their responses were correct or incorrect.
- In the third step (see Figure 5), students were shown the judgments they had made about the text in Step 1 and asked to judge how well their judgments matched those of the expert.

A second round of assessment with a new group of students indicated that the student responded very positively to the new version of the module.

5.2 Lesson Two

Assessment of the initial versions of the audience module also revealed a serious problem with the instructional section. In the discussion on defining terms, the module suggests that words such as torque, enzyme, maser, titration, and entropy may require definition when included in texts for a general audience. Some of our participants said that we were being too hard on the audience and that most would know those words. Clearly the module was not being sufficiently persuasive about one of the central principles that the module addresses,

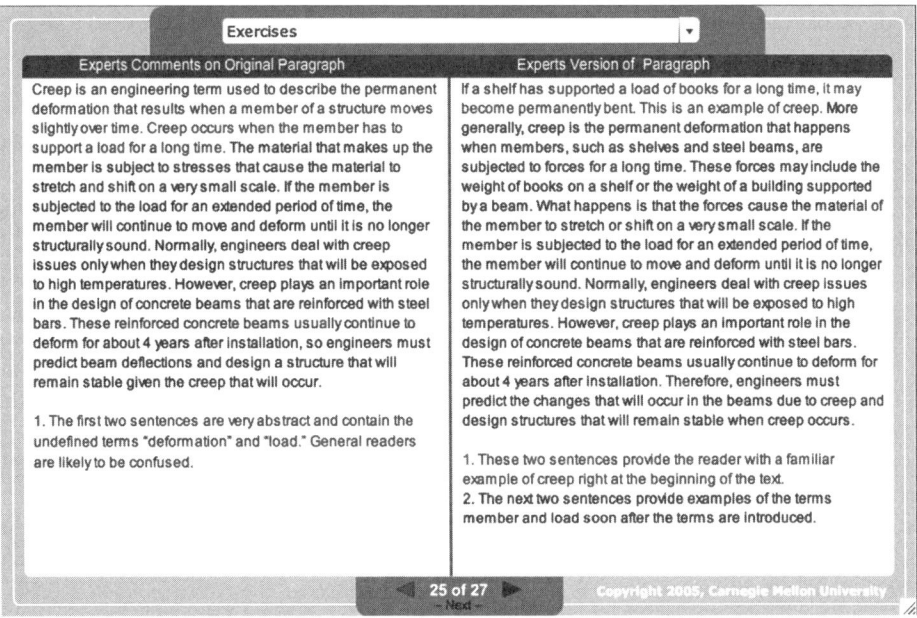

Figure 4: On the left, students are shown an annotated version of the original text. The numbered comments are color-coded to indicate which parts of the text they refer to. On the right, students are shown a revised version of the text. Comments explaining why changes were made in the color-coded sections of the text may be viewed below the text.

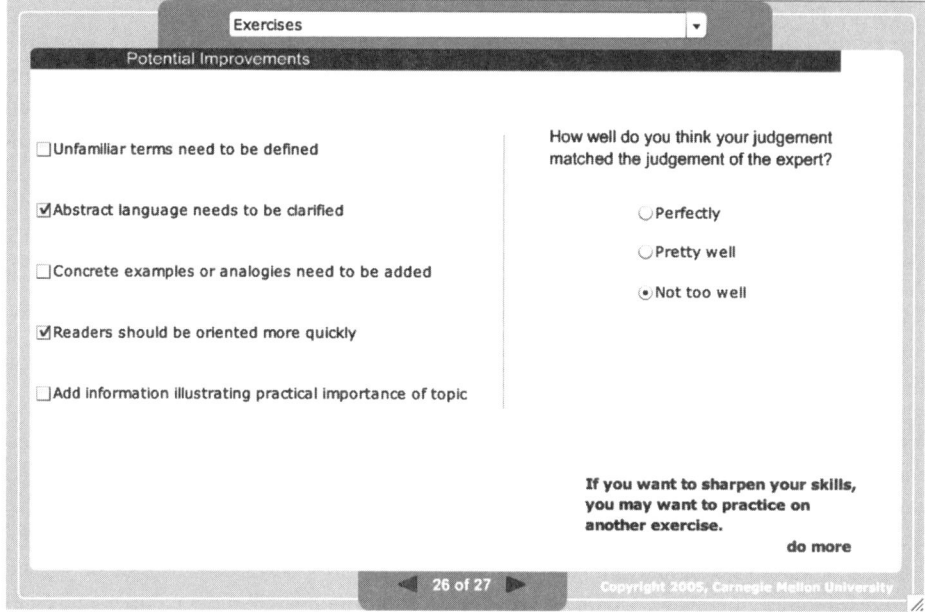

Figure 5: On the left, students are shown the diagnosis of the text's problems that they made before seeing the expert's revision. On the right, they are asked to judge how well their judgments match those of the expert.

namely, writers with technical backgrounds may overestimate what general audiences know about their specialty.

An earlier study by Hayes, Schriver, Spilka, and Blaustein (described in Hayes, 1989) provided evidence that having knowledge can make it difficult for a writer to predict what would be unclear to a reader who does not have that knowledge. In this study, student writers were asked to read texts on statistics or autism and underline any passages that they thought a general audience member who was unfamiliar with the topic would find confusing. For each topic there were two versions; an unclear one and a clear one that explained many of the things that were confusing in the unclear text. In half of the cases, the writers read the clear version before the unclear version and in the other half of the cases, they read the unclear version before reading the clear one. The researchers found that the writers underlined only half as many passages if they had read the clear version earlier as they did when they read the unclear version first. This was true even though the writers had received the information that helped them to understand the unclear text just five minutes before making their judgments. They concluded that if the writers understood the text themselves, they were inclined to believe that others would understand it too.

We believed that this principle also applied to the estimation of other peoples' familiarity with technical terms. To see if this hypothesis was correct, we carried out a study with a very simple design. Twenty participants were given two lists of technical terms. For the first list of 33 words, participants were asked to estimate on a scale from 0 to 100 what percentage

Indicate the percent of first year college students you believe understand this word

Amalgam	0	10	20	30	40	50	60	70	80	90	100
Amorphous	0	10	20	30	40	50	60	70	80	90	100
Apogee	0	10	20	30	40	50	60	70	80	90	100
Arboreal	0	10	20	30	40	50	60	70	80	90	100
Aurora Borealis	0	10	20	30	40	50	60	70	80	90	100
Boron	0	10	20	30	40	50	60	70	80	90	100
Calorimeter	0	10	20	30	40	50	60	70	80	90	100
Cardinal number	0	10	20	30	40	50	60	70	80	90	100
Centripital	0	10	20	30	40	50	60	70	80	90	100
Cephalic	0	10	20	30	40	50	60	70	80	90	100
Corollary	0	10	20	30	40	50	60	70	80	90	100
Diffract	0	10	20	30	40	50	60	70	80	90	100
Elucidate	0	10	20	30	40	50	60	70	80	90	100
Emulsion	0	10	20	30	40	50	60	70	80	90	100
Finite	0	10	20	30	40	50	60	70	80	90	100
Geodesic	0	10	20	30	40	50	60	70	80	90	100
Igneous	0	10	20	30	40	50	60	70	80	90	100
Kinetic	0	10	20	30	40	50	60	70	80	90	100
Lithium	0	10	20	30	40	50	60	70	80	90	100
Mach Number	0	10	20	30	40	50	60	70	80	90	100

Figure 6: Test form on which participants estimated audience knowledge of technical terms.

of *college freshmen* would know the term (see Figure 6). For the second list of 52 words participants were asked to estimate on a scale from 0 to 100 what percentage of *college graduates* would know the term. Next, the participants were given these same two lists of words again and asked to rate their own familiarity with the terms on a four point scale: (1) not at all familiar, (2) I've heard of it, (3) I think I know it, (4) I'm sure I know it. (see Figure 7).

The two lists of words were selected from *The living word vocabulary: a national vocabulary inventory* by Edgar Dale and Joseph O'Rourke, 1981 (Chicago: World Book-Childcraft International) which tabulated the percentage of individuals in various populations in the U.S., e.g., college freshmen, college graduates, who knew each word. Dale and O'Rourke's criterion for knowing a word was that a person was able to choose the most appropriate definition of that word from a set of three. Using this data, and compensating for guessing, we estimated the proportion of the population that actually knew the appropriate definition. Using these estimates, we were able to calculate for each participant the degree to which he or she overestimated or underestimated the percentage of people who understood the terms in the two populations.

Figure 8 shows the relation between the participants' own familiarity with particular terms and their tendency to over- or under-estimate other peoples' familiarity with those terms. Analysis of variance reveals a highly significant effect of familiarity on overestimation ($F = 61.556$, $df = 3$, $p < .0001$). On average, our students estimated that college graduates were more likely than freshmen to know the terms but the difference was not statistically significant.

Indicate how familiar you are with each of these words

Amalgam	not at all	I've heard it	I think I know it	I'm sure I know it
Amorphous	not at all	I've heard it	I think I know it	I'm sure I know it
Apogee	not at all	I've heard it	I think I know it	I'm sure I know it
Arboreal	not at all	I've heard it	I think I know it	I'm sure I know it
Aurora Borealis	not at all	I've heard it	I think I know it	I'm sure I know it
Boron	not at all	I've heard it	I think I know it	I'm sure I know it
Calorimeter	not at all	I've heard it	I think I know it	I'm sure I know it
Cardinal number	not at all	I've heard it	I think I know it	I'm sure I know it
Centripital	not at all	I've heard it	I think I know it	I'm sure I know it
Cephalic	not at all	I've heard it	I think I know it	I'm sure I know it
Corollary	not at all	I've heard it	I think I know it	I'm sure I know it
Diffract	not at all	I've heard it	I think I know it	I'm sure I know it
Elucidate	not at all	I've heard it	I think I know it	I'm sure I know it
Emulsion	not at all	I've heard it	I think I know it	I'm sure I know it
Finite	not at all	I've heard it	I think I know it	I'm sure I know it
Geodesic	not at all	I've heard it	I think I know it	I'm sure I know it
Igneous	not at all	I've heard it	I think I know it	I'm sure I know it
Kinetic	not at all	I've heard it	I think I know it	I'm sure I know it
Lithium	not at all	I've heard it	I think I know it	I'm sure I know it
Mach Number	not at all	I've heard it	I think I know it	I'm sure I know it

Figure 7: Test form on which participants estimated their own knowledge of technical terms.

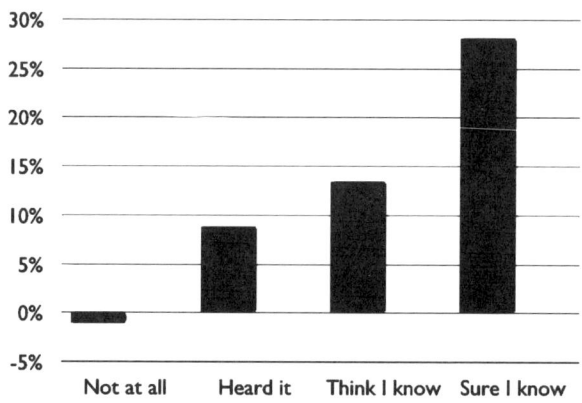

Figure 8: The relation of the participants' own knowledge of terms to the percentage by which they overestimate others' knowledge of those terms.

We used the results of this study to create an exercise for inclusion in the tutor designed to convince students that they tend to overestimate other people's knowledge of the words with which they, themselves, are familiar. To do this, we identified those terms for which our participants overestimated other peoples' familiarity most strongly. We then used these

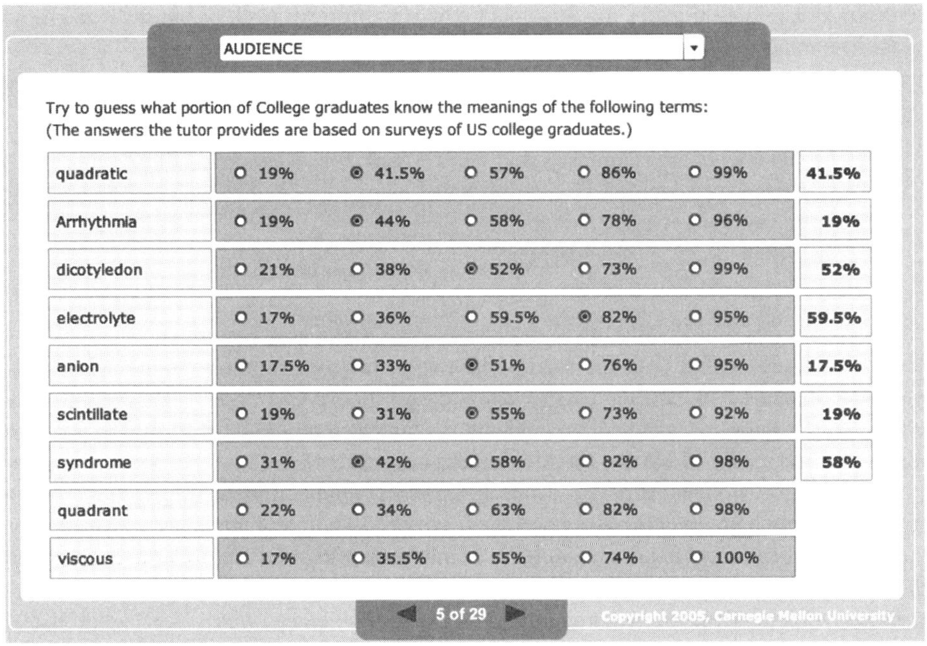

AUDIENCE						
Try to guess what portion of College graduates know the meanings of the following terms: (The answers the tutor provides are based on surveys of US college graduates.)						
quadratic	○ 19%	● 41.5%	○ 57%	○ 86%	○ 99%	**41.5%**
Arrhythmia	○ 19%	● 44%	○ 58%	○ 78%	○ 96%	**19%**
dicotyledon	○ 21%	○ 38%	● 52%	○ 73%	○ 99%	**52%**
electrolyte	○ 17%	○ 36%	○ 59.5%	● 82%	○ 95%	**59.5%**
anion	○ 17.5%	○ 33%	● 51%	○ 76%	○ 95%	**17.5%**
scintillate	○ 19%	○ 31%	● 55%	○ 73%	○ 92%	**19%**
syndrome	○ 31%	● 42%	○ 58%	○ 82%	○ 98%	**58%**
quadrant	○ 22%	○ 34%	○ 63%	○ 82%	○ 98%	
viscous	○ 17%	○ 35.5%	○ 55%	○ 74%	○ 100%	

5 of 29   Copyright 2005, Carnegie Mellon University

Figure 9: Students are asked to estimate the proportion of college graduates who know each term. When they respond, they are given feedback (indicated in the last column) indicating the actual proportion of college graduates who know the term.

terms as items in the test shown in Figure 9. Students using the tutor are asked to estimate college graduates' knowledge of these terms, and are then given a feedback as shown in Figure 9.

5.3 *Summative Assessment*

Before the tutor project is complete, we will carry out summative assessment of each of the modules to establish that they actually improve students' writing.

One aspect of all of the modules that might be considered problematic is that they teach students to evaluate other writers' texts but do not give them practice in evaluating their own texts. But it is known that writers may respond differently to their own texts than they do to other peoples' texts. For example, Bartlett (1981) has shown that sixth graders are better at editing other peoples' texts than they are at editing their own texts. Thus, there is a serious question whether teaching students to evaluate other peoples' texts will transfer to their evaluations of their own texts. Wallace et al. (1996) have addressed this question directly in the case of revision. Wallace and Hayes (1991) had earlier demonstrated the effectiveness of a strategy for improving college students' skill in revising other peoples' texts. Wallace et al. (1996) demonstrated that the strategy also worked when writers were revising their own texts. Although the success of the Wallace et al. study is encouraging, we must demonstrate transfer to the student's own writing for each of the skills taught in the various modules.

At this time, we have summary assessment data for just one of the modules: the framing statement module. This module teaches four principles:

1. Framing statements are statements that tell the reader what the text will be about.
2. They help readers to decide whether or not they want to read the text, and if they decide to read, they help the reader to understand the text.
3. They should be placed early in the text.
4. Pointers, that is, explicit statements such as "I intend to show" and "The purpose of this memo is" enhance the effectiveness of framing statements.

To assess the effectiveness of the module in a real classroom setting, we compared students' use of thesis statements in two presentations of the same course. In one presentation, Fall, 2004, the tutor was available to students, and in the other, Fall, 2002, it was not. The course, "Introduction to Intelligence in Animals and Machines," is a large introductory course that draws students from all of the colleges on campus. In this course, students are required to write a five-page research paper on any one of roughly 30 topics in psychology. The instructions for writing the paper were identical in 2002 and 2004, and indicated that 5% of the grade would depend on providing a clear thesis statement. In 2004, the instructor announced that the thesis statement module was available on the course website but that its use was not required. In addition, in section meetings, the teaching assistants encouraged students to use the module when writing their papers. At the beginning of the Fall, 2002 and Fall, 2004 semesters, we asked students for permission to copy the first page of their essays for research purposes. We then copied the first pages of the essays and removed any marks identifying the student and the semester. The first pages were then randomly intermixed and blind-graded for the presence or absence of a thesis statement and the presence or absence of a pointer. Table 2 shows the percentage of thesis statements and the percentage of pointers in 2002 when the module was not available and in 2004 when it was available. The difference in the percent of thesis statements was significant ($\chi^2 = 16.153, df = 1, p < .001$) as was the percent of pointers ($\chi^2 = 4.807, df = 1, p < .05$).

The improvements in both the use of thesis statements and of pointers are substantial from an instructional perspective. We feel that these gains would be even larger if students had been required to use the tutor rather than simply having it available.

We plan to carry out assessments for each of the modules in two settings. First, we will assess each module in the controlled setting of the laboratory to determine if the module can teach the targeted judgmental skills to students under careful supervision. Second, we

Table 2: Percentages of thesis statements and pointers employed by students who did and did not have the tutor available.

	% Thesis Statements	% Pointers
2002 Tutor not available	39.5	19.4
2004 Tutor available	61.9	30.2

will assess each module in classroom settings to determine if the judgmental skills transfer to the student's own writing.

6 Various Ways in Which the Tutor May be Used

We anticipate that the tutor may be used in a variety of ways:

1. Individual science and engineering students who are concerned with their writing skills may choose to use the tutor on their own.
2. Science and engineering instructors may urge their classes to use the tutor before a writing assignment.
3. Instructors may direct students who have specific weaknesses in writing to use particular tutor modules, for example, the module on organization.
4. The tutor may be used as supplementary instruction in writing centers.
5. The tutor can be used as a reference. For example, students can consult the punctuation or the citation module to refresh their memories on these topics.
6. The tutor can also be used in the workplace either as an online reference or as a training tool for employees who are moving into professional writing positions.

To help instructors keep track of students' tutor use, the tutor can provide a certificate indicating the student's level of performance on each module. If they wish, instructors can require that students turn in the certificates so that they can check on students' tutor use.

7 Who can Benefit?

Potentially, the tutor can help many students who are now not receiving adequate writing instruction. Because the tutor will be readily accessible through the web, it can be used by science and engineering students in all the two-and four-year colleges in English-speaking countries. It can be used to reduce the workload of human tutors in writing centers. Further, it can be used by professional writing groups in industry or government as a reference or a training tool. We believe that many engineering and science students will be able to improve their communication skills by using the tutor. Students in other fields may benefit as well. For example, a history major or a music major writing a research paper might benefit from the modules on punctuation, on citation practices, and on preparing charts and graphs. However, those who are likely to receive the greatest benefits are under-prepared students and students for whom English is not their first language. Educational institutions will also benefit because the tutor is a very cost-effective way to deliver writing instruction.

Chapter 9

The Implications of Blogs for Professional Writing: Speed, Reach, Engagement, and the Art of the Self in the Participatory Web

Doreen Starke-Meyerring

This chapter examines blogs as a growing and contested space for professional writing and situates blogs in the context of recent shifts toward a participatory, collaborative "read-and-write" Web. Using Gurak's (2001) framework for Internet communication, the chapter then shows that blogs represent a critical disruptive shift in workplace writing, contributing to a new transparency (Tapscott & Ticoll, 2003) that alters how workplace professionals communicate with customers, investors, and other stakeholders. Specifically, the personal, independent, and spontaneous ethos of blogs is bound to clash with traditional, highly controlled corporate PR discourse. The chapter argues that companies will need to understand the shift in communication the blogosphere represents, design communication policies that are conducive to the open and participatory ethos of the blogosphere, and make systematic attention to writing instruction a key component of a knowledge infrastructure that empowers employees to engage customers and other stakeholders in the participatory web.

When Jeff Jarvis, a Dell customer, took to his blog to write about his ordeal with Dell customer service over a malfunctioning laptop, he attracted thousands of fellow customers with similarly negative experiences, who subsequently posted their comments to his blog, sharing their negative experiences with Dell for the world to see. On Jarvis's blog, Dell customer service, which had at some point been the hallmark of the company, was quickly redefined as "Dell Hell," a label that spread through the Internet in no time. His "Dell hell saga" quickly made the news in the mainstream media, ranging from the *New York Times* and *The Guardian* to the *Wall Street Journal* and *Businessweek Online*. The latter speculated about the damage to the brand resulting from Dell being "in the bloghouse" (Lee, 2005), which

---

Written Documents In The Workplace
Copyright © 2007 by Elsevier Ltd.
All rights of reproduction in any form reserved.
ISBN: 978-0-080-47487-8

Starke-Meyerring, D. (2007). The implications of blogs on professional writing: Speed, reach, engagement, and the art of the self in the participatory web. In G. Rijlaarsdam (Series Ed.) and D. Alamargot, P. Terrier, & J.-M. Cellier (Vol. Eds.), Studies in Writing, Vol. 21, Written Documents in the Workplace, 125–138.

according to a market analyst study (Market Sentinel, Onalytica, & immediate future, Inc., 2005) will be significant and long lasting.

Jarvis's blog is not unique. Quite the contrary: Technorati, one of the main blogosphere tracking services, currently (in April 2006) tracks more than 35 million blogs. In addition, as its 2006 report *The State of the Blogosphere* notes, the number of blogs doubles every 6 months, with a new blog being created every second of each day. Over the last 3 years alone, the number of blogs has grown sixty-fold. As the number of blogs grows, so does their coverage in the mainstream media. In fact, news about blogs abounds, reporting about employees losing their jobs over their blogs or—conversely—becoming more influential in the blogosphere than their CEOs, about CEOs knowing or not knowing how to blog, and about businesses changing their products or their labor or environmental practices in response to customer protest in the blogosphere. As Miller and Shepherd (2004) and Herring, Scheidt, Bonus, and Wright (2005) point out, these reports of disruption are a clear indication that new genres are emerging—that new communication practices are being worked out as organizations grapple with the new potentials and constraints blogs present. In Miller and Shepherd's words, "The appearance of a new genre is an event of great rhetorical interest because it means that the 'stabilized-enough,' negotiated balance between innovation and decorum has broken down and a new one is under development" (n.p.). Thus, blogs are an indication that writing on the web is undergoing a deep shift—one that involves considerable disruption in the workplace and in workplace writing.

This chapter examines this shift and its implications for businesses and consequently for workplace writing. Given the purpose of this handbook, however, the chapter cannot provide an in-depth or comprehensive analysis of this burgeoning communication technology; instead, the purpose of the chapter is to provide an introduction to blogs as a growing and contested space for professional writing, to situate them in the context of recent shifts in writing on the World Wide Web, and to begin assessing their implications for business and consequently for workplace writing. Since the focus of the handbook is on workplace writing, the chapter concentrates on blogs written by professionals in the workplace or by customers and other stakeholders about businesses or about their experience interacting with businesses.

1 Defining Blogs

At their core, blogs, or web logs, are web sites whose main component consists of a list of—usually date-stamped—postings, which can include text, photos (photoblogs), videos (vlogs), podcasts, or visual and textual messages from mobile devices (so-called moblogs or mobile blogs). What is significant about this core element of blogs is that the list of postings is automatically presented in reverse-chronological order, so that the most recent posting always appears first. In contrast to traditional web sites, blogs therefore are expected to be updated frequently and regularly—sometimes several times a day. In addition, unlike traditional web sites, blogs often invite reader comments on postings; provide opportunities for visitors to subscribe to the postings, via so-called web feeds; and offer numerous other linking features that integrate them into the conversations occurring on the web (Blood, 2002; Herring et al., 2005; Miller & Shephard, 2004; Walker, 2003; Wikipedia, 2006).

Blogs emerged in the 1990s as a tool for web designers and software engineers to keep track of their work online. The first use of the word "web log" is often attributed to Jørn Barger, who used it in his blog *Robot Wisdom* (http://www.robotwisdom.com) for the first time in 1997 and defined it as "a sort of personal newsmagazine on the Web" (http://www.robotwisdom.com/weblogs/orientation.html). Originally, the popularity of blogs was limited because their design required knowledge of hypertext markup language and access to server space. However, their popularity surged when free instant blogging software began to emerge in 1999, such as LiveJournal.com, MoveableType.com, and the popular blogspot software by Pyra Labs, one of the first free blogging services available. When Google, the popular search engine company, decided to buy Pyra Labs in 2003 and to offer its blogspot software as a Google service (now at blogger.com) along with free server space, public attention to blogs increased again, as did their popularity.

In contrast to the beginning, when blogs served predominantly as tech journals or as personal diaries, they now serve a dizzying array of purposes for different people or groups—individuals, public citizen groups, and businesses. For individuals, citizens, and public groups, blogs can, for example, serve as personal diaries helping friends and family members keep in touch, as citizen journalism blogs presenting alternative views of mainstream media news, as political campaign blogs soliciting candidate support, or as social activist blogs working to involve citizens in addressing pressing social issues. Likewise, in the workplace, blogs can serve just as many divergent purposes; for example, they can serve as work-team blogs helping team members keep track of their projects and share information, as tech-support blogs keeping customers up to date and supporting their use of a company product, as employee blogs adding a human touch to customer interaction, as crisis blogs providing continual updates on the crisis and its solutions, as CEO blogs aspiring to provide intellectual leadership in the industry, or as direct e-commerce blogs promoting and creating interest in company products and services.

Given this array of purposes, it is perhaps not surprising that their potential for redefining workplace practices and in particular workplace writing is considerable. However, to understand the shift blogs represent in professional writing, it is important to contextualize their emergence in the larger changes that have recently occurred on the Internet, especially in the participatory Web.

2   Situating Blogs in the Context of the Participatory Web

Although blogs have so far received perhaps the greatest news coverage and have had the greatest influence on the workplace, they are part of a larger shift toward a more collaborative and participatory web—what some have come to call Web 2.0 (O'Reilly, 2005). In its early stages, the World Wide Web was mostly an information resource in which those with sufficient knowledge of coding language or appropriate web design software published their content. To a large extent, the early web was mostly a reproduction of practices from the print age: content was prepared, published, and remained fairly static for others to read. Since the late 1990s, however, the web has turned from a "read-only" (at least for most people) into a "read-and-write medium" in which anyone with a web browser can now instantly write anything they like or collaborate with other web users. Unlike in read-only times, people now do not need web design software or knowledge of coding languages, nor do they need to purchase server space. They simply use one of the freely available web-based software tools (e.g. www.blogger.com) from their browser and can start writing, collaborating, and communicating with other "netizens" on the web.

This shift toward a read-and-write medium has also been characterized by the increasing emergence of web-based (rather than computer-based) writing and collaboration software, some of it created in open-source spirit, with software developers contributing their time and expertise to the development of software that is freely available for everyone to use. Often referred to as "Web 2.0" or "social media" in popular Internet lingo, the array of social networking sites and software is dizzying. Web2.0awards.org, a site dedicated to rating these new sites, alone lists more than 300 winners and honorable mentions of Web 2.0 sites, including free web-based collaborative writing software (e.g., Writely at www.writely.com, Rallypoint at http://rallypointhq.com, or ThinkFree Office Online at http://online.thinkfree.com); online real-time collaboration software (e.g., campfire at campfirenow.com); collaborative map creation software (e.g., wayfaring.com or frappr.com); photo, music, and video sharing sites; peer news production sites (e.g., newsvine.com, digg.com); as well as software designed to help users create, sort through, rate, and keep track of collaborative web sites (e.g., wetpaint.com, jot.com, mediawiki.org, wordpress.org, technorati.com, blogniscient.com, bloglines.com).

According to Tim Berners-Lee (2000), inventor of the WWW's architecture, this shift toward a participatory read-and-write web was the original intent behind its design. Early on, Berners-Lee lamented that the first browsers predominantly allowed for reading, but less so for writing and editing. As Berners-Lee noted, "the web is more a social creation than a technical one. I designed it for a social effect—to help people work together—and not as a technical toy" (p. 123). It is in the context of this shift toward a participatory "read-and-write" WWW that blogs have emerged and through which they exert their influence on business and consequently on workplace writing.

To examine the shift blogs represent, I use Gurak's (2001) cyberliteracy framework of key Internet concepts—speed, reach, interactivity, and anonymity—which was derived from her Internet research in order to determine how the Internet alters communication compared to previous media. As Gurak notes, these concepts are "the functional units by which most internet communication takes place. These terms help us understand how cyberspace functions, how this technology is the same as and different from others before it, and how we can work with the technology to become cyberliterate" (p. 29). However, Gurak's analysis was focused on the early Internet, when blogs were relatively unknown. While her analysis was accordingly designed to examine the shift in communication on the Internet compared to previous media, I use the framework here to examine the shift in communication on the early web compared to the current participatory web, specifically blogs, to understand what constitutes the shift that has given rise to what Miller and Shepherd refer to as the breakdown of the "negotiated balance between innovation and decorum" (n.p.). For this purpose, I briefly discuss each concept, using them as lenses through which to read blogs. I then apply the framework to a brief discussion of reported blogging cases to assess their impact on businesses and professional writing.

2.1 Speed and Reach

Speed and reach, according to Gurak (2001), are two of the key concepts that redefine communication on the Internet. As Gurak notes, *"with the split second it takes to press a single key, text, sounds, or visual information can be sent across the globe*" (p. 30). News stories about the speed with which emails, for example, have been forwarded, spread, and posted to discussion boards abound. As Gurak notes, however, this speed has numerous implications, ranging from redundancy and repetitiveness to expectations of a more spontaneous, and therefore more casual, conversational, and perhaps less crafted or edited communication style.

Reach, according to Gurak (2001), is "the partner of speed" (p. 33). As she explains, "one keystroke can send a message to thousands of people. This message can be sent on to others, posted to a web site, posted to Usenet newsgroups, and sent into countries with travel restrictions but no restrictions on incoming electrons" (pp. 33–34). Drawing on Kaufer and Carley's (1993) theory of communication and distance, Gurak emphasizes the multiplicity of Internet reach—the possibility of instant one-to-many, one-to-one, as well as many-to-many and many-to-one communication. In addition, what makes communication on the Internet unique compared to previous media is that once sent, these messages tend to be difficult to constrain, contain, retract, or even erase. Finally, as Gurak observes, the reach of the Internet also allows individuals to find and form communities with like-minded people regardless of their physical location as long as they have Internet access.

Blogs intensify the speed and reach of the Internet and take it to new levels for a number of reasons. First, with regard to speed, thanks to freely available and easy-to-use blogging software, blogs can be created and updated within minutes compared to the considerable time that was required to create a traditional web site. Second, with a listing of updated postings in reverse chronological order at their core, blogs beg regular updates. Indeed, for many authors, timely updates are the hallmark of blogs, whereby timely is understood as daily, or even several times a day, but at least once a week (Blood, 2002). The expectation of timeliness is so great that blogging handbooks advise bloggers to notify their readers if they for some reason, such as a vacation, plan to be away from their blog for a longer period of time (Blood, 2002).

Third, many blogs provide web feeds or machine readable content subscriptions made available to visitors through RSS (Really Simple Syndication), Atom, or other formats. Subscribers can then use news aggregator software to compile web feeds from multiple blogs, mainstream media sites, or other sources, thus always receiving the updates to a blog automatically rather than checking the various blogs manually. As a result, web feed subscribers to a blog receive new postings immediately and automatically and can immediately visit the updated blog and post a comment, or they can write a response on their own blog. The subscribed blogger in turn will likely also have subscribers, so that a message is spread much like an immediate chain reaction—clearly more quickly than through traditional web sites in the past.

Moreover, web feeds increase the reach of blogs to subscribed bloggers and beyond, whereas a traditional web site typically relied on visitors passing by or searching for it with a search engine. In contrast to other Internet technologies such as email, blogs have a greater reach because their messages are constantly available, and they are available to anyone who happens onto the blog—whether as a subscriber, through a search engine, or through a link. Likewise, other technologies such as usenet groups or discussion groups have tended to be more contained in themselves.

Fourth, blogs tend to have a more intricate linking structure than most other Internet technologies and therefore are much more networked throughout the web. For example, blogs often facilitate conversations or connections through such components as permalinks, which allow other bloggers to link to a posting in a reliable way, or trackbacks, which allow blog readers to link to other blogs that have created a link to the posting. Depending on the purpose or function of the blog, links within a posting also connect the blog to other blogs or other web sites. In fact, for many blogs, links to other blogs and web sites with the author's personal commentary even become the main staple of the blog (Blood, 2002; Wikipedia, 2006). Finally, blogs also commonly provide links along the margins for constant access to sites the author or authoring group considers particularly relevant or important as well as a blogroll—a list with links to important blogs the author or authoring group follow on a regular basis. As a result of their intricate linking structure, blogs are not only well networked, but they also achieve high rankings on Google searches because the search engine uses the linking structure of web sites to determine their possible relevance to a search query.

Altogether, blogs clearly intensify the speed and reach of messages, so that what a well-networked blogger writes about has the potential to be spread much faster to a much greater number of readers than was common of other traditional Internet technologies. As a result, professional writers interacting with one customer are in fact potentially interacting with thousands of other customers—if the customer is a well-networked blogger—without possibly being aware of the speed and reach of the communication.

2.2 *From Interactivity to Participation and Engagement*

As Gurak (2001) points out, one of the most important concepts that distinguish the Internet from previous media such as print and television is its multidirectional communication and interactivity. Unlike television or traditional print media, the Internet allows for instantaneous "talking back" (p. 44) and joining into conversations with other individuals and groups. In addition to interacting with a web site through its hyperlinks, traditionally, this interactivity involved, for example, sending an email to a web site author; filling out a web-based form on an e-commerce web site; posting a product review on an e-commerce site; joining a usenet group, a discussion board, or a listserv; meeting in synchronous chatrooms; and, more recently, instant messaging with friends or colleagues.

Blogs, however, have not only intensified interactivity, they have also redefined it. As Blood (2002) observes, blogs are all about building "social alliances" (p. X/10). Indeed, they deeply reflect the collaborative nature of the participatory web, which Berners-Lee distinguishes from the interactivity of the early web as follows: "We should be able not only to interact with other people, but to create with other people. *Intercreativity* is the process of making things or solving problems together. If *interactivity* is not just sitting there passively in front of a display screen, then intercreativity is not just sitting there in front of something "interactive" (p. 169).

Unlike traditional web sites, then, blogs are less about publication than they are about participation (O'Reilly, 2005), the co-creation of knowledge, and the building of relationships and connections. They accomplish this shift in a number of ways: they often facilitate an open genre structure that allows for participation and co-creation (Starke-Meyerring, 2005), they are usually built around an intricate linking structure that is deeply social, and they have given rise to an intricate and deeply social blogosphere committed to tracking conversations, networks, and influence.

Most blogging tools facilitate blogs with an open genre structure in that they enable blogging authors to invite others to contribute postings to the blog or to add comments to a posting, ultimately allowing audiences to participate in producing discourse. In this respect, blogs differ greatly from print genres, such as books or manuals, which foster a relatively clear distinction between writers and readers or users, requiring writers to analyze readers in order to produce a document that typically excludes readers or users from participating in the production of the document. Even early Internet genres, such as web sites and e-mail, are relatively closed in that user participation in their production is limited. In contrast, blogs contribute to the shift toward open systems (Spinuzzi, 2002; Spinuzzi, Bowie, Rodgers, & Li, 2003; Spinuzzi & Zachry, 2000), with communication shifting "from a consumer model of documentation-as-product towards a citizenship model in which citizens contribute to and collaboratively develop information" (Spinuzzi, 2002, p. 194). This open genre structure blurs the boundaries between writers and readers more so than in earlier Internet technologies.

In addition, as mentioned earlier, blogs rest on an intricate linking structure, including links within the postings, along the margins, and in the blog roll; trackbacks; and permalinks for postings. What is most important about this intricate linking structure, however, is its deeply social nature designed to facilitate networked and participatory communication. Their links within their postings, for example, tend to weave a network with other blogs and Internet sites, which differ sharply from traditional websites, especially commercial ones. As Blood (2002) emphasizes, for example, "commercial websites spent years chanting the mantra of stickiness: the ability to get visitors who came to their sites to stay there, even creating policies that prohibited the inclusion of external links anywhere on their sites" (p. 9). In contrast, on blogs, Blood explains, "It is the link that creates the community in which weblogs exist" (p. 19). With blogs, then, interactivity is not limited to an email to a web site or to a self-contained usenet group, discussion board, or chatroom. Instead, their intricate linking structure enables an ongoing conversation across the web.

Finally, blogs reshape the interactive nature of the Internet because they have given rise to an intricate and deeply social blogosphere committed to tracking conversations, networks, and influence rather than simply finding published information—the main purpose of most traditional search engines in the early web. Technorati, perhaps the most popular blogosphere tracking site, for example, keeps track of the most popular blogs, ranking them according to the number of unique incoming links in the last 6 months as an indication of active readership and thus blog influence. Bloggers can also set their blogging software to ping the site or other such sites—that is, to notify the site whenever a new message is posted to the blog, so that others in the blogosphere can track the most recent postings. In addition, bloggers can "claim their blogs" to add their profile, have their blogs featured, and create watch lists that allow them to keep track of incoming links and thus of conversations between blogs. Finally, the site tracks the most frequently linked news items, movies, personal videos, and books. Other blogosphere tracking sites similarly facilitate the tracking, ranking, and networking of blogs. Blogstreet.com, for example, offers a blogback feature, which allows bloggers to see blogs that have included them in their blogrolls; a blog neighbourhood feature, which allows bloggers to discover related blogs; and a "blog influence quotient," a type of ranking that is in turn based on the influence (not the number) of the blogs that include the blogger on their blog roll.

As this analysis of blogs through the lens of interactivity shows, blogs represent an important shift in interactivity compared to communication in the early web: while traditional business web sites may have been able to get by with the limited interactivity of email addresses, web forms, or isolated reviews by customers, in the blogosphere, this interactivity is turned into "intercreativity" (Berners-Lee, 2000) and participation, calling for the engagement of readers in open genres—an engagement that reduces social distance and blurs the boundaries between readers and writers. In the blogosphere, then, writers create documents not as much *for* readers as *with* them.

Moreover, participation in the blogosphere also means writing in an emerging attention economy, in which "*a superabundance of information*" makes attention the scarcest resource (Lankshear & Knobel, 2001, 2003). This scarcity of attention has numerous implications for professional writing. Reviewing several theories of the attention economy, Lankshear and Knobel point in particular to the need for considerable discursive sophistication—what they call "*powerful writing*," the ability to gain influence in a highly competitive attention market.

2.3   *From Anonymity to the Art of the Self*

Drawing on rhetorical theory, Gurak (2001) notes that the controlling factor in persuading or influencing people is not the appeal to logic or even to emotion, but rather to the projected character and credibility of a speaker—what rhetoricians call ethos or ethical appeal. To a large extent, people make decisions about what to believe based on the projected character or trustworthiness of the speaker, which in turn must be perceived as reflecting the values of the community. As Gurak emphasizes, however, the problem is that on the *Internet*, it is relatively easy for people to conceal their identity—at least barring court subpoenas to Internet Service Providers for server records. Similarly, as Turkle (1997) observed, on the Internet, people can more easily assume any identity and project any character they would like. Accordingly, Gurak considered anonymity as another key concept in Internet-based communication.

In contrast to the early web, however, blogs redefine anonymity because they exist in a blogosphere that is characterized by a scarcity of attention and a concomitant focus on influence, which in turn depends on discursive sophistication, in particular in the projection of a credible self or ethos. While it is certainly possible to project a compelling ethos anonymously, the ethos of blogs depends to a large extent on the inclusion of personal and private details about the daily interactions of the blogger(s). Such an ethos can be more difficult to achieve with an anonymous identity, as it is much more easily questioned and less trusted. Accordingly, as Miller and Shepherd (2004) conclude from their analysis of blogs as emerging genres, "the blog-as-genre is a contemporary contribution to the art of the self" (n.p.), a conclusion that is consistent with the views of long-time bloggers.

Jørn Barger, for example, explained that "one of the greatest pleasures of reading weblogs is getting to know their editors" (http://www.robotwisdom.com/weblogs/index.html). Similarly, blogging handbooks emphasize that one of the hallmarks of blogs is their projection of a strong ethos, including a strong personal voice and the discussion of personal experiences—perhaps even such minutiae as whom the blogger met or what he or she had for lunch. In her blogging handbook, Blood (2002) likewise emphasizes, "The appeal of each weblog is grounded thoroughly in the personality of its writer: his interests, his opinions, and his personal mix of links and commentary" (p. 6). As she explains, what makes a blog influential is the "point of view, discrimination in choosing links, and experience of the writer. It is the writer's unique fusion of interests, enthusiasms, and prejudices—her personality—that makes a weblog compelling. In short, a weblog's quality is ultimately based on the authenticity of its voice" (p. 59).

Blood's observations are consistent with those of other researchers. In their study of a random sample of almost 300 weblogs, Herring et al. (2005) found personal content on more than 70% of the blogs. Similarly, Miller and Shepherd (2004) contextualize blogs in a cultural moment of an increased desire "to catch the intensely private moments of others" (n.p.) as expressed in the intense media obsession with the private lives of public figures and the emergence and high popularity of reality TV shows, which allow for an extended voyeuristic gaze on the private lives of ordinary people. According to their analysis, projecting a personal ethos in this highly personalized environment, or in Miller and Shepherd's words, an "intensified, mediated identity" constitutes "the rhetorical achievement of the blog" (n.p.).

Granted, like much in communication, the specific expectations of a credible ethos will depend on the particular community in which the blogger participates and on the particular situation in which he or she engages; nevertheless, bloggers seem to draw on two resources in particular to project a credible ethos: their choices of links and their independence in presenting alternative views to those of mainstream practices, institutions, and media. As Blood (2002) points out in her handbook, "it is the link that gives weblogs their credibility by creating a transparency that is impossible in any other medium" (p. 19). According to Blood, bloggers who maintain a subject-focused blog especially realize that the links they provide reflect directly on their credibility. Not surprisingly, then, Blood notes, "few people are willing to put just anything on their page" (p. 31). And as Miller and Shepherd (2004) remind us, drawing on Aristotle, "character is manifested in choice, as Aristotle had it" (n.p.).

It is perhaps for this reason that a blogger's independence in selecting links and choosing items to blog about is so important. As Blood (2002) stresses, "the weblog's strength is fundamentally tied to its position outside of mainstream media: observing, commenting, and honestly reacting to both current events and the media coverage they generate" (p. 23). As such, weblogs can be expected to resist traditional, highly controlled institutional discourse. In the case of communication with businesses, the ethos of blogs may even represent the antithesis to the centrally controlled and marshalled discourse of public relations (PR) departments.

Situated in a vast blogosphere, bloggers, then, depend on considerable discursive sophistication, especially in "the art of the self," to gain attention and influence. Given that their projection of a credible ethos may well depend on a personal perspective, independence, and alternative communication practices compared to those of the mainstream, their ethos may likely clash with traditionally controlled organizational communication practices.

3 Implications for Businesses and Professional Writing

As the analysis above shows, blogs constitute a new rhetorical space characterized by intensified speed and reach as well as open, participatory, highly networked communication. With these characteristics, blogs facilitate what Tapscott and Ticoll (2003) refer to as the increasing transparency of business practices, which they define as "the accessibility of information to stakeholders of institutions, regarding matters that affect their interests" (p. 22). Blogs give stakeholders of corporations unprecedented access to information about corporate practices, allow them to spread such information to fellow stakeholders around the world in mere seconds, and enable them to self-organize across locations and to take action on this information. As Tapscott and Ticoll put it, stakeholders "probe deep into a company's supply chain to expose environmental and human rights practices, then demand and force change" (p. 19). For this purpose, blogs can provide customers with new ways of organizing that which are decidedly different from those in the past: "In the past, consumers were isolated. A few joined quaint consumer groups; others talked to neighbors about products they might buy, or read the main source of objective advice, Consumer Reports. Today, they self-organize" (p. 19). For corporations, one of the challenges becomes how to engage diverse stakeholders in dialogue about company products, practices, and performance by participating in the blogosphere. This involvement in the blogosphere affects how both managers and employees engage customers, investors, and other stakeholders as well as how these stakeholders in turn engage businesses.

3.1 Implications for Manager and Employee Communication with Business Stakeholders

Both managers and employees are expected to engage customers and other stakeholders in the blogosphere. Managers in particular are expected to provide intellectual leadership, for which developing an influential blog becomes an essential task. In the blogosphere, influence, however, depends not as much on position as on "the art of the self"—the projection of a compelling authentic and personal ethos. It is thus very likely that an employee can become more influential than a CEO, thus becoming potentially a more important influence on customer or investor decision-making than a CEO.

For some CEOs, however, the ethos of blogs is difficult to master, so that their blogs remain steeped in the hyperbolic promotional ethos of press releases. In the blogosphere, their struggles with the new ethos of blogs easily stick out like a sore thumb and easily become the subject of news satire. Thus, Stephen Evans (2005) from BBC News, for example, cites General Motors corporate management's blog (http://fastlane.gmblogs.com) as one example of a CEO blog that remains stuck in PR ethos with statements such as, "I am enthusiastic about the Buick Lacrosse ... It's wonderfully executed, has fabulous workmanship, is dead-quiet, and, with the sport suspension and for the four-cam V-6, has sensationally good dynamics." In contrast, the blog of SUN CEO Jonathan Schwartz (http://blogs.sun.com/roller/page/jonathan) is frequently noticed for its projection of a blogging ethos that transcends past controlled corporate PR and instead of mere self promotion also offers industry analysis, directions the company is pondering, conversations Schwartz has had with various government officials, including the President of Brazil, or speeches he has given. The blog provides the rationale for company decisions and initiatives as well as insights into the daily schedule and acitivities of its writer. A glance at some of the recent post titles on his blog reveals a concern with issues beyond those of SUN alone and shows his attempt at providing analysis of larger trends, e.g., "The Brazil Effect" (a posting about his meeting with the Brazilian president), "The Network is the Computer," or "Why Free Standards Matter."

Nevertheless, employee blogs can become more popular than those of CEOs. They may become even so well subscribed to that the employee becomes the de facto mouth piece of the company, attracting an entire international fan community as in the case of Microsoft's Richard Scoble's blog on Microsoft products and software development (http://scobleizer.wordpress.com). The popularity of such influential employee blogs ultimately may make it almost impossible or at least difficult for companies to dismiss their writers without upsetting hundreds of thousands of customers who subscribe to their blogs. Scoble's blog, for example, achieves a high Technorati rating of number 21 out of 36 million blogs tracked by the site (http://www.technorati.com/pop/blogs/, April 22, 2006). Not surprisingly, then, for many subscribers, this employee, rather than the company's PR department or even the company CEO, has become the mouthpiece of the company, despite the blog's disclaimer that "Robert Scoble works at Microsoft (title: technical evangelist). Everything here, though, is his personal opinion and is not read or approved before it is posted. No warranties or other guarantees will be offered as to the quality of the opinions or anything else offered here."

At Microsoft, currently more than 2000 employees are blogging (see http://blogs.msdn.com/Bloggers.aspx) and building relationships with customers. The number alone suggests an openness that is beyond the control of centralized, carefully controlled PR initiatives. In essence, then, instead of a specially trained select group of PR professionals, any employee with a blog can become a powerful PR advocate or disaster for their company, depending on their discursive sophistication, the training they receive, and the extent to which their corporate policies mesh with the open, independent, participatory, and spontaneous ethos of the blogosphere.

Unfortunately, employees currently seem to receive little support as they are learning how to navigate the new speed and reach, participatory nature, and the "new art of the self" in the blogosphere. According to media reports, a number of employees have lost their jobs as a result of their blogs. Widely publicized cases include the case of the Wells Fargo receptionist who was fired over blog comments criticizing a supervisor, the Delta Airlines employee who was fired over the pictures of herself she posted on her blog, an associate product manager at Google whose blog had included comments about the shortcomings of the company's health plan, or a contractor at Microsoft who had included comments about newly purchased Apple computers on his blog (Armour, 2005; Deutsch, 2005). In fact, a new term, "being dooced," has emerged to refer to employees who have been fired for their blogs. Created by a web designer in the U.S. who was fired for her blog (www.dooce.com) when she mentioned co-workers in her blog entries, the term has come to represent the clash between traditional and new communication practices that surrounds the emergence of blogs in the workplace.

3.2 Implications for Stakeholder Engagement of Businesses

While blogs created internally by both managers and employees present a radical shift away from past practices of centralized, carefully vetted, and controlled PR messages, external blogs created by customers and activist groups may have an even greater impact on business and workplace writing. Increasingly, such blogs are used to share dissatisfaction with customer service, discuss problems with company products or unethical practices, or launch sustained activist campaigns designed to push for corporate change, for example in labor, environmental, or social practices. And businesses are only beginning to understand the shift in the ways their customers and stakeholders communicate, oftentimes underestimating the speed and reach of blogs or attempting to draw on traditional controlled PR messages, even though such messages represent the antithesis to communication in the participatory web.

As mentioned in the introduction, perhaps one of the most widely publicized cases illustrating the role of blogs in customer service communication is that of Jeff Jarvis (www.buzzmachine.com), a former TV critic, who began blogging about his experience of buying a defective Dell laptop and trying to obtain customer service. Jarvis wrote about his "saga," sparing no details about his interactions with Dell customer service, PR, and technical representatives, thus ultimately, giving them an audience much larger than himself. As an influential blogger, Jarvis attracted thousands of customers with similar experiences, who also shared their experience in lengthy comments on his blog. In addition, he captured his experience with the shortcut "Dell Hell," thus creating a meme—a catchy idea that spreads rapidly on the Internet (Lankshear and Knobel, 2003). Enabled by RSS, blog tracking sites, and other network mechanisms, the increased speed and reach of blogs allowed the idea to travel quickly, so that it was soon covered by mainstream media around the world. The Dell response was reported to be somewhat slow. The company eventually closed its once popular customer service forums, and in a media interview, Michael Dell was quoted to have said, "We don't want anyone to have a bad experience, whether they are a blogger or anyone else" (Moltzen, 2006), indicating that Dell had not yet distinguished between a customer and a blogging customer.

In addition to pushing for better customer service, blogs have also taken on questionable corporate practices such as privacy violations. The Kirkville Blog (http://www.mcelhearn.com), authored by Apple fan and multiple author of Apple books Kirk McElhearn, for example, recently was one of the leading blogs questioning and protesting Apple's newly revised iTunes product. Apple had introduced a new service called MiniStore™, which recommended potential additional songs for purchase. For this purpose, the service involved collecting information about a user's songs—without notifying the user—as soon as the user clicked on a song, regardless if the song had been purchased from iTunes. As McElhearn noted in his blog, "Apple has overstepped its limits, and this spyware (because it sends information to a server) and adware (because it displays information to attempt to sell you products) is a very serious breach of the trust I have long had in Apple's products" (n.p.). McElhearn's blog was not the only one to criticize Apple; some of them had quickly created a meme to capture their protest—"iTunes—spyTunes"—and had begun to disseminate it in the blogosphere. Apple responded immediately, apologizing for its mistake and quickly issuing a new version of the MiniStore™, which now alerts users to the feature, allowing them to disable it and providing them with the option to opt in or abstain from having their personal data transmitted. Clearly, the company had distinguished between a customer and a blogging customer and had realized the need for a fast response.

Businesses also increasingly face a growing number of networked "watch" blogs attempting to influence corporate practices. These blogs are often set up specifically with the express purpose of pushing for the reform of labor, environmental, or other corporate practices in corporations. As the largest corporation, Wal-Mart, a U.S.-based retail chain, has increasingly attracted such organized protest. Wal-Mart Watch, for example, unites a number of organizations, including such groups as the American Independent Business Association,

National Council of Women's Organizations, Sierra Club, Interfaith Worker Justice, Campus Progress, Teamsters, and others. The organization identifies itself as a "nationwide public education campaign" designed to "challenge the world's largest retailer to become a better employer, neighbor, and corporate citizen." (http://walmartwatch.com/home/pages/about). In addition to a basic web site, the site offers a blog (http://walmartwatch.com/blog), which provides updates and commentary on Wal-Mart corporate practices, thus creating an ongoing dynamic community with new postings and updates, and comments from visitors who thus remain continually involved. In response to its negative publicity from such blogs, Wal-Mart has begun an initiative of contacting influential bloggers with positive views of the company, asking them to blog about company news—often before the news is transmitted to mainstream media (Barbaro, 2006).

4 Conclusion

Blogs have become an important discursive space for professional writing—one that represents a critical shift in Internet communication in the context of the participatory. As a part of this shift, blogs with their regularly updated postings, web feeds, and intricate social-linking structure intensify the speed and reach of communication. Moreover, as open genres that allow for the co-creation of discourse, they emphasize participation and ongoing conversation over publication, thus blurring the distinctions between readers and writers and demanding engagement with others. In this way, they contribute to a new transparency (Tapscott & Ticoll, 2003) that alters how professionals in the workplace communicate with and engage customers, investors, and other stakeholders. Specifically, the personal, independent, and spontaneous ethos of blogs will likely clash with traditional, highly controlled institutional discourse.

For businesses, this shift and the concomitant renegotiation of communication norms have a number of implications. First, there is a difference between a customer and a blogging customer who knows how to use the participatory web to engage other like-minded customers. In the participatory web, then, customers, investors, and other stakeholders will unlikely wait for government legislation to regulate service, environmental, labor, or other corporate performance standards. They will instead, as Tapscott and Ticoll (2003) note, take to the blogosphere to engage in dialogue with each other as well as with companies directly. Second, to engage stakeholders, both managers and employees are increasingly expected to participate in the blogosphere. In fact, given the ethos of openness that characterizes the blogosphere, companies that remain closed and do not open up to the blogosphere may increasingly be viewed with suspicion. Third, to participate in the blogosphere, companies will need to understand the shift in communication the blogosphere represents, and they will need to design communication policies that are conducive to the spontaneous, open, personal, participatory, and independent ethos of the blogosphere. Finally, in the participatory web, there is also a difference between an employee and a blogging employee. Depending on their discursive sophistication, any employee with a blog can potentially become an influential mouthpiece for a company, helping inform and shape customer and investor decisions, or they can become a PR disaster. Because influence in the blogosphere depends considerably on discursive sophistication, or "powerful writing"

(Lankshear and Knobel, 2001), blogs also issue a renewed call for the study and teaching of professional writing.

Given the disruption the participatory web, and here specifically the blogosphere, represents for the business environment, however, this call for the study and teaching of professional writing cannot be one for "quick fix-it" blogging workshops. For just as a "quick fix-it" workshop on a particular accounting procedure is unlikely to turn an employee into a sophisticated accountant, a "quick fix-it" workshop on a particular writing technology cannot turn an employee into a sophisticated writer. Rather, the case of blogs and the disruption they represent in the workplace are an indication of how central and influential an activity writing has become. With blogs, the speed and the reach of writing have increased exponentially, and carefully controlled centralized messages are being undermined by a participatory ethos of openness and transparency. The disruption resulting from the participatory web also vividly illustrates what is at stake in professional writing: its impact can range from dismissal to guru status for employees or from costly PR nightmares to engaged customers. Instead of "quick fix-it" workshops, therefore, discursive sophistication in the workplace requires systematic, regular, and research-based instruction in writing; it requires considering such instruction as a part of a company's knowledge infrastructure, along with technology, technological support, and policies that empower employees to engage customers and other stakeholders in the participatory web.

Chapter 10

The Production of Work Instructions in an Industrial Workplace: The Impact of a Functional Writer's Work Context on the Outcome of His Activity

Véronique Barret, Isabelle Clerc and Sylvie Montreuil

In this chapter, we stress the significant influence produced by the work context on the activity of a writer of work instructions in an industrial workplace, as is shown in the case of a content specialist employed by his company as a process engineer. Most models of written production describe the immediate context as being the work environment. However, in order to accurately grasp the constraints confronting a functional writer (i.e., a non-expert writer) in the workplace, the writer's work context must be examined from within a broader perspective. Some effort will have to be dedicated to sketching out the different circles in which the individual initially hired for his or her technical knowledge must operate.

As it turns out, the functional writer's instruction-writing tasks have never ranked as a top priority. They have instead grown out of his numerous obligations, which themselves have arisen in response to constraints of both an internal and external nature. By way of illustration, we describe the activities of a functional writer whom we observed in a manufacturing firm located in Quebec, Canada.

1 Research Problematics

Communication in the workplace is, at this time, an emerging field of research, particularly since the integration of the human resource-centred management approaches known as High Commitment Management (Tremblay & Simard, 2005; Wils, Labelle, Guérin, & Tremblay, 1998; Wood, 1996), which ascribe a predominant role to communication and, with this, the language-based component (linguistic basis) of work. In addition to the advent of this new vision of management, there is also the development of the global economy and the implementation of international quality standards designed, in particular, to guarantee the traceability of manufacturing operations. "In any company, the decision to undertake a quality program targeting certification implies a transformation in the relationship to language at the workplace. These transformations are compelled by the need to describe the procedures followed and to explicate the rules that must be complied with in order to complete the different tasks" (Olivesi, 2002, p. 141). In turn, these transformations of the work context mean that writing is, more than ever, a mainstay of corporate activity. The volume of technical writing is practically incalculable and its social impact is vitally important in many different ways. For example, in 1986, the explosion of the space shuttle *Challenger* was caused in part by a poorly understood memo (Roy, 2000, p. 34). Furthermore, for businesses the costs associated with the production of poor-quality technical texts are very high: "According to US government estimates, the losses in productivity resulting from employees' difficulties reading and writing amount to $225 billion annually" (Reese as cited in Roy, 2000, p. 36).

If in the scientific community technical texts are the subject of some interest, the focus of research has, however, been more on measuring reader comprehension than on analysing the work performed by the writer. As has been stressed by Heurley and Ganier (2002, p. 247), "Research into the production of technical texts shows a significant lag in comparison with research into use." Furthermore, until now, little research has been devoted in social sciences circles to the writing of technical texts in the industrial sector—and, specifically, to the *in situ* observation of the production context surrounding these texts.

In his model of the writing process dating from 1995 (an updated version of the model developed in Hayes & Flower, 1980), Hayes has defined the context of production in the following terms: "The *Context of production* component, under which is located *Social components*, as represented by the professor and the target reader, and the *Physical components* element, namely, the text that the student writer is in the process of writing, other texts, and a writing aid such as word-processing" (Hayes, 1995, p. 52). This model was developed on the basis of classroom situations and does not address in any great detail the external constraints under which the writer must operate in a work context. Heurley (2001, p. 67) noted that "The situations of design/production and use fall within broader frameworks—institutional, linguistic, religious, economic, etc.—that define numerous external constraints [...]." This being said, these external constraints are not explicated in his work. Schneider (2002) briefly describes various studies that have been performed on texts in context—namely, studies showing the impact of an organizational culture and the social context on components of the final text; studies showing the impact produced by the text production process and texts on a business organization or on efforts to achieve a consensus on a business's mode of organization. In research conducted by Schneider (2002), Brant (1992) and Doheny-Farina (1986), demonstration is provided, in particular, of how the social context and the social structure influence the act of writing. Leplat (2004) notes that only a scant number of studies have been conducted in real work situations, a conclusion confirmed by Smeltzer and Thomas (1994) in a meta-analysis of research performed in context on the manager as writer. As they point out, the existing data have been constituted from questionnaires because access to company premises has been difficult. It would thus seem quite apparent that the context of text production in the workplace has not been adequately documented.

In addition, among the studies that have analysed the writer's work context, the subject has often been professional and technical writers or, on the other hand, actors from the school sector such as students or principals. Functional writers have attracted less attention on the part of researchers probably because they have to be observed at their places of work, into which it is often hard to gain access (aside from the difficulty of finding the time required to integrate an intern in workteams and answer his or her questions, there is also the question of industrial espionage that, understandably, gives pause to a company's upper management when contemplating the prospect of hosting a researcher).

As was noted above, where the process and output of writing is concerned, the concept of context is focused more on the writer's work environment than on what might be called the meta-context. Thus, with a view to gain a new perspective on the work of a functional writer in the workplace, the following questions warrant reflection and analysis, namely: *What is the overall context surrounding the production of technical texts by a functional writer? What is the impact of this context on the demands and constraints bearing on the work of a functional writer? What are the steps involved in the process of producing work instructions for use on a production line?*

In industry, functional writers may include all types of employees, ranging from the plant manager to the employees. Functional writers are specialists of content rather than of writing (Beaudet, 1998). As part of discharging their duties, they must, on a more or less regular basis, produce technical texts bearing on their field of work—e.g., procedures, manufacturing instructions, plans of action, books of specifications, test reports, etc. The primary (or main) work activity of a functional writer is not writing. Rather, writing is a secondary activity coming within the framework of this employee's primary activity, which is defined on the basis of the duties he or she discharges within the company. Thus it is important to approach a functional writer's text production activity within a context that is broader than that of the writing task itself and, accordingly, of the immediate context surrounding this writing activity. First and foremost, the focus should be placed on the writer's primary task so as to contextualize and thereby gain further insight into the writing task under which it has been subsumed. In addition, to genuinely grasp the role of the overall context on the secondary activity consisting in writing, and thus into the writer and the text object itself (the outcome of the writing-oriented work activity), it is necessary to analyse the particular context of the company in which the primary activity is integrated. Furthermore, in the context of the global economy, it is also important to have a picture of the context in which the company itself is operating (in this instance, the manufacturing company's entire output is subject to market fluctuations—e.g., competition from Asia, the exchange rate (CAN$ vs. US$), etc.). Figure 1 is intended to illustrate the overlap occurring among the various contexts.

The *world context* encompasses factors that fall outside of the company's purview—namely, economic factors (e.g., sector-wide trends), political factors (e.g., laws, regulations, standards, etc.), as well as geographic and sociocultural factors. It is these factors that shape the *company's context*, which in turn shapes the primary context surrounding the work activity of the employees. The company's context encompasses the company's upper management; the organizational culture and corporate objectives; the available financial, material and human resources; and the work organization. The *primary context* is that in which the work activity of individuals is carried out—namely, the activities that are directly related to the job held within the company, or, in other words, that are immediately connected to the competencies

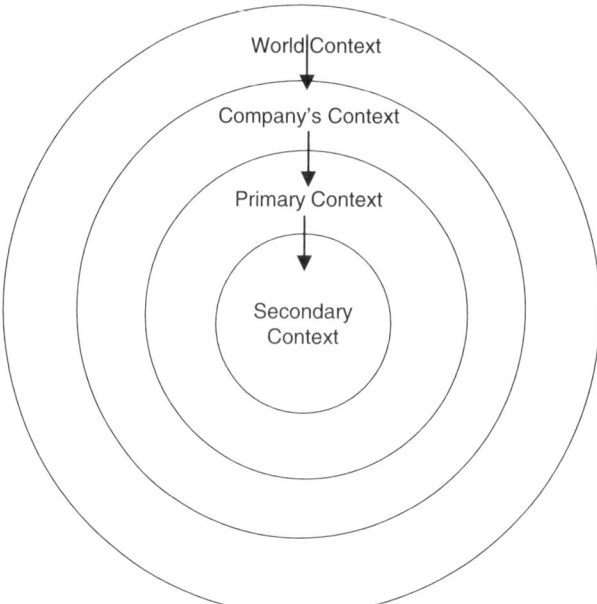

Figure 1: Overlapping of contexts.

for which a given individual was hired. The *secondary context*, which is shaped by the primary context, is the more specific context surrounding a secondary activity stemming from the numerous obligations arising in connection with the primary activity. For the functional writer observed, the activity of producing texts is a secondary activity.

2 An Analysis of the Overall Work Context (Meta-Context) Governing a Functional Writer and His Work Activity: A Case Study

To illustrate the impact of the work context on the production of technical texts in a real work situation, a process engineer at a Quebec industrial plant was followed over 12 consecutive months. The following sections present the conceptual framework developed for this study, the methodology used and a description of the observation process.

2.1 Conceptual Framework

Studying the production context of a functional writer presupposes that this person may be observed *in situ*. It is not enough to simply analyse examples of written production or of discourses of production and reception that have been gathered in the field. Not only must one be able to observe the various activities, one must be integrated into them so as to grasp the constraints, demands, numerous unforeseen obstacles, problems of all kinds, as well as everything that occasionally goes unspoken. In order to observe the writer's work activity as part of a structured, systemic process that also accounted for the social aspects of the work in question, it was necessary to locate a conceptual framework designed for analysing work situations in the workplace. For observation purposes, the most operational of such frameworks draws on ergonomics fundamentals to focus on work activity (Guérin, Laville, Daniellou, Duraffourg, & Kerguelen (2006). It is worth noting at this point that ergonomics research focusing on work activities is primarily conducted in the French-speaking nations and indeed is the approach favoured by a majority of ergonomics researchers in Quebec (De Montmollin, 1995); moreover, this current differs from human factor ergonomics, a predominantly American current that generally serves as a model worldwide. Borrowing from Guérin et al. (2006), it is important to carefully distinguish between the following three realities: the task, the work activity and the work assignment.

In ergonomics, a task is a theoretical construct, previously identified by the units of a company, "whose objective is to reduce to a minimum any unproductive work (i.e., unproductive in terms of performance indicators used at the company), and to optimize productive work. Such objectives can be achieved by eliminating poor work habits or methods and by seeking out and implementing best practices" (Guérin et al., 2006, p. 48). In a nutshell, a task can be defined in terms of what has to be done, which tools and methods are to be used, under what conditions the task will be performed and which employees will be charged with completing it.

Work activity consists of the mobilization of a working individual under conditions of variation or fluctuation. This working individual enacts strategies of regulation and compromise in order to deal with such difficulties or unforeseen departures from plan as may crop up, considering that the conditions governing the performance of work often differ from those prescribed or defined by the task. "Work activity" is used here to mean what the "operator" (the term used by Guérin to describe anyone who performs a work activity)[1] does in relation to the task. Here, "in relation to" is intended to signify that the task and the activity performed by the operator are not fully commensurate with one another: the target objective may be achieved with a varying degree of success, whereas compliance with the prescribed technical and organizational means, standards and contract terms and conditions may occur to a greater or lesser extent. "Activity" is thus used to express the compromise that is achieved by the operator between: "[…] the predefined production objectives, his or her own traits and characteristics, as well as his or her capabilities in respect of reaching these objectives, considering the conditions for carrying out his or her activity made available to him or her by the company, the social processes involved in accrediting employee qualifications, and the governing terms and conditions negotiated in the form of a labour contract" (Guérin et al., 2006, pp. 51–52). The notion of activity refers to "[…] the cognitive, physiological, perceptual, social and psychic strategies used by operators to execute their work as well as the means at their disposal for accomplishing the work" (Lamonde & Montreuil, 1995, p. 721). While the "work activity" current of ergonomics views the operator as an individual who performs a work activity, this is not to say that the individual's behaviours are perforce defined, reductively, in terms of socio-objective finalities alone, however much the latter may be core to any definition (Fillietaz,

---

[1] In our case, a functional writer is as likely to hold the position of an operator as that of an engineer.

2002, p. 75). Other more subjective aspects, such as those identified during the analyses of the activities of employees working under conditions of risks to their safety (Brun, 1992) or in relation to user services (Falzon & Lapeyrière, 1998), have shown that the notion of operator, as applied in ergonomics, also comprehends socio-subjective dimensions.

The work assignment (job) is defined in terms of: the work activity; the real conditions applying to its performance; and the actual outcomes, whether positive or negative, produced by this activity.

2.2 Methodology

To describe the overall context of the work of a functional writer and his or her work activity, we drew on data from the following sources: documents about the company along with its inventory of work instructions; *in situ* observation of work, accompanied by interviews and note-taking; full semi-structured interviews and *ad hoc* interviews about work instructions. Over a 12-month period, Barret spent 85 days in the workplace on a regular basis. The researcher was integrated into the process team (i.e., the team responsible for developing work methods, in particular). She went on guided tours of the plant and carried out an observation session lasting 75 min on a production line. Barret conducted 29 *ad hoc* interviews (lasting from 20 min to 2 h) and 11 semi-structured interviews with company actors at various levels of management (lasting from 1 to 3 h).

This study was conducted on the work premises of a manufacturing company located in an urban centre in the province of Quebec, Canada.[2] The company has a workforce numbering about 300, operates 24 h a day and is certified *ISO 9000*:2000. Both short-run production and mass production characterize the company's operations. Our analysis was developed in the plant used for mass production. For more than a year now, workstations have been organized into production lines for service in mass production. The work organization is modelled according to the principles of taylorism, a doctrine of scientific management founded in the early 20th century by Frederick Taylor, an engineer keen to eliminate inefficiencies and to improve worker productivity. "The tenets of scientific management called for using time-and-motion studies in order to optimize the use of equipment and machinery, rationally planning and sequencing tasks, eliminating unproductive jobs by using a stopwatch to determine the optimum timing of motions, etc." (adapted from "taylorisme" appearing in the *Grand dictionnaire terminologique*, file dated 1984). One of the distinguishing characteristics of taylorism was to distinguish between the design or set-up of tasks and the actual performance of a given job.

In the case of the Quebec manufacturing outfit whose activities we had the opportunity to observe, the newly hired operators often have no experience, a lack which the company was able to overcome thanks to its own training school. The company is constantly undergoing change and functions according to the orders it receives from its clients. These orders are subject to sudden modification, thus potentially entailing frequent changes—occasionally without any prior notice—to the way production is organized. Production is managed according to the principle of "just-in-time," according to which a system of production is

---

[2]By agreement with the company directors, we are unable to name the firm here for reasons of confidentiality.

geared to orders received and not to inventory on hand. Inventory management is performed according to the production principle of tight flow—in other words, the volume of parts and consumable materials is adapted to the volume of goods to be produced in order to satisfy client demand within the agreed times. Management by the company is impacted by the price of the raw materials entering into the fabrication of its products. The company's mostly American clients have, in the last two years, demanded a discount on the products they purchase, owing to the increase in value of the Canadian dollar versus the American dollar. As never before, clients' expectations oblige the company to be highly competitive in terms primarily of its prices, delivery and product quality. The organization of work in all of the company's units and divisions has been modified as a result.

The operator[3] observed within the framework of this study was a functional writer, in addition to being a process engineer on the process team. He was 28 years old and had been trained as a mechanical engineer. He had been working in the company for five years at the time of our research and had held several positions: project estimator, engineer on the research and development team, and engineer on the new products team. He had been a member of the process team for three years. He was on day shift.

2.3 Work Instructions

The functional writer we observed wrote several types of technical documents, but the study that is presented herein deals with the production of work instructions. There were several rationales behind this choice. To begin with, effective work instructions help not only to avoid work accidents but also to cut production costs by reducing the risks of nonconformity and delays in shipment. Secondly, they contribute to the implementation of best-manufacturing practices—e.g., ISO 9000, Six Sigma, etc. (Pillet, 2004). Thirdly, they contribute to quality assurance, particularly in respect of the transfer of knowledge required to consolidate a company's fund of expertise. Fourth, effective work instructions ought to help reduce the risks of human error (Lin & Salvendy, 1999).

In ergonomics, it is generally agreed that work instructions constitute means, supplied by the company and made available to employees[4] to the same extent as other tools, machines or equipment (Guérin et al., 2006). Work instructions may be designed and adapted to the work activity of employees with varying degrees of success. In the context of this study, work instructions are endowed with a dual status: first, as the outcome of the work of the writer and second, as a tool supplied to employees. The need to set out work instructions would, it appears, flow out of the "gap occurring between the competencies required to perform a particular task, on the one hand, and those competencies either held or presumed to be held by the employees charged with performing this task" (Leplat, 1998, p. 7). Work instructions are designed to "define a method to be complied with when carrying out a given activity, such that the

---

[3] As this text sets out the results of the analysis of the actual activity of a functional writer, the term "operator" has, in keeping with Guérin's terminology, been reserved for this person.

[4] As it so happens, these employees have turned out to be "operators" who also perform a work activity. As this text sets out the results of the analysis of the actual activity of a writer, the term "operator" has been reserved for this person, whereas the operators at the plant who use these instructions (and whose work activity was not analysed within the framework of this study) will be referred to elsewhere in this article as "employees".

operations in question are performed as planned, no deviations from the prescribed procedure occur, modifications can be made to the task as necessary, and target results are indeed obtained" (Mazeau, 1998, p. 7). Work instructions may also be useful as an employee training tool, a set of guidelines, a baseline for task performance and a checklist of prescribed actions (Veyrac et al., 1997, p. 389). Work instructions also appear to be a valuable tool for preserving "corporate memory," facilitating the transfer of knowledge from departing seasoned employees (managers and employees) to young or newly hired employees.

In everyday usage, the terms "procedure" and "instruction" are frequently employed as synonyms. In the industrial sector, however, a very high proportion of companies subscribe to ISO (International Organization for Standardization) standards, which clearly distinguish procedures from instructions.

> "**Procedure**," according to the ISO document *ISO 9000* (2005, p. 12), is defined thusly:
> specified way to carry out an activity or a process (3.4.1)
> NOTE 1 Procedures can be documented or not.
> NOTE 2 When a procedure is documented, the term "written procedure" or "documented procedure" is frequently used.
> document (3.7.2)[5] that contains a procedure can be called a "procedure document".

> "**Process**," on the other hand, is defined in the same series *ISO 9000* (2005, p. 11) as:
> set of interrelated or interacting activities which transforms inputs into outputs
> NOTE 1 Inputs to a process are generally outputs of other processes.
> NOTE 2 Processes in an organization (3.3.1) are generally planned and carried out under controlled conditions to add value.
> NOTE 3 A process where the conformity (3.6.1) of the resulting product (3.4.2) cannot be readily or economically verified is frequently referred to as a "special process".

> As to the definition of "**work instructions**," they are to be found in the document *ISO/TR10013* (2001, p. 1):
> "detailed descriptions of how to perform and record tasks
> NOTE 1 Work instructions may be documented or not.
> NOTE 2 Work Instructions may be, for example, detailed written descriptions, flowcharts, templates, models, technical notes incorporated into

---

[5]"Document information (3.7.1) and its supporting medium
EXAMPLE Record (3.7.6), specification (3.7.3), procedure document, drawing, report, standard.
NOTE 1 The medium can be paper, magnetic, electronic or optical computer disc, photograph or master sample, or a combination thereof.
NOTE 2 A set of documents, for example specifications and records, is frequently called "documentation".
NOTE 3 Some requirements (3.1.2) (e.g., the requirement to be readable) relate to all types of documents, however there can be different requirements for specifications (e.g., the requirement to be revision controlled) and records (e.g., the requirement to be retrievable)." (*ISO 9000*, 2005, p. 14).

drawings, specifications, equipment instruction manuals, pictures, videos, checklists, or combinations thereof. Work instructions should describe any materials, equipment and documentation to be used. When relevant, work instructions include acceptance criteria."

Thus, according to the ISO, work instructions and procedures are, most often, two distinct documents, although it is conceivable that work instructions be included within procedures (i.e., the former are always subordinated to the latter). When instructions exist (which is not necessarily obligatory, it all depends on the company's needs), they refer to procedures and vice versa. In the ISO system, "Documented procedures generally describe activities that cross different functions, while work instructions generally apply to tasks within one function" (*ISO\TR10013*, 2001, p. 5). Thus, for every task involving critical activities,[6] work instructions have to be developed, published and regularly updated. The degree of precision characterizing a set of instructions varies according to the company's needs, the complexity of the work at hand, the methods deployed, the training sessions given to employees and the skills and qualifications of the staff. According to the ISO standard, work instructions may take on a great variety of forms (e.g., narrative text, drawings, videos, etc.), for there is no one set framework or model for the instruction genre.

In the present case study, the following definition has been elaborated for the purpose of gathering examples of instructions and of describing the text object produced by the functional writer.

Work instructions written in an industrial setting are technical texts that precisely and specifically prescribe the critical activities involved in accomplishing a particular task. Work instructions are not developed according to any preestablished format; instead, they may take on the form of a descriptive text, flowchart, technical note, etc.; they can be integrated into drawings, photos or videos, and can figure in a book of specifications, a checklist, or in an equipment instruction manual; they may also combine one more of these means. Linguistically speaking, work instructions most often consist of a succession of infinitive or imperative verbs and use a single word or a small group of words to convey either the action to be accomplished (e.g., "Clean") or not to be accomplished (e.g., "Do not stack more than two items at a time"). They may also take the form of a definition (e.g., "Neoprene in the form of a self-adhesive tape or sheet provides protection from die marks."). Work instructions are used by an individual or a group of individuals to perform, directly or indirectly, to best effect (e.g., "Products from incomplete batches are to be laid on the 'incompletes' shelf or, in the case of oversize items, on the red carts (while waiting to fill incomplete batches)."). They should enable an employee to achieve immediate, failsafe results from the very first time out. In an industrial firm, they aid in ensuring that runs go according to plans, specifications

---

[6]"Work instructions should be developed and maintained to describe the performance of all work that would be adversely affected by lack of such instructions. […] Work instructions should describe critical activities. Details which do not give more control of the activity should be avoided" (*ISO/TR10013*, 2001, p. 6).

and standards and that the safety and security of human and material resources are sufficiently protected.

2.4 Summary Description of the Work of an Engineer Belonging to the Process Team

According to a corporate document, the task assigned to the process team by the company is as follows:

1. Defining and validating the optimal fabrication technique: process, instructions and standards.
2. Providing technological watch.
3. Presenting the optimum technology to senior management.
4. Implementing new processes.
5. Carrying out continuous improvement projects.
6. Offering technical support to the other departments.

These tasks are carried out in response to the order of a client for a mass-produced product. The process team's work comes into play at different stages of handling the order, primarily: the production of estimates; prototyping, in the case of a new product; the identification and selection of manufacturing processes; the training of plant employees; the completion of production runs; and the provision of customer service activities.

The process engineer whom we followed worked an average of 9 h daily and summed up usual daily activities as follows: 1 h developing plans of action for "client complaints"; 4 h providing technical support in the plant and in the other departments of the company; 2 h communicating (e.g., email, phone calls, meetings, etc.) and 2 h carrying out continuous improvement projects (e.g., instructions and various reports). All these activities of his overlap one another.

Requests for technical support come from several different units of the company: sales, estimation, new product development, production, maintenance, occupational health and safety (OHS), client service and employee training. These requests are as numerous as they are diverse; likewise, response times can vary considerably. As such, requests can be categorized as follows: locating the best means (choice of material, purchase of a new machine, toolmaking, modifying work organization and planning, etc.) according to the context (cost, available space, compatibility of technologies, order flow management, health and safety, etc.) so as to be able to produce and deliver the product in conformity with client specifications. Relative to the manufacturing process, the origin of requests may be as far upstream as estimators or as far downstream as the client service team. The following two examples are intended to illustrate what is entailed by support requests.

The new product development team is in charge of prototyping. Once the prototype has been trialled according to plan, it is then transferred to the process team, which is then made responsible for developing the work methods to be used in the mass manufacturing of the product. To aid them in this transfer, the process team uses a project management procedure that prescribes the involvement of several actors. In turn, these various management activities require a great many actions: estimates, data searches in the various bases of the company, drawings of the product line set-up, meetings with various company actors, etc.

Requests from the production team are varied, and may originate with the Vice-President for Operations, the account manager at the client service unit, the production manager, maintenance technicians, foremen and even plant employees. Requests may be related to spoiled units, breakdown of machines, etc. Once production has been given the go-ahead, the functional writer whom we observed takes charge of handling a portion of client complaints, which is to say that he conducts an investigation and develops a plan of action so as to return the situation to normal. He must see to solving the problem.

The diversity of these requests and of the people making these requests gives a good idea of the broad range of work performed by this process engineer and of the numerous interactions between actors and activities. One of the outcomes of this situation is that modifications are regularly made to operations planning. For example, in the opinion of the writer whom we observed (and whose views we were in a position to concur with), the time allotted for conducting continuous improvement projects, which encompassed the completion of work instructions, was constantly being foreshortened. Requests for technical support often wind up with an order to produce a document. By his own estimation, this engineer spends 50% of work time drafting documents such as: reports, experimental designs, summaries of experiment findings, replies to client complaints, plans of action, emails, work instructions, etc. The members of the process team seldom work together, as they each have their own projects. They do collaborate with one another when the need arises—sharing technical advice, for example.

The instruction drafting process begins as soon as the manufacturing methods have been identified and selected, and ends once the product is no longer produced by the company. Work methods are most often developed during the preproduction phase surrounding a new product. Preproduction is the phase when a complete check is made of all manufacturing actions with a view to optimizing runs once a prototype has been cleared for production by the new product development team. For a certain time, a predetermined number of parts or components are produced. This is followed by the actual production of the product. Based on the observations noted at this stage, the trainers work out a basic framework for the work instructions yet to be developed. Indeed, the training staff are valued contributors, all the way from the very first reflection process concerning methods to the end of production runs. In the capacity of technical experts, they are contacted by the process team for advice and input on the choice of production method. At a later stage, trainers take part in the decisions concerning the layout of production lines and design-specific training sessions for the manufacturing processes to be used for products. To produce work instructions, it takes the sustained collaboration of the functional writer, the trainers, plant employees, foremen and the OHS advisors. During the preproduction step, the trainers provide support to plant employees, validate the work method, and define the main framework of the future work instructions. They also make sure that the production line is well balanced (determining the cycle time at each workstation so as to optimize production flow) and rule on the standards adopted (cycle time, number of employees per workstation, quantity of components produced, etc.). The manufacturing methods selected vary according to the product targeted for manufacturing, the availability of machines, the size of the physical premises, etc.

Once the process team has finished setting up production of the product, work instructions have to be developed. The training staff sends the main outlines of these instructions to the writer. Initially, the instructions will be used by trainers as a support during the training sessions given to plant employees. The process team is the team responsible for producing work instructions and, more often than not, the writer whom we met was the person placed in charge of drafting them.

2.5 The Practical Context Surrounding Work Instructions in the Workplace

For three years now, work instructions have been the responsibility of the process team. The team has attempted to standardize a model, or to structure the instruction writing and revision process, but the planning of work instructions remains a short-term thing. However, the instructions used in the workplace encompass highly varying models that were likely developed long before this team was given this duty. In the absence of any prior consensus, various units proceeded to produce instructions that, in the time since, have not necessarily been updated in terms of either content or form. Some sets of instructions continue to be used, and others not. Any existing updates were produced in response to production requirements arising in the last three years. All instructions have been archived in a computer file and, according to the writer, are now due for some serious weeding-out and updating.

Work instructions are produced primarily by the engineer whom we observed. According to the team co-ordinator, there is no official instruction-writing mandate, which cannot, moreover, be considered as constituting a priority. The engineer reckons that he devotes 2–4 h per month to the task of instruction-writing, an insufficient amount of time in his opinion. The current situation, which he believes to be normal, can be described as follows: his work docket holds 40 sets of instructions waiting to be drafted, not to mention approximately 40 additional sets currently being used and for which he should produce updates, for these work instructions normally bear on the manufacturing process surrounding a specific product, which in turn bears a direct relationship to the orders of specific clients.

It may happen that a given set of instructions is not available when the order is given to start up the production of a product. As the writer explains: it is likely he did not have enough time for developing instructions, as the time requirements associated with readying the production line necessarily impinge on the time normally reserved for writing. In addition, the writer occasionally needs to develop greater command of his subject and, moreover, the process team wishes to check whether the work method chosen for a new line of production is the right one. The need for instructions is deemed as being less urgent whenever production resumes for a product that was previously manufactured in the absence of any instructions. When instructions do not exist, the trainers and the plant employees involved in manufacturing a similar product are looked to as references. In situations of this kind, the trainers give the plant employees the requisite explanations orally. Oftentimes, moreover, a plant employee will turn to his or her peers to learn how to perform a task or to validate his or her understanding.

The work instructions can be found on the company's intranet and may be accessed only by the foremen, the trainers and the process team. If the plant employees wish to consult a particular instruction, they must request permission to do so from their foreman. During the last several months, the functional writer has laid the groundwork for a project to implement work instructions in a production line. Three official meetings were held for the purpose of presenting this project to (1) the trainers, (2) the process team and, for a second time, to the trainers; and (3) a foreman, a number of expert plant employees[7] assigned to the production line in question, and the OHS preventionist. Finally, a short presentation on the project was given during the monthly meeting of the OHS committee. A fifth meeting for all of the plant employees concerned is scheduled for a short time prior to the implementation of the instructions on the production line. The process team co-ordinator, who gave the project his go-ahead and who identified the particular production line on which work instructions were to be implemented, attended all of the employee mobilization meetings. The plant employees who had been invited to voice their opinion at meetings as well as those employees who were interviewed within the framework of this case study generally took a positive view of the "impending" arrival of instructions on the production line. Many of them considered work instructions to be useful for their work; they adhered to the underlying principle, but would withhold judgment until seeing how it would translate into practical results. No one at the company was able to say when this project would be brought to completion. Over the past three years, the process team has attempted to formalize the position of work instructions in the production process. Periodic changes in the process team's order of priorities stem from the receipt of orders requiring urgent attention and the short turn-around times they must manage with as part of supplying technical support to the production line.

2.5.1 The representation of the target reader by the functional writer   Work instructions are used by several different people for various reasons, but ultimately there is only one final target reader: the plant employee. For the writer, the target reader is, moreover, a plant employee who has attended a training session given by one of the company trainers. He or she is familiar with the main techniques required to do his or her job and has been working at the company for at least one month. This representation of the target reader necessarily determines the amount of details provided for each activity. In the functional writer's mind, the plant employee will, ideally, use the work instructions to perform his or her duties unassisted. In reality, however, the writer has observed that a new plant employee always turns to his or her co-workers to learn how to perform a given task or to validate whether he or she has grasped the work instructions and is able to perform the activity according to the prescribed timelines and cycle times.

2.5.2 The range and diversity of the target readership   The main target reader of work instructions is the plant employee, who possesses his or her own personal characteristics (gender, age, physical and cultural traits, etc.), varying levels of experience and training, etc. He or she is also in a momentary state or condition of varying nature and intensity. A plant employee's state or condition is determined by biological rhythms, fatigue, life outside of the workplace, etc. In addition, this state is variable and has an impact on the work activity in hand. A number of these factors influence the comprehension of work instructions. For example, the personal characteristic of being "a plant employee having a mother tongue other than French, not having acquired proficiency in reading French, and understanding oral

---

[7]Experienced operators who aid the trainers during training sessions for new employees or whose assistance is called on in the production of new products, for example.

French with difficulty" might well have an impact on the comprehension of work instructions. If a writer fails to adapt work instructions in accordance with the levels of education and experience possessed across a range of potential target readers, the result may seriously jeopardize employee health and safety as well as the quality of output (e.g., substandard products).

The steps in the instruction-writing process are described in the next several sections. From beginning to end, the process occurs over periods of varying length, especially owing to the interruptions resulting from the other work activities that the functional writer must also perform in his capacity as process engineer.

2.6 The Key Steps of Producing Work Instructions

The key steps involved in producing work instructions are as follows: the gathering of technical data; the processing of the information thus gathered, which includes translating the information into text, and formatting (including the integration of visual elements); verifying the conformity of instructions with the agreed sequence of procedures; and feedback and information management, including such aspects as integration into the work activities of the target readers, access, medium of dissemination, the dissemination process proper (posting/publishing) and monitoring and follow-up. Each of these steps is described in the following section.

2.6.1 Gathering of technical data for the production of work instructions The technical trainers forward, via email, a general outline of the instructions, including a description of the steps to be followed during the production of the product, or merely the parameters appearing on a plot taken from the production line. Then, in order to better visualize the production of the end product, the writer supplements this drawing with technical drawings that are produced by the designers and posted on the company intranet. The writer adds health and safety-related information into the work instructions, drawing on the data forwarded to him by the OHS advisor in the form of personal protective equipment sheets and workstation risk identification sheets. However, not all of these sheets are available or up to date. In that case, the writer produces his instructions to the best of his knowledge and asks the OHS advisor to check them for accuracy and completeness.

2.6.2 Processing of information According to our observations of the workplace, the functional writer divides the activity of information processing into the following two steps.

- Translating information into text

Upon receiving the basic outline of the instructions to be drafted, the writer sets about ordering this collection of sentences. To reformulate his content, he begins his sentences with a verb of action, followed by a direct object along with a phrase indicating the manner in which the action is to be done (e.g., "Wipe die with a clean cloth"). He makes a point of using short sentences and eliminating jargon. As much as possible, he "francisizes" his text (the practice, in Quebec, of using standard French terminology in place of English or English-derived vocabulary or *in lieu* of inappropriate regionalisms specific to Quebec French), as the company must follow the recommendations of the *Office québécois de la langue française* (the Quebec government agency charged with protecting and promoting the use of French throughout all spheres of Quebec society). He divides up the sentences so that each one contains only a single action (i.e., one step per sentence). According to his understanding of how the product is produced, he checks for any missing steps and adds in the relevant information as needed. He does not go and view the set-up of the production line prior to producing the work instructions. This will be performed at a later stage.

- Formatting and integration of visual elements

Following the text production step properly, the writer then proceeds to format his document. Since early 2006, the company has been managing its documentation on a wiki-style Website.[8] For the work associated with this step, the writer uses a new model built around the programming language employed on wiki sites. For the writer, this innovation has meant gaining proficiency in the system's programming language. More than ever, he finds it hard to delegate the drafting of work instructions to another employee. The new model was presented to the various actors concerned at employee mobilization meetings centring on the project to implement work instructions on the production line. At first glance, everyone seemed to be satisfied. The previous model was developed using Open Office Impress, a type of presentation software equivalent to PowerPoint. The text is accompanied by photos illustrating each of the steps to be followed and is spread over two columns. It is the writer's view that a well-done presentation is an aid to comprehension. The model now being used is the product of a long (two-year-long) reflection, several trials and numerous modifications. For example, the first version had no photos. Noticing that the text was not always read by its target readers, the writer thus decided to add photos to it. Work instructions are apportioned according to the particular workstation, with each workstation receiving one set of instructions. Previous to this approach, all of the manufacturing activities were divided up according to the tasks performed at each workstation but assembled into a single volume of instructions. The first page of this document featured a diagram showing the production line and the machines; the sequence of actions involved in producing the product; and the number of plant employees and their position along the production line. The end result was a hefty document that plant employees had difficulty finding their way around in. Further, given his desire to provide sufficient details, the writer was prompted to include more information in the work instructions than less. In his superiors' opinion, work instructions should be able to fit on a single page and, considering the little time available for producing such documents, they encouraged the writer to simplify the document as much as possible. In their view, an over-lengthy document goes unread. While the writer continually strives for concision, it must be said that the contents of a given set of instructions do not always fit onto one page.

The next step consists in adding photos (taken by himself or by the trainer) to illustrate the various activities. The formatting has to be readjusted as a result. The writer then integrates

---

[8] A wiki is a kind of collaborative Website whose most distinguishing characteristic is to facilitate the process of writing content in HTML and placing it online—this, in combination with allowing all users having access to a wiki to make changes to any of the pages thus posted, with a record of such modifications being continuously maintained and readily viewable. A wiki simplifies the tasks of structuring, communicating, disseminating and searching for information. Though occasionally interpreted as being an acronym for "What I Know Is," the word wiki stems from the Hawaiian *wiki wiki*, which means quick or fast.

icons representing the various types of personal protection equipment (PPE) to be used when performing any given activity. He also includes icons and basic explanations in connection with certain workstation-related risks for OHS. Currently, the integration of OHS content is embryonic: of approximately 50 work instructions consulted, only four sets of instructions feature PPE icons and notices such as "WARNING: sharp edges." The writer is working on a new model of work instructions that he hopes will be simpler.

2.6.3 Verifying conformity of instructions Once the work instructions have been completely formatted, the functional writer makes sure that he has fully understood and reproduced the gist of what the trainer had first written in the outline form; in particular, he checks against the potential sequence of operations. As soon as he deems his version of the document to be final, he sends it on to the trainers and thereafter to the other members of the process team. He requests that each person checks the portion of the instructions of concern to him or her. Following approval by all the parties, the work instructions are then distributed.

2.6.4 Feedback and information management The new work instructions are announced via email to the foremen, trainers from the training team and the process team. The email contains the intranet link to the work instructions. The system displays a directory listing of the instructions in pdf format. Documents pertaining to a product are classified by client name. The trainers are responsible for organizing, in collaboration with the foreman, training sessions for plant employees. During the training period, the instructions are tested by the trainers, foremen and plant employees. If modifications have to be made to the work instructions, a trainer will forward this information to the writer, who will proceed to modify and redistribute the instructions. Feedback is given on only two occasions, during training and the initial run of product. Any changes made subsequently to the work instructions are not reported, which means that no monitoring or follow-up is performed.

3 Conclusion

To begin with, it is worth recalling that the case study has been presented here with a view to bringing a new perspective to the context of text production in the workplace and, as a result, to obtaining some elements of response to the following questions: *What is the overall context surrounding the production of technical texts by a functional writer? What is the impact of this context on the demands and constraints bearing on the work of a functional writer? What are the steps involved in the process of producing work instructions for use on a production line?*

In this instance, the process of drafting work instructions is performed by a functional writer, who is himself a process engineer. This process grows out of the identification and selection of manufacturing methods by the process team and ends whenever the particular product is no longer manufactured by the company (or, to be more precise, whenever the company's client drops this product from its product line). The determination of work methods figures among an extensive, necessary set of production-oriented activities. The key steps involved in producing work instructions are to: (1) gather technical information; (2) process the various data, a step that includes both translating this information into text and formatting (including the integration of visual elements); (3) verify the conformity of the instructions; and (4) feedback and information management, including integration of the end document into the activities of the target readers, access, the medium of dissemination, the dissemination process proper, and monitoring and follow-up. These activities are conducted over periods of varying duration, especially owing to the interruptions resulting from the other work activities that the functional writer must also perform in his capacity as process engineer. It was shown that the functional writer's work activities are highly diverse and that they vary considerably in terms of the conditions under which they are to be performed. As has also been shown, the process of producing work instructions is a collective, co-operative activity, bringing together a number of actors to accomplish the same objective in a relationship of mutual dependence. The functional writer must deal with: the different individuals concerned by this task; the company's values and image; the policies and rules specific to the firm; the work context; quality standards; OHS norms, IT limitations, etc. (Henry & Monkam-Daverat, 1998; Mazeau, 1998).

It has clearly emerged from this study that the functional writer is competent and is not the origin of work instruction-related problems. The steps of the process to which he adheres are indeed those that are recommended in works on professional copyediting and in models of the writing process. The writer also accounts for the needs of the target reader not only in terms of the selection and ordering of information, but also of the wording and the illustrations used to describe the key steps.

The reality, in the case presented here, is that the functional writer is obliged to operate under several constraints of an organizational nature, appearing in the form of limitations on the time and human resources allocated to instructions. At this stage of our study, it appears that one of the major constraints confronting the writer stems from one of the company's management principles, according to which all corporate activities must demonstrate their cost effectiveness. Given the current context of global competition—in which companies struggle to remain in operation and to satisfy lending institutions and shareholders alike, downsizing is *de rigueur*, and "doing more with less" is the order of the day—the production of work instructions is not viewed as a value-added activity. In short, the message conveyed by senior management concerning work instructions amounts to this: although the instruction project is useful and necessary, the company has neither the time nor the resources required to make it a top priority. Thus, production of instructions has to be fit into day-to-day operations, such that improvement will occur little by little. The company has therefore taken the risk of "making do" with the strict minimum where work instructions are concerned. In a context in which the company has opted for a short-term management approach, it is unlikely that a long-term improvement project such as the one involving instructions will be pursued readily.

As is shown by the context in which the manufacturing company operates, this collective, co-operative activity is strongly influenced by production imperatives of the "just-in-time" variety—and especially by the management of orders for quick delivery. In the effort to satisfy these demands, any plans for completing medium- or long-term tasks, such as drafting and implementing work instructions, are necessarily prone to disruption or, at the very least, constant rescheduling. This project must, whenever possible, be integrated into the day-to-day activities of the process team. More often than not, any hoped-for modifications to the order of priorities set for the process team and even for the overall organization of production are impacted by the receipt of urgent, frequently unplanned-for orders or by changes in orders, the installation of new equipment, or repairs on machinery. In short, and to take the worm's eye view of the workplace reality, this manufacturing plant is inevitably confronted with having to weigh the requirements related to the setting of production targets against those pertaining to the identification and mobilization of the available resources—all with a view to carrying out production activities under the best conditions possible in respect of deadlines and delivery specifications.

The failure to implement work instructions on production lines (when, indeed, instructions can be had for the implementing) stands out as a problem of vital importance, for two reasons primarily. First, owing to the management approach favoured by senior management and focusing on empowerment (Conger & Kanungo, 1988; Honold, 1997; Psoinos & Smithson, 2002), the employees have been entrusted with an increasing number of management-related responsibilities. Middle management, which includes the foreman, is directly concerned by measures designed to foster empowerment. His role as manager reduces the time available to him to directly supervise plant employees. The lack of presence "on the shopfloor" is compounded by the fact that plant employees do not enjoy direct access to the instructions and must go through him in order to obtain them. Secondly, as work instructions are valuable in terms of preserving "corporate memory"—especially the company's fund of expertise and know-how—and as a support in training sessions, it is critical to assure their availability. Considering that the company operates in a context of orders requiring attention, to the point of occasionally entailing one-time hirings (the company boasts a 300-strong workforce but can hire up to 45 employees at once), considering also the relative shortage of skilled manpower in its segment of the employment market, instructions should, logically, represent a source of added value for the company. In addition, the production of work instructions can represent a tool for mobilizing employees from different teams around a shared objective and, in the process, of generating a consensus that accounts for the needs and constraints faced by each person to be involved in the activity for which instructions are being developed. A project of this kind can help improve communication at the workplace.

Writing at work[9] is the outcome of a process of complex interactions involving issues of import to the very culture of a company and its future development (Minzoni-Déroche, 1998). Through the use of an ergonomics-based conceptual framework centring on work activities (Guérin et al., 2006), it has been shown that a comprehensive vision of context is vital to fully grasping the stakes and issues surrounding writing at work in a manufacturing company—particularly as has been illustrated in the case of work instructions. It is therefore clear that communication problems related to writing at work cannot be solved solely through an investigation of the text object or of the writer in his immediate work context. From this point of view, there is a need to enrich and supplement the portion of text production models dealing with the context. To this end, a first step will consist in expanding the very notion of context, moving beyond the immediate context centring on the writing activity to a more comprehensive sort of context. The immediate context of writing (here referred to as the secondary) is shaped by other contexts. As has been shown in this case study, the secondary context is influenced by the primary context, which itself is conditioned by the context of the company. In turn, the company's context is determined by the world context. Each of these contexts possesses its own specific characteristics. As well, each determines

---

[9]"'Writing at work' may be used to refer to a set of documents originating in a company and, more broadly speaking, in any public or private production-oriented organization" (Fraenkel, 2001, p. 113).

the constraints that frame the production and the use of technical texts, not to mention the texts themselves.

A second step will consist in conducting further field research so as to fully grasp the very essence of these multiple contexts and their intertwining influence both on production activities and on research results. This research should be interdisciplinary rather than multidisciplinary in nature and scope. To gain a comprehensive grasp of an object of knowledge, it is necessary to foster genuine interactions between specialists—i.e., a thoroughgoing pooling and selection of concepts, methods and analytical frameworks. Such an approach calls for a process of cross-fertilization that cannot be achieved by merely juxtaposing the angles of analysis that are trained on a given object by a set of disciplines having no contact with one another otherwise.

Acknowledgements

This study was made possible thanks to the financial contribution of the ARUC-ITE (*Alliance de recherche universités-communautés/Innovations, travail et emploi*, Department of Industrial Relations, *Université Laval*, Québec City, Canada), the GIROST (*Groupe interdisciplinaire de recherche sur l'organisation et la santé au travail*) and the IRSST (*Institut de Recherche Robert-Sauvé en Santé et en Sécurité du travail du Québec*). We should also like to thank the management and employees of the host company for graciously accepting to participate in this study.

SECTION 3:

UNDERSTANDING DOCUMENTS

Chapter 11

Situation Models and Their Role in Comprehension: The Need to Study Their Internal Structure

Isabelle Tapiero and José Otero

Understanding a text requires building a coherent mental representation, commonly called the situation model (Van Dijk & Kintsch, 1983) or the mental model (Johnson-Laird, 1983). What are the objects that compose the situational level of representation and what are the relations among them? In this chapter, we describe the different types of formalisms that have been used to represent meaning: schemas (Schank & Abelson, 1977), propositions (Kintsch & Van Dijk, 1978), tokens in scenarios and pointers (Sanford & Garrod, 1981) and cognitive categories such as states and events (François, 1991; Trabasso & Van den Broek, 1985). We also present an alternative view, that is, the representation of the structure of situation models as amodal (Gernsbacher, 1990), or in terms of analogical structure to that of the states of affairs it represents (Johnson-Laird, 1983). Within this view, the structure of the model should result from the analogy in entities and relations between the represented world and the representing world. This latter conception highlights the perceptive component of the representation.

There is a large consensus on the idea that discourse comprehension involves two main levels of reader's mental representation in memory (Van Dijk & Kintsch, 1983; Just & Carpenter, 1987; Kintsch, 1988): textbase and situation model. The textbase representation captures the meaning conveyed by the text, independently of its surface formulation, but remains closely tied to the text formulation. The situation model or referential representation of discourse consists in "the reader's representation of the world the text refers to (Just & Carpenter, 1987, p. 195)" or "the cognitive representation of the events, actions, persons, and in general the situation, a text is about (Van Dijk & Kintsch, 1983, pp. 11–12)". It refers to a construction in episodic memory of the event or situation a text is about, that is, a subjective representation of a fragment of reality in the reader's mind. Johnson-Laird (1983)

Written Documents In The Workplace
Copyright © 2007 by Elsevier Ltd.
All rights of reproduction in any form reserved.
ISBN: 978-0-080-47487-8

Tapiero, I. & Otero, J. (2007). Situation models and their role in comprehension: The need to study their internal structure. In G. Rijlaarsdam (Series Ed.) and D. Alamargot, P. Terrier, & J.-M. Cellier (Vol. Eds.), Studies in Writing, Vol. 21, Written Documents in the Workplace, 161–175.

and other researchers have used the term "mental model" to refer to analog representations of situations and events in the world that fulfill different roles in comprehension and reasoning. We will use both terms interchangeably to refer to readers' mental representation although it is important to note that each of these constructs have differential structural and functional characteristics.

There are several reasons why situation models are needed to account for discourse comprehension (Van Dijk & Kintsch, 1983). One of the arguments is based on the idea that a discourse may be viewed from different perspectives and different points of view, just as it may modify those perspectives or points of view. The facts, events and situations are interpreted, described and told by different persons, from different viewpoints, although they remain the same. The situation model, which is independent of the current discourse and of the point of view adopted, accounts for this discrepancy. The notion of situation model also accounts for the different interpretations of a text generated by two persons. It does not necessarily refer to distinct textual representations, but can correspond to differences between the concerned situation models. Using this notion leads one to dissociate the semantic content from the situational content of a text and to causes the model constructed to be dependent upon the reader's prior knowledge. Indeed, under some circumstances, when the representation of the text content (i.e., semantic representation) is difficult to construct, people remember the situation model evoked by the text rather than the representation of the text itself. Conversely, there are some situations in which the text is recalled, but not the situation model, particularly for novices in a specific domain described in the text. These two distinct situations can be explained by two factors: coherence and prior knowledge. In the former, non-coherent text content may lead to difficulties in the construction of a semantic representation, although the reader may reach a "certain level of coherence" for the situation evoked by the text. In the latter situation, the amount of domain-specific knowledge the reader has is closely related to the level of difficulty in building a situation model. The greater the amount of knowledge about the events depicted in the text, the easier it is to elaborate a situation model. The reordering of information is another reason why situation models are necessary. A story in which the order of events has been modified often tends to be recalled in the canonical order rather than in the actual order of the story itself (Kintsch, Mandel, & Kozminsky, 1977). This phenomenon can be explained in two ways, both of which imply recourse to the notion of situation model. First, it is likely that during recall, the story is reconstructed from the situation model formed as the story was being told and not from the text itself. An alternative is that the text representation follows the "natural" order, despite the presentation order. However, the only way to proceed in reconstructing the story is to build a canonical situation model, and then to use that model to re-order the textbase information. In both cases, the reorganization of the events presupposes the construction of a situation model. But a text does not always lead to the construction of a new situation model. More frequently, an existing model is modified using information in the new text. This is done, for example, during the updating of knowledge from reports (Van Oostendorp, 1996) or when the reader has a specific goal such as a learning goal (see Mannes & Kintsch, 1987).

However, more is known about the role of situation models or about the mechanisms underlying their construction than about the objects and relations that constitute them. Langston, Kramer, and Glenberg (1998, p. 247) point to this problem: "In essence what is meant by a mental model is a representation of what the language or text is about, rather than a representation of the language itself. Apart from this essence there is little agreement as to how to characterize a mental model. Is it an image? A schema? A set of propositions?" Our intention is to review in this chapter some theoretical and empirical arguments on the nature of objects in situation models and on the relations among these objects.

1 The Internal "Objects" of Situation Models

Situation models are one kind of representational system. Any representation system relates two elements: a represented world and a representing world (Rumelhart & Norman, 1988). Both of these worlds may be conceptualized as consisting of a set of objects, and a set of relations among those objects. However, no clear evidence for one specific type of object in situation models has been demonstrated yet. What follows provide an overview of the objects in situation models as well as the relations between these objects.

1.1 The Predicate-Argument Schema

The construction of meaning is central to discourse representation and to the understanding of the nature of objects in situation models. Although different kinds of formalisms have been used for representing meaning (e.g., feature systems, frames, schemas, scripts), the predicate-argument schema, that is, the proposition, has been widely proposed as the building blocks of meaning representations and as compound units of situation models. According to Kintsch (1998), a propositional representation of meaning has advantages over other forms of representation because it is flexible enough to subsume the alternative systems. Schemas, associative networks or production rules can be expressed in this notation. The author postulates the construction of a situation model, in which text-based propositions (the textbase) and knowledge-based propositions are related to form a situation model evoked by the text. He also assumes that a flexible process of constraint satisfaction supplies a good mechanism by which such an interpretation can emerge.

Building a situation model requires the use of prior knowledge. In Kintsch's theory (Kintsch, 1988, 1998), knowledge is also represented as a network of propositions (i.e., associative network). The network nodes can refer to propositions, schemas, frames, scripts or production rules, which can all be written in the formalism based on the predicate-argument schema. Thus, this unique format makes the task easier when knowledge and text representations are integrated to form the situational level of representation (see Kintsch, 1988, 1998).

However, although situation models have been represented propositionally sometimes (Haenggi, Kintsch, & Gernsbacher, 1995; Tapiero & Otero, 1999), the existence itself of the amodal symbol (e.g., propositional representation) has been questioned. Other formalisms have been developed given that the mental representation that a reader/listener constructs relies on the structural identity of the represented and representing worlds. In other words, how individuals perceive the real-world situations should have a large influence on words interpretation (Gernsbacher, 1990; Johnson-Laird, 1983). In line with this assumption, a new approach in cognitive science brought some relevant insights on the potential nature of representational units. Within this view, situation models are viewed as experiential simulations of the described situation (Barsalou, 1999), where affordances derived from sensory-motor simulations are essential for semantic processing. Zwaan also stressed the importance of vicarious experiences in narrative comprehension for defining situation models (Zwaan, 1999). This latter view puts a strong emphasis on the general assumption that cognition is inherently perceptual, with a common representational system for perception and cognition (Barsalou, 1993; Glenberg, 1997; Miller & Johnson-Laird, 1976). We will now turn to the discussion of approaches that assume other representative units than propositions to define the content of situation models.

1.2 States, Events and Actions as Core Elements of Situation Models in Narratives

Situation models refer to the cognitive representation of events, actions, persons and the situation a text is about (Van Dijk & Kintsch, 1983). Consequently, the representation a reader constructs while reading a text may be organized around these conceptual categories. Cognitive semantics attempts to identify these conceptual categories and to provide a description that structures mental and linguistic representations in terms of states, events and actions (Baudet, 1990). States are considered as preservations of properties of a system's components as well as preservations of the stative relations (e.g., spatial relations) among these components, within a temporal interval. Events are defined as changes in status of components within the system (see Baudet, 1990). These categories are supposed to be activated from long-term memory during text comprehension, and a subset of this information is instantiated as inferences in the situation model (Graesser & Zwaan, 1995).

The differential influence of states and events on the comprehension process has been demonstrated. Graesser, Robertson, Lovelace, and Swinehart (1980) showed that readers of familiar stories have more difficulty to infer states than to infer events. Also, Molinari and Tapiero (2000) investigated the influence of these categories on readers' mental representations. In a study, high and low knowledgeable subjects had to learn a text about a scientific topic (i.e., the neuron) described in terms of states (e.g., the unequal distribution of electric charges on the two sides of the neuron membrane) and events (e.g., the opening of the sodium channels in response to depolarization). Before the reading phase, these two groups had to study an outline designed to provide them with concepts related to the text domain. The task subjects had to perform just after the learning of the outline induced them to activate either a semantic representation (i.e., summary) or a situation model (i.e., schema) of the outline. The main results indicated that beginners focused more on states compared to experts, while the two knowledgeable groups did not differ in the processing of events. The authors also found that the activation of the outline's semantic representation (i.e., summary) facilitated subsequent event information processing, while the activation of the outline's situation model (i.e., schema) facilitated the processing of states. Thus, it appeared that the integration in memory of the category "state" is highly related to the activation of a situation model. This reflects that, in scientific texts, states could play the role of "reference point" or "conceptual anchor" around which the corresponding events would "gravitate". Thus, it is likely that the notions of individual, state, event and action are central to understand the internal structure of situation models.

The importance of events and actions for defining the mental representation elaborated from stories has also been emphasized in the Event-Indexing Model developed by Zwaan, Langston, and Graesser (1995). The authors proposed that events and intentional actions of characters are the focal points of situation models of narrative texts. As each incoming story event or action is comprehended, readers monitor and update the current situation model by constructing five indices: temporality, spatiality, protagonist, causality and intentionality. In 1998, Zwaan and Radvansky proposed a more sophisticated version of the Event-Indexing Model and distinguished among three characteristics of situation models: a situational framework, situational relations and a situational content. The situational framework is conceived of as a spatial-temporal framework and establishing it is a necessary step during the construction of a situation model. Situational relations are optional relations on the five situational dimensions previously mentioned (see Zwaan et al., 1995). Finally, the situational content includes entities represented as tokens in a situation model (i.e., protagonist and object) and their properties (e.g., physical and mental attributes) (Zwaan & Radvansky, 1998). According to the authors, entities and properties are optional as they are included in a situation model only when they are central for understanding the situation, except for protagonist, which is an obligatory part of the representation of narratives. Finally, in some cases, situation models can become very complex and not all information can be stored in the token or with the properties. To solve this problem, the authors propose the existence of pointers, part of the token, that refer to a more generalized information about an entity. Whenever more information is necessary for the situation model, references to this generalized information, via the pointers are made. This is consistent with both Sanford and Garrod's (1981) and Glenberg and Langston's (1992) approaches of situation models.

1.3 Tokens and Pointers as Representational Units of Situation Models

The theory proposed by Sanford and Garrod (1981) attempts to explain how knowledge is used when readers interpret texts, and brings complementary information about the objects constitutive of situation models. According to the authors, the situation model built requires knowledge activation at least partly script-based (Sanford, 1987; Schank & Abelson, 1977). When faced with a text, the reader has first to identify an appropriate domain of reference (i.e., setting and situation), loosely corresponding to what the text is about. Then, he/she has to use the identified domain to interpret the subsequent text. This approach underlies the evidence of a scenario matching (Sanford & Garrod, 1981): Knowledge of settings and situations constitutes the interpretative scenario behind a text. Thus, what is remembered of a text is a knowledge-based model of the situation.

Assuming a dynamic view of reading, Sanford and Garrod (1981) argue that as the text unfolds, there will be only a limited set of fore-grounded entities explicitly mentioned in the text, in conjunction with a particular scenario. The authors refer to entities and objects mentioned in the text as being in explicit focus, as long as they are represented in working memory. In contrast, the information provided by the current scenario is described as being in implicit focus. Representations in memory of entities and objects are called tokens. These tokens are defined as representational elements of situation models that are maintained in focus (see also, Glenberg & Langston, 1992). By contrast, representations of scenarios are composed of slots and default specifications (i.e., in implicit focus). Thus, when a new entity is mentioned in a text, a token for it is constructed in explicit focus. These tokens serve as discourse pointers to information no longer active in memory and prime contextually relevant information in long-term memory in an automatic manner (i.e., implicit focus).

Thus, within this approach of the comprehension process, the reader's mental representation is viewed as a set of entities and scenario tokens, plus a number of pointers that specifies the roles of entities in the various scenarios. When an incoming text is integrated with information in focus, contextually relevant information in long-term memory is also connected to new information. In this way, new information is mapped onto relevant information in both active memory and long-term memory. As Glenberg and Langston (1992) pointed out, such a mechanism is quite powerful because it allows the reader to check and maintain coherence at both local (against information in focus) and global (against relevant information in long-term memory) levels. The occurrences maintained in explicit focus (usually, the protagonist in narratives) would serve as pointers and would prime the relevant information of the scenario in implicit focus. The relations between these pointers are significant since mental models can be updated by introducing new pointers or by rearranging the existing ones to reflect the situation evoked in the text. When an existing pointer is moved or that a new pointer is introduced, the attention is orientated toward this pointer.

In conclusion, what we presented above shows that the reader's situation model built is made from entities or events called tokens that allow, via discursive pointers, to relate the currently processed information with knowledge readers have of the situation evoked in the text. This mapping process is automatic and emphasizes the role of readers' knowledge activation on the construction of the mental representation. Other formalisms involving knowledge activation assume that the mental representation should reflect the way individuals perceive the world: The structure of the model should result from the analogy in entities and relations between the represented world and the representing world. This latter conception highlights the perceptive component of the representation.

1.4 Situation Models Defined as an Analog Relation Between Symbols and Referent

In Gernsbacher's Structure Building Framework (1990), the goal of comprehension is to build coherent mental structures and substructures (i.e., representations), and comprehenders' success at building mental structures depends on their ability to envision real-world situations. In this model, representations are introduced at two levels: the micro- and the macro-levels. At the micro-level, representations are memory cells, conceptualized quasi neurologically as individual cells with a base activation level. At the macro-level, there are the abstract structures and substructures that represent episodes, sentences and clauses. However, Gernsbacher did not adopt an intermediate level of representation such as the propositional level.

The Structure Building Framework (Gernsbacher, 1990) has an amodal approach. Thus, the medium of mental structures must handle non-linguistic as well as linguistic input. This requires a theory that proposes a variety of compatible representational media and Van Dijk and Kintsch (1983) and Johnson-Laird (1983) theories could account for this variety. As we already discussed above, according to Van Dijk and Kintsch (1983) the semantic and situational levels can both be represented in terms of propositions. According to Johnson-Laird (1983), information is represented as propositions ("strings of symbols that correspond to natural language"), mental models ("structural analogs of the world"), or images ("the conceptual correlates of mental models from a particular point of view"). However, Johnson-Laird argues that the propositional representation is not sufficient to represent mental models mainly because, the organization of its elements is governed by the principle of structural identity: The structure of the model is identical to that of the state of affairs it represents. Thus, for a particular text, the structure of the model reflects the structure of the situation described in the text.

Johnson-Laird proposes two types of models: the physical model that represents the physical world, and the conceptual model that represents abstract things. Within the physical model, the author distinguishes between five categories of models that highlight the crucial role of relations: relational simple, spatial, temporal, kinematic and dynamic. He also includes another type of model: the image, which rather than a model *per se* stresses its instrumental function for the mental simulation. However, according to Johnson-Laird (1983), mental models and images contain information relative to one or several objects, that is structured is a non-arbitrary way and reflects the structure of the object.

Thus, both Gernsbacher and Johnson-Laird assume that comprehenders mentally represent the physical situations expressed by language and that they develop relatively iconic representations of the physical situations conveyed by the texts. In other words, readers build their mental representations on the basis of structural identity between the represented and the representing world or on their perception of daily-life events.

Therefore, what we discussed earlier indicates a relatively large consensus on the idea that the construction of readers' mental representation should closely match the way readers attribute relevance to world events. This conception leads to reduce inevitably the "distance" between cognition and perception.

1.5 Situation Models as Analogical Correspondence between Symbols and Referents

Assuming that the representation of knowledge requires to respect the analogical relationship between symbols and referents, some theorists developed another symbolic system, that is, the perceptual-based approach or the embodied explanation. The proponents of this approach (Barsalou, 1999; Glenberg & Robertson, 2000; Zwaan, 1999, 2004) make the assumption that cognition relies on the use of perceptual and motor representation, rather than on abstract, amodal and arbitrary mental representations such as the propositional format (Barsalou, 1999; Glenberg, 1997). This assumption is supported by empirical data collected mainly on visual and spatial representation, and by recent findings from neuroscience, indicating that the perceptual and motor representations activate previous traces stored in these specific brain areas (see Damasio, 1989).

One crucial hypothesis in perceptual symbol systems relies on the existence of an analogical correspondence between symbols and referent. First, each referent has a perceptual representation that is created from a series of perceptual symbols, each one of these being constituted of features (e.g., shape, color, orientation) that define the referent (i.e., those relevant for comprehension). These features, once combined, constitute the unified representation of the object called the simulation (Barsalou, 1999). Thus, any change in one component of the object should cause a change in the specific perceptual symbol, and consequently should have an effect on the representation. Perceptual symbol systems also predict an interaction between mental representation (i.e., the simulation) and their referents due to the affordances of the object, since any transformation the referent undergoes may cause an analogous transformation in the simulation. Thus, if the referent is an object (e.g., a pencil) and if the orientation of the referent changes, so too the representation. Stanfield and

Zwaan (2001) also argued that, if any change in the referent produces similar modification in the simulation, an alteration in the simulation should as well have implications for the interpretation of the referent.

Perceptual symbols do not exist independently of one another in long-term memory; instead, related symbols become organized into a simulator that allows the cognitive system to construct specific simulations of an entity or event in its absence (Barsalou, 1999). Within this theory, a concept is equivalent to a simulator and a given simulator can produce limitless simulations of a kind, with each simulation providing a different conceptualization of it. For instance, the simulator for chair can simulate many different chairs under many different circumstances, each one offering a different conceptualization of the category (see Barsalou, 1999).

Simulators bear important similarities with schemata, and contain two levels of structure: (1) An underlying frame that integrates perceptual symbols across category instances (i.e., generating mechanisms), and (2) the potentially infinite set of simulations that can be constructed from the frame. Together, a frame and the simulations it produces constitute a simulator. According to Barsalou, mental models are also related to simulator although they are not identical (Johnson-Laird, 1983). Whereas a simulator includes two levels of structure, mental models are roughly equivalent to only the surface level, that is, simulations of specific entities and events. Mental models tend not to address underlying generative mechanisms that produce a family of related simulations (see Barsalou, 1999).

2 Relations among Objects in Situation Models

Situation models are representing structures built during the process of discourse comprehension (Gernsbacher, 1990). These structures include objects and relations among objects. The latter depend on how objects, the building blocks of situation models, are conceived. As noted above, situation models have been represented propositionally sometimes. Relations between propositions, such as argument overlap, may be quite different from relations among objects in non-propositional situation models. In the following sections we review some of the theoretical and empirical findings on relations, both for propositional and non-propositional situation models.

2.1 Propositional Situation Models

Van Dijk and Kintsch (1983) and Kintsch (1998) describe the relations existing among objects in propositional situation models. Kintsch (1998, p. 39), in particular, distinguishes three types of relations. First, there may be indirect coherence: Propositions are related because they are part of the same episode, that is, they share time, place or an argument. In this case, the relations between propositions in the situation model are defined in terms of perceived relations in the world. Second, there may be direct coherence when propositions refer to the same episode, as in indirect coherence, but in addition the relation is marked by clauses or sentences. Here, a sign for the relation is explicitly found in the surface structure of discourse. The relation that may be created by a reader among propositions at the situation-model level is like the one considered above: The propositions are recognized as being part of the same episode. Third, there may be relations among propositions signaled by subordination. In this case the relation between objects is one of specification, for example, the manner of an action or the property of a participant.

Although relations in propositional representations take into account corresponding relations in the world, as in the case of indirect coherence considered above, the former seem to have quite different properties than the latter. For example, with regard to relations based on shared space or time, no variability in the strength of the spatial relation or temporal relation between propositions, caused by the temporal or spatial distance between the corresponding facts in the world, should be expected. In this respect, relations in this type of representing world are quite different from relations in the represented world. Because of this, in contrast to the propositional approach, situation models have been conceptualized by many researchers as analogical representations, that is, as structural analogues of the world (Johnson-Laird, 1983). The analogical character of situation models implies a parallelism between represented and representing relations that needs to be examined in detail. We review below some theoretical and empirical findings regarding relations in non-propositional situation models.

2.2 Non-Propositional Situation Models

Three main types of relations between objects in non-propositional situation models, mainly of narratives, have been distinguished (Zwaan, Magliano, & Graesser, 1995): spatial, temporal and causal. Although these relations have been frequently studied isolated from each other, looking at one at a time (Zwaan & Radvansky, 1998), they have been found to interact in defining the strength of the total relation among objects in situation models (Rapp & Taylor, 2004). The characteristics of these three types of relations are presented next.

2.2.1 Spatial relations Spatiality has been the most frequently studied dimension in situation models. The reason for this may be the clear difference in the representation of world spatial relations in analog and propositional models. Two events or objects spatially near each other in the represented world may be situated farther apart in the surface or textbase representation. However, they would be expected to be near each other if the situation model is really an analogic representation. And according to several research results, this is what happens indeed. It has been widely shown that the mental representations constructed from descriptive texts reflect the spatial properties of the environment described in these texts. In particular, when subjects have to memorize the location of different objects in a complex environment, the accessibility of the objects tend to decrease with the distance to the protagonist's location, where subjects should think that they are located (Morrow, Greenspan, & Bower, 1987). Also, when subjects mentally explore distances between objects for which the location has been specified by a verbal description, the mental exploration durations appear to be longer as the distance between objects increases (Denis & Cocude, 1992).

However, it seems unreasonable to reduce spatial models to a singular or simple view of the described environments. Presumably, they are situated at a more abstract level and codify a "multi-perspective" rather than separate scenes from a unique point of view. Taylor and Tversky (1992) compared two texts that described the same spatial environment with two different perspectives, route versus survey. Subjects' task was to judge inferences on the spatial layout. The results showed that judgments were as fast and correct, independent not only from the perspective adopted by the subject for judging inferences but also from the reading perspective. Thus, the spatial model built is not "biased" by the particular perspective adopted during reading. This model is general, abstract and flexible and allows the adoption of different perspectives. It is equivalent to a "structural description", that is, an abstract representation that specifies the relations between the different parts of an object (Tversky, 1991). Another important result concerns the accessibility of spatial dimensions: Are all of the dimensions in situation models equally accessible, as they are in the world? In order to investigate which spatial dimensions are best represented in spatial models, Franklin and Tversky (1990) carried out a study in which subjects processed texts that described a set of objects located along several spatial dimensions (i.e., front/back, left/right, up/down). When subjects had to retrieve the location of each object from memory, it appeared that not all spatial dimensions were equally accessible. Some, such as the vertical dimension, were dominant over others: Subjects found very rapidly the information relative to the position of objects located above or below them, according to the description they have memorized. Also, although the dimension front/back appeared to be strongly asymmetric, the dimension left/right did not show any asymmetry and appeared to be the dimension on which subjects were less proficient. Franklin and Tversky (1990) concluded that the ways people canonically perceive the world influence the comprehension of spatial terms. Localization on the vertical dimension is the easiest to discriminate because it implies two strong sources of asymmetry: gravity and canonical position of the body. The front/back dimension is also very well discriminated because the perceptive and motor activities involving objects are strongly affected by the position of these objects on the given dimension. Finally, the discrimination between left and right is the most difficult to represent because no salient differentiation cues are available. Thus, mental models of tri-dimensional environments are not only simple figurative representations of texts describing these environments. The models constitute some " working space" in which subjects are able to make calculations on the relations that are not directly mentioned in the text that permits to generate it (Tversky, 1991).

Thus, what we presented above indicate that some dimensions are more easily detected than others, and this shows the great influence of knowledge and perceptivo-motor experience in the construction of spatial models. In addition, it seems that building a spatial model is not a very "natural task" for subjects and they need to be guided in order to do so. Zwaan and Van Oostendorp (1993) showed that without specific reading instruction, readers are not strongly involved in the construction of a spatial situation model. Also, in a study of Gray-Wilson, Rinck, McNamara, Bower, and Morrow (1993, Experiment 3), subjects built detailed situation models only when the specific tasks requirements force them to focus on spatial information during reading. Thus, there is no doubt that people create spatial models of a situation conveyed in texts. However, whether or not they represent all the entities of the environment described with their relations may evolve over time and is strongly dependent on the focus of subjects' attention on specific parts of information, e.g., entities or relations (see Zwaan & Radvansky, 1998), on the relevance they give to some spatial relations taking into account their prior knowledge, goals and strategies or self-estimation of the comprehension level of the situation. This reflects the relative complexity of spatial models or, in other words, the possibility for situation models to embed different levels of complexity (see Johnson-Laird, 1983).

2.2.2 Temporal relations The comprehension of temporal relations among events described in a text (precedence, succession or size of time intervals) and how they are represented in situation models has received relatively little attention (Zwaan & Radvansky, 1998). However, time has an important role in the creation of situation models. In two experiments, Salmeron, Canas, Kintsch, and Fajardo (2005) explored the role of reading strategies in hypertext comprehension in terms of reading order and amount of information accessed, with the main assumption that the former influences the reader's situation model while the latter has an effect on the textbase. The authors' main results supported the hypothesis that participants that read the text in different order get different learning outcomes at the situation-model level. In particular, differences due to the reading order appeared to rely on two different variables: nodes accessed and coherence between node transitions. To construct an appropriate situation model, a minimum number of nodes must be read. In addition, participants that read the contents in a high-coherent order formed a better situation model of the text than those who read the contents in a low-coherent order.

Changes in the time dimension determine the identification of event boundaries in narratives (Speer & Zacks, 2005), and consequently are central in representing events, the focal points of situation models of narratives according to the Event Indexing Model (Zwaan, Langston, & Graesser, 1995). Some studies have focused on the influence of the time dimension in the availability of information in situation models. Distance along the time dimension has a similar effect to spatial distance on the availability of events in situation models. For example, Carreiras, Carriedo, Alonso, and Fernández (1997) used short narratives where the protagonist was initially described as holding an occupation, such as economist, or, in an alternative version, as having held it. Recognition responses to the probe word denoting the occupation were faster for the version where the protagonist was holding the occupation, compared to the version where the protagonist was no longer holding it. So, in essence, the findings point to a diminution of the availability of information corresponding to past temporal frames.

Bestgen and Vonk (1995) studied the influence of temporal markers on this availability. They found that information preceding connectives like "and" is more easily retrieved than information preceding connectives like "then". Temporal markers seem to divide situation models in temporal sections, being the earlier sections less available than the later. In extreme cases, when there is an important time interval between narrated events, readers build separate situation models (Anderson, Garrod, & Sanford, 1983). One possibility is that readers interpret temporal adverbs in a temporal framework as cues for temporal coherence. When they are inappropriate, as in the case of Anderson et al.'s study (1983), they cannot match the information provided within their mental structures they develop and have to shift to a new structure or substructure (see Gernsbacher, 1990). Separation of situation models is operationally defined in terms of the fan-effect paradigm (Radvansky, Zwaan, Federico, & Franklin, 1998): An increase in retrieval time is to be observed when several facts refer to several situation models compared to the case when all of them refer to a single situation model.

Given the previous results, the central problem is to find out how temporal relations are represented in situation models. Two possibilities have been considered.

Representation in a spatial dimension. First, temporal relations could be represented in a spatial dimension. Glenberg and coworkers (Glenberg, Kruley, & Langston, 1994; Langston et al., 1998) have proposed that mental models are built in a spatial medium, analogous to three-dimensional space. Consequently, spatial relations in the world would be naturally represented in this space. But, in addition to this, dimensions like time would be represented spatially too. For this, it is necessary to map time on a spatial dimension. In one experiment testing this view, Glenberg and Langston (1992) presented subjects with texts that described four-step procedures like writing a paper (1-2-3-4). The middle two steps, 2 and 3 were to be performed simultaneously. But, obviously, they had to be presented sequentially in the text. To enhance the creation of situation models, the experimenters provided half of the subjects with pictures that represented the temporal relations between the steps of the procedure. According to the hypothesis, temporal relations should be translated into spatial relations in the situation model and the pictures should help in this. Subjects were tested so that they had to judge if two steps should be performed in the order in which they were presented. The results agreed with the predictions: Subjects that were provided with pictures performed equally well in pairs 1-2 and pairs 1-3; subjects in the no-picture condition performed better in pair 1-2 than in 1-3. These results are consistent with a situation model that includes temporal relations that are represented spatially.

Schaeken, Johnson-Laird, and d'Ydewalle (1996) analyzed the representation of temporal relations like "before", "after" and "while" in mental models. In this study, a situation like:

a happens before b
b happens before c
d happens while c

was translated into a static mental model with spatial properties as follows:

a   b   c
*   d*

The authors studied situations with a definite representation, like the latter, and indeterminate descriptions resulting in more than one representation. Subjects had to answer questions on determinate or indeterminate descriptions. The results support the mental model account, against another based on formal rules. Subjects in the experiment seem to create static mental models where temporal relations are translated into spatial relations, as shown above.

The previous studies focus on the ordinal character of the time scale, that is, on temporal precedence or succession. A second problem concerns the representation of time on an interval scale. This could be done in a static spatial situation model by translating time intervals into distances in the representing medium. One possibility mentioned by Schaeken et al. (1996, p. 207) is to represent time corresponding to a world event, or sequence of events, directly in terms of time in the situation model. This possibility is examined next.

Representation in a temporal dimension. The temporal dimension of situations and events may be directly translated into a corresponding temporal dimension in situation models. In this case, an event's duration would be represented by the corresponding duration of a mental simulation of the event, one of the crucial functions of mental models (Rumelhart & Norman, 1988, p. 556). It should be noted that the time scales in the represented world and representing world do not have to be the same. These models are termed "temporal" in a classification proposed by Johnson-Laird (1983, p. 422). One subtype of these models is composed of a discrete sequence of spatial frames, in the same temporal order as the temporal order of events. Some students' representations of geological time correspond to such a discrete temporal model (Hidalgo & Otero, 2004). The second subtype corresponds to temporal models where the sequence of frames is psychologically continuous. These are called "kinematic" models by Johnson-Laird (1983, p. 422). Discrete temporal models may represent the ordinal aspect of time only, while kinematic models would be the only temporal models where time intervals could be represented.

As is the case with spatial relations, temporal relations in situation models share some of the characteristics of perceived temporal relations in the world: The availability of events in memory depends on the temporal distance of these events in narrative discourse. Also, an important time shift in discourse causes readers to replace a situation model by a new one. Temporal relations have been proposed to be represented in two basic mediums: spatial and temporal. Analyzing in detail the implications of these alternatives would shed some light on the internal structure of situation models.

2.2.3 Causal relations There is ample evidence that causal relations play a central role in the construction of a coherent mental representation in narratives (Black & Bower, 1980; Omanson, 1982; Trabasso, Secco, & Van den Broek, 1984; Trabasso & Van den Broek, 1985; Van den Broek & Lorch, 1993). It has been widely demonstrated that recall probability of an event depends on whether that event is on the causal chain or not (Black & Bower, 1980; Omanson, 1982), and also on the number of causal relations it has with others (Graesser & Clark, 1985; Trabasso & Van den Broek, 1985). In addition to this, causal connections have been found to lead to better recall than other types of connections (Myers, O'Brien, Balota, & Toyofuku, 1984).

Four criteria can be used to determine whether a causal relation exists between two statements (Mackie, 1980; Van den Broek, 1990; Trabasso et al., 1984; Trabasso, Van den Broek, & Suh, 1989). Two properties are required: temporal priority (a cause never occurs after its consequence) and operativity (a cause must be active when its consequence appears); and two properties determine causal strength: necessity and sufficiency. Necessity reflects the fact that if a cause would not have happened, the consequence would not take place given the circumstances. Sufficiency reflects the fact that if a cause appears, the consequence will probably appear, given the circumstances. Four types of causal relations have been identified in the literature (Trabasso et al., 1989; Van den Broek, 1990): physical causality, motivation (a goal motivating actions), psychological causation (events/actions bringing about internal states such as goals or emotions) and enablement. The different properties of these types of causal relations were examined by Trabasso et al. (1989). Participants read several stories, and then rated pairs of story events according to either a criterion of necessity or a criterion of causality. Pairs of events were selected from each of the four types of causal relations. The results showed that the types of causal relations differ in their connection strength. Physical causality usually has the higher connection strength, followed by motivation and psychological causation, and then enablement. This latter relation was considered necessary but not causal by the participants. Thus, necessity seems to be a less demanding criterion than causality, and causal relations have to satisfy both necessity and sufficiency. But the distance between two statements in the text surface structure can affect the perception of possible causal relations, as a function of their importance for the success or goal failure (Van den Broek & Lorch, 1993). Tapiero, Van den Broek, and Quintana (2002) have investigated properties of the four causal relation types (physical causality, motivation, psychological causation and enablement) and how these properties affect their representation. They varied two criteria, necessity and sufficiency, and the distance (adjacent versus non-adjacent) between the elements causally related to examine the influence on readers' judgments of the strength of the relation. Readers evaluated the strength of the relation between pairs of sentences extracted from narratives constructed according to the Recursive Transition Network model (see Trabasso & Van den Broek, 1985). Strength ratings were made without reading the narratives, after a single reading of the narratives, or after a double reading of the narratives. The results showed, first, that the criterion of sufficiency appeared to be a more causal criterion than necessity (see Trabasso et al., 1989). Second, a causal strength hierarchy according to the type of causal relation and distance appeared. For adjacent pairs, the authors replicated the pattern previously obtained by Trabasso et al. (1989): Physical causality had the higher connection strength, followed by motivation and psychological causation, and then enablement. For non-adjacent pairs, the patterns of strengths for the different types of relations differed both from the Trabasso et al.'s study and from those for adjacent pairs. Relations that involve a goal or internal state (either as a cause or as a consequence) were considered strongly connected even when the elements of the relation were separated in the text structure. This suggests that readers tried to connect all the sentences to the goal, paying special attention to information that can indicate goal success or failure. In contrast, physical causalities were not relevant for the text theme. These relations possessed the strongest causal connections when adjacent to their consequences because the cause was still operative but became very weak when their operativity declined in the non-adjacent distance. This study also showed the importance of distance in interaction with criteria and reading conditions. Sufficiency appeared to be more sensitive to distance than is necessity and the judgments on the non-adjacent pairs denote a loss in the causal strength. Perceived relational strengths also differed across the reading conditions. In the reading conditions (single reading, double reading), causal rating values were greater than in the non-reading condition. In the non-reading condition, the reader can only assess the relation against his or her own knowledge about the social world and relations frequently will be very weak at best. Thus, stories provide rating circumstances that increase the causal strength between pairs of statements.

Thus, readers use their naive theory of causality to understand a text and to form a coherent representation. We highlighted the importance of the four criteria that determine whether a relation is causal or not in relation with distance (adjacent and non-adjacent) between elements causally related. However, readers probably involve more than the causality per se in the construction of their representation. We described in this section the contribution of three main relations (i.e., dimensions) in this elaboration but other dimensions than the one discussed here are likely to be involved (see Zwaan, Langston, & Graesser, 1995). In addition, although most research have emphasized the characteristics of each dimension separately, further investigations have to be done to account more specifically for their mutual influence.

3 Conclusion

This chapter was aimed at providing an overview of the elements defining the internal structure of situation models: objects and relations among objects. Our description of objects and relations within propositional and non-propositional systems evidences for all the richness and complexity of situation models, as well as underlies the different assumptions regarding the nature of readers' mental representation. We now return to the main question raised in this chapter: Is there a preferential system that defines "ideal" units or entities in situation models? This question cannot be answered in a simple way. However, in order to best capture the complexity of what we define as the deepest level of representation, that is, the situation model, an integrated theory of comprehension should account for a combination of systems or formats that would be called upon in a dynamic and "contextual" way, depending on situational factors and the reader's prior knowledge. This implies incorporating the main features of the objects, the relationships among them and affordances with the world, along with the experiential relationship between the reader and the world evoked in the text. Although fictitious, this world is assumed to share many characteristics with the real-world situations experienced by readers.

Chapter 12

The Effects of Interaction with the Device and Text Structure on the Mental Representations Derived from the Procedure

Patrice Terrier, Virginia Diehl and Julie Lemarié

Procedural texts, which interleave reading and doing, appear to be distinct from narrative and expository texts. Studies investigating the effects of interaction with the task device provided evidence that measures that are intended to tap either the textbase or the situation model (Van Dijk & Kintsch, 1983) are sometimes dissociated and sometimes related. Readers usually draw on their knowledge of both representations to do any text-related task (e.g., using knowledge of the text to perform the task). Effectively transmitting the situation model may be especially important with procedural text. Text structure variables often encourage item-specific processing as opposed to relational processing (Einstein & Hunt, 1980). Signals in the text may assist the reader in locating needed information, but at the cost of overall topic organization, and they appear to increase memory only for marked information. The material-appropriate processing framework (McDaniel & Einstein, 1989) and the transfer-appropriate processing principle (Morris, Bransford, & Franks, 1977) are useful models for integrating these results.

An important approach to text comprehension (Van Dijk & Kintsch, 1983) is based on the assumption that there are two main components of the memory representation derived from reading a text: the textbase and the situation model. The first component, which represents the propositional information contained in the text itself, is the primary contributor to tests such as text recall. The second component represents the situation described by the text, and is formed by the merging of text propositions with inferences derived from the reader's background knowledge. The situation model is regarded as the primary contributor to tests that go beyond recall of the propositional content of the text.

Environmental factors can influence the nature of comprehension processes, causing differences in performance on measures that tap different levels of representation (e.g., Mannes & Kintsch, 1987). This chapter explores whether this also occurs in the case of procedural texts, which are characterized by interleaving reading and doing, and discusses the extent to which components of the representations in memory can be mapped onto different measures, and how the structure of the text can influence the memory representation. To comprehend a procedural text is, in practice, to be able to carry out a task having certain demands. These demands may result in a differential relationship between levels of representation. Enacting the instructions may require a correct representation of both the information contained in the text itself and the situation described by the text. These demands may also influence whether the text is processed in parts or as an organized whole. For example, an assembly task with a stepwise structure may not invite the processing of the entire procedure, even if the writer has included visual signals in the procedure to help the building of a hierarchical representation.

In the first part of the chapter, we concentrate on the effect of interaction with the device. We will suggest that in the case of instructions, the distinction between the textbase and situation model is generally useful. However, they (and their corresponding measures) are not always distinctly dissociated from each other. In the second part, we explore how text structure variables (that may contribute to the construction of the textbase by facilitating macrostructure development) have their effect, with special emphasis on memory recall. We will argue that there is an important distinction between processing a global representation of the text and selective access to pieces of information—which is a more probable impact of text variables.

1 Task Orientation

According to the text-representation model (Van Dijk & Kintsch, 1983), the textbase and situation models are developed as the reader reads. Studies have demonstrated that these representations can develop to different extents; factors that lead the reader to pay more attention to certain aspects of the text can differentially affect the dependent variables that measure the two representations (e.g., Mannes & Kintsch, 1987). Most studies have used narrative or expository texts. However, when using procedural texts, the reader usually wants to get the task done, and might therefore pay special attention to the building of an accurate situational representation. Informed by the evidence that reading goals differentially affect the strength of the textbase and situation model, we should consider the possibility that the strength of the situation model could sometimes be greater than the strength of the textbase. Dissociations between textbase and situation-level measures may be the exception rather than the rule for texts that have their focus getting the task done, assuming that different measures could be equated with different representation levels.

1.1 Dissociations Between Textbase- and Situation-Level Measures

Mills, Diehl, Birkmire, and Mou (1995) looked at the effect of readers' purpose for reading on their ability to do the task and remember the text, and showed that the importance of the information to task performance interacted with the reading objective. Texts describing a task (e.g., making a children's windup toy) were provided. While reading a text, participants read with the purpose of either doing the task (Read-to-Do) or recalling the text (Read-to-Recall). Participants then recalled the text, and completed the task. Task-oriented readers (i.e., Read-to-Do) performed the task faster but recalled less than those who read to recall the text. The texts' idea units were split into high and low importance for performing the task. Read-to-Do participants recalled more of the more important units than the less important, but there was no effect of importance in the Read-to-Recall condition. The Read-to-Do participants sped up their reading rate for the less important ideas (particularly on the second reading), whereas the Read-to-Recall subjects did not. These results support the notion that those with a task orientation pay more attention to the parts of the text that are important to getting the task done, which implies that their chief concern is the building of an adequate situation model. Those who read with a "text orientation" do not appear to make such distinctions.

Diehl (2004) investigated whether the accuracy of the situation model for procedural texts is influenced by access to the corresponding object's affordances. The participants either read and did the task or only read the two sets of instructions. They then rated the difficulty and kinds of problems (if any) each sentence had. In general, given only a procedural text (reading and not doing), participants tended to focus on the textbase and to identify grammatical problems. On the other hand, when readers were asked to do the task while reading, they focused on getting the task done and therefore noticed when sentences were not well ordered. Also, the results from the sentence difficulty ratings were consistent with the idea that perceptions of difficulty depended in part on the condition the subject was in.

Another study that seems to support the notion of a dissociation between the textbase and situation models is by Diehl and Mills (1995). They demonstrated a situation in which one variable (adding action to the reading objective) increased performance on one measure (doing the task) and decreased performance on a second measure (recalling the instructions). Note that this double dissociation provided evidence for a negative effect of enacting the instructions on recall, a result that is perfectly consistent with the prediction the authors had derived from the text-representation theory: task-oriented readers will recall less because they will pay less attention to the text itself and will concentrate more on the building of a situation model.

Results observed by McNamara, Kintsch, Songer, and Kintsch (1996) and Diehl and Mills (1995) are used to argue for the conceptual separation between the situation model and textbase, but these results are not always found. Successful performance of a task from a set of instructions usually requires one to both understand the textbase and have an accurate situational model (Geiger & Millis, 2004). Logically, there should be a close relationship between the levels of representation. Consequently, as the next section will discuss, textbase and situation-level measures can be associated as a function of a given variable.

1.2 Weak Support for Dissociation between Textbase- and Situation-Level Measures

Glenberg and Robertson's (1999) subjects listened to a description of the parts of a compass and a map. While listening, some watched a video in which a hand pointed to the parts as they were described (listen and index). In another condition, subjects could not see the objects, but they read the description after listening to it (listen and read). Subjects in the listen and index conditions scored higher on measures that tapped the situation model (e.g., later task performance and a transfer task). Although subjects in both of these conditions learned a great deal of abstract knowledge about maps and compasses (as measured by a multiple choice pre-and post-tests), they did not differ from each other either before or after the manipulation. Those participants who had the parts pointed out showed evidence of having a better developed situation model, but the two conditions did not differ on their knowledge of the abstract concepts from the text (textbase).

Diehl and Mills (1995, Expt. 2) had some subjects read a procedural text while looking at the device (read and see). In this condition, the results did not show a double dissociation between recall and task performance. The participants who saw the device while reading showed task performance very similar to that of those who read while doing the task. However, they recalled more than the read-and-do subjects. Diehl and Mills (1995) explained these results by suggesting that the read-and-do participants were preoccupied with getting the task done, and neglected the text in the process. Participants in the read-and-see condition were oriented toward the task (and therefore did well on later task performance), but were able to pay more attention to the text than the read-and-do subjects (and therefore formed a more accurate representation of it).

Duggan and Payne (2001) also demonstrated that manipulations that improve the situation model (as measured by later task performance) do not always negatively impact the formation of the textbase (as measured by text recall). In three experiments using a videocassette recorder simulation, they compared chunking instructions (in which three or four steps were read and then performed) with single-step conditions. In the first experiment, readers in the chunking condition made more errors and took more time to do the procedure during learning, and made fewer errors and took less time at test. In contrast, chunking did not affect text recall. In the third experiment, chunking was only encouraged, not forced: in order to consult the written instructions, subjects in the high-cost condition had to engage in several mouse movements and clicks. In the low-cost condition, the instructions were always available in full. Subjects in the high-cost condition chunked more than subjects in the low-cost condition. The cost manipulation influenced task performance in terms of errors and time to complete the task, with a better performance in the high-cost (and larger chunk) condition. However, there was no effect of this manipulation on text recall. Although showing single (rather than double) dissociations, these results can still be interpreted as supporting the conceptual separation, in that one measure was not influenced (recall) whereas the other was (task performance).

However, there is also evidence for *associations* between measures. Returning to the study by Diehl and Mills (1995, Expt. 2), readers who watched the experimenter do the task recalled more than read-and-do participants (a result consistent with the text-representation theory and with the conceptual separation between the textbase and situation model), *but* they also performed the task faster (a result inconsistent with the text-representation theory and the conceptual separation). This result represents an instance of association between textbase and situational model. In other words, readers who watched the experimenter do the task did better than those who did the task themselves on both recall and task performance. Diehl and Mills (1995) explained this result, in retrospect, as being due to the fact that the subjects who saw the experimenter do the task did not have to figure out how to do the task correctly. Errors during training were not corrected in the read-and-do condition, and may have led to longer task performance times at test (as compared to the read and watch the experimenter do condition).

1.3 When the Focus of the Text is Getting the Task Done: Where Does it Leave Us?

With procedural texts, the distinction between memory for the procedure and memory for the instructions themselves does not always map directly onto a distinction between situation model and textbase. We consider three lines of arguments in support of this notion, and then discuss the enactment effect.

First, in most cases, successful enactment benefits from both attention to the textbase, which supplies information about how to do the task, and an embodied representation of the task, which would be part of the situation model (Geiger & Millis, 2004). Consequently, as we have just seen, textbase and situation-level measures can be associated as a function of a given variable. Duggan and Payne (2001) have argued that empirical dissociations between the textbase and situation model are dependent on the degree to which the textbase and situation model are inferable from each other: "Where there is a very close relation between textbase and situation model, a participant might use memory for whichever representation they favor during training to infer the other at test" (Duggan & Payne, 2001, p. 298).

Second, although two tasks may be dissociable, they may still reflect a single source of information (Dunn & Kirsner, 1988): a reversed association would provide stronger support for inferring that more than one process is operating. A reversed association occurs when both a positive association and a negative association between two tasks (or measures) are observed across different conditions (i.e., when the relationship between the two tasks is non-monotonic). Moreover, in practice, processing assumptions are usually tested by observing performance on the task, using the "transparency assumption" (Dunn & Kirsner, 1988). This assumption states that observed performance directly reflects the operation of its underlying mechanisms. For example, one might assume that textbase and situation-level processes map directly onto recall and task performance. The view that recall draws exclusively on the textbase representation, and task performance exclusively on the situational representation ignores the possibility that different tasks may draw, to a greater or lesser extent, upon any number of processing resources. We doubt that a memory task can be process pure, and would only reflect the textbase or, more generally, the semantic level. For example, a recognition task has been used to reveal multiple levels of representation of a text (Fletcher & Chrysler, 1990; Kintsch, Welsch, Schmalhofer, & Zimny, 1990; Schmalhofer & Glavanov, 1986).

Third, newer theoretical perspectives on embodiment in discourse comprehension (Barsalou, 1999; Glenberg, 1997; Zwaan, 2004) and past research showing the effect of the described situation on recall (Bransford, Barclay, & Franks, 1972) both clearly suggest that memory performance can reflect the situation level. Barsalou and Wiemer-Hastings (2005) have suggested that situational information would be important in a number of tasks (e.g., recall, recognition, lexical decision, verification tasks) and would require many different cognitive processes (episodic memory, conceptual processing, visual cognition, language processing). Other theories assume that language processing involves a set of cues that the comprehender uses to create a mental simulation (perception plus action) of the described situation (Barsalou, 1999; Glenberg, 1997; Zwaan, 2004). In this approach, there is no need to assume a one-to-one correspondence between measures and levels of representation.

As Duggan and Payne (2001) have pointed out, showing an advantage for reading and doing over only reading (on a task performance measure) has no practical application, and so, consequently, it is not this effect that needs additional empirical investigation. Under circumstances where procedural texts (which have as their focus getting a task done) are being used, a comparison of the "read and do" and "read and watch experimenter do" conditions will be more informative. As noted earlier, such a comparison has shown that under the condition of watching the experimenter do the task (which is clearly task oriented), an improvement in the (putative) textbase measure can be coupled with an increment in the (putative) situation model measure (Diehl & Mills, 1995, Expt. 2). This parallel effect suggests overlap in the processes contributing to performance on the two kinds of measures.

The observed advantage the recall test for the read-and-watch experimenter do over the read-and-do condition, while consistent with the text-representation theory, is at odds with the large body of results on the "enactment effect". Numerous studies have investigated memory for actions (for review, see Engelkamp, 1998). In the typical paradigm, simple action phrases like "break the match" or "scratch your head" are learned under various encoding conditions. Participants enact the instructions, watch somebody doing so, or simply learn them verbally. The conditions in which actions are carried out typically lead to better recall than other encoding conditions; this is the enactment effect. Consider for the moment that equating tasks with processes (transparency assumption) is correct. If so, how could the enactment effect be explained? One possibility is that the memory advantage for enacted (individual) instructions reflects an improvement of the textbase and has nothing to do with the situation level. This seems unlikely given that successful memory of what is comprehended would necessarily involve the retrieval of a representation of the state of affairs described in a text (Zwaan & Radvansky, 1998, par. 1). Further, assuming that referring words and phrases to objects is crucial for comprehension of procedural texts, there is room for perceptual and experiential information in comprehension, even at the level of background knowledge (Glenberg & Robertson, 1999).

A common explanation for the enactment effect is that enactment encourages item-specific encoding (Engelkamp, 1998). Relational processing, or organizational processing, involves focusing on similarities or shared themes among disparate pieces of information. Item-specific processing focuses on properties that are distinctive or unique. Here, we reason the way procedural texts are generally used favors selective processing of instructions—or item-specific processing, rather than relational-information processing (Einstein & Hunt, 1980; Hunt & Einstein, 1981; Hunt, 2003). Because many procedural texts have a stepwise structure, we can read a single step and then execute it before reading the second step. These conditions have been pointed out previously (Duggan & Payne, 2001; Guthrie & Mosenthal, 1987; Vermersch, 1985), and we conjecture that they can be appropriately applied to the enactment effect. Consequently, a positive-enactment effect should be observed even when instructional steps are related. Later we will see that the same manipulation that had depressed memory recall in the Diehl and Mills (1995) studies has been shown to improve memory recall. But first, we discuss the role of text structure variables that provide much evidence for item-specific or local processing.

2 The Impact of Text Structure

In this section, we discuss the role of signals as markers of text structure, before considering other structural variables. Coupled with the way procedural texts are used (i.e., interleaving reading and doing), item-specific processing of instructions (rather than relational) could often be encouraged both by the task orientation and the text structure. We will argue that there is an important distinction between processing a global representation of the text and selective pieces of information; the latter is more likely to be affected by text variables. This distinction could help in understanding how several text structure variables have their effect.

2.1 Relevant Features of Procedural Texts

Some characteristics of procedural texts are particularly relevant to text structure. As Ockerman and Pritchett (2000) point out, the main purpose of procedural texts is to reflect the task structure. The task structure has its origin in the conceptual structure as represented in the mind of the writer. This conceptual structure has to be translated in the text by means of linguistic and/or visual cues to form the text structure. The text structure may be defined as the main ideas of the text and their relationships. The construction by the reader of a situation model that maps onto the conceptual representation of the writer may be particularly crucial with procedural texts, because an error may have serious consequences. For that reason, the writer has to cue the text structure in an explicit way to avoid ambiguities. However, procedures used by task experts can be less comprehensive and detailed than those used by novices (Ockerman & Pritchett, 2000). Expert workers rely on their own conceptual representation and use the procedure as a guide for action. But, in the case of readers with poor background knowledge, it is necessary to be explicit and non-ambiguous. Frequently, the writers of procedural texts are experts with the task and device, and so they cannot anticipate the comprehension difficulties the reader may encounter (Fayol, 2002a,b; Wright, 1977). Accordingly, procedural texts are sometimes implicit and too vague for the reader (Richard, 2002). If the writer leaves out linguistic cues such as connectives or importance indicators, the reader may not be able to use her or his background knowledge to infer the semantic and hierarchical relationships between ideas. In this case, the text's visual structure may serve as a very important cue for the reader to infer the structural relationships between the text segments (Lorch, 1989).

The text's visual structure may play a crucial role when there is a lack of explicit structural cueing. It is also clearly useful for procedural texts, which are generally consulted for specific information. Moreover, their consultation is rarely a linear reading of the whole text but rather an interleaving of reading -and doing (Duggan & Payne, 2001; Ganier, 2002a; Vermersch, 1985). This particular consultation mode of procedural texts affects which format improves their ease of use. Because many procedural texts have a stepwise structure, it is possible to execute the procedure while reading with a minimal load on memory. Reading a single step and then executing it before reading the next step may be low on effort, but is also low on transfer-appropriate practice and will therefore lead to poor retention (Duggan & Payne, 2001; Schmidt & Bjork, 1992).

A writer can facilitate the reader's task by using a variety of devices to signal relevant information (Meyer, 1975; Van Dijk & Kintsch, 1983). Signals are writing devices (either visual or linguistic) that point out the importance of an idea in a text and/or reveal the content relationships (Meyer, 1975; Spyridakis, 1989a). Numbering, highlighting, underlining key words or phrases, explicit use of connectives, importance indicators (e.g., "It is important to note…"), preview sentences, headings, and paragraphs can be used. Signals represent distinctive processing, and distinctive processing is defined as the simultaneous processing of organizational (or relational) and item-specific information (Hunt, 2003). In making the prediction of increased recall for participants who read a text with signals because signals should support the building of a hierarchical framework in memory, one is probably implicitly predicting a benefit from relational or organizational processes at the expense of item-specific information.

Although technical communicators rely heavily on signaling devices, empirical studies on this topic are few and contradictory (Spyridakis, 1989a, 1989b). Signals should help the reader form a hierarchical framework in memory that will facilitate the retention of superordinate content, and serve as an organizer of subordinate content. Spyridakis (1989a) suggested a reason why few studies consistently support the effect of signals in this process: The likelihood of demonstrating strong and consistent results for signaling increases when one uses texts of some length and difficulty on unfamiliar topics. Why do few studies support the effectiveness of signals in the process of building a hierarchical framework? We now develop two arguments. First, signals may only be useful when they provide necessary background knowledge and/or disambiguate information, and not when they are redundant with text content. Second, signals are not routinely used to build a global representation of the text by the reader—even in the reading-to-learn context of narrative or expository texts that place demands on memory—and consequently no overall recall advantage is observed for texts containing signals. Rather, the effects of signals are selective effects and point to the importance of considering task demands.

2.2 Do Signals Just Strengthen the Text Structure?

Signals in expository texts are devices that visually enhance the text macrostructure that is mostly cued by explicit textual segments like macropropositions or thematic expressions. Consequently, in these cases, visual signals may be considered as agents facilitating the construction of the textbase. But procedural texts may often represent cases where semantic relationships between text parts are implicit (Richard, 2002) or ambiguous. Indeed, frequently, authors are experts, and cannot anticipate novice's comprehension difficulties (Fayol, 2002a,b). We illustrate the difference between signals that serve to strengthen the text structure and those that disambiguate with the example below that describes the list of documents necessary to ask for a passport renewal (Figure 1). In the case where the coordinating conjunction "or" is included, the fact that "a tax assessment" is an instance of residence proof is explicit and there is no ambiguity with respect to the number of documents required. The fact that "a tax assessment" is located on the same line as "a residence proof: a gas, electricity bill, or a tax assessment" reinforces the semantic relationships between the text segments. If the

---

Documents required to renew a passport:
a previous passport,
a recent residence proof: a gas, electricity bill, **(or)** a tax assessment,
a full face bare headed 2x2 inches in size photograph
a 30 € tax stamp (tobacconist's shop, tax centre, tax office).

Figure 1: List of documents necessary for a passport renewal.

conjunction "or" is deleted from the text, the fact that "a tax assessment" is an instance of a residence proof is mainly cued by the position of the text segment in the enumeration. Indeed, if the segment was located at the beginning of the following line, a reader with poor background knowledge on these types of documents could think that the tax assessment is not a residence proof but another required type of document, and this could affect the reader's action.

As signals in expository and procedural texts have mainly been studied as something that strengthens a semantic structure that is already cued by the text content, it is not surprising that their effect on comprehension has not been clearly demonstrated. On the other hand, when signals disambiguate a procedural text, they should have an effect at the situational level as well as at the textbase level. In addition, the semantic value of different signaling devices could differ and could result in different levels of memory performance. Virbel (1985, 1989) has noted that some of a text's visual properties are meaningful because they reflect the author's structural intentions. In terms of writing models (e.g., Hayes, 1996), visual properties are assumed to form part of the complex representational act of considering one's audience. However, not all visual properties are meaningful; some of them are just consequences of the physical page layout. For example, beginning a new line may be due either to the intention to cue a topical change (as in the example) or to the limits of the page. The text sequencing observed in a text, although related to the linearity imposed by the layout, may be used by the author to reflect a temporal sequencing, especially in the case of procedural texts. Consequently, one might expect that text-sequence information could be related to comprehension. Interestingly, Therriault and Raney (2002) provided several pieces of evidence that text-sequence memory is related to comprehension, whereas place-on-the-page memory is not. A possible explanation may be the differential semantic value of these different cues.

2.3 Signals have Selective Effects on Recall

Although an important motivation for using signals is to convey the text structure, there is little evidence that the processing of relational information is enhanced by text format. We briefly consider the difficulty in substantiating the prediction of an increased overall recall for those participants who read a text with signals. Clearly, this prediction has been mainly tested in the reading-to-learn context of expository texts, and reviews generally do not cite many studies that have used procedures (see Spyridakis, 1989a). Drawing on one type of text to test an assumption made with another type of text may be risky (as described in the next section). We assume, however, that a similar effect could be expected in the reading-to-do context of procedural texts, due to the importance of locating specific information in a document.

It is possible that the reader would adopt a structural strategy that focuses on the processing of topical relationships when the text is signaled (e.g., Loman & Mayer, 1983). One example of this idea is the "strategy-switch hypothesis".[1] Because authors use signals to help readers encode the text's overall structure, signaling should affect overall recall (e.g., Lorch & Lorch,

---

[1] The "strategy-switch hypothesis" states that readers do not routinely encode a text's overall structure in the absence of signals. Rather, they encode the text as a temporally organized list of facts or events to be learned. Signals entail a switch of the text encoding strategy from a list strategy to a structure strategy, with readers elaborating a representation that reflects the hierarchical organization of the text and the relative importance of its conceptual content (Loman & Mayer, 1983; Lorch & Lorch, 1995; Meyer & Poon, 2001).

1995; Meyer, 1975). However, overall recall has typically not been found to differ in texts containing signals (e.g., Meyer, 1975); signals may facilitate the recall of the information they mark by inhibiting recall of unsignaled information. These selective effects on recall have been reported for many signaling devices including highlighting, underlying key words or phrases, numbering, and combinations of signals such as preview sentences, headings, connectives (Glynn & Di Vesta, 1979; Irwin & Pulver, 1984; Loman & Mayer, 1983; Meyer & Rice, 1982). Even organizational signals (e.g., headings, overviews, topical summaries), which are designed to emphasize the structure of expository texts (Lorch, 1989), have been shown to affect the distribution of recall of text content rather than the quantity of content recalled (Loman & Mayer, 1983; Lorch, Lorch, & Inman, 1993; Lorch & Lorch, 1996). In sum, the prediction of increased recall for those participants who read a text with signals is difficult to substantiate in the reading-to-learn context of expository texts. We suggest that the same situation will occur in occupational contexts, where locating specific information in written documents is prerequisite to reading-to-do (Guthrie & Mosenthal, 1987).

Locating information in a document involves detecting a specific subset of information within a large array that is displayed for visual inspection (Guthrie & Mosenthal, 1987). When the task of locating information is considered, building a representation of the hierarchical structure may or may not be critical. Is the availability of a representation of the text's topics and organization critical to the development of an efficient selective search strategy? Klusewitz and Lorch (2000) concluded that there was no evidence that participants used information about the hierarchical organization of the text to guide their page inspection when different types of headings were compared. Although headings had clear effects on page inspections (look times decreased when headings were added), look times were *not* shorter in the structure headings condition than in the topic headings condition (there was a consistent tendency in the opposite direction). Klusewitz and Lorch (2000) concluded that in search tasks, readers appear to use the headings on a page to facilitate the inspection of the page. This use of headings benefits inspection, but at the cost of interfering with the construction of a topic-structure representation. This study appears to be at odds with demonstrations that headings encourage the construction of a topic-structure representation (Lorch & Lorch, 1995, 1996; Lorch et al., 1993), but those demonstrations involved tasks that placed greater demands on memory than search tasks. This conclusion is reminiscent of what has been demonstrated for hierarchical presentation of information in an assembly task (Zacks & Tversky, 2003).

2.4 Hierarchical Structure of Instructions

Cellier and Terrier (2001) investigated the effect of visually segmenting and grouping the instructions from a procedural text. Text format was either in block form or structured in spaced paragraphs corresponding to the major steps of the assembly task, where each paragraph included a sequencing of instructions (with bullets and spacing). Visually sequencing and grouping the instructions significantly decreased inspection time of the text when subjects did the task at encoding—time to complete the task later did not vary. The sequencing and grouping of instructions had no positive effect on recall. Rather, the less structured text was recalled marginally better. In a related study (Denis & Veyrac, 2002), recall was significantly improved when the structure of the procedure was presented in a less explicit mode (when a flow chart or a reduced text were compared with an original extended text).

Zacks and Tversky (2003) examined whether an interface designed discretely and hierarchically would facilitate memory in the context of an assembly task. Instructions were segmented, presented hierarchically, and organized by objects and actions, consistent with the theory of event cognition (Zacks, Tversky, & Iyer, 2001). An interface designed discretely and hierarchically facilitated memory for assembly of a musical instrument but interfered with memory for assembly of a toy. The authors suggested that the explanation for the difference lies in the demands of the assembly tasks. Hierarchical structure facilitated the task when a certain order of assembly was required, but it interfered when the task afforded several possible assembly orders.

Cailliès and Tapiero (1997) compared two procedures that described the use of Microsoft Word™, a teleological hierarchy, wherein the goal and the outcome were directly linked and the actions were subordinated to the goal, and a temporal-causal version wherein a goal led to a sequence of actions, which eventually produced an outcome. They showed that a hierarchically organized procedure (teleological version) facilitated comprehension (as measured by cued recall) for participants who were advanced in the domain to be acquired (text editing), whereas beginning and intermediate participants benefited more from the procedure that was organized temporally and causally. The interaction was explained by the overlap between the participants' prior knowledge, and the semantic coherence of the text: prior knowledge of advanced participants is teleological, thus they benefit from the teleological organization; prior knowledge of beginner participants is organized in a temporal-causal chain, thus they benefit from the temporal-causal organization of the procedure. More recently, Cailliès, Denhière, and Kintsch (2002) used a primed recognition task to further clarify this explanation. They analyzed the relationships subjects established between a goal, four actions, and the obtained outcome. They concluded that beginner participants did not establish a relation between the goal and the outcome during reading (the target recognition time varied with the distance between the prime and the target in the text), whereas the goal and the outcome were directly connected in the prior knowledge structure of advanced participants (the outcome was always recognized faster than the actions).

Informed by the research on narrative texts, Diehl and Mills (2002) used procedural texts to investigate the relationship between three structural variables (i.e., on vs. off the causal chain, active vs. static information, and hierarchical structure) and difficulty rating, importance rating, reading time for first and second readings, and true-false. Although different dependent variables were used, the results for causal chain and active/static were consistent with previous research with narrative texts (e.g., Trabasso & Van den Broek, 1985). Sentences on the causal chain were judged to be more difficult and important, and were read more slowly. Active sentences were read more slowly and judged to be more important. However, the results with the hierarchical structure variable were predicted to show a different pattern with instructions than with narratives. With narratives, the highest level of sentences is read more slowly and judged to be more important (Cirilo & Foss, 1980). However, with procedural texts—at least with those used in Diehl and Mills (2002)—the majority of the *task steps* were on the second level, so they predicted that this level would be read most slowly and judged as most important. Although the results with reading time were unclear, the latter prediction was confirmed. The confirmation of this prediction is important in that it illustrates that models of narrative text understanding do not accurately predict results for procedural texts when relevant procedural text characteristics differ from those of narrative texts.

In addition, models of narrative text understanding do not accurately predict recall for procedural texts when the "argument overlap" level effect (Walker & Meyer, 1980) is considered (Mills, Diehl, Birkmire, & Mou, 1993). In the referential model (Van Dijk & Kintsch, 1983), texts that have a more argument overlap (e.g., nouns, adjectives) among propositions are assumed to be more locally coherent than texts with less argument overlap. Thus, the propositions that are superordinate (high level in the textbase) have a higher probability of recall and recognition than subordinate propositions. Mills et al. (1993), using procedural texts, reported a reversal of the level effect: lower-level propositions were recalled better than superordinate propositions.

To sum up, the effect of relational markers of text structure is not undisputed in the literature. Signals have a selective effect on recall of expository texts: they facilitate the recall of the information they mark but a global memory effect is not generally observed. Also, when the activity of locating information—often required in work settings—is considered, it is unlikely that relational markers are used to elaborate the global representation of the text. The way procedures are used (with the interleaving of reading and doing), coupled with the list-like structure of most procedural texts, makes it likely that they would benefit from item-specific processing more than relational processing. Hierarchical structure and level effects suggest that, with procedural texts, task demands should be considered before applying predictions that have been supported with narratives.

3   Text Structure and Task Orientation: Material-Processing Interactions

Material-processing interactions also reveal the importance of a task analytic approach. The effect of text structure may show up only under certain circumstances (i.e., only for a given orientation or processing condition). Following Cellier and Terrier (2001), the effect of visually segmenting and grouping the instructions of a procedural text was investigated using an enactment manipulation (Terrier, Lemercier, Cellier, & Mojahid, 2004). An assembly task was used, and enactment was manipulated in a within-subject design. A positive-enactment effect was predicted for a procedural text, based on the assumption that the way procedural texts are used (i.e., processed step-by-step) favors item-specific processing. Also, the experiment explored whether the enactment effect could be sensitive to the text structure, thereby revealing the cognitive impact of the text structure on item-specific processing. The text was either blocked or structured with paragraphs that corresponded to the steps of the building task. The experimenter and the subject alternatively enacted the instructions of the assembly task (building a model of a blower) at encoding, while the instructions were always read aloud one-by-one by the subject. Then subjects recalled the instructions. The experiment indicated an enactment effect in the context of an assembly task: subject-performed instructions were better recalled than experimenter-performed instructions. But this enactment effect was observed only with the blocked text, not with the structured text. In the latter condition, the recall of experimenter-performed instructions increased and became as good as the recall of subject-performed instructions. These results suggest that the processing of item-specific information (in this case, encouraged by doing the task) is important with procedural texts, as evidenced by the observation of an enactment effect when instructions gave no information about the text's structure. This is contrary to the negative-enactment effect found by Diehl and Mills (1995, Expt. 2) and predicted by the text-representation theory (Van Dijk & Kintsch, 1983).

Mills et al. (1995) studied both text structure and goals when they examined comprehension for one "list-like" and one "narrative-like" procedural text and gave participants one of the two goals for reading—to recall or to perform the action described in the text. The structure of the text did not affect recall (or performance) and did not interact with the goal. This would suggest that text structure is not important for procedural texts. Recently, a different pattern emerged with similar material (Geiger & Millis, 2004). In the study by Geiger and Millis (2004), text coherence was held constant when procedural or descriptive versions of a text were compared as a function of task orientation: to perform the procedures, to summarize the passages, or to answer questions. The texts described how to build simple objects or machines. The procedural versions contained enumerations of the steps ("first, second") and the reference to the reader ("you"), while the descriptive versions did not. In addition, in Experiment 2, a "list-like" version of the procedural text was designed in which each step of the procedure was explicitly numbered. The list-like text was compared with the more "narrative" procedural version in which there were some enumerations that used words. The first experiment (Geiger & Millis, 2004, Expt. 1) failed to replicate past research that showed readers' goal differentially affects the textbase and situation models (Diehl & Mills, 1995; Mills et al., 1995; Schmalhofer & Glavanov, 1986). Although the procedural and descriptive texts did not differ as a function of idea units recalled, a main effect of the goal was observed: the perform goal led to better recall than the question-answering goal. This pattern was the same for the procedural and descriptive text. When textbase and situation model question accuracy (on a true–false test) was analyzed, there was still no main effect of text type and no interaction involving text type. Goal affected performance: the perform goal led to better comprehension than the question-answering goal. Also, question type had an effect: subjects scored higher on textbase than situation model questions. In a second experiment (Geiger & Millis, 2004, Expt. 2), a drawing measure revealed that the text structure (narrative or list-like) affected comprehension, but the results suggested that the direction and statistical significance of the difference may be goal-specific. A textbase and situation model drawing score was calculated for each participant. When participants read to perform the instructions, both textbase and situation model scores were higher for the narrative procedural text rather than for the list-like text. In contrast, a non-significant trend showed the opposite pattern for the question-answering condition.

Two key findings emerged from this study. First, comprehension was better (although not significantly) both at the textbase and situation level with narrative texts when the text was read for performance—the finding suggest associations between the true/false and drawing scores. Second, a goal-specific effect of text structure was observed: when the text was read in order to perform the task, comprehension was best when the text was written in a narrative style as compared to a list of steps. Importantly, the pattern of recall (and drawing scores) is consistent with the claim that more elaborative processing occurred when the text structure did not match the perform goal (narrative-procedural text and perform goal) than when text structure and reading objective did match (list-like procedural text and perform goal). Because the prediction of superior recall performance following a material-appropriate task (essentially a material-encoding mismatch task in this case), relative to a material-inappropriate task (a material-encoding match task), follows from the material-appropriate processing framework (Einstein, McDaniel, Owen, & Coté, 1990; McDaniel & Einstein, 1989), one possible framework for dealing with this and other material-processing interactions (e.g., goal-specific effect of text structure variables, interactions between text structure and expertise, or between signals and text difficulty) could be the material-appropriate processing framework. This framework holds that accurate recall will increase when the processing goal encourages processing attributes that are not invited naturally by the stimuli. Overall recall will be increased only when participants perform encoding tasks that attend to the non-obvious characteristics of the stimuli. For example, Geiger and Millis (2004) suggested that, in their study, the perform goal emphasized local processing, thereby enhancing memory as a whole. In this case, the perform goal provided extra item-specific processing on top of the relational processing encouraged by the narrative version of the text, and recall was enhanced. Of course, the idea of additive effects of relational and item-specific information (Einstein & Hunt, 1980) with technical texts requires further empirical findings to reach any firm conclusion.

The pattern that occurred for the perform condition (the narrative-like procedural text led to better comprehension than the list-like text on textbase and situation level measures), which was reversed (but not significant) for the question-answering condition, suggested that the perform goal is of important practical concern in the design of the structure of a procedure. With the perform goal of procedural texts, can some difficulties be introduced for readers in the manner advocated by Schmidt and Bjork (1992) and as demonstrated by McNamara et al. (1996) with expository texts? Duggan and Payne (2001) clearly highlighted this possibility in their study on chunking, when they showed that, with procedural text, performance during learning does not always predict later performance. Moreover, they also explicitly showed the relevance of the transfer-appropriate processing principle (Morris, Bransford, & Franks, 1977) in explaining why, for McNamara et al.'s (1996) high-knowledge readers, the texts that were less coherent improved the situation model measures.

4 Conclusion

When considering the effect of interaction with the device described by a procedural text, the textbase and situational representations sometimes map directly onto different measures (e.g., recall and task performance), but such a one-to-one correspondence has not been consistently demonstrated. When there is a close relation between textbase and situation model, as we assume for procedural texts, empirical dissociations could be the exception rather than the rule, because one level may be easily inferable from the other, and the transparency assumption will not be supported.

Because many procedural texts have a stepwise structure (e.g., assembly tasks), we proposed that the way procedural texts are used often favors item-specific rather than relational processing because of the interleaving of reading and doing. This is not to say that relational information is not important in some procedural texts. For example, in inspection tasks, clearly explaining how the current action is positioned within the single procedure or the set of procedures is one of the locational procedure context guides that may be provided with task guidance systems (Ockerman & Pritchett, 2004; Ockerman, this volume). Locational procedure context clarifies the relationships of each procedure step to other steps and to the procedure as a whole (Ockerman & Pritchett, 2004). According to Hunt (2003), relational or organizational processing specifies, at least, the context defining an event, and the item-specific processing specifies unique properties of a particular item within the event. Consequently, beyond the assembly tasks that are often used in procedural text research, inspection tasks (and locational procedure context) would be an interesting way to further examine the participant's reliance on item-specific processing versus relational processing. We would expect to find that the user is aware of more than just a series of isolated commands.

It is often assumed that a global processing of the text (and consequently of the task to be performed) can be encouraged solely by revealing the text structure, and that this type of processing will automatically result in better comprehension. In the second part of this chapter, we explored how text structure variables (that may contribute to the construction of the textbase by clarifying the macrostructure) have their effect, with special emphasis on memory recall. We have seen that the role of signals as markers of text structure is not undisputed (even with expository texts) and have argued that signals may encourage item-specific processing (i.e., a selective effect on recall is observed). Other structural variables have also been studied in procedural texts. The hierarchical and levels effects suggest that the influence of structural variables is task specific, or more generally, goal specific. Also, interactions between task orientation and text structure that clearly show the goal-specific effect of text structure support the importance of the distinction between global and local processing.

Although there is not much published data on this topic, what is available suggests that the interaction between text structure and task orientation may have important implications for the use and design of procedural documents. Recently, in the domain of expository hypertext comprehension, where locating information is an important aspect of document use, Salmerón et al. (2005, Expt. 2) have shown that manipulating an overview (low coherence overview and high coherence overview) did not improve the situation model. Rather, it appeared that the reading order selected by the reader influenced coherence, which, in turn, led to a stronger situational representation of the information. However, background knowledge interacted with reading order: readers with low knowledge benefited from a more linear reading order, whereas high knowledge readers did best with a less linear strategy. Further, Salmerón, Kintsch, & Cañas (in press) showed that the reading strategy that was selected depended on characteristics of both the text and the reader. These findings suggest that the study of procedures should take the reader's attributes (e.g., prior domain knowledge) into account, and that those may influence the use of different strategies.

To conclude, understanding the interaction between task orientation and text structure variables is fundamental for an account of how procedural texts can best be written. Relational and item-specific processing (Einstein & Hunt, 1980), the transfer-appropriate principle (Morris et al., 1977), and the material-appropriate processing approach (McDaniel & Einstein, 1989) can provide a framework to approach this interaction.

Chapter 13

Comprehension Processes in Translation

Pedro Macizo and Maria Teresa Bajo

We review comprehension processes involved in translation. These processes range from lexical access (recognition of isolated words), sentence understanding (extraction and combination of syntactic information to obtain a sentence interpretation) to discourse-level processes (integration and interpretation of successive sentences to arrive at a global mental representation). The results of studies comparing translation and normal reading provide strong support for a horizontal view of the translation task: Translation includes code-switching processes that start before full comprehension of the source text has been achieved. In addition, translation places increased demands on working memory relative to those in ordinary comprehension during reading. These findings have implications for training professional translators.

1 Introduction

An individual who knows two or more languages has not necessarily acquired the communicative skills to reformulate a source language (SL) into a different target language (TL). It is still true that bilinguals under everyday circumstances produce "natural translations" without any special training in translation tasks. This natural translation has been considered a product of bilingualism, and the degree of translation competence a function of the bilingual's ability to use two languages (e.g., Harris, 1977). However, beyond considering bilingualism the foundation of the translation ability, translation competence could not be necessary a consequence of bilingualism. Natural translation contrasts with professional translation where performance is the result of years of training and learning of translation strategies (problem identification, linguistic analyses, text inference and reasoning, etc., Gerloff, 1986). Moreover, cognitive processes in natural and professional translation may be quite different. For example, the cognitive representation of strategies learned by professional translators could become attached to lexical units (Shreve & Diamond, 1997), making different the understanding of the SL.

Written Documents In The Workplace
Copyright © 2007 by Elsevier Ltd.
All rights of reproduction in any form reserved.
ISBN: 978-0-080-47487-8

Macizo, P., & Bajo, M. T. (2007). Comprehension processes in translation. In G. Rijlaarsdam (Series Ed.) and D. Alamargot, P. Terrier, & J.-M. Cellier (Vol. Eds.), Studies in Writing, Vol. 21, Written Documents in the Workplace, 193–204.

The research that we review in this chapter examines language comprehension with professional translators. We describe the varieties of translation and the main theoretical perspectives in this area and afterwards, we examine lexical, sentence and discourse processes in translation. Two critical issues are addressed in the chapter. First, the controversy between the parallel vs. sequential processing of SL and TL in translation; second, the role that working memory (WM) plays when translators comprehend the SL.

2 Varieties of Translation and Theoretical Perspectives

The term translation has been used in both a broad sense and a narrow sense (De Groot, 1997, p. 25). The broad sense of translation refers to any task where a SL is reformulated in a TL. In this perspective, translation is equivalent to interpretation since no differences are established between the written and the oral modalities of the SL. In the narrow sense, however, the term translation is restricted to any task where the SL to be translated is written (text, sentences, etc.). Thus, under the narrow view of translation, a "SL mode" dimension would distinguish between translation and interpretation: translation referring only to written SL texts and interpreting denoting only the reformulation of SL speech (see Figure 1). In our opinion, the narrow sense of translation would be preferred since translation and interpretation differ from a cognitive perspective. For example, the memory demands in rephrasing SL speech (e.g., simultaneous interpreting) are higher than the memory resources needed for reformulating written SL texts (e.g., Gile, 1997).

In addition, translation tasks could be classified according to a "perception-production delay" continuum (see Figure 1). This dimension refers to the time elapsed between the input and the corresponding output, which can be understood as the degree of overlap between the SL comprehension and the TL production. This dimension has been called ear-voice-span (EVS) in circumstances where both the input and the output are orally formulated (Barik, 1969). The simultaneity of processing and the EVS are negatively related; hence, shorter EVS would reflect more co-occurrence of processes at the same time. The translation version with the shortest perception-production delay is *sight translation* (or simultaneous translation, McDonald & Carpenter, 1981). In this type of translation the professional rephrases the SL text aloud while reading it (Gile, 1997). Sight translation is not paced by the SL speaker since the input is a written text; however, the memory demands remain high because the translator has to continuously produce the text in the TL under time pressure. Although *semiconsecutive translation* has not been referred in the literature, we could consider it as the counterpart of semiconsecutive interpreting for written SL texts. In semiconsecutive translation the written text has to be orally produced in the TL, but, in contrast to sight translation where the professional has to read and rephrase the SL text simultaneously, in this type of task the translator alternates between reading and speaking periods.

Finally, in the *written* form of *translation* the input and the output are both written text. In this translation version, professionals use external helps (e.g., dictionaries, reference works) and strategies such as comparing the SL/TL texts or choosing between two equivalent solutions, without the time pressure imposed by other forms of translation.

There is also a task mixture of sight translation and simultaneous interpreting where both text and speech are presented. In *simultaneous interpreting with text*, the speaker reads the text

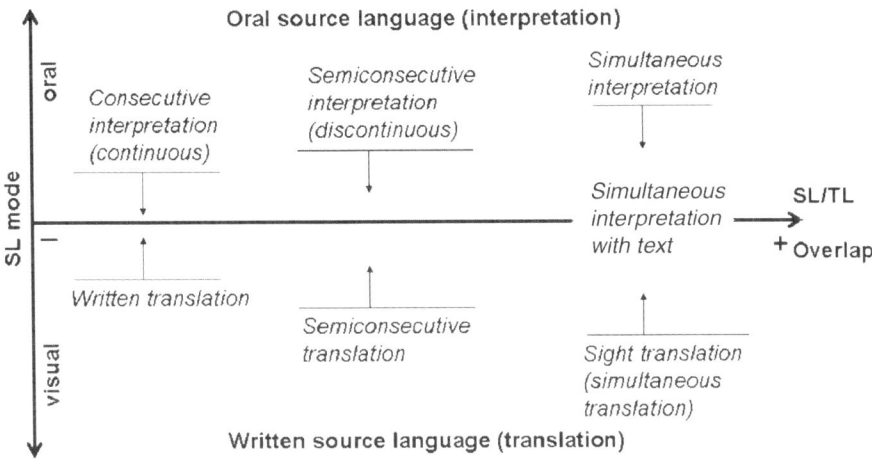

Figure 1: Forms of translation and interpreting arranged in two dimensions. The horizontal axis refers to the simultaneity of the SL comprehension and TL production (SL/TL overlap). The vertical axis denotes the written or visual nature of input (SL mode).

and the translator has the text also available. The translator has to listen to the speaker and compare the spoken SL with the text message before translating the information into the TL.

Two different forms of translation can also be considered when the direction of the translation and the translator's languages are taken into account. In forward translation, the translators rephrase from their first language (L1) to their second language (L2). In backward translation, the professionals reformulate from L2 to L1. Forward translation has been also referred as active or inverse, whereas backward translation has been called passive or indirect (Fabbro, 1999). Empirical evidence has shown that forward translation is slower and more error prone than backward translation (Kroll & Stewart, 1994; Sánchez-Casas, Davis, & García-Albea, 1992). This asymmetric pattern has been explained by the revised hierarchical model (Kroll & Stewart, 1994) as a consequence of the asymmetry in the strength of the lexical/semantic connections of the bilingual two languages. Translation from L1 to L2 is more likely to engage time-consuming conceptual processing than translation from L2 to L1 and thus, backward translation would be faster than forward translation (Kroll & Stewart, 1994).

Despite these differences among the translation tasks, all of them engage three major processes: analysis and understanding of SL text, switching between two linguistic codes and production of TL text. However, it has been proposed two opposing views of how these processes work during translation. One of them, the horizontal/parallel approach, considers that translation involves reformulation, that is, establishing semantic matches between the lexical and syntactic entries in the two languages involved (Gerver, 1976; see Danks & Griffin, 1997, for a similar approach). The TL lexical units are supposed to be activated and checked in a continuous parallel manner, before SL meaningful chunks are fully comprehended and integrated into the discourse representation (see Figure 2). Opposed to this view, the vertical/serial approach considers that translation is the result of the processes of analysis and understanding of the input message (Seleskovitch, 1976). The translator's task

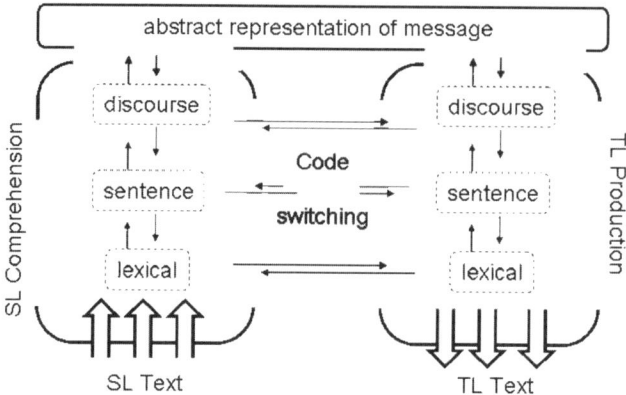

Figure 2: A proposal of cognitive processes in translation. The model depicts the principles of the horizontal views of translation. SL: Source language; TL: Target language.

is to give lexical expression to the "meaning" extracted from these processes: full comprehension of the input is needed before the constructed meaning is reformulated in the TL. Thus, understanding and reformulation proceed in a discrete serial manner.

In addition, the two approaches differ in the role that they assign to WM during different processes involved in the translation task. Although there is not a general agreement about what WM is (see Miyake & Shah, 1999), one of the most influential perspectives suggest that it is composed of three components: The phonological loop is needed to process and maintain phonological information, the visual/spatial sketchpad performs similar functions for visual and spatial inputs, and the central executive is a limited capacity attention system (i.e., the supervisory attention subsystem of Norman and Shallice, 1986) which includes attention processes (e.g., the capacity to focus attention, the process of dividing attention, etc.). The phonological loop and the central executive are particularly involved in translating a text. The phonological loop is required to maintain the SL text until reformulation in the TL takes place. The executive functions are needed to coordinate the translation processes, to switch between the SL and the TL and to avoid the interference produced by the subvocal rehearsal of the SL when speaking in the TL.

Although WM is needed for translating a text and many theories has emphasized its role in producing the TL text (Gile, 1997; for a review of WM in translation see Macizo & Bajo, 2005), the vertical and horizontal perspectives pose different predictions of the role of WM in comprehension during translation. According to the vertical approach, although the input and the output of the translation task involve different linguistic codes, the primary process in translation is comprehension. The translators, as all readers, interpret the source text against their background knowledge and use their WM resources to access the meaning of individual words, the syntactic structure of the sentences or to integrate meaning into higher structures. Once these processes have being carried out, production in the TL proceeds. Thus, for the vertical view, comprehension in reading and comprehension during translation involve similar demands and these comprehension processes do not overlap with production in the TL. According to the horizontal approach, reformulation from one linguistic code to another would consume resources that would add to the resources needed for normal comprehension (De Groot, 2000; Gile, 1997). These resources would be needed to access lexical entries in the TL, to hold the input message during translation, to store the partial results of the reformulation process and to distribute resources among all these concurrent operations (De Groot, 1997, 2000; Gerver, 1976; Gile, 1997). Hence, according to the horizontal view, comprehension for translation would engage more WM resources than within-language reading. Several studies have provided support for both the parallel processing of the SL and TL and the high WM demands in comprehension for translation (Macizo & Bajo, 2006; Ruiz, Paredes, Macizo, & Bajo, 2004). In the next sections, we discuss these studies and organize them according to the level of processing in comprehension.

3 Comprehension in Translation

Language comprehension in both, within-language (e.g., reading) and between-language tasks (e.g., translation) includes at least three levels of structure, associating specific cognitive processes with each level. Word processing includes encoding visual features of words into abstract representations (e.g., graphemes) and the retrieval of word form and meaning from long-term memory (lexical access). The processes at the sentence level include syntactic operations that interpret clauses semantically and integrate the word meanings in the sentence to obtain a sentence interpretation. Finally, discourse processes include the integration and interpretation of successive sentences by using textual cues and the reader's world knowledge to arrive at a global mental representation (the text main topic).

3.1 Word Processing

Comprehension in translation starts accessing to lexical properties of words. Recent psycholinguistic research with bilinguals and professional translators provide evidence that lexical information in the SL and the TL is related. When bilinguals and translators recognize words, information from both languages is activated in parallel (La Heij, De Bruyn, Elens, Hartsuiker, & Helaha, 1990; Macizo & Bajo, 2004a; Miller & Kroll, 2002). For example, Miller and Kroll (Experiment 1) used a stroop-type interference paradigm in a word translation task. Spanish/English bilinguals were instructed to ignore a distractor word while translating an L1 target word. Distractor words were presented in the L2 language and were related to the meaning or to the lexical form of the L1 word to translate. They found significant effects of the distractors on translation performance. Semantically related distractor words produced interference, whereas form-related distractor words produced facilitation, demonstrating that access to L2 language occurs early in translation. These data have been considered into models of lexical processing (i.e., the bilingual interaction activation model, BIA, Dijkstra & Van Heuven, 1998) under the assumption that when words are read in one language, the lexical forms representing these words are activated in both the SL and the TL. In addition, the non-selective access of lexical information has been corroborated in studies with professional translators examining the processing of cognate words in translation tasks. Macizo and Bajo (2006) compared a group of highly proficient Spanish/English bilinguals without training in translation and a group of Spanish/English translators having more than two years of experience in their profession. Participants translated from Spanish to English both cognate and non-cognate words. Cognate words are words with the same meaning and shared orthographic and phonological properties across languages (e.g., *piano* in English and Spanish). Each individual word was presented in isolation and translation latencies were recorded. If the lexical forms in the SL and TL are activated in parallel, cognate words would be translated faster than non-cognate words because of their similarity across the two languages. The results supported this hypothesis indicating that both bilinguals and translators were faster at translating cognates than non-cognate words.

In addition to the non-selective activation of lexical information, recent evidence shows that translators understand SL words in such a proficient manner that permit them to efficiently handle the interfering effect of concurrent articulation while trying to comprehend the SL (Bajo, Padilla, & Padilla, 2000; Padilla, Bajo, & Macizo, 2005). For example, Padilla et al. (Experiment 1) compared the number of words recalled by experienced professional interpreters, a group composed of highly competent professionals in language-related disciplines and a group matched in WM span to the group of interpreters. All participants were presented words to be studied in isolation or under the concurrent uttering of the syllable "bla" (suppression condition). The two groups of non-interpreters showed a decrement in the number of words recalled in the suppression condition compared to the control condition (articulatory suppression effect), while this effect was practically absent in the interpreter group. Thus, translators were able to cope with the interference of simultaneously understanding and producing. Moreover, the translators' ability to handle the task was not directly related to their WM capacity since control participants matched in WM span showed interference under suppression conditions. A possible reason of this better performance by the interpreters is that they overcome the interference through the support of long-term language-specific knowledge. The use of this linguistic knowledge led the translators to comprehend words efficiently even in circumstances where understanding is difficult because of the simultaneity of perception and production. A key source of evidence of this long-term knowledge activation comes from the Padilla et al.'s study (Experiment 3). In this experiment, a group of interpreters was asked to study lists of words or non-words silently or under articulatory suppression conditions. If the presence or absence of the articulatory suppression effect was related to the support of linguistic knowledge, no articulatory suppression effect would be expected when words were studied; however, it would be found for non-words because they lack prior knowledge. Results confirmed these predictions, participants recalled fewer non-words but equal number of words under articulatory suppression conditions. Thus, although the concurrent articulation of irrelevant speech prevents the normal refreshing of words in WM, knowledge of the lexical/semantic properties of these words may help to maintain the information.

3.2 Sentence Processing

Beyond lexical access, the meaning of individual words has to be combined using syntactic rules to understand sentences for later translation. Sentence processing is particularly relevant in translation tasks since translators do not produce their output instantaneously, but they wait to produce the translation until sufficient information has been comprehended and integrated in a meaningful unit (Goldman-Eisler, 1972).

It has been widely demonstrated that WM plays an important role in reading sentences and that sentence processing is constrained by the resources of WM. Research on within-language reading has yielded evidence that WM resources are critical for sentence parsing, comprehension of syntactically complex structures, maintaining alternative interpretations of ambiguous sentences, etc. (King & Just, 1991; Mitchell, 1994; Waters & Caplan, 1996). However, some empirical and theoretical work suggests that WM demands are higher when sentence understanding is directed to later translation. Additional WM resources are needed in translation as compared to within-language sentence understanding to change the attention between the source and the TL, to coordinate perception and production processes and to cope with the interference of the dual activation of two languages (Danks & Griffin, 1997; Gile, 1997). One way to demonstrate the higher WM demands in sentence processing during translation is to evaluate within and between language tasks while manipulating the SL complexity. Recent studies have investigated this complexity by either embedding homograph words into sentences (Macizo & Bajo, 2006, Experiment 1) or using difficult relative sentences (Macizo & Bajo, 2004b). For example, Macizo and Bajo (2004b) compared comprehension in reading and comprehension for active and passive translation of sentences presented word by word, while online reading times were recorded. Spanish/English professional translators were asked to comprehend and repeat and to comprehend and translate sentences from either Spanish to English (active translation) or English to Spanish (passive translation). Cognitive demands on WM were explored introducing object relative sentences (e.g., The judge that the reporter interviewed dismissed the charge at the end of the hearing). Sentences with this opaque syntactic structure are difficult to process because the reader cannot assign thematic roles until the subordinate verb appears in the sentence. Therefore, until the verb *interviewed* is encounter, readers cannot assign either the role of patient to the first noun (*judge*) or the role of agent of the relative clause to the second noun (*reporter*). In comprehension for translation, slower online comprehension for relative clause sentences was expected because of the increase on WM demands, especially at the point where the relative clause verb was encountered and role assignment had to be performed. The results confirmed this hypothesis; reading times were slower at the boundaries of the relative clauses during understanding for translation in both forward and backward directions. When professional translators were actively translating from Spanish to English, they spent more time processing the end of the relative clause than when they understood for repeating. This effect was of approximately the same magnitude when participants understood for passive translation from English to Spanish. Therefore, the results suggest that within-language understanding and understanding for translation differ in the amount of WM resources that they require and, possibly, in the processes that they involve. As we earlier described, the horizontal view of translation proposes that comprehension for translation involves the parallel activation of the SL and TL (code-switching processes), and this would increase the WM demands during comprehension. This view contrasts with the vertical perspective where comprehension and recoding are performed in a sequential order with no direct links between SL and TL at the lexical/syntactic levels of analysis. A couple of studies have confronted these two perspectives of translation following the same reasoning: if translators engage in partial reformulation processes and activate lexical entries in the TL while understanding for translation, some linguistic properties of the TL should show an effect when understanding SL sentences (cognate status of words, lexical frequency of words in TL). Macizo & Bajo (2006, Experiment 2) explored the access to the TL during sentence comprehension manipulating the cognate status of words located at either the beginning or the end of sentences presented word by word in Spanish. Professional translators read three types of sentences for either repeat in Spanish or translate them into English: sentences starting with a cognate word (e.g., the zebra has black and brown colour skin similar to the skin of the caterpillar); sentences ending with a cognate word (e.g., the steed has black and brown colour skin similar to the skin of the zebra); and sentences without cognate words at the beginning or at the end (e.g., the steed has black and brown colour skin similar to the skin of the caterpillar). When translators understood sentences for repeating, no facilitation effects were found for cognate words; however, when they read the sentences for later translation, the reading times for cognate words (*zebra* in English, *cebra* in Spanish) were faster than the control words located at the end of sentence (*caterpillar* in English, *oruga* in Spanish). This different pattern of cognate effect when comparing comprehension for repeating and comprehension for translation directly supported the horizontal theories of translation proposing that, when reading for translation, units in the SL and the TL become activated in parallel. However, this study did not clarify the nature of the TL activation during the SL sentence processing since it is unclear whether the cognate effect is located at the lexical or semantic level of processing. Although cognate words share lexical properties across languages (orthography and phonology), it has been suggested that cognate words also have more overlapped semantic features than non-cognate words (De Groot & Nas, 1991). The Ruiz et al.'s (2004) study provided direct evidence that at least, lexical properties of the TL become active during SL comprehension. In the study, they examined the frequency of usage whose effect has been clearly located at the lexical level (e.g., Balota & Chumbley, 1984). Following the same design described above, Ruiz et al. selected Spanish words with the same frequency of usage in Spanish (*esquina/corner*, *escalera/stair* in Spanish/English respectively) whose frequency of usage in English was either high (*corner*) or low (*stair*). As in the Macizo and Bajo's study, these critical words were located at the beginning or the end of Spanish sentences, and professional translators had to understand them for repetition or translation in English. Online comprehension of Spanish words (*esquina*) with high frequency in English (*corner*) was faster than the processing of Spanish words (*escalera*) with low frequency in English (*stair*) when they were embedded at the end of sentence and participants read them for later translation. However, when the translators understood and then repeat the sentences no differences were found between high- and low-frequency words in English. Thus, comprehension of SL is sensible to TL properties of critical words embedded in the sentences to be translated. Cognate words and high-frequency words at the end of the sentences facilitate reading comprehension when translators read and translate, but these effects are not found when translators are reading for repetition in the SL. This opposed pattern of results based on the goal of reading is in agreement with horizontal theories of translation suggesting that activation and switching between the two languages involved proceeds in parallel to processing and understanding of the SL. In addition, the presence in both studies of facilitation at the end of the sentences and its absence at the beginning of them indicates that code switching and TL activation do not proceed until a minimum unit of information has been processed (Goldman-Eisler, 1972).

3.3 Discourse Processing

Little research has been done in translation and interpretation at the level of discourse processing. However, some studies in translation and interpreting have explored differences in understanding narrative and expository texts (Dillinger, 1994; Macizo, 2003). Narrative texts are poems and novels, and their purpose is to entertain; whereas, expository texts are textbooks and newspapers, and their purpose is to inform (Weaver & Kintsch, 1991). It have been claimed that narrative and expository texts differ at the discourse level. Narrative discourse fosters more knowledge-based inferences because it is easily related to the reader's everyday experiences, whereas expositions are often decontextualized and they tend to address topics far from the reader's world knowledge (Graesser, 1981). These differences result in narrative texts being easier to read than expository texts. Overall, narrative texts are better recalled and understood than expository texts in reading (e.g., Graesser & Riha, 1984).

In relation to translation, Dillinger (1994) explored possible differences between these types of text on interpreters. The author selected a narrative and an expository text (described as a sequence of procedures) that only differed in their semantic properties (frames). Professional and inexperienced interpreters were required to interpret from English to French and afterwards to recall each text, while oral protocols were recorded. The protocols were transcribed and later categorized as a function of the number of SL propositional information included in the interpreters' TL productions. In addition, to study the effect of text properties, these propositions were sorted based on their importance for the discourse organization of SL text. The frame propositions were the most complex information structures, whereas non-frame structures were less relevant for text organization. The results showed that participants translated more propositions of the narrative text than of the expository one. Moreover, participants selected more frame than non-frame propositions from the narrative text; however, there were no differences in the type of proposition translated from the expository text. This interaction suggests that interpreters understood the discourse structure of the narrative text, but they were not able to extract the high-level organization of the expository text. Dillinger matched the texts in all dimensions (number of words, clauses and propositions) but discourse-level variables (narrativity). Hence, any difference between texts served as evidence that interpreters go beyond sentence meanings to integrate them into a text structure, which is rich and better organized in narrative texts. However, based on these data, it is unclear whether translators process the discourse in translation as they do in reading. Dillinger's study was intended to explore comprehension on novice and trained interpreters without comparing within and between language tasks.

It is assumed that building cognitive representations that capture the ideas of the text imposes a cognitive load during comprehension. Thus, it would be interesting to know how translators deal with these demanding processes when they carry out tasks that differ in complexity (reading vs. translation). Macizo (2003) compared these tasks using an exploratory approach to study discourse processing. Ten narrative texts and ten expositive texts written in Spanish were presented word-by-word while professional translators were required to either read aloud or translate them into English. Word reading times were analyzed in multiple regression analyses introducing predictor variables at the lexical, sentence and discourse levels of processing. Discourse level included the paragraph boundary and the serial position of the sentence in the text. In addition the type of text (narrative and expository) was also analyzed. The sentence boundary variable specified whether the words were located at the beginning or at the end of paragraph. Readers use ends of paragraphs both to integrate explicit ideas embedded in the paragraph, and to infer new information based on their previous long-term knowledge and the knowledge already extracted from the text. The abstract representation of the text is not static, but develops as the person reads the text. Thus, sentences at the beginning of the text reflect the foundation of the text representation, whereas sentences at the middle or the end of texts have to be integrated into the growing representation. The regression results indicated that the effect of discourse factors depended on the task. The paragraph boundary significantly predicted RT variance in reading and translation. Online comprehension was slower at the end of paragraph; however, the effect was higher at the beginning of the text in translation whereas the paragraph boundary effect had the same magnitude across all the text regions in reading. Similarly, the sentence position effect was modulated by the tasks. Overall, final sentences were read faster than those in initial positions. However, the serial position effect was more pronounced in translation than in reading. Finally, narrative texts were read faster than expositions during both reading and translating. The higher effect of paragraph boundary and serial position of sentences in translation suggests that the creation of a text representation and the inter-sentence integration becomes harder in translation than in reading. It has been suggested that discourse processes are demanding on cognitive resources at the very beginning of the text when the reader activates knowledge relevant to the text (Haberlandt & Graesser, 1985). Therefore, the pronounced effect of text variables at the beginning of comprehension in translation seems to be related once again to the relative higher WM demands in between-language tasks. Furthermore, the results replicate Dillinger's study by showing better performance for narrative than for expositive texts in translation. However, these differences were similar for reading and translation despite the difficulty to create a text representation in the latter task.

4 Conclusions

Comprehension involves lexical, sentence and discourse processes that are performed in both within-language (e.g., reading) and between-language tasks (e.g., translation). However, the study of comprehension during translation should be considered as a separated but closely related area since comprehension is modulated by the task goal. Studies on word processing have demonstrated that there is non-selective access of lexical information across the translators' two languages and that the meaning of words to be translated is retrieved through the parallel activation of SL and TL. A consequence of this non-selective activation is that cognate words with shared orthography and phonology across languages are translated faster than non-cognate words. In addition, the translators' long-term knowledge provides support to word processing, which led them to cope with the demands of WM in translation. We have reviewed studies showing that processing capacity requirements are higher in comprehension during translation than in within-language reading. These higher demands in translation make difficult to understand complex sentences due to the presence of either ambiguity (homographs, Macizo & Bajo, 2006) or opaque syntactic structures (object relative sentences, Macizo & Bajo, 2004b). In addition, some studies have demonstrated that SL comprehension is mediated by TL characteristic. As described earlier, online reading and comprehension of Spanish words embedded at the end of sentences is facilitated when these words are cognate vs. non-cognate words (Macizo & Bajo, 2006). This evidence supports the horizontal view of translation pointing out that SL processing and SL to TL code switch co-occurs. Although there have been only few studies that have examined discourse processing in translation, the findings suggest that WM demands constrain in high-level comprehension processes. However, further research is clearly needed to explore discourse processing in translation. Finally, the construction of a situation model, which integrates background knowledge with the information contained in the SL, seems to be determined by all comprehension processes discussed here (lexical, sentence and discourse processes). Macizo (2003) observed that lexical, sentence and discourse factors made a unique contribution to the comprehension performance during the translation of texts: When lexical, syntactic and discourse complexity increased comprehension slowed down. In addition, we observed that translators use their word knowledge efficiently so that they can comprehend even in circumstances where understanding is difficult because of the simultaneity of perception and production (Padilla et al., 2005). It is, therefore, possible that building a situation model may benefit from the translators' ability to activate their background knowledge.

Most of the knowledge available about comprehension in translation comes from the analysis of different linguistic tasks. The comparison between tasks is relevant since it lets us to explore how comprehension is modulated by the goal of understanding (e.g., translation consumes more WM resources than reading). Furthermore, these differences based on the tasks are in agreement with the language-mode hypothesis. Language mode refers to the relative state of activation of a multilingual's two or more languages (Grosjean, 1997, 1998). The extreme situations are those where either only one language is active (monolingual mode) or two or more languages are simultaneously active (bilingual/multilingual mode). However, Grosjean proposes that between these two extreme modes, there is a continuum where the relative activation of two languages depends on factors such as the topic of the conversation or its purpose. Therefore, an individual who knows two languages is able to retrieve the components of each language, as he/she needs them, these components being speaking, writing and understanding. Grosjean (1998, p. 137) applies the notion of language mode to reading comprehension: If individuals reading in one of their languages in a monolingual mode notice they have to use the other language, they would move to positions close to the bilingual mode. Thus, comprehension processes would depend on the characteristics of the situation such as the translator's tasks (e.g., reading or translation) and, in turn, these characteristics may explain differences between within-language understanding and comprehension in translation.

In addition to the language-mode hypothesis, it is possible that the activation of different task schemas makes the distinction between within-language comprehension and comprehension in translation (Green, 1998). A task schema details the action sequence required to perform linguistic tasks. Thus, the reading schema specifies that only a language has to be activated to understand and produce the message, whereas the translation schema drives the lexical activation of two languages to understand the SL and produce in the TL. Although task schemas are supposed to compete for selection, the appropriate schema selection occurs because individuals maintain the task as a goal. The existence of reading and translation schemas may explain some of the empirical data discussed in this chapter (e.g., the different pattern of TL activation during reading and translating sentences). Thus, translators have the reading and translation tasks as two different goals and activation of the respective schema may produce differential activation of the TL. In addition, the continuous use of translation schema by expert translators could be at the base of the distinction between natural and professional translation discussed in the introduction. These translation schemas may underlie the automatic performance of translation skills.

The topics discussed in this chapter have applied implications for training professional translators. A recent approach in teaching translation is called the "process-oriented perspective" (Gile, 1994). According to this view, students of translation receive training in the cognitive processes involved in translation and interpreting. For example, the sequential model of translation proposed by Gile is a pedagogical view of training translators by focusing on two main phases: comprehension and reformulation. From this chapter it can be drawn that translation places increased demands on WM relative to those in ordinary comprehension during reading. Therefore, low WM demanding strategies should be learned to help translators' performance without increasing cognitive load in translation. For example, Agrifoglio (2004, p. 61) suggests that one of the most effective strategies to reduce WM demands in translation would be to mark key elements before translating the text to identify grammatical structures that differ markedly between the SL and the TL. Gile (1995) describes a similar strategy based on the use of slashes and brackets to separate subordinate clauses from main clauses. Probably, the activation of these grammatical structures might facilitate the translation processes without increasing cognitive demands. In addition, the novice translators' memory skills should be trained so that they can use external aids such as summaries or annotations without having an extra cost in processing. These memory skills might include training in coordinating comprehension and production and practicing tasks to improve the capacity of activating two linguistic codes simultaneously (i.e., articulatory suppression situations where translators have to articulate words while trying to comprehend the source message, Padilla et al., 2005).

Acknowledgments

This work was supported by Grant (BS02002–00159) from the Ministry of Education and Science of the Spanish Government. Pedro Macizo was supported by the research program "Ramón y Cajal" from the Spanish Government.

Chapter 14

How Reading Strategies Affect the Comprehension of Texts in Hypertext Systems

R. Ignacio Madrid and José Cañas

The use of hypertext as a relatively new technology for presenting expository texts has emerged as an alternative to traditional linear prose. One of the main points of hypertext is that it gives the reader easy access to different sources of information on a particular topic. In this context, readers faced with an expository text in hypertext have to develop a particular strategy in order to determine which information they will read and in which order they will access it. However, this possibility introduces new ways of processing information that can affect its comprehension either positively or negatively. In this chapter we revised a series of studies exploring the strategies that readers use when reading a hypertext and how these strategies influence text comprehension. Data reveals that some aspects from navigation behaviour such as the amount of information accessed and the coherence between transited nodes affect comprehension and are modulated by individual differences on cognitive factors.

1 Introduction

Hypertext is replacing traditional linear text in important areas such as education, communication and commerce. Together with the speed and ubiquitous access to information, there is a claim that hypertext improves the learning and/or comprehension processes compared with linear text. However, the advance of hypertext has not been accompanied by research results supporting benefits of hypertext for comprehension or learning in comparison with linear text (Dillon & Gabbard, 1998; Chen & Rada, 1996). Therefore, it is important to better understand how readers comprehend information presented in hypertext format to obtain an understanding of the real benefit of using hypertext for comprehension or learning.

From the point of view of cognitive ergonomics, navigation and reading in hypertext is related to the interaction between a user (the reader) and an artefact (the hypertext). In this way, we can say that there exists a mutual dependency between human cognitive functions and the properties of the interface where the information is provided (Cañas, Salmeron, & Fajardo, 2004). From a user-centred perspective (Unz & Hesse, 1999), we should understand this interaction process, that is, how the reader interacts with the hypertext system for comprehension. Therefore, we have to know which variables, both from the system and from the reader, determine a better comprehension.

In this chapter, we review the research that has been conducted on the effect of reading strategies that readers follow on hypertext comprehension, and how variables related to reader's cognitive functions modulate it. This review would allow us to propose a framework for understanding reading comprehension in hypertext systems that could be used to find explanations for some contradictory results found in the research literature and to improve hypertext design in order to take advantage of its characteristics.

2 Cognitive Tasks Involved in Hypertext Use

Does comprehending text in hypertext format involve the same processes and abilities as those involved with linear-text comprehension? When using hypertext we have not only to read the information contained in text nodes, we also have to move between information units that compose it, following a path guided by the specific task for which we are using hypertext. There are different subtasks that conform the task of reading hypertext, which not only differ in their contents but in their cognitive requirements. Oulasvirta (2004) examines content and navigation-orienting tasks pointing out that, from the memory point of view, these tasks are dissimilar in the deepness of the processing that readers carry out, being shallower for navigation-orienting tasks.

Therefore, a good experimental strategy may be to analyse cognitive processes involved in each task separately. In this way, Kim and Hirtle (1995) classified cognitive tasks related to hypertext into three groups: informational tasks, navigation tasks and task management. Informational task is performed by the reader to comprehend the text presented in the hypertext system, while navigation and management tasks are performed to access the information units distributed among the different nodes and to coordinate accessing and reading tasks.

2.1 Comprehension or Informational Tasks

Reading and comprehending the concepts included in text nodes and the relations between them are the main informational tasks related to hypertext. From a theoretical point of view, there is a lack of specific models that cope with the special features of hypertext comprehension and learning. Therefore, researchers have worked making assumptions based on cognitive or learning models well established in linear-text research. In spite of the increase of task control falling on the reader and the cognitive constraints added by the hypertext system, it has been assumed that the basic processes involved in reading a linear text (working memory span, reading rate, word access, etc.) are the same on hypertext (Wenger & Payne, 1996), and the way of perceiving, processing and storing textual information is guided by the same principles as that in linear-text reading.

The Construction-Integration (C-I) model of text comprehension (Van Dijk & Kintsch, 1983; Kintsch, 1988, 1998) has been used extensively for conducting research in the field of hypertext comprehension (Foltz, 1996; Hofman & Van Oostendorp, 1999; Potelle & Rouet, 2003). The C-I model of Kinstch (1988) has shown to be very useful in explaining several topics that affect comprehension like previous knowledge of the reader (McNamara & Kintsch, 1996), the effect of advance organisers and system structure (Lorch & Lorch, 1985) or the role of text coherence (Foltz, Kintsch, & Landauer, 1998). So we can think that these topics are important in hypertext comprehension too.

The model distinguishes three levels of mental representations that a reader forms from the text: the surface level, a verbatim representation of the text; the textbase, a hierarchical propositional representation of the information within the text; and the situation model, which integrates that information with readers' prior knowledge. According to the C-I model, many factors contribute to text comprehension, but coherence and prior knowledge are the main factors.

We can say that text coherence exists when two propositions of a document share arguments and therefore are semantically related. Research results have shown that the level of coherence of a text has different results on comprehension depending on the prior knowledge of the reader. If the reader has not an adequate level of the domain's knowledge, the constructive processes needed on comprehension can be impaired or limited, especially when low-coherence texts are used. When readers with low-domain knowledge read a highly coherent text, they construct better situation models than when they read a low-coherence one. If the propositions of the two texts do not share arguments, bridging inferences must be done by accessing background knowledge in order to fill the lack of information. Regarding high-knowledge readers, no differences are found when they read a low- or a high-coherent text. This is explained by assuming that for high-knowledge readers, coherence gaps allow them to make inferences, building rich elaborations and compensating the lack of explicit information with a deeper processing at situation-model level (McNamara, Kintsch, Songer, & Kintsch, 1996; McNamara & Kintsch, 1996).

Additionally, hypertext coherence could be viewed from two perspectives. From a discourse production perspective, text coherence is as a property of text reflecting an author's coherence structure. In linear text, the author tries to design a coherent text with topic continuity, but this has no bearing on hypertext since the reader chooses the order and number of texts to read. From a discourse comprehension perspective, coherence can be viewed as a property of the mental representation constructed by the reader from the text read (Storrer, 2002). From this last perspective, it makes sense to ask for the importance of navigation for comprehension on hypertext environments, since the reading order of text nodes affects coherence and therefore comprehension. The studies designed to explore the role of coherence on comprehension have shown that comprehension on hypertexts is higher if they were read in a coherent manner (Foltz, 1996), and coherence between nodes transitions was responsible for differences in knowledge acquisition at situation-model level (Salmeron, Cañas, Kintsch, & Fajardo, 2005). This issue is of great importance from a design perspective, since hypertext designers can influence in the coherence-building process despite the fact that hypertext users select the reading order by themselves.

2.2 Hypertext Navigation and Management

The way in which the information is provided to the reader may be of great importance since in hypertext fragments are organised on text nodes that can be accessed using the navigation tools that the interface provides. Navigation on hypertext includes planning and executing routes through hypertext, deciding reading order and selecting links.

Therefore, navigation and informational tasks have to be coordinated for achieving interaction goals successfully. User and system features can influence each other since problems related to navigation can affect text comprehension. For example, Nauman, Waniek, and Krems (2001) found that the more navigational problems there are the less content can be recalled.

One of these problems is cognitive workload, that can be defined as the amount of cognitive resources that a person needs to perform a task (O'Donnell & Eggemeier, 1986). When cognitive workload is high (cognitive overhead), performance is affected. One of the causes of cognitive overhead on hypertext may be the discontinuous text-processing characteristic of hypertext reading (Storrer, 2002). Reading is only continuous within the same node, and then readers have to choose between nodes and pay attention to the navigation interface, reducing cognitive resources available for text comprehension. The additional cognitive load would mean that less-skilled readers get a lot of additional interference hindering the fulfilment of the inference (Foltz, 1996).

It seems that orientation and navigation problems occur when switching between tasks or integrating the necessary information for comprehension. In this line of research, Waniek, Brunstein, Naumann, and Krems (2003) ran an experiment aimed to examine factors relevant to orientation and navigation in hypertext, testing three kinds of electronic texts: linear text, linear text with overview, and hypertext. Their hypothesis was that a hypertext reader not only constructs a text-content representation for comprehension, but a text-structure representation for navigation. Through navigation, the reader creates a cognitive map with the relation between the different nodes linked to the mental representation of the text contents. This representation is essential for orientating and navigating through the hypertext, and for acquiring knowledge. Results of their experiments showed that orientation and navigation problems appear as a result of a clash between the two representations in some of their dimensions.

To overcome these problems associated with hypertext management and navigation, it has been proposed that system structure could be improved by using structural overviews that specify the relations between the information nodes. This can provide a guide for low-domain knowledge readers without affecting freedom of navigation, based on the hypothesis that visualization of the structure of the text could enhance their text structure's mental representation (Waniek et al., 2003). In fact, evidence exists showing that the overviews facilitate text comprehension, especially when the text is long, complex and unfamiliar (De Jong & Van der Hulst, 2002; Shapiro, 2000). However, some studies show null or contradictory results (Brinkerhoff, Klein, & Koroghlanian, 2001; Naumann, Waniek & Krems, 2001; Quathamer & Heineken, 2002; Shapiro, 1998; Waniek et al., 2003).

However, these contradictory results may only be apparent, since there are many variables that could be affecting the benefit of using overviews. In a recent revision, Shapiro and Niederhauser (2004) concluded that the effectiveness of a certain type of structure or overview hinges on interactions between learner's prior knowledge, goals and the activity level of the learner approach. Well-defined structures may be of help for achieving a good textbase and guiding low prior-knowledge readers, but ill-structured systems promote deep learning and the seeking of coherence within the system, especially for high-knowledge readers. However, the benefit of an ill-structured hypertext will disappear if the learning of reading strategy adopted by the reader is passive.

3 The Effect of Reading Strategies on Reading Comprehension in Hypertext Systems

It seems that the reading strategies that readers follow to select the reading order can affect comprehension indirectly by leading the reader to process a particular text in a particular way. To be precise, reading strategies could determine the amount of information a reader accesses, and the reading order of the different sections. Therefore, a reader's navigation behaviour could be considered as one of the main factors affecting comprehension outcomes. When readers are confronted with a hypertext, they have not only to decide what sections or nodes to access but also have to choose in which order they are going to do so. In this way, using a hypertext has much to do with problem solving (Foltz, 1996), and these reading strategies in hypertext can be considered the decision rule that a reader follows to navigate through the different nodes of a hypertext. But what is the exact effect of these navigation or reading strategies on comprehension?

First, we have to note that there are some methodological issues affecting the answer of this question. As we have seen in the later section, the disagreement about the joint effects of reading strategies and system and user features on hypertext comprehension could be explained by the fact that experimental variables tend to interact in the complex hypertext environment, leading to confounding results (Shapiro & Niederhauser, 2004). For that reason, there are some proposals for clarifying the state of the art in the field by including pre-testing of prior knowledge (Dillon & Gabbard, 1998), using several measures of text comprehension (Hofman & Van Oostendorp, 1999) and deepening the understanding of the interdependence between navigation behaviour and the learning performance (Unz & Hesse, 1999).

In relation to the last proposal, Salmeron et al. (2005) have conducted a set of experiments in order to examine the differential effect of reading strategies on comprehension outcomes. The results of the experiments showed the importance of controlling reading strategies in order to avoid the confounding of their effects with those related to text characteristics that could be predicted by text-comprehension models.

In the first experiment, they found that an increase in the amount of information read in a hypertext facilitates the construction of the textbase, whereas the reading order through sections was associated with differences in the construction of the situation model. In the experiment, participants had to read an expository text on atmosphere pollution adapted to hypertext that consisted of 24 nodes, which can be accessed through a hierarchical overview. Coherence between nodes was analysed using latent semantic analysis (LSA) (Foltz et al., 1998). Before the reading phase, readers were pre-tested for knowledge on atmospheric pollution. The post-test of atmospheric-pollution knowledge was conducted with text-based questions for measuring knowledge acquisition at textbase level, and cued association task and inference questions for measuring knowledge acquisition at situation-model level.

The analysis of reading strategies was done by focusing on the navigational path of the reader, using multidimensional scaling techniques for identifying similar groups of navigational paths and analysing differences between groups. In this way, participants were assigned to one of the three reading order groups after examining node-transition matrixes: the first grouped subjects that followed a linear order, the second, grouped those that followed overview in a top-down order and the third grouped those that followed a combination of the other orders or a different order. Results showed that knowledge acquisition at textbase level was predicted by the amount of information read (different nodes accessed). This was only true for low-knowledge readers but not for high-knowledge readers. The amount of nodes accessed had no effect at situation-model level. On the contrary, reading order had a main effect on cued association and inference questions scores, but not on text-based questions scores. In order to explain the differences between readers' orders, the three different groups were compared on different dependent measures. Reading order groups did not differ on previous knowledge, but it did on the nodes accessed and on coherence between transitions. It seems that a minimum number of nodes must be read in order to construct an appropriate situation model, but when a similar number of nodes are read, differences on the learning outcomes were due to differences with the reading order.

In a second experiment, Salmeron et al. (2005) tried to replicate the effect of knowledge and coherence (McNamara et al., 1996; McNamara & Kintsch, 1996) on hypertext. Their hypothesis was that low-knowledge readers benefit more from a high-coherent text then from an incoherent one, and on the contrary, high-knowledge readers learn more from a low-coherent text. In this experiment, subjects read all the nodes with the aid of one of the two overviews (high- and low-coherence). Additionally, the coherence of the reading order (high- and low-coherence) was measured. Results showed that the effect of knowledge and coherence was replicated on hypertext only if the reading order was taken into account.

So, people using different reading strategies follow a different reading order and, as a consequence of that, focus on different aspects of the text, and that could affect the comprehension of the relations between the different sections of a text. Although this was a well-known relation reported in the literature of linear text (Magliano, Trabasso, & Graesser, 1999; McNamara, 2004; McNamara & Scott, 1999; Trabasso & Magliano, 1996), we need to better understand the type of strategies that hypertext readers follow when their main purpose is to comprehend a text in hypertext format (Unz & Hesse, 1999).

One possible reading strategy is maintaining coherence. In an experiment conducted by Foltz (1996), subjects were instructed to read the texts that compound a hypertext in silence but describing what they were thinking when making any node transition. Analysis of verbal protocols showed that subjects used strategies for maintaining the global coherence of the text, and it seemed that they relied on the map and node titles for guiding their decisions. But, this could not be the only possible strategy since reading strategies can go further on hypertext than in linear text and could depend on hypertext navigation tools and on the goals of the readers.

Some studies differentiate between reading strategies by describing the criteria followed by participants for the selection of the reading order. For example, Lawless and Kulikowich

(1998) suggested three kinds of hypertext user: knowledge seekers, feature explorers and apathetic hypertext users. Other descriptions of possible reading strategies on hypertext were provided by Balcytiene (1999), who conducted a study examining processes of knowledge construction with hypertext. In this study, subjects using a hypertext for learning on "Gothic style" were filmed during navigation and interviewed after the task was completed. Three main reading patterns were identified: systematic reading, exploration due to individual preferences (interest) and systematic versus explorative reading. It was found that the two former patterns were more successful than the latter for learning.

In a set of experiments, Salmeron, Kintsch, & Cañas (2006) have followed an approach aimed to identify the main reading strategies followed by hypertext readers and their interactive effect with previous knowledge. They first identified three reading strategies on hypertext readers: coherence strategy, interest strategy and easiness strategy. Coherence strategy (Foltz, 1996) consisted of selecting the reading order in order to maintain global coherence, choosing the link most related to the text just read. When following an interest strategy, readers first choose the links that they considered most interesting. Finally, the easiness strategy was followed by readers who first selected the links they considered easiest.

In the first experiment, they used a hypertext about atmosphere pollution with 27 nodes. After reading each node, participants have to freely choose between two nodes: the one with the lowest coherence with the previous text and the one with the highest coherence. They answered a pre-test about the topic, and after reading all the contents of the hypertext they had to answer a text-based questionnaire and inference questions, and to perform a judgement-related task for measuring knowledge acquisition. Finally, participants were asked about the criteria used for selecting the links. Participants were grouped according to the following criteria: coherence, interest and linear strategy groups. They were divided into low- and intermediate-knowledge groups according to their pre-test score.

The results showed that low-knowledge readers following the coherence strategy scored higher in the two situation-model measures (judgement-related task and inference questions) than those of the interest strategy, and the same pattern was observed when compared with a linear selection of contents. This was not true for high-knowledge readers. There was only an effect of previous knowledge on textbase knowledge but no effect of strategy was found, supporting previous research that showed that textbase was affected by the number of nodes accessed (Salmeron et al., 2005) but not by the reading order of the text nodes (Naumann, Waniek, Brunstein, & Krems, 2003; Salmeron et al., 2005).

So, for low-knowledge readers, coherence strategy seemed to be the best, but for high-knowledge readers there were no differences between strategies. These results for participants with prior knowledge can be explained by the use of strategic processing. It is assumed that when reading a hypertext, there are both a strategic influence derived from the use of a particular reading strategy and a text-induced influence related to text coherence changes due to the reading order (Salmeron et al., 2005). In order to select a coherent link, readers have to process the semantic relation between the previous text and the links presented, and consequently to engage in an active processing of the text that allows high-knowledge readers to overcome the shallow processing than can be induced otherwise by a high-coherent order.

In a second experiment, participants in one group were instructed to follow a particular strategy (coherence or interest) and their performance was compared with that of two control groups in which participants read the texts linearly in either a low- or high-coherence order. Results of this experiment supported the results of Experiment 1: low-knowledge readers using a coherence strategy performed better than readers using an interest strategy both in the related judgment task and in inference questions. This effect was not found with intermediate-knowledge readers. Analysis of text-based questions showed no differences between groups. Interestingly, the analysis of the control groups showed that low readers learnt more from a high-coherent reading order, whereas intermediate knowledge readers learnt more with a low-coherent reading order. No differences were found for text-based questions.

The most interesting result of Experiment 2 was obtained when comparing the strategy groups with the control ones. The authors hypothesised that the differences between a strategy group and its control group could be interpreted, assuming that the comprehension effect of a particular strategy is not only text-induced by reading order, but also independent of it. The results showed no differences between strategies and control groups for low-knowledge readers, and between interest strategy and their control group for intermediate knowledge readers. Even though, intermediate participants following the coherence strategy learnt more than those reading a high-coherence order without link selection linearly.

Therefore, the conclusions of this study was that the effect of the type of reading strategy for low-knowledge readers on comprehension seems to be produced indirectly by the coherence of the reading order selected. Otherwise, there is a strategic processing effect for prior-knowledge readers using the coherence strategy that forces them to engage in active processing compared with those that read the high-coherence text without selecting the order. No strategic effect was found for intermediate-knowledge readers following an interest strategy, but authors were careful to make strong conclusions about that, due to the difficulty of creating optimal conditions in which readers follow an interest strategy and at the same time follow a high-coherent reading order.

Therefore, strategic processing effects seem to be responsible for the benefit observed in advanced learners in several studies comparing hypertext and linear text. Similar conclusions can be extracted from the Cognitive Flexibility Theory (CFT) (Spiro, Coulson, Feltovich, & Anderson, 1988). From the CFT point of view, prior knowledge has to be first deconstructed and then reconstructed, and this implies flexibility to apply this knowledge to every new case or situation. Predictions of this theory have some implications for hypertext comprehension and learning (for a revision, see Shapiro & Niederhauser, 2004). Concretely, hypertext offers the possibility of accessing the same document from several perspectives, so one text can be accessed repeatedly from multiple different nodes, and this can enhance the ability of the reader to use his knowledge in a more flexible way.

In summation, the evidence in this section pointed to a joint effect of prior knowledge, reading strategies and navigation pattern for explaining differences on comprehension outcomes with hypertext. Different reading strategies may lead to different navigational patterns, varying the global coherence and amount of text read and then affecting knowledge acquisition. Additionally, the effect of reading strategies on hypertext seems to be different, depending on the level of prior knowledge of the reader.

However, a further step in explaining hypertext comprehension processes would be to find out why readers follow a particular strategy and no other. In the next section we examine user and system characteristics that are related to readers' navigational and reading strategies in order to explore this issue.

4 What Determines Reading and Navigational Strategies?

As we have already seen, navigating hypertext for comprehension is similar to problem solving. The information contained in the hypertext has to be extracted in a meaningful way, and this depends mainly on two groups of factors: the conjunction of reader knowledge, abilities and skills, and the way in which the system is structured and the navigation tools that it provides, which could enhance or hinder the comprehension process. All these factors affect both the adoption of a particular reading strategy on hypertext, before reading starts, and then its necessary updating during the reading process. For example, readers can adopt a coherence strategy for reading a hypertext, but an ill-structured system structure can abort this strategy if readers are low-knowledge and cues for searching coherence are not explicit. So, reading and navigational strategies can be modulated, modified, enhanced or impaired by system features and/or cognitive requirements of the task.

There is a broad range of readers' characteristics that could affect their reading strategies, including prior domain knowledge, reading abilities, personality traits, cognitive styles and cognitive factors (working memory span, spatial abilities, perceptual speed, etc.). The specific learning or cognitive style of the reader has been proposed to be an important factor in determining the adoption of a particular reading strategy on hypertext. Hypertext readers could adopt navigational behaviours consistent with their cognitive styles.

For example, Chen and McRedie (2002) have made a distinction between field-dependent and field-independent readers. In a series of experiments conducted by these authors, the results showed that field-independent readers take an active approach, exploring their own navigation patterns, whereas field-dependent readers get lost easily and bring their attention to the more salient signals regardless of their relevance. This is the reason why field-dependent readers follow the overview provided by the system passively. In a similar approach, Balcytiene (1999) differentiated between self-regulated and cue-dependent learners. Self-regulated learners tend to extract information in a systematic way, starting first with the construction of the mental model for guiding the learning process from a problem-solving framework. In contrast, cue-dependent readers are not consistent in their reading behaviour and need to be guided in their learning process. Other differences in reading behaviour on hypertext have been found in the literature between verbalise and image-cognitive style (Graff, 2005), analytical-sequential and holistic-intuitive (Calcaterra, Antonietti, & Underwood, 2005) or between holist and serialists cognitive styles (Ford & Chen, 2000).

With regard to cognitive factors that could affect the adoption of a particular reading strategy, we can see that from the beginning, research on hypertext has been led by the idea that hypertext may reflect the basic principles of the functioning of human mind (Bush, 1945; Jonassen, 1990; Delany & Gilbert, 1991). Therefore, researchers have worked with the premise that hypertext navigation is intuitive "*per se*", since using associative retrieval paths (links) is similar to the way retrieval is performed in memory (Foltz, 1996). Although this might be true, references to orientation and navigational problems on the hypertext literature have been found frequently (Boechler, 2001; Diaz & Souza, 1997; McDonald & Stevenson, 1996; Ransom, Wu, & Schmidt, 1997). Those problems could be explained by the excessive cognitive requirements created by the interaction with the hypertext system.

For example, Juvina and Van Oostendorp (2004) performed an experiment aimed to determine cognitive predictors of user navigation. Results showed that cognitive factors, like spatial ability, working memory and episodic memory were related to some aspects of navigational behaviour. Specifically, low-working memory capacity was a predictor of orientation problems meanwhile spatial ability predicts task performance. Some other studies have also shown the important implication of spatial cognition on hypertext navigation. For example, Dahlbäck, Höök, and Sjölinder (1996) have found a strong correlation between the performance on image rotation tests and navigation task timing. These results are consistent with the data of a meta-analysis performed by Chen and Rada (1996) that showed a consistent effect of spatial abilities on hypertext efficiency measures. If we define spatial cognition as an ability that comprises the knowledge and the mental representation of spatial structure (Liben, 1981), we can say that the spatial cognitive component of navigation implies the knowledge and mental representation of the hypertext structure, together with knowledge about how to use this information for task performance, and the capacity of thinking in hypertext mental representation.

Obviously, working memory has an important role in managing hypertext tasks. As in linear text, the contents of a working memory required for text comprehension include sensorial aspects, linguistic expressions, propositional structures, situational models, goals, lexical knowledge and schemas, which are necessary for making inferences (Van Dijk & Kintsch, 1983; Kintsch, Patel, & Ericsson, 1999). However, working memory requirements are greater in hypertext than in linear text (Conklin, 1987; Tardieu & Gyselinck, 2002), and the balance of cognitive resources is different, with more importance placed on relational and spatial process than on hypertext (Wenger & Payne, 1996). Naumann et al., (2003) have found that in hypertext reading high-working memory load would lead to more navigation problems and less-acquired knowledge, since navigation in hypertext consumes working memory resources and working memory capacity is limited. Furthermore, when hypertext is attached with graphics, images and other media (hypermedia, multimedia) the cognitive requirements of the task increase. For example, Tardieu and Gyselink (2002) have shown that when using multimedia material, users get new constraints related to working memory on integrating and comprehending information.

However, these studies failed to address the interactive effect of cognitive factors and the navigation pattern (strategy) followed by the reader. Only recently, Madrid, Salmeron, Cañas, and Fajardo (2005) have examined the role of nine cognitive factors on the navigational pattern of the reader. The hypothesis of their experiment was that cognitive factors associated with navigational variables can modulate hypertext comprehension. They found that spatial abilities are related to the amount of information read (nodes accessed) and that the level in which readers follow the structural overview provided for navigation was affected by their working memory capacity. The results were in agreement with a limited capacity view in which a task that exceeds our cognitive resources has a negative impact on our performance. Therefore, cognitive requirement increases in hypertext when readers have to switch between informational and navigation tasks for acquiring knowledge.

We might conclude that there are some user and system features that influence hypertext use and comprehension. Navigating behaviour and individual differences in prior knowledge and cognitive factors/styles/abilities seem to play an important role in knowledge acquisition on hypertext. However, more research is needed to explore how these cognitive factors determine the adoption of a particular reading strategy.

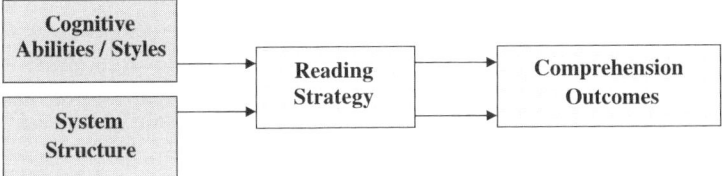

Figure 1: General framework on hypertext comprehension.

5 Conclusion

This chapter tries to bring attention to several system and reader features that can affect hypertext comprehension and learning. It was shown consistently that the reading strategies of the reader affect comprehension indirectly by means of their navigation pattern, and directly by the adoption of an active processing approach. As Salmeron et al. (2006) showed the selection of the reading strategy can be very important especially for low-knowledge readers, because reading strategies that make the readers follow an incoherent pattern brings poor comprehension outcomes.

The adoption of a particular reading strategy depends on several aspects both concerning the reader and the system structure. However, the complexity of having many factors involved in hypertext comprehension may lead to confusing results and erroneous conclusions, so we propose that the relation between user and system features, navigating behaviour and comprehension outcomes must be analysed carefully. The research results reviewed in this chapter show that it is not possible to make cognitive predictions about hypertext comprehension if we do not take into account the individual differences and navigational pattern of the hypertext readers. Therefore, we could propose a general framework for conducting research on hypertext comprehension and for understanding the user and system factors that affect it, such as the one represented in Figure 1. In this framework, the two basic ideas are as follows: (1) any variable that is thought to be affecting reading comprehension must be examined in relation to the particular reading strategy that the reader adopts; and (2) that strategy must be explained by the interaction of reader cognitive characteristics and the hypertext system design features.

As this framework shows, results obtained on experiment testing the influence of cognitive abilities and system structure on comprehension outcomes may be overshadowed by the effect of reading strategy.

This schema has clear implications for the design and use of hypertext documents in the workplace. Enhancing the use of technical documents on hypertext requires that system structure fits different reading strategies and cognitive abilities for better comprehension outcomes. In this way, adaptive hypermedia systems have been suggested to overcome problems related to individual differences (Brusilovsky, 2001).

Chapter 15

Task-Guidance Systems and Procedure Context: Enabling Procedures to Enhance Worker Performance

Jennifer Ockerman

Procedures are widely used in many industries to provide for safety and consistency in task completion. Procedures can benefit workers at tasks such as inspection, maintenance, and assembly by structuring the task and supporting the worker's memory of task steps. The introduction of light, inexpensive electronics has provided the opportunity to investigate how this technology can improve the use of procedures in the work place. These electronics provide for the development of task-guidance systems (Ockerman & Pritchett, 2000). Task-guidance systems can further aid workers in procedure following by addressing shortcomings of paper procedures and presenting procedure context (Ockerman & Pritchett, 2000; Ockerman & Pritchett, 2004). This chapter provides a brief background on the use of procedures, a description of task-guidance systems, and an explanation of procedure context, including results of some empirical investigations into their efficacy. All three can provide greater levels of benefits to workers if they are well designed and integrated.

1 Procedures

A thorough description of the potential benefits and pitfalls of procedure use can be found in Ockerman and Pritchett (2000), a briefer description is provided here as background. Ultimately, a procedure takes a large, complex task, capable of being approached in many different ways, and presents it as a sequence of manageable, communicable steps. The importance of procedures in high-risk domains with little leeway for non-procedural actions is highlighted by the fact that lack of or improper procedure following can dramatically impact safety and efficiency (Marsden, 1996; Mosier, Palmer, & Degani, 1992; Palmer & Degani, 1991; Pearl & Drury, 1995). Although important in many situations, it is important to note what a procedure does—and does not—know. Implicit in a procedure is pre-determined knowledge about the task at hand; this information may include directive information specifying immediate actions, feed-forward information highlighting upcoming steps, and feedback information specifying checks and confirmations to make on just-completed steps (Drury & Prabhu, 1996; Patel, Drury, & Lofgren, 1994). What is missing, however, is any current knowledge of the environment and any assessment of the state of the system of interest or task object, which is a specific subset of knowledge of the environment. This real-time assessment of the environment and the task object remains the responsibility of the worker at all stages—initiating a step, completing a step, and examining feedback from the environment to confirm the step has been completed properly.

In industrial settings, procedures can benefit employees in tasks such as inspection, maintenance, and assembly because they provide an effective, tested, and proven structure by which to complete a task. Procedures can be found in almost all industries, and in many referring to a written procedure is a sign of professionalism. In sum, procedures may serve as a guideline for expert workers or they may provide a list of directives to be followed exactly; either way, procedures can serve to structure a task, aid worker memory, and ensure consistency and safety in task completion.

2 Task Guidance Systems

In work practice, the term "procedure" almost always refers to a written document. Several factors necessitate the written form of the procedure: a need to communicate and share it; an inability to remember a long procedure; and a desire to confirm how to perform important actions and verify that they have been completed correctly.

Physical instantiations of procedures are usually intended to be easy to use, acting as a one-way memory cue to the worker that requires nothing in return beyond the flip of a page or a check beside each step as it is completed. While paper checklists can be easy to use and meet several basic needs, they are not perfect. Studies of paper checklists have identified several types of errors in their use: losing track of the "current" step, and therefore skipping steps; skipping items due to interruptions and distractions; intentionally skipping an item and forgetting to return to it; and stating that an item has been completed when it has not (Palmer & Degani, 1991).

The use of paper checklists has also faced physical challenges. If the procedure is long and complex, the written checklist may be large, bulky, heavy, and distributed over several volumes. When procedures must be updated, both providing new documentation and rigorously eliminating old documentation can be a difficult process. Paper checklists may not hold up well and be difficult to use in many environments, such as cold, wet, dirty, or windy. Paper procedures may also be difficult to access in positions where the worker needs his or her hands free or the space around him or her clear. Finally, when the procedures require the worker to jump forward and backward in the list of steps, navigating through paper procedures may not be easy, especially if steps to be performed sequentially are not co-located physically in the same list. These difficulties can lead to non-compliance by workers because the procedures are too burdensome to use. In addition, difficulties in updating procedures can lead to inconsistent and inaccurate procedures. Unfortunately, in too many instances, procedures have been found to be faulty. For example, Marsden (1996) summarized two studies of procedure following in the nuclear industry. The first (INPO, 1986) reported that, of the 48% of incidents initially attributed to "failures of the human factor", almost 65% involved a procedural deficiency. The second reviewed almost 700 incidents and concluded that faults in procedures were implicated in 69% (Goodman & DiPalo, 1991).

The term "task-guidance systems" applies to electronic worker aids that, without any sensing of the environment at hand, can serve as a reference and guide to the worker. New technological capabilities (e.g., wireless handheld or wearable computers) make such systems practicable. Inspection and assembly tasks often require hands-free operation; task-guidance systems can now talk and listen to the worker. These tasks often require the worker to be mobile during a task; task-guidance systems can now be carried—or worn—around with relative ease. These tasks require the worker to traverse many—sometimes hundreds—of procedure steps; task-guidance systems can now store and display them in a consistent format and in the right order. Finally, these systems are now sufficiently inexpensive that their widespread use is conceivable in communities of mechanics and factory workers where no such electronic assistance has been provided before, if they are designed well enough to have a clear, demonstrated benefit to workers.

However, for task-guidance systems to be beneficial, they must be developed with the worker's task in mind. A number of problems may occur, ranging from the system interfering with the primary task and being ignored, to the worker over-relying on the system in conditions where its underlying procedure is inappropriate or incorrect. Conversely, on a positive note, if the task-guidance system is viewed as more than just an electronic version of a paper checklist, it may use its display flexibility and memory store to provide a powerful assistant to a worker. The following sections enumerate the benefits that task-guidance systems can provide.

2.1 Establishing Task Structure

A procedure establishes a structure for the task, and a task-guidance system helps communicate that structure to the worker. At the simplest, the task-guidance system may present the steps to the worker as they are requested. A more informative system may also provide a conceptual understanding of the task structure. This conceptual presentation could be global to the task; for example, for a walk-around aircraft inspection a task-guidance system may indicate to the worker where he or she has been, should be (at the current step), and will be relative to the aircraft, allowing him or her to see how far he or she has progressed. The presentation may also be local to the current step, such as providing some anticipatory information about upcoming steps (Ockerman, Thompson, & Najjar, 1997). Ordinality, necessity, irreversibility, and temporal considerations may also be described; for example, at each step, the subsequent steps that depend on this step may be noted, so that the worker is aware of the consequences of skipping a step or changing the order of the steps.

Providing information about task structure may be particularly useful when the structure is complex. For example, procedures may have hierarchical structures, in which high-level procedures refer the worker down to low-level, detailed procedures; likewise, procedures may contain conditional statements at which point the procedure may fork in different directions. In such conditions, the task-guidance system may be designed to allow the worker to review where in the task structure he or she is currently, and the steps that led there (Converse, 1994; Elm & Woods, 1985). In addition, the user might be provided with information explaining the reasoning behind the procedure's structure. For example, a walk-around preflight inspection procedure is structured for efficiency in movement.

2.2 Supporting Memory

Like paper procedures, task-guidance systems can provide an external representation of a list of steps too long to remember. In addition, task-guidance systems can also help workers keep track of their current location within the task. For example, if the system requires a cue from the worker when each step is concluded, then the system can provide an external, persistent memory of location within the task that is robust to memory lapses and interruptions. Likewise, task-guidance systems may record when the worker elects to skip a step and later allow the worker to review the skipped steps when desired, or remind the worker later in the task that their current step depends on completing a previous step that was skipped and is not yet completed. Not only do preliminary research results suggest that such features help prevent known memory problems (Ockerman & Pritchett, 1998), but they may also decrease the apparent need for a worker to follow the procedure's steps in the order written and thereby enable the worker to tailor their actions to immediate conditions.

2.3 Supporting Consistency and Safety

Not only may task-guidance systems help workers complete a procedure thoroughly and reliably, as just described, but they may also then be given an easy mechanism to record that the task was completed, and how it was completed. Such records may then be downloaded to data-keeping applications, thereby providing detailed records without requiring data entry after the task (Ockerman, Najjar, & Thompson, 1999). Such an institutional knowledge, resident at a common source of downloads, may also enable a more structured and reliable means of communication between team members. Completed steps, skipped steps, and pending steps can potentially be communicated between workers' task-guidance systems, or uploaded from a central data-record at the start of a shift.

2.4 Supporting Worker Expertise

While workers may have considerable expertise, any worker can always learn more about a task if motivation exists and means are provided. Task-guidance systems can easily allow the worker to access more detailed information, if the programming investment of putting this information into the system is made (Ockerman et al., 1999). This information may be about the task at hand, such as describing to a mechanic how an engine part will move in operation in order to facilitate detecting if the part wear is out of range; or, this information may be about the procedure, such as describing the rationale for asking the mechanic to look at this engine component at this point in the procedure and how it fits into the higher level "general" procedure (Catrambone, 1990).

Once confident in their knowledge, the worker may then benefit from the ability to select less information about each step, reducing the time reading and processing task information.

Allowing the de-selection of information gives the individual worker control over the detail of their procedure, while keeping its underlying structure consistent between all workers.

2.5 Supporting Effective Task Strategies

A procedure may serve as a "lock-step" sequence of directives or as a "guideline", depending on the procedure's comprehensiveness and detail, and on the worker's expertise. Beyond the just-mentioned self-calibration by the worker to the procedure's detail, task-guidance systems may be able to indicate to the worker an effective and appropriate strategy, explicitly or implicitly. For example, a procedure step which serves as guidance may not only be worded as such, but also may allow the worker to view other possible actions, the rationale for each step, and other such supportive information. On the other hand, a step that absolutely must be performed as specified may be presented as a directive, perhaps with the accompaniment of an aural alert, and with the rationale given for performing the step exactly. The operator might not be allowed to check any subsequent steps as complete until the directive is checked by the worker.

Likewise, task guidance may be able to encourage anticipatory strategies in procedure following. Possible mechanisms range from consistently providing the worker with a preview of upcoming steps, to identifying dependencies between steps that an anticipatory strategy can build upon, and showing, on a step-by-step basis, future steps that will be impacted by current actions.

2.6 Mitigating Unintentional Non-Compliance

While mitigating unintentionally non-compliance may be an important goal in designing a task-guidance system, achieving this goal may be more accurately viewed as a standard objective in good system design. By providing a task-guidance system that clearly indicates the current location within the task, many causes of unintentional non-compliance, such as interruptions, losing track of current location in the procedure, and forgetting which steps were skipped, can be eliminated. In addition, good system design should avoid the many hazards of difficult to read and understand instructions that may lead to errors in procedure following, such as unreadable print, inconsistent terminology, and variable formatting of information (Pearl & Drury, 1995).

2.7 Mitigating Intentional Non-Compliance

Intentional non-compliance can arise when the worker perceives more drawbacks to following a procedure than benefits; unfortunately, many procedures currently being used meet this description (Drury & Prabhu, 1996; Drury & Sarac, 1997; McCarthy, Wright, Monk, & Watts, 1998; Patel et al., 1994; Thomas, 1995). One rationale given by workers for intentional non-compliance is that the procedure (or its physical instantiation) is too burdensome to be beneficial (see Ganier & Barcenilla, this volume). In studies in the nuclear power industry, Park, Jeong, and Jung (2005) have identified several kinds of procedural complexity, including step-information complexity, step-logic complexity, step-size complexity, abstraction level of knowledge required, and level of engineering decision, which can increase the cognitive burden and thus affect the compliance of operators. This is similar to studies on under-reliance on automation. For example, Kirlik (1993) demonstrated that automation that requires significant interaction and workload from its operator may not be used if the operator perceives he or she can complete the task more easily on his or her own.

A second reason provided by workers for intentional non-compliance is that they do not believe the procedure sufficiently or efficiently addresses the task to be completed. For example, some airline inspectors have claimed they do not refer to an inspection procedure because they do not think it provides a thorough inspection of an aircraft (Pearl & Drury, 1995). Park and Jung (2003) found that nuclear power operators with intermediate work experience (10–13 years) were most likely to not follow some procedures by either skipping redundant actions or modifying action sequences. In addition, procedure steps with intermediate complexity were most likely to be altered. They reasoned that workers with intermediate experience have just enough knowledge to understand some of the process and thus felt they could make changes to the procedure that would not be detrimental but not enough experience to understand all the potential consequences of not following the procedure exactly. Furthermore, the procedure steps with intermediate complexity were complex enough to be changed but not so complex that it was difficult to figure out how they might be changed without negative consequences. Workers sometimes do not agree with what they perceive to be the purpose of the procedure (deBrito, 1999; McCarthy et al., 1998; Zach, 1980), and at an extreme, view procedures as "a system of work control designed essentially to protect the company in the event of an accident" (Marsden, 1996). Of course, if the underlying procedure is truly inefficient or ineffective, then this perception cannot and should not be mitigated by a task-guidance system, no matter how well designed.

When the procedure provides a good foundation for a task-guidance system, system design decisions can have a powerful impact on the burden perceived by the worker in using it. At its worst, the physical instantiation of a procedure may be physically burdensome, such as maintenance manuals comprising several thick volumes, making it both difficult to port the procedures to a work location and also difficult to find the appropriate procedure for the current context (see Ganier & Barcenilla, this volume). Task-guidance systems can potentially be quite light and small, possibly eliminating any physical burden. However, poorly designed task-guidance systems may impose a cognitive burden with characteristics such as poor legibility or overly complex operation.

To encourage an appropriate level of compliance, task-guidance systems may be purposefully designed to help the operator understand the benefit of the procedure. For example, by presenting the overall intention of the procedure, the rationale for each step, and an illustration of the task structure, the worker may be able to develop a more accurate perception of the procedure's worth than if it is just presented as a series of steps to be taken on faith.

Intentional non-compliance may also arise when the worker perceives that the organization condones, or encourages, non-compliance. For example, when the company's philosophy and policies conflict with company-provided procedures (Degani & Wiener, 1997), operators may be confused about how to follow procedures as well as conform to company policies. Investing in task-guidance systems and encouraging their use can stress an organization's desire for all workers to follow procedures when that desire truly exists and is reflected in all aspects of management, pay and compensation, punitive actions, and the work environment.

Finally, workers may not comply with procedures when they fear the procedure is inaccurate. Unfortunately, workers sometimes have difficulty judging the appropriateness of the procedure for the current situation (Jeffroy & Charron, 1997; Schutte & Trujillo, 1996). Task-guidance systems may enable the worker to recognize when a specific step is faulty or inappropriate for the situation through providing the worker with sufficient information about each step (e.g., its intention, the conditions under which it is assumed to be accurate, etc.) so that he or she can judge its merits. However, such a design goal may be difficult to achieve, as the decision to follow a procedure can be very brittle. Once a fault has been perceived (whether the perception is right or wrong), the entire procedure may be stereotyped as untrustworthy rather than having each step judged for its individual merits. This effect is similar to the effects of automation faults on operator trust and reliance (Lee & Moray, 1994; Muir, 1987) and of false alarms on operator conformance to subsequent alerting system commands (Hasse, 1992; Pritchett, 1999).

2.8 Mitigating Over-Reliance on the Procedure

Just as workers may not trust a procedure once it has failed, so might they not mistrust it before a failure. This may lead to over-reliance on the procedure, a condition where the worker incorrectly follows a procedure that is "wrong-for-the-situation". Analogies may be drawn from research on automation (Parasuraman & Riley, 1997), in which over-reliance remains a sizeable concern. A procedure may be "wrong-for-the-situation" in four ways. First, the procedure may be technically correct but have a different intention, and therefore different outcome than the worker desires. Second, a procedure may be technically correct and have the desired intention, but may have been designed to work within a limited range of environmental boundary conditions, which are currently not satisfied. It is reasonable to hypothesize that a task-guidance system may help mitigate these two causes of over-reliance by making the worker an educated follower of the procedure through providing sufficient information about the procedure to judge its appropriateness to the situation at hand.

The third potential problem with a procedure arises when the worker follows it using an inappropriate strategy. For example, an aircraft inspection task typically has an associated checklist that asks the worker to inspect the most important aircraft components and the most likely sources of faults; however, knowing that no one procedure can foresee every possible problem with the aircraft, the inspector is expected to use the checklist as a guideline, while remaining observant for anything else that may appear out of order. For the inspector to execute this checklist exactly, yet miss observable faults, represents a form of over-reliance on the procedure. Such over-reliance may stem from carelessness, which a task-guidance system cannot mitigate, or it may stem from a lack of awareness of the intended role of the procedure, which a task-guidance system can help prevent through two non-exclusive approaches. First, the "warning label" approach may have the task-guidance system explicitly remind the worker when any of the steps is only a guideline, or sample, of a large set of tasks, reducing complacency and communicating expectations. Second, the "cognitive being" approach attempts to situate the worker better in the task, so that he or she can see the layout of the suggested inspection tasks, know the upcoming tasks so that he or she can work towards them, and thereby actively use the task structure of the procedure as a basis for how he or she approaches the task.

Finally, the fourth potential manner in which a procedure may be wrong is when a step is erroneous; that is, in which the step does not meet its stated intention within its allowable boundary conditions. Like a mechanical fault in an automated system, this is a problem that should be tested for and prevented during the design and update of the procedure, as it requires substantial expertise and confidence to identify in operational conditions.

3 Procedure Context

The last two benefits of task-guidance systems, mitigating intentional non-compliance and over-reliance, led to the formulation of the concept of procedure context. Procedure context illustrates to the user not only the current action that is required, but also situates it in the larger purpose and organization of the procedure and the current task. Thus, the user is aware of more than just a series of isolated commands (Swezey, 1987) and the user can use the procedure as guidance to anticipate future actions of the system and/or other operators within a complex system (Pritchett & Yankosky, 2003). In addition, procedure context may provide a window on the thought processes of the procedure designer, and thus insights on how the procedure applies to the current situation.

Although procedure context was conceived of by reviewing the design goals of task-guidance systems, a few empirical investigations illustrate that procedure context transcends task-guidance systems and applies to all procedures, not just those presented on a task-guidance system. This section defines procedure context and ends with descriptions of the empirical investigations, which show procedure context's more universal applicability.

3.1 Definition

The concept of procedure context highlights an underlying basis, providing a framework, for suggestions from many studies in the current literature on procedure information elements that might prove beneficial to procedure followers. These suggested information elements are often omitted in existing paper procedures and by new electronic procedure systems, particularly the prototypes of small portable electronic procedure systems that tend to show the procedure steps one at a time. It is hypothesized that providing procedure context to users might improve their overall performance by making them aware of the meaning and structure of the entire procedure.

Procedure context consists of several elements. These individual elements are either known early in the procedure's life cycle or are implicitly part of a completed procedure; as such, procedure context is not adding information to a procedure but making the relevant pieces of information explicit to the user.

3.2 Procedure Context Categories and Elements

The specific elements of procedure context have been identified through a review of literature and procedures. This is most likely not an exhaustive list but provides a sufficient basis to begin to evaluate the possible benefits of procedure context.

As the list was developed, it was noted that the procedure context elements identified fell into two categories: explanatory and locational. These categories and their elements are described in the following sections.

3.2.1 Explanatory procedure context category The explanatory elements provide meaning, purpose, relationships, and conditions, which provide a background for the procedure. This category of procedure context is a window into the procedure designers' reasons for the current procedure, providing information about reasoning, conditions for use, and a strategy for using the procedure. The explanatory procedure context lets the user know when the procedure does not match the current situation and can aid the user in determining other ways of accomplishing the task in a different but safe manner.

In terms of the design guidelines for task-guidance systems proposed earlier, explanatory procedure context elements can aid in establishing a task structure for the user and supporting the user in selecting an appropriate task strategy. In addition, having access to and understanding the background of a procedure and its individual steps can increase a user's expertise and possibly mitigate intentional non-compliance. Finally, explanatory procedure context elements might mitigate over-reliance due to a lack of awareness of why the procedure is designed the way that it is.

Explanatory procedure-context elements are frequently not included in the procedure, but might be covered when the worker is trained on the procedure or on the job. However, explanatory procedure-context elements are presumably known to the designer of the procedure, since the designer would use this type of information to design a procedure. The designer must convert the dynamics and structure of a task and its relationship to an external, changing environment into an understandable and effective static representation that can be used over and over. Unfortunately, all this knowledge is rarely explicitly published in the final procedure and is often effectively "lost" to the user. It has been noted that sometimes a significant amount of time transpires before a worker might realize why the procedure is designed as it is (Hutchins, 1995), and even then there is no guarantee that he or she has figured it out correctly.

To incorporate these elements into task-guidance systems requires direct communication with the designer(s) of the procedure or inferring them from the procedure and knowledge of the task, environment, and task object. This is not a problem for procedures being newly created for task-guidance systems but could be a difficulty for already existing procedures that are being retooled for task-guidance systems.

Explanatory information about the task, such as intention and rationale, has been shown to increase the rate at which each step is read, aids in recalling the steps of the procedure at a later time, and improves performance when performing the task without the procedure (Smith & Goodman, 1984). In addition, knowing the background of a procedure can ease worker resistance to a procedure by providing insight into the relevance of the procedure to effective task completion instead of as a way to control the worker (deBrito, 1999; McCarthy et al., 1998; Wright, Pocock, & Fields, 1998).

Each of the explanatory elements is defined and described separately below.

3.2.1.1 Intention The intention element of procedure context makes the user aware of the overall goal of the procedure; that is, the final state to be achieved once the procedure is complete. Knowing the intention of a procedure might allow the user to determine the appropriateness of this procedure for the current situation. This element spans the entire procedure.

3.2.1.2 Rationale The rationale element provides the reason for each procedural step; that is, why this step is included in the procedure. In one study, inspection of a commercial pilot's own copy of procedures found that 38% of the annotations made by the pilot could be classified as notes on "why a procedure is the way it is" (Wright et al., 1998). Knowledge of a step's rationale can aid the user in understanding when this particular step is appropriate for the current situation and improve his or her knowledge about the procedure.

3.2.1.3 Boundary conditions The boundary condition element represents information that informs the user about the conditions for which the procedure is applicable. It includes information such as the type of training and experience that the user is expected to have, the type of equipment needed, and the type of environment and system for which the procedure is valid. The boundary condition class makes the user aware of the limitations and expectations of the procedure or individual steps of the procedure.

3.2.1.4 Triggering conditions The triggering conditions element of procedure context is information about the events that signal the starting or stopping of a procedural action. Triggering conditions are events that are external to the procedure. For example, in a process-control procedure, the completion of a sub-process might trigger a control action of opening a different valve. Making task-guidance users aware of triggering conditions can help them to determine not only when a step should be done but also provide insight into the relationship between the environment and the task.

3.2.1.5 Temporal construct The temporal construct element provides the time criticality for an action; that is, the window of time when the action can or should be performed. For example, in construction there are often time limits on how long a chemical mixture (e.g., concrete or grout) can be 'worked' before it is no longer suitable for use. In addition, the temporal construct element might be useful in predicting future activity and future states of the task.

3.2.1.6 Ordinality The ordinality element defines any order requirements; that is, when an action must be done before or after other actions. For example, the clutch must be depressed before starting standard transmission automobiles: otherwise the transmission would be damaged. The ordinality differs from the temporal constructs and triggering conditions elements in that it only concerns the order of the procedure steps, not their exact timing or their relation to external events. There are situations where the order of steps can be very important, and needs to be made clear to the worker.

3.2.1.7 Necessity The necessity element informs the user about the necessity of a particular procedure action to safe and effective completion of the task. For example, in air traffic control procedures, this instruction is given at the beginning of the controllers' handbook: "a. *Shall*, or an action verb in the imperative sense, means a procedure is mandatory. b. *Should* means a procedure is recommended. c. *May* or *need not* means a procedure is optional" (FAA, 1995). If task-guidance users understand the necessity of a particular step they can make judgments about whether a step must be done and reason about what the impact will be if it is not completed.

3.2.1.8 Reversibility The reversibility element presents information about risk and whether the action can be reversed if it is done incorrectly, that is, the consequences of an action. For example, in a cake making procedure mixing the batter is an irreversible action: the batter cannot be unmixed. Carroll (1998) demonstrated improved learning performance when users knew they would be supported in reversing or recovering from an error; that is, that errors are reversible. Awareness of the reversibility of a procedure step can aid the user in reasoning about that step when they encounter a different situation.

3.2.1.9 Appropriate specificity The appropriate specificity element refers to whether the instruction lists everything that must be done or just illustrates a sample of the total actions required. For example, in an inspection task a high-specificity statement might be "inspect the switchboard switches and connections", while a low-specificity statement might be "inspect the switchboard (switches, connections, etc.)". The first statement gives the impression that only the switches and connections need to be checked, while the second statement makes it clear that switches and connections are simply examples of items that need to be checked. However, it is important to note that appropriate specificity can only be rated in direct comparison to the actual action that needs to be completed. For example, if only the switchboard switches and connections need to be inspected then listing both of them makes the intent clear to the user. If, on the other hand, items on the switchboard other than the switches and connections should be inspected then it is important to convey this to the user through proper wording or by listing them all out. The procedure user needs to know when the procedure writer is simply suggesting what might need to be done and when the procedure writer is saying exactly what needs to be done. Appropriate specificity provides information about the detail level of the procedure and thus insight into an appropriate strategy of following the procedure (e.g., as guidance or "lock-step").

3.2.2 Locational procedure context category Locational procedure context locates an individual step within both the local and global structure of the procedure or procedures of which it is a part. Locational procedure context can aid in establishing the task structure and supporting an effective task strategy. The locational elements of procedure context are inherently part of procedures and are obvious when the full procedure is known but can be hidden to the user in the middle of a task. This is especially true for mobile users who are often using small visual displays. Locational elements, due to their availability in existing procedures, can be incorporated into task-guidance systems explicitly. This category of procedure context, when provided explicitly, may prove to reduce over-reliance during everyday normal conditions by providing the ability to look ahead and know where one is in the procedure, instead of following each individual step in a vacuum.

3.2.2.1 Previous actions The previous action element provides information on what actions have been completed just previously to the current action. The previous action element provides a memory aid when interruptions have occurred and the user has momentarily left the task cognitively and/or physically. Several literature sources support the idea that knowing the most recent steps can improve performance in various ways (Converse, 1994; Elm & Woods, 1985; Hoecker, Corker, Roth, Lipner, & Bunzo, 1994; Jeffroy & Charron, 1997). For example, Elm and Woods (1985) demonstrated that it might reduce the instance of "getting lost" in computerized procedures, while the other studies have suggested that it aids through hindsight of what has been done and thus what needs to be done.

3.2.2.2 Following actions The following actions element provides information on the actions that are coming up immediately after the current action. This information can provide "flow information", allowing the user to blend actions together in a fluid motion. In addition, the following action element can provide intermediate goal information. Intermediate goal information shows what the current action(s) should result in. For example, in an assembly task, the following actions might show what the item should look like for the next assembly step. Intermediate goal information is helpful for tasks where the task object is changing in some physical manner (e.g., assembly and repair tasks).

In addition, following action information can implicitly provide information about the ending point of the current step. For example, in a cooking procedure, if the next step begins with "when boiling…" then the cook knows that the current step includes getting the mixture to boil. Several studies provide some support for the theory that providing future actions may prove to be useful to the users of the procedure aids (Converse, 1994; Hoecker et al., 1994; Jeffroy & Charron, 1997; Laughery & Persensky, 1994; Ockerman et al., 1997).

3.2.2.3 Location indication The location indication element is information on how the current action is positioned in the entire procedure; this might be a single procedure or a whole set of procedures that are used simultaneously to complete a task. This can be conveyed on one or more scales, such as a physical, duration, or number-of-steps scale. For example, duration location indication information would provide a measure of how much time has gone by and approximately how much more time remains. As such, location indication information can provide insight into progress being made on the task itself. This information has been thought to be useful in several studies (Converse, 1994; Jeffroy & Charron, 1997; Marsden, 1996).

3.2.2.4 Forking The forking element provides information about forks or branches that occur in the procedure. Forks or branches might occur in hierarchical procedures where the user is periodically directed to lower more-detailed procedures or might be caused by conditional statements that redirect the user. For example, in emergency cockpit procedures there is often the need to go through a troubleshooting procedure that then directs the pilot to go to another procedure. Forking information, similar to location indication above, must tell the user when and where the forks are and how to backtrack through them if necessary. Thus, the forking element information provides the user with an overview of future and past forks in the procedure they are using. The need for this type of information, and the ability for computerized systems to offer it, was mentioned as an asset of computerized systems by Converse (1994).

Procedure context provides a supporting framework for each step of a procedure, making clear how each step fits into the overall procedure and its purpose. Procedure context can aid in establishing a task structure, support worker's expertise and effective task strategies, and possibly mitigate intentional non-compliance and over-reliance. Explanatory procedure context provides reasoning, conditions for use, and a strategy for using the procedure, explaining items such as why the step is done, when the step is appropriate, and when the step needs to be done. Locational procedure context situates an individual step in the overall procedure structure and with its immediate neighbors. By providing procedure context the users are more aware of the entire procedure and can become cognitive beings that are thinking about the actions that they are taking, rather than giving task-guidance systems authority to dictate the course of action.

3.3 Empirical Investigations

There have been three empirical investigations into the effect of procedure-context elements on worker performance. All three have shown some positive impact on worker performance. A brief summary of each investigation is provided below.

3.3.1 Preflight inspection of general aviation aircraft In this investigation locational procedure context elements previous actions, following actions, and location indication were manipulated in a procedure that defined preflight inspection of general aviation aircraft (Ockerman & Pritchett, 2004). The results showed that the presence of previous and following actions increased the amount of interaction (the number of touches) that pilots had with the aircraft during preflight inspection but did not improve the pilots' ability to identify faults on the plane being inspected. It is thought that pilots' usual experience of finding their planes fault-free may have hindered their ability to find the substantial number of faults planted on the plane used in the experiment. However, the pilots had a more continuous inspection of the plane and touched the plane in more locations (which is often required to find faults such as loose connections) when they had access to previous and following procedure steps in sight of the current step that they were completing.

3.3.2 Evaluation of emergency descent plans In this investigation the explanatory procedure-context elements rationale, triggering conditions, and ordinality were manipulated in a procedure that provided guidance on how to fly an emergency descent to an alternate airport (Ockerman & Pritchett, submitted). Thirty-two airline pilots were asked to quickly assess several emergency descent procedures for accuracy and report if they would follow each or not. The results showed that the procedures with rationales led to a more correct reasoning by the pilot for acceptance or non-acceptance of a procedure. The pilots also reported that they liked being provided with the rationale of a procedure. However, overall the pilots were little better than chance at distinguishing procedures that corresponded to a trajectory leading to a safe landing from those that did not.

3.3.3 Airport approach procedures This investigation examined the addition of the explanatory procedure-context elements rationale, temporal constraint, triggering conditions, and location indication to a standard airport approach plate (Landry & Jacko, 2006). The results indicated that the presence of procedure-context elements eliminated nearly all the large lateral errors by the pilots and aided them in staying within the boundaries of the approach. The pilots also had improved situation awareness, which implied that their ability to keep track of their location in the procedure was improved.

4 Conclusion

Procedures are an integral part of many work environments. They provide a structured and tested method of completing an often-complicated task. With the miniaturization of highly capable technology, it is possible to provide procedures on small, easily transported electronic devices that have been defined as task-guidance systems. Task-guidance systems have been shown to be feasible and effective, but care needs to be taken in their design to ensure this outcome. Procedure context has been suggested as one important component of well-designed procedures, and has also been shown to positively impact worker performance when presented to the worker, either in a task-guidance system or other format.

This is just a small start to the research that is needed to truly understand task-guidance systems and procedure context, and how they can improve worker performance in a variety of tasks and domains.

Acknowledgments

Compilation of this chapter was funded by a Stuart S. Janney Fellowship from the Sabbatical Fellows and Professors Committee of the Johns Hopkins University Applied Physics Laboratory.

Chapter 16

Animated Documentation: A Way of Comprehending Complex Procedural Tasks?

Richard K. Lowe

Acquiring understandings of how complex dynamic systems operate can be very challenging, particularly for novices in the relevant information domain. Traditional approaches for explaining these systems use print-based documents containing occasional static illustrations. However, this form of documentation cannot provide a direct, analogue representation of the situational dynamics involved in operating a system. Users must infer the actual dynamics from what is merely implied by the text and graphic representations, a task that is prone to error. Modern computer-based documentation represents situational dynamics explicitly by animated depictions of operational processes. Unfortunately, this development has been accompanied by simplistic assumptions about the intrinsic efficacy of explanatory animations. However, recent research indicates that complex animations can impose their own processing demands on users that may interfere with comprehension of the presented information. This chapter examines the potential strengths and limitations of animated explanations, and then discusses research-based suggestions for improving their design.

The design of effective documentation relating to complex procedural tasks and processes poses considerable challenges for technical communicators. Such documentation is used to support a variety of performances, including how to assemble a device, how to operate a system, how to repair a product, or how to analyze problems occurring with a process. With the increasing pace of technological change, there is growing pressure for documentation to communicate new information more efficiently and effectively than ever before. One way in which technical communicators can respond to these rising expectations is to move from traditional print-based materials to more electronically based forms of documentation. These new formats offer a wider range of options for enhancing the presentation and distribution of information. While there can undoubtedly be advantages in terms of distribution efficiencies, it is unclear whether all aspects of electronic documentation are equally effective in communicating the required information. One of the possibilities for electronically enhancing documentation is to complement written material with explanatory animations. This is a radical departure from the existing approaches, and is not informed by the heritage of practical experience and empirical research that underpins traditional forms of documentation. From a technological point of view, we certainly *can* produce animated documentation; but *should* we produce it? And if so, what issues need to be considered when designing the documentation's animated components?

Users depend on documentation to provide a high level of support for task performance, particularly if they are novices in the relevant domain or if new information is being introduced. Much documentation is concerned with procedures and how to carry them out successfully. A procedure can be defined as an ordered sequence of steps and successful execution of procedures typically requires the user to perform a particular series of actions. In the first place, documentation needs to supply users with fundamental information about relevant visual and spatial characteristics of the subject matter in its context (Bieger & Glock, 1986). For example, in the case of documentation about how to assemble a device, users need to be able to recognize the different components to be brought together during the assembly procedure, and to know what the device should look like once it has been assembled. However, as can be seen from the examples mentioned above, information about *dynamic* aspects of the task also needs to be communicated effectively. For instance, users need to acquire information about the actions required to assemble the device, and generally the order in which those actions must be performed. However, as Zacks and Tversky (2003) have noted in contrasting their saxophone and model bug assembly tasks, order may or may not be crucial for procedures, depending on the particular nature of the task concerned (see also Terrier, Diehl, & Lemarié, this volume).

1 From Documentation to Mental Models

It is not sufficient for documentation merely to provide the necessary information; it should also present that information to the user in an efficient and effective way. The ultimate effectiveness of an information presentation is determined by how well it can be acquired and internalized by the user as a basis for the required performance. For example, the order in which the user processes the presented information and the nature of the internal representation built as a result can influence performance success. Presentation environments, in which the user has a substantial degree of choice as to the information pathway chosen, such as with hypertext (see Madrid & Canas, this volume) or pictorial displays, pose particular challenges for documentation designers. There is increasing evidence that a crucial factor in the effectiveness of information presentations is the basis for their design. Narayanan and Hegarty (1998, 2002) concluded that designing materials according to principles consistent with how people process information is of fundamental importance for both traditional and electronic presentation formats. Thus it is important for document designers to appreciate the nature of such processing.

It will be assumed that in order to understand a process or carry out a procedure successfully, a user must build an appropriate mental model of the subject matter (Johnson-Laird, 1983; Kieras & Bovair, 1984). Users do this while processing the information contained within the external representations that comprise the documentation (see also situational models, Tapiero & Otero, this volume). Mental models have been characterized as internal representations that individuals construct in their minds to stand for external subject matter that is either experienced directly or else is encountered indirectly via descriptions and depictions. Information is represented in such a model by a system of mental tokens that internally maps the entities and relationships present in the external referent situation. In the case of documentation containing, say, instructions for operating a piece of equipment, the information available in the documentation would be the basis for constructing a mental model of the equipment and its operation. The mental model so constructed would then shape how the user conceptualizes the equipment and its operational processes, carries out procedures involving the equipment, interprets the responses of the equipment to the user's actions, and deals with novel situations that arise during its operations. By this analysis, the effectiveness of the user's interaction with the actual equipment will depend on the quality of the mental model that the user has built with the assistance of the equipment's documentation. Such mental models can be built from either the documentation alone, or from both the documentation and the equipment itself.

2 External and Internal Representation

It is important to make a clear distinction between the information presented in an external representation (such as documentation) and the internal representation (mental model) a user constructs from that externally presented information (Scaife & Rogers, 1996; Schnotz & Bannert, 2003; Schnotz & Lowe, 2003; Schnotz, 2001). The provision of accurate, comprehensive information in the documentation does not by itself guarantee that the mental model a user constructs on the basis of that documentation will be satisfactory. We must also consider the user's capacity to deal with that information appropriately. For example, if key aspects of the necessary information are not properly extracted by the user and appropriately internalized, the resulting mental model will be of low quality. This in turn would reduce the effectiveness of mental processes that are carried out by the user on the basis of that mental model. If the components of a mental model or its representation of the referent situation's dynamics are inaccurate or incomplete, it will be reflected in the results of cognitive computations. Operational errors and failures in inference or prediction could come about as a consequence of the model's deficiencies in representing the equipment. The documentation designer's role can therefore be conceptualized as to provide information in a form that is capable of helping the user to build a high quality mental model of the subject matter.

Mental models can represent either static content (such as structures and concepts) or dynamic content (such as procedures and processes). In order to represent static content effectively, the tokens comprising the constructed mental model need only capture unchanging entities and the fixed relationships between them. For this type of subject matter, a static internal representation will clearly suffice. However, an essential feature of mental models that are constructed for dynamic content is that they can also adequately represent changes in the component entities and relationships over time. In this case, a *dynamic* mental model is required, one that can be 'run' backwards or forwards so that the individual can generate appropriate inferences and predictions about the behaviour of the referent system. This mental processing involving the dynamic characteristics of the represented situation may be applied either to the existing mental model or to one representing some hypothetical alternative version of the referent (as with '*What if …?*' scenarios). The running of a dynamic mental model has the potential to support effective problem-solving processes and productive exploration of hypothetical possibilities but only if the model is of high quality.

We have seen that the adequacy of a mental model depends on the quality of the information used for its construction. Two primary sources of such information are (i) what the user already knows (internal information held as existing background knowledge), and (ii) what information is available to the user in the environment (external information presented in a system and its documentation). When users consult a system's documentation in order to perform a task, we can assume an essentially fixed level of background knowledge. This means that the information extracted using the documentation provided with a system is fundamental to the building of a satisfactory mental model. The information so extracted can come from either the documentation itself or from the system as the user explores it as a consequence of what is covered by the documentation. In both cases, a prime role of the documentation should be to facilitate users' extraction of the required information. This raises the question of how effectively documentation can provide such facilitation, particularly with respect to dynamic aspects of the subject matter.

3   Text and Illustrations

Traditional approaches to documentation rely on static representations of information to guide users through the relevant processes and procedures. These typically consist of a blend of printed text and illustrations that address both visuospatial and dynamic aspects of the subject matter. In well-designed documentation, these blends offer complementary sets of representations in which responsibility for providing the necessary information is carefully partitioned between the text and illustrations, with the aim of maximizing overall effectiveness for the user. This partitioning allows the documentation designer to take advantage of the distinctive strengths of each type of representation, while avoiding their respective weaknesses. For example, the linear sequential structure of text can provide the user with an orderly progression through a body of information and a range of clear signals about the hierarchical nature of the content. Text features such as headings, subheadings, and paragraphing perform a signalling function and indicate overall organizational aspects to the reader (Lorch & Lorch, 1995). They can facilitate user search processes by cueing the location of key ideas and can also explose the structure. It should be noted, however, that mere inclusion of these features does not necessarily facilitate the user's building of a satisfactory internal representation of the topic structure (see Terrier, Dielh, & Lemarié, this volume). A further advantage of text is its ability to represent information about concepts and generalizations that are difficult to capture pictorially because of the inherent specificity of graphic representations (Schnotz, 2001).

Conversely, illustrations have their own particular representational strengths. For example, depictions can provide a much more straightforward representation of complex visuospatial relationships than is possible with text (c.f. Denis, 1996). They are able to capture a myriad of visuospatial characteristics in a direct and economical manner whereas attempts to describe such relationships with the text tend to be clumsy and imprecise. Without resorting to highly extended and convoluted description, it is often difficult for words alone to give much more than a very rudimentary specification of these aspects. Because text is a linear sequential system of representation, events that occur simultaneously can only be expressed sequentially when represented in written documents. Clearly, the resulting linearization (Levelt, 1982) means that a text representation distorts the subject matter's true visuospatial and temporal characteristics. Further, human information processing theory suggests that pictorial representations can have advantages over text in terms of the demands they make on users, particularly with respect to the processing of visuospatial information (Larkin & Simon, 1987). The suitability of illustrations for visual and spatial information helps to explain why they are also used within documentation to represent *changes* that occur in such information. This dynamic aspect is added to the fundamental visuospatial information by means of arrows and other auxiliary graphic devices that indicate changes in form and position occurring in the subject matter over time.

However, even the best-designed traditional documentation contains what may be considered a serious constraint on its capacity to represent procedures and processes. Neither texts nor static illustrations are capable of providing a full specification of temporal change. This constraint is a result of the fundamental mismatch between the static nature of such text-illustration combinations and the dynamic character of the subject matter. For example, while the addition of auxiliary graphic devices to a static illustration gives an indirect indication of the situational dynamics, it does not provide specific micro-level information about the temporal changes involved (Tversky, Bauer Morrison, & Bétrancourt, 2002) and so its proper interpretation can require extensive inference. Further, graphic devices commonly used to indicate dynamic information in static depictions vary in how effectively they can specify the intended dynamics (Lowe & Pramono, 2006). Even with those that tend to be more effective, there can be no guarantee that users will make the necessary inferences about the situational dynamics represented. As a result, documentation that offers only static information about dynamic aspects of the subject matter runs a risk that users' understanding of procedures and processes will be incomplete or impaired.

Until quite recently, the limitations of available technology and cost imperatives meant that there was little practical alternative to supplying documentation in traditional print-based format. However, with advances in technology and plummeting costs of convenient alternatives to print, this situation has changed radically. A particularly significant change has been in the area of dynamic representations. Software and hardware advances now make it possible to produce and display animated graphics with relative ease, while global communications infrastructure permits these materials to be distributed almost instantaneously around the world. While animations are likely to be more suitable for some content areas and topics than others, they appear to be particularly well suited to the explanation of procedures (Park, 1994). At first glance, it might be expected that animated documentation should offer considerable advantages over traditional static approaches because it is far better matched to the characteristics of dynamic subject matter. The following section explores the basis for such an expectation.

4 Animated versus Traditional Documentation

We have seen that the static text-illustration combinations found in traditional types of documentation cannot fully represent all aspects of a complex dynamic situation. They are intrinsically incapable of representing the component changes over time in a direct, analogue fashion and instead represent dynamic information indirectly and partially. This typically results in broad specifications only of temporal changes and a consequent lack of precision. Because the changes are under specified and imprecise, successful interpretation relies on the user being able to elaborate the actual situational dynamics by making appropriate inferences. This may be a challenging undertaking, particularly with complex content where the user lacks the background knowledge on which such inferences need to be based. Under these circumstances, attempts to elaborate the given static information in order to construct a dynamic mental model are likely to result in an internal representation that is incomplete and inaccurate. The flawed understandings that are a consequence of such faulty constructions prejudice the user's capacity to carry out procedures successfully or to react appropriately to crucial process indicators.

An obvious potential advantage of animated depictions is their capacity to provide an explicit analogue representation of situational dynamics in which visuospatial and temporal information are presented in a closely coupled manner. Animations save users from having to generate a mental animation that can internally represent relevant dynamic aspects of the subject matter (Hegarty, 1992). Instead, users have direct temporal information already provided for them in the external representation. Their task then becomes one of *extracting* the required dynamics for incorporation into a mental model rather than generating those dynamics. Given the limitations on human information processing capacity, it would seem beneficial to save users the cognitively demanding task of having to generate a mental animation from static information. This would allow cognitive resources to be devoted instead to tasks such as understanding the situational dynamics, and making effective decisions based on that understanding. In addition, animation has the potential to provide other benefits such as gaining attention and serving a cosmetic function. However, merely providing users with external animations on the assumption that this will facilitate their building of dynamic mental models fails to recognize the challenges that users may face in extracting the required information. The very characteristics of animations that on one hand offer advantages through the direct representation of situational dynamics, on the other hand may make information extraction more difficult. Processing tasks such as the perception, selection, and comparison of important information can be particularly challenging with animation because of its fleeting nature (Anglin, Towers, & Levie, 1996).

Effective extraction of information is a requirement for static as well as animated depictions, and can be a resource-intensive process in both cases. The mere act of presenting a depiction does not automatically mean that users will process the information it contains in an effective manner. For example, the extraction of task-relevant information from a static depiction relies on the viewer's success in carrying out appropriate spatial search processes (Winn, 1993; Lowe & Munt, 1999). However, in order to extract information from animations, there is the added challenge of performing successful temporal search. To appreciate why extraction of information from an animation may be particularly demanding, it is revealing to contrast the processing of animations with the processing of static graphics.

5 Processing of Animations

Because comprehension of static graphics and comprehension of animated graphics both rely on the same set of fundamental human processing capacities, they necessarily share a great deal in common. However, a key difference is the animation's inclusion of the temporal dimension, which from a theoretical perspective is likely to have both advantages and disadvantages in terms of processing. Until quite recently, animations were typically displayed to the viewer in a pre-determined, continuous manner with the viewer having no control over the pace, direction, or continuity of the presentation. The technical system displaying the animation (film or television) controlled the presentation regime and this was typically constant across all viewing occasions. In this section, we will consider system-controlled animations, and then later in the chapter shift our focus to the more recent development of user controllable animations.

The processing demands involved in trying to follow an animated explanation can be considerable, particularly if it deals with complex subject matter (Lowe, 1999). In such cases, the challenges faced can be thought of as potentially stretching the viewer's processing capacities beyond their limits. Reasons why animations may be more demanding to process than static graphics include:

- **Amount of information.** Because animation depicts change via multiple frames, each containing some different information, the total amount of information presented to users is necessarily greater than that contained in the 'single frame' of a static depiction.
- **Limited processing time available.** The 'continuous change' effect in animation depends on the presentation of each frame of information for a very limited time only. Consequently the time available for users to process each new unit of information is quite restricted.
- **Distributed simultaneous change.** In an animation of even modest complexity, changes occur simultaneously in different parts of the display. Forming a coherent interpretation requires that users both attend to these distributed changes and relate them to each other.
- **Transitoriness of information.** Because previous frames of information are not constantly available, users must hold relevant information in memory to relate it to new information and to integrate material that is presented in different frames of the animation.

When users lack background in the subject domain and the information presented is complex, they run the risk of being overwhelmed by the processing challenges stemming from these characteristics of animation. To manage this situation and so maintain processing, the user needs to limit the amount of information from the animation that must be dealt with per unit time.

6 Consequences of Animation's Processing Demands

In a general sense, users can accommodate animation's demands by adjusting their processing approach to make the presented information flow more tractable. Fine-grained empirical investigations of the way viewers deal with complex animations suggest that their primary response is to invoke selective attention (Lowe, 2001). Rather than attempting to process all of the available information, they select a subset of what is presented and direct their resources to dealing with those aspects. However, the subset of information that viewers select is not necessarily particularly relevant to the building of an appropriate mental model. When subject matter depicted in the animation is relatively unfamiliar to the user (as presumably is the case in much documentation), there is a tendency to process the presented information largely on the basis of its perceptual characteristics. Lacking the requisite background knowledge, viewers have little alternative but to adopt this domain general approach in order to maintain their processing. It appears that under these conditions, extraction of information from an animation is dominated by the information's perceptual salience rather than its relevance to key themes in the subject matter. Information that for some reason differs markedly from its surroundings in a perceptual sense is likely to be noticed irrespective of its importance. Conversely, aspects of the display that are perceptually inconspicuous will tend to be glossed over, even if they are of high thematic relevance to the subject matter being represented.

Both visuospatial and temporal characteristics seem to play a role in determining which aspects in an animation are noticed and which are neglected. For example, as can be the case with static depictions (Lowe, 1993), attention is likely to be directed to graphic entities that have a distinctive size or shape. Under such circumstances, these conspicuous entities may become the perceptual 'field', with the remainder of the display acting as the 'ground'. However, in animations the visuospatial characteristics of the display are not constant as they are in a static depiction so that animation introduces a different class of field-ground effects. The change in visuospatial characteristics over time introduces an additional and powerful type of perceptual driver that may have a strong influence on what information in the display is attended to by viewers. When this occurs, it appears that a *dynamic contrast* effect comes into play whereby direction of the viewer's attention is captured not only by contrast amongst the visuospatial characteristics of the display's graphic entities but also by relative changes in the position and form of those entities. By analogy with the perceptual division of a static display into a field and ground on the basis of contrasts in visuospatial characteristics, the dynamic contrasts across an animated presentation appear to result in its division into a *dynamic* field and ground. For example, an entity undergoing rapid change in its position or form while the rest of the display remains relatively stable will tend to capture the viewer's attention. However, it is also possible that a single unchanging entity surrounded by a sea of changes in the rest of display will also be noticed to the neglect of other information. In other words, it is the contrast that matters rather than dynamic characteristics *per se*. As with the visuospatial characteristics of a display, there is no necessary correspondence between heightened perceptibility due to dynamic contrast and the thematic relevance of aspects that therefore tend to be noticed.

7 User Controllable Animation

It has been suggested that giving users control over an animation can ameliorate the potential negative effects associated with strict system control as mentioned above. This suggestion is based upon the notion that user-controllable animations allow individual users to shape interrogation of the presentation to match their processing capacity. For example, if the animation presents information too rapidly, the user could simply slow it down to make the presentation more tractable (Hegarty, Narayanan, & Freitas, 2002). Similarly, if a single playing of a particular section of the animation was insufficient for all the desired information to be extracted, the user could then play that section repeatedly. There is some evidence that such user control of dynamic presentations can facilitate extraction of relevant information for simple tasks in everyday domains such as knot tying. Schwan and Riempp (2004) found that knowledge acquisition from interactive video instruction, in which viewers could utilize stop, reply, and review functions, was superior to that from traditional noninteractive video. However, this may not be the case for more complex tasks in specialized domains such as meteorology (Lowe, 2003), where the subject matter is far more abstract and unfamiliar. Even extensive user control does not seem to compensate for the effect that a lack of background knowledge has on how users extract information from animations. This suggests that perceptual processing plays a key role in domain novices' efforts to comprehend the presented information. The perceptual salience of components in the display continues to dominate processing, with inconspicuous but thematically relevant information still tending to be neglected. The problem appears to be that users are simply unaware of what types of information are important, and where such information is likely to be spatially and temporally located within the animated sequence. The animation alone does not provide reliable guidance on what to notice, or where and when to look for it (Lowe, 2004). As a result, unless users already have considerable background knowledge about the subject matter of the animation and its dynamics, merely providing them with control may not be particularly helpful. In animation, individual pictures that are in fact closely related in a conceptual sense (such as repeated instances within cyclical processes) may be presented so they are separated in time. This makes indexing these pictures difficult because of low temporal contiguity (regarding cross-representational indexing, cf. Mayer & Anderson, 1991). When the subject matter is complex and unfamiliar, users are likely to require support to help them interrogate the animation productively.

8 Animation with Verbal Information

As with traditional documentation, it is unlikely that documentation featuring animations would be able to rely on the graphic component alone to present all aspects of the required information. Rather, it seems that some aspects would probably be better handled by words than pictures. However, this raises the issue of how such words should be presented to the documentation user. We have already seen that animations by themselves can impose considerable information processing demands so that the addition of verbal information has the potential to increase these demands even further. This would be the case if such information were presented via written words (on or off screen) because of competition within the single visual processing channel. It is clearly important to avoid such a split attention effect if possible so that the advantages of presenting information by both words and pictures can be obtained with a minimum of disruption to productive processing (Mayer & Moreno, 1998). Fortunately, the aural channel provides an alternative route for words that appears to operate without providing appreciable competition to the visual channel. Complementing an animation with narration (Mayer & Anderson, 1991) is therefore likely to have advantages for providing verbal information compared with written text. However, because this means that both words and pictures would then be transitory, this approach brings with it other types of processing challenges that would need to be addressed when designing documentation.

Verbal information (whether spoken or written) could serve a number of distinct roles in animated documentation. In addition to providing an appropriate format for additional information that is more suited to expression as a verbal representation, it could be used to improve interrogation of user-controllable animation. As discussed earlier, aspects of an animation that have compelling perceptual characteristics can divert the viewer's attention away from more relevant but less conspicuous aspects. It may be possible to ameliorate this tendency by using written or spoken text to direct user attention towards spatial and temporal locations that contain low salience information of high thematic relevance. In effect, the intention would be to reduce the exploratory freedom that is typical of current open-ended approaches to user control and constrain interrogation to more productive avenues. This use of text for a directive purpose contrasts with the standard approach in which words are used to provide additional information about the subject matter. It is possible that a careful mixture of directive and informative text could be used to increase the effectiveness with which users extract thematically relevant information from animations. A further possible role for verbal information is to provide broad strategic guidance about general approaches that may be useful during interrogation. For example, it may be that playing a specific section of an animation at a variety of different speeds will reveal additional patterns of change amongst the depicted entities that are missed if only a single playing speed is used. Such an approach is likely to be valuable for complex subject matter that contains important hierarchical dynamic relationships.

9 Realism in Animation

One consequence of technological advances in the field of animation production is that it is now possible to produce highly realistic depictions of complex dynamic subject matter. On the surface, this may appear to be a most desirable prospect because it allows for close matching of the subject matter and its representation in terms of both appearance and behaviour. It could be argued that as a result, less interpretative processing would be needed than with a lower level of realism. However, the history of how explanatory graphics have evolved in practice indicates that realism has been largely abandoned in order to increase the explanatory power of depictions. For example, diagrams have long been established as the fundamental means of depiction across a wide variety of technical domains. In diagrams, the characteristics of the subject matter are portrayed in a highly selective and manipulated manner. Only essentials of the referent situation are included in the depiction. These selected aspects are depicted in ways intended to facilitate user processing of the relevant information rather than maintain a close superficial resemblance to the referent.

The production of animated documentation would in many cases require the types of illustrations used in traditional documentation to be converted into animations. Where diagrams and other abstract depictions are involved, the question arises as to whether the temporal characteristics of the subject matter should be given the same level of selective and manipulative treatment as is applied to visuospatial characteristics. If there is to be the same concern with facilitating user processing, should the *behaviour* of the subject matter in its depiction be altered extensively to parallel the extensive alterations of *appearance* that are accepted practice for static diagrams? This does not appear to be happening with the way explanatory explanations are designed at present. While animated diagrams continue to be depictively unrealistic, their dynamics in contrast tend to be portrayed realistically. This approach of preserving *behavioural realism* makes no allowance for the processing challenges faced by users when dealing with dynamic information that were canvassed earlier in this chapter.

The current preoccupation with behavioural realism in animations may be a passing phase that is partly driven by designers' temporary fascination with the technological capacity of recent hardware and software to produce ever more (dynamically) realistic depictions. This may be coupled with a naïve view that realistic representations in general have a privileged effectiveness. However, in the realm of static graphics, many different techniques are routinely applied to modify the subject matter's visuospatial characteristics, often in quite extreme ways. Use of these modifications is firmly established in the graphics employed by many professions, presumably because they have been found highly effective. A major goal of these modifications is to alter the perceptual properties of certain aspects of the display so that the viewer's processing will be more efficient and effective. Underlying such modification is many years of accumulated experience about what users find easy and difficult when processing explanatory graphics as well as which approaches result in users making fewer errors. While this craft knowledge has not been formalized across disciplines of practice, it nevertheless appears to embody principles consistent with the characteristics of human information processing. For example, by omitting information and manipulating the portrayal, aspects with high natural perceptual salience but low thematic relevance can be de-emphasized so they are less likely to attract user attention. Conversely, modifications are also applied to add visual emphasis to inconspicuous aspects that are of high relevance. In the realm of animated explanation, it seems likely that a similar emphasis on functional rather than physical fidelity may also have positive effects on comprehension. Indeed, there is evidence that quite extreme manipulation of an animation's temporal characteristics facilitate the building of more appropriate mental models of mechanical devices (Fischer, Lowe, & Schwan, 2006).

10   Animated Documentation: Fantasy or Frontier?

There is no doubt that from a purely *technological* perspective, it is now possible to include animation as an integral part of user documentation. In addition, compelling psychological arguments can be advanced that animations have the potential to greatly facilitate users' processing of the required dynamic information by depicting it directly and explicitly. However, like all forms of representation, animation is a two-edge sword that brings its own set of processing challenges, particularly when the subject matter is complex and unfamiliar to the user. These are the very circumstances under which animation is most likely to be considered for inclusion in documentation. While intuitively appealing, the use of animations in such cases needs to take proper account of the powerful perceptual factors that can play such a central role in how users extract information from dynamic displays. A principled approach to animation design based on an understanding of the pervasive influence of these factors (rather than intuitions) is required. This should inform decisions about how information will be presented by an animation and what support will be given to help the user process that information efficiently and effectively.

At present, our understanding of how users process explanatory animations is in its infancy so that authors of these resources lack a principled basis for their design. There are major issues likely to impinge on designs that have thus far received little or no attention from researchers. For example, when a static graphic is converted to an animated depiction, it appears likely that there will be interactions between visuospatial and temporal effects on perception that may have profound implications for the animation designer (Lowe & Pramono, 2006). In addition to the need for more empirical research on how users process animations, a robust theoretical framework is required that offers an integrated view of the perceptual characteristics of static and dynamic graphics, the consequences that their similarities and differences are likely have for information processing, and the implications for design practice.

A fundamental design choice to be made when contemplating the use of animations for presenting aspects of procedural information is the suitability of animated depiction for the intended purposes. Animation is not a universal panacea, even for dynamic content because it is capable of imposing its own processing demands on the user that may be harmful to comprehension rather than helpful. Designers should therefore not automatically choose animated graphics for depicting procedures just because they are dynamic. In one sense, the transitory nature of animations severely constrains the user's information processing opportunities relative to those available with static graphics. While the provision of animations with user control may appear to compensate for these constraints, handing over such control to the user can generate its own problems. Potential challenges for user comprehension of animated documentation appear more likely to occur if the subject matter is highly specialized, complex, and abstract. Under such circumstances, designers need to take account of the possibility that perceptual demands could be a dominant factor shaping the way users approach the interpretation of explanatory animations. Indeed, the compelling perceptual influence of an animation's dynamic aspects may compete with important visuospatial information for the user's attention. If the design of an explanatory animation ignores this possibility by giving priority to a behaviourally realistic approach to depiction, users may neglect key information. An alternative to behavioural realism is a design approach that emphasizes functional aspects and manipulates the display regime in order to expose and foreground information of prime thematic relevance. For animated documentation to be effective, the approach to design must extend beyond the animations themselves. These dynamic components need to be considered in the broader context of visual and verbal support that can help to guide user attention to key spatial and temporal locations. If animations are both well designed in terms of matching human processing capacities and tightly integrated into a coherent information presentation system, they have great potential to greatly enhance the comprehensibility of documentation.

Chapter 17

The Impact of Cognitively Based Design of Expository Multimedia

N. Hari Narayanan

Designers, engineers and technical writers at work are often asked to describe and explain causal systems in technical documents. The focus of this chapter is on how such expository documents can be created in a way that helps the reader better understand the systems that the documents describe, based on the premise that understanding complex causal systems requires building accurate mental models. This chapter first characterizes causal systems and discusses difficulties associated with understanding causal systems from external verbal and visual representations. A cognitive model of comprehension that elucidates processes of mental model construction is then presented. Various guidelines and principles for the design of effective multimedia documents are derived from this model. Finally, an example is provided to illustrate the cognitively based design and structure of a multimedia document. Information in this chapter will serve both designers of technical documents looking for practical guidance and researchers interested in cognitively based design of expository multimedia.

1 Introduction

Causal and dynamic systems—systems that change internally or effect changes externally, and whose operations or behaviors can be explained in terms of causal mechanisms—are important constituents of the world that we live in. Machines with electrical, mechanical, and hydraulic components, from abacus to zeppelin, operate on causal principles. Instances of causal and dynamic systems abound in engineering and technical disciplines. So it is not surprising that designers, engineers, and technical writers at work are often asked to describe and explain complex causal systems in technical documents on paper or on the computer (using interactive multimedia). The focus of this chapter is on how such expository documents can be created in a way that helps the reader better understand the causal systems

Written Documents In The Workplace
Copyright © 2007 by Elsevier Ltd.
All rights of reproduction in any form reserved.
ISBN: 978-0-080-47487-8

Narayanan, H. (2007). The impact of cognitively based design of expository multimedia. In G. Rijlaarsdam (Series Ed.) and D. Alamargot, P. Terrier, & J.-M. Cellier (Vol. Eds.), Studies in Writing, Vol. 21, Written Documents in the Workplace, 243–259.

that the documents describe, based on the premise that understanding complex causal systems requires building accurate mental models.

Causal and dynamic systems may be seen as particular types of mechanisms (Machamer, Darden, & Carver, 2000) composed of entities and activities that produce a series of internal or external state changes that are explainable by causal laws, beginning with an initial condition or state and ending in a final condition or state. Developing an accurate mental model of causal systems is important to comprehension. However, understanding causal systems is difficult because many aspects of such systems are dynamic, invisible, and interdependent (Feltovich, Coulsen, Spiro, & Dawson-Saunders, 1992). Erroneous preconceptions and naïve beliefs can interfere with comprehension, by preventing the development of correct mental models. So in the next three sections, we provide a characterization of causal systems, illustrate this with an example, and discuss some of the difficulties associated with understanding causal systems from descriptions and depictions in technical documents containing visual and verbal representations. We then present a cognitive model of multimedia comprehension that elucidates processes of mental model construction from external representations. Various design guidelines and principles for the design of effective multimedia documents are derived from this model. Finally, an example is presented to concretely illustrate how such cognitively based document design can be achieved. Our hope is that this information will serve both document designers looking for practical guidance and researchers interested in information design guided by cognitive theories.

2 Characterization of Causal and Dynamic Systems

Causal and dynamic systems of interest in this article can be characterized as follows.

(1) Systems are hierarchically structured with subsystems and components. Engineered systems are generally designed and analyzed in a hierarchical fashion (Rasmussen, 1985). Modules and submodules of a system form a hierarchical structure such that the overall function of the system is achieved through contributory functions of its modules. For example, it is instructive to describe the function of a gear-train module as transmitting power from the engine module to the wheel assembly module. Natural systems, such as the human body, are also often explained and understood in terms of subsystems like the respiratory system, circulatory system, etc.

(2) Subsystems at each level of the hierarchy, and basic components at the lowest level, exhibit various behaviors that accomplish natural or designed functions. For instance, the function of a brake pad in an automobile is to dissipate the kinetic energy by turning it into heat through friction. This function is accomplished through the behavior of the brake pad pressing against a rotating surface of the wheel assembly. As another example, in the human body, the expansion and contraction of lungs accomplish the function of moving air in and out of the lung cavities.

(3) The behaviors of subsystems and components influence (trigger, prevent, or modify) the behaviors of other subsystems and components. For example, the movement of a brake pad against the drum of a wheel reduces the rotational velocity of the wheel. These influences or dependencies are governed by physical or other kinds of laws and principles.

(4) The propagation of these influences creates chains of events, which we call "lines-of-action", in the operation of the overall system, and these event chains give rise to the overall behavior or function of the system.

(5) These chains of events extend in temporal and spatial dimensions. For example, the downward movement of a brake pedal, initiated by the driver of an automobile, causes a variety of electrical and mechanical behaviors of other components, ultimately causing the brake pads in the vehicle to push up against the wheel drums. Similarly, the movement of the diaphragm, through a series of other behaviors, causes blood in the lung capillaries to be enriched with oxygen and depleted of carbon dioxide. Sometimes such event chains are linear, i.e. a behavior influencing another, which in turn influences a third, and so on. But more often cause-effect event chains branch and merge. Furthermore, the event chains can be traced in the spatial dimension, i.e. the affected components are distributed within the spatial structure of the overall system, and also in the temporal dimension, i.e. events coincide with or follow one another in time. Causal systems in which multiple lines of action (or series of events) branch and merge in both space and time are particularly hard to explain in documents, and difficult to understand and reason about. But understanding and being able to predict these event chains is an extremely important aspect of comprehending causal and dynamic systems.

3 Example: An Everyday Device

In this section we describe an example of a causal and dynamic system. The purpose is not only to illustrate the previously described characteristics in concrete terms, but also to provide the reader with a specific system to keep in mind while reading the following sections on cognitive modeling and design principles. The flushing cistern (Figure 1) is a mechanical

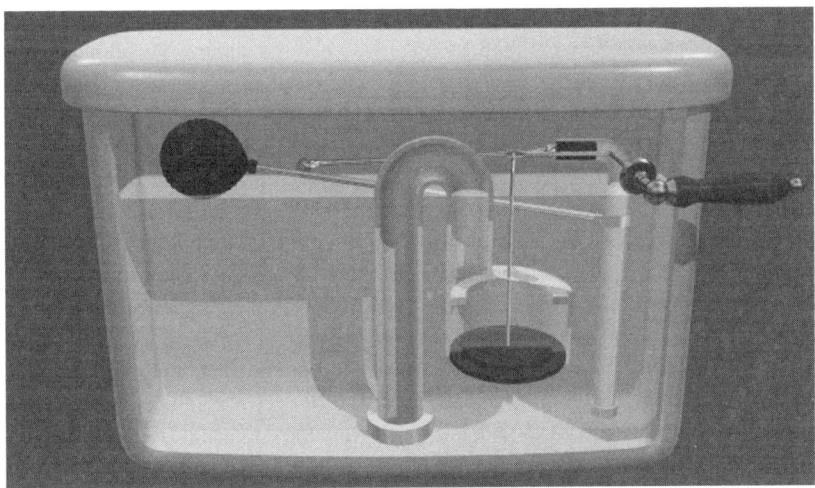

Figure 1: A mechanical device with branching and merging lines-of-action.

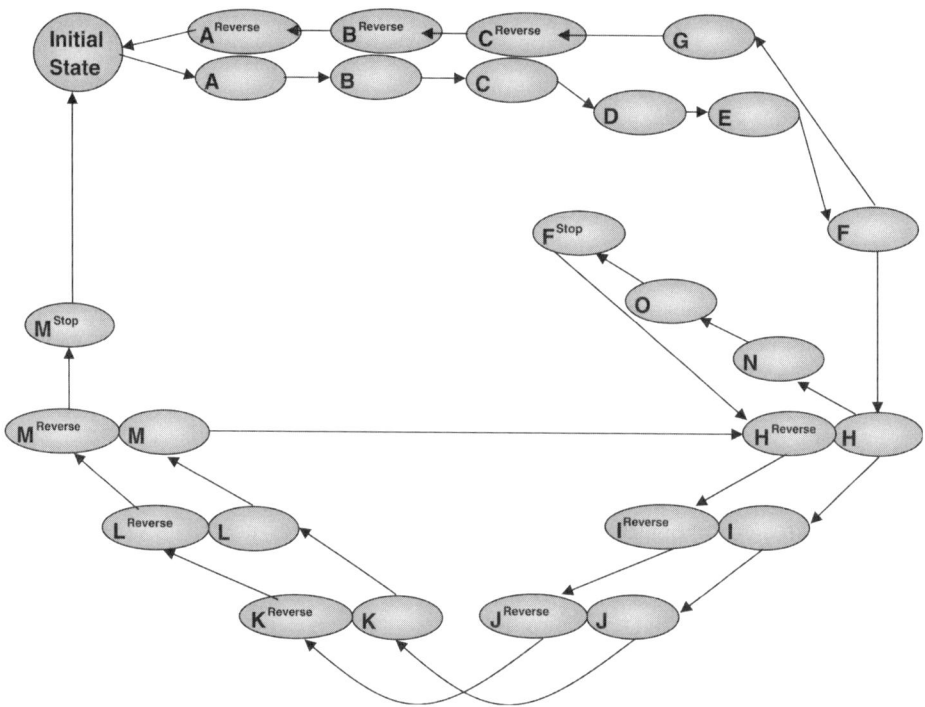

Figure 2: Branching and merging lines-of-action in the flushing cistern device.

device that most will recognize. Although this is a common device, its internal structure and operation are not obvious to people. It is a complex causal system with two external and observable behaviors. It has a handle that can be turned or pulled, and this action results in a certain amount of water being forcefully ejected out of the cistern. This device consists of two subsystems: a water outlet system that expels water and a water inlet system that refills the tank. The water outlet system consists of the following components: handle, connecting lever, vertical rod, lower disk, upper disk, and siphon pipe. The water inlet subsystem consists of the following components: float, connecting rod, lever, valve, and inlet pipe. Figure 2 shows the branching and merging lines-of-action in the operation of this device. The various causal events that constitute these lines-of-action are explained next.

The operation of the water outlet system is triggered by the clockwise turning of the handle, which generates a chain of cause-effect events that culminate in water exiting the chamber through the siphon pipe. These events are denoted by letters of the alphabet in the following discussion. The rotation of the handle (A) moves the connecting lever upwards (B). This motion is transmitted through a mechanical linkage to the vertical rod. When the vertical rod is pulled up (C), it presses the lower disk (which is connected to its end) against the upper disk and pulls the lower and upper disks together upwards with it (D). This results in water being pulled into the siphon pipe from the tank below the disks, water rising and filling the siphon pipe, and eventually flowing over the curve and downward, and out of the siphon pipe into the toilet bowl (E). This creates the siphon effect, which continues to pull water from the tank and expel it through the siphon pipe (F). Thus, A–B–C–D–E–F is one line-of-action.

Meanwhile the lower and upper disks fall back down to their initial position at the bottom of the siphon pipe (G), while water continues to flow through the holes in the lower disk and around the edge of the upper disk (its diameter is smaller than that of the bell pipe). This reverses the motions of the vertical rod ($C^{Reverse}$), the connecting lever ($B^{Reverse}$), and the handle ($A^{Reverse}$), i.e. the handle returns to its original position. Thus, F–G–$C^{Reverse}$–$B^{Reverse}$–$A^{Reverse}$ is another line-of-action.

The operation of the water outlet system is triggered by the outflow of water from the tank (F). This outflow causes the water level in the tank to drop (H). This results in the floating ball moving down (I), rotating the lever attached to it in the counterclockwise direction (J). This rotation pulls the hinged rod attached to this lever out of the inlet pipe (K). This movement of the rod opens up the inlet valve more and more (L), resulting in more and more water flowing into the tank (M). Thus, F–H–I–J–K–L–M is another line-of-action. Note that F is a branch point at which the initial single line-of-action splits into two.

Now there are two opposing influences on the water level in the tank. It drops (H) due to water outflow through the siphon pipe (F). It rises ($H^{Reverse}$) due to water inflow from the inlet valve (M). Thus H is a merge point at which two separate lines-of-action merge, exerting two opposing influences on the same event. As the siphon pipe is larger than the inlet valve, the outflow rate of the water from the tank exceeds the inflow rate. Therefore, the water level keeps dropping (H). Eventually, the water level drops below the mouth of the bell part of the siphon pipe (N). This allows air to enter the siphon pipe and break the siphon effect (O). This empties out the water in the siphon pipe and stops the outflow of water (F^{Stop}). At this point, the floating ball is in its lowest position, i.e. the inlet valve is fully open. Further inflow of the water makes the water level in the tank rise ($H^{Reverse}$). This in turn reverses the motion of the floating ball ($I^{Reverse}$), the lever it is connected to ($J^{Reverse}$), and the hinged rod attached to this lever ($K^{Reverse}$). The reversed movement of this rod starts closing the inlet valve ($L^{Reverse}$), which in turn causes less and less water flowing into the tank ($M^{Reverse}$). Eventually, the water level in the tank will reach its original position, at which the inlet valve is completely closed and water inflow stops (M^{Stop}). Thus, H–N–O–F^{Stop}–$H^{Reverse}$–$I^{Reverse}$–$J^{Reverse}$–$K^{Reverse}$–$L^{Reverse}$–$M^{Reverse}$–M^{Stop} is another line-of-action which brings the tank back to its initial state.

4 Difficulties in Comprehending Causal and Dynamic Systems

There are several difficulties associated with understanding how complex causal systems function. One source of difficulty is their hierarchical levels of organization with both local interactions and dependencies across levels. Many causal systems consist of multiple levels of organization that often depend on local interactions (Ferrari & Chi, 1998; Wilensky & Resnick, 1999). The relationships across these levels are not intuitively obvious. For example, in learning about ecological systems, one needs to envision how genes, individuals, populations, and species interrelate. An ecosystem can be viewed from the level of the individual organism to the level of the environment as a whole (Wilensky & Resnick, 1999). In human biology, phenomena occur at the anatomical, biochemical, and physiological levels. For example, respiration occurs at a cellular level as well as at the organ system level. The levels are interdependent on each other. When cells need oxygen, not only does the lungs move more deeply than usual but also the heart may beat faster to get more oxygen to the tissues. In an ecosystem, animals provide carbon dioxide needed by plants for photosynthesis and plants provide oxygen needed by fish to utilize energy. A disturbance at one level or component of the system can easily affect others.

A second source of learning difficulty is that novices tend to focus mainly on perceptually salient aspects of systems, leading to inaccurate and incomplete mental models. So invisible, dynamic phenomena that are typically present in complex causal systems pose considerable barriers to understanding (Feltovich et al., 1992). Experiments in the domain of meteorology (Lowe, 1994, 1999) indicate that novices have poor comprehension of both static and animated weather maps. In both cases, the information they extract is perceptually salient rather than thematically relevant, and inappropriate causal attributions are made to changing weather phenomena. For example, novices erroneously ascribe cause–effect relationships to weather phenomena visible in typical meteorological animations based on temporal relationships alone. Other studies of complex systems also demonstrate that understanding focuses on perceptually available structures (Gellert, 1962; Hmelo, Holton, & Kolodner, 2000; Hmelo-Silver & Pfeffer, 2004).

A third problem is the significant working memory load imposed by mental animation (Hegarty, 1992) and simulation, cognitive processes that come into play in reasoning about causal systems. The functioning of such systems involves simultaneous events and interactions, and these pose a substantial load on working memory because of the mental simulation process and rule-based inferences needed to construct a complete mental model (Graesser, 1999; Narayanan & Hegarty, 1998, 2002). Moreover, making connections among different levels of a complex system places added demands on working memory. This is particularly true because many systems are characterized by complex causality; and there may be many nonlinear, intermediate steps that intervene between cause and effect (Perkins & Grotzer, 2000).

A fourth learning bottleneck is that complex systems may have emergent properties that are not fully predictable from the behavior of individual components (Wilensky & Resnick, 1999). Thinking about emergent phenomena involves the recognition that a system can have multiple causal factors, and these occur at both micro and macro levels.

Fifth, novices tend to develop simple mental models even for complex systems. A review by Perkins and Grotzer (2000) found that students tended towards very simple causal explanations of complex phenomena. When they reasoned about effects, they missed the connectedness within the system and the complex causal relationships because they tended to focus on the structure of systems rather than on the underlying function. This is consistent with expert-novice comparisons of complex systems thinking (Jacobson, 2001). Jacobson interviewed undergraduate students and complex systems experts and found that students favored simple causality, central control, and predictability. Expert explanations demonstrated decentralized thinking, multiple causes, and the use of stochastic and equilibration processes. This suggests that students' mental models tend to be overly simplistic, often affected by what is perceptually salient.

A sixth source of learning difficulty is that complex systems often involve concepts that can be in conflict with learners' prior experience. For example, Resnick and Wilensky (1998) found that most people have what they referred to as a "centralized mindset", preferring explanations that assume central control and single causality even for systems that are distributed and emergent.

Finally, there are deep principles that explain behavior in complex causal systems and account for the relationships across levels. But learners have difficulty in applying principles to infer behaviors of such systems. Chi and colleagues (Chi, DeLeeuw, Chiu, & LaVancher, 1994) asked students to read a passage about the circulatory system. The functional aspects of the system were implicit and difficult for students to infer. Only students engaged in self-explanations could make those inferences.

In the rest of this chapter we will address the issue of how multimedia explanations of complex causal systems can be designed to overcome some of these difficulties, aid comprehension, and support the building of accurate mental models. The suggested approach involves designing multiple expository representations, built using the technology of interactive multimedia. The design of educational multimedia is often based on informal intuitions of the designer, and seldom based on sound design principles. The approach presented in the following sections is a case study of principled design, starting from a cognitive process model of understanding causal systems, applying the model to design and evaluate interactive multimedia documents, and through this process deriving both an empirically tested structure of expository multimedia documents and a set of design guidelines and principles.

5 A Cognitive Process Model of Comprehending Causal and Dynamic Systems

Narayanan and Hegarty (1998) developed a model of how learners comprehend multimodal (visual and verbal) documents that explain how mechanical systems work, and applied it to designing multimedia expository presentations in the domains of computer algorithms and mechanical devices. This model, similar to Kintsch's construction-integration model of discourse comprehension (Kintsch, 1988), views comprehension as a series of processes by which the learner uses his or her prior knowledge of the domain and integrates it with the presented information to construct first a static, and then a dynamic, mental model of the system being explained. The resulting internal representation is a mental model (Gentner & Stevens, 1983) in the sense that there is a direct correspondence between parts of the representation and components of the dynamic system that it represents. Moreover, the model is "runnable" in that it contains information that allows the learner to mentally simulate or animate a system and generate predictions about its operation. Mental model construction, according to this model, involves several stages of processing, as described below.

5.1 Decomposition

A complex system typically consists of individual components and structures. Pictorial representations of these contain several diagrammatic elements such as geometric shapes and icons that represent various parts of the system. The first step in comprehension is to parse the external representations into units that correspond to meaningful elements of the domain. This decomposition process is guided both by prior knowledge about the system and its components (a top-down influence), and by visual properties of the external representation such as use of different colors or textures to show different components in a diagram (a bottom-up influence).

5.2 Constructing a Static Mental Model

Another stage in comprehension involves making representational connections among the visual and symbolic units identified during decomposition, and making referential connections. The learner must make connections between the visual and symbolic elements identified in the previous stage and their referents. The learner must also represent the relations between different parts of the system. In a mechanical system for instance, this involves understanding the physical interactions (connections and contact) between components. When illustrations are accompanied by text, these different representations must be integrated to construct a mental model of the system being described. An important process in this integration is co-reference resolution, i.e. making referential connections between elements of the different representations that refer to the same entity. This is similar to the processing of co-references in natural language discourse (Gordon & Hendrick, 1998). Successful co-reference resolution requires that visual and verbal information about a common referent must be in working memory at the same time in order to be integrated.

5.3 Knowing and Applying Basic Laws

Complex systems work according to basic laws (such as the laws of physics). Some users, especially novices, may lack an understanding of these laws. Even when novices are able to articulate basic laws governing the operation of a system, they may be unable to apply the laws to produce correct inferences. In such cases, providing explanations of these fundamental laws in the context of the system being described is necessary to improve understanding.

5.4 Inferring Lines-of-Action

Another stage of comprehension involves identifying the chains of events that occur in the operation of the system, events that are dependent on each other due to logical, causal or other kinds of influences. Previous studies (Hegarty, 1992; Narayanan, Suwa, & Motoda, 1994a, 1994b, 1995a, 1995b) have shown that people tend to infer events in the operation of a system along the direction of causal propagation. In complex mechanical systems with cyclical operations or branching and merging causal chains, finding the causal chains requires knowledge of both the spatial structure of the system and the temporal duration and ordering of events in its operation. This can introduce errors both in hypothesizing event chains and in integrating event chains of interacting subsystems (Hegarty, Quilici, Narayanan, Holmquist, & Moreno, 1999; Narayanan et al., 1995a).

5.5 Constructing a Dynamic Mental Model

The final stage of comprehension is that of constructing a dynamic mental model by inferring the behaviors of individual components of the system, and integrating this information to understand how the components work together. Cognitive and computational modeling in the mechanical domain (Hegarty, 1992; Narayanan & Chandrasekaran, 1991) suggest that this is often accomplished by considering components individually, inferring their behaviors due to influences from other connected or causally related components, and then inferring how these behaviors will in turn affect other components. Thus, if asked to predict the motion of a machine component from that of another component in the system, learners make more errors and take more time if the components are farther apart in the causal chain (Baggett & Graesser, 1995; Hegarty & Sims, 1994). This incremental reasoning process causes the static mental model constructed in earlier stages of comprehension to be progressively transformed into a dynamic one. This stage can involve both rule-based inferences that utilize prior conceptual knowledge (Schwartz & Hegarty, 1996) and visualization processes for mentally simulating component behaviors (Narayanan et al., 1994a, 1994b, 1995a, 1995b; Schwartz & Black, 1996; Sims & Hegarty, 1997).

The cognitive model described above was originally proposed by Narayanan and Hegarty in 1998. Subsequently, it was further refined and applied to the development of interactive hypermedia presentations intended for novice students, in the domains of machines and computer algorithms (Narayanan & Hegarty, 2002). In several experiments involving both domains, presentations that were designed according to the model were found to be more effective than conventional printed materials and conventional multimedia presentations. The construction and testing of several interactive hypermedia presentations not only served to validate the model, but also led to several design guidelines and principles for multimedia explanations of causal systems. These are presented in the next section.

6 Designing Multimedia Explanations of Causal and Dynamic Systems

The processes of cognition posited by the model described previously led to predictions about potential sources of comprehension difficulties that a reader who is trying to understand a causal and dynamic system from a multimedia explanation may face, and a corresponding set of design guidelines for multimedia documents.

6.1 Design Guidelines

Diagrams and animations do not always make clear how the system being explained can be parsed or separated into subsystems and components. Accurate decomposition is a precursor to the development of an accurate mental model of the system, therefore, this is a potential source of comprehension difficulty that readers face in trying to understand complex causal systems from static or animated pictorial representations. The corresponding design guideline is that visual representations that the reader sees should provide explicit support for accurate parsing or decomposition of the system into its subsystems and components. For example, a multimedia document about a machine could include an exploded diagram that shows its components separated in space or an animation that shows how the system can be separated into (or put together from) its components and subsystems. Color coding, grouping, and highlighting boundaries are some of the visual techniques that can be used by the designer to aid decomposition.

Lack of prior knowledge about system components is another comprehension difficulty that a novice might encounter. This can lead to unidentified or misidentified system components in one's mental model. Therefore, if readers are not expected to have sufficient prior knowledge to understand the conventions of the domain, connections to prior knowledge should be provided as part of the presentation. For example, a multimedia document about a machine could contain realistic depictions of components to facilitate accurate identification and recall of prior knowledge. Another way to help readers in making connections to prior knowledge is to hyperlink graphical components and technical symbols in the interactive document to detailed explanations of the entities that they depict so that novices have access to background information that more expert readers can skip.

For any system, how its components are connected or related to each other is an important determinant of how the system behaves or operates. Therefore, an accurate representation of these connections is a critical part of constructing an accurate mental model of the system, and this is a third source of potential comprehension difficulty. Hence, multimedia presentations should be designed to make explicit the connections or dependencies among system components and component behaviors. For example, if all component interactions in a machine occur in a single plane, a cross-sectional diagram of the machine should be provided to explicate the physical and spatial connections among its components. If the component connections and interactions occur in multiple planes however, a single cross-sectional diagram may not be sufficient to accurately convey the nature of these connections and interactions. In such a case, other diagrams such as orthographic or isometric projections may be necessary.

Multimedia explanations often provide multiple visual and verbal representations to describe and explain the same object or concept. For example, the synchronized combustion of gasoline inside the cylinders of an internal combustion engine may be explained by a textual description or spoken narrative accompanied with a labeled cross-sectional diagram, illustrated by an animation of the cross-sectional diagram, and further illustrated with video footage of an actual running engine. When multiple representations refer to the same entity or concept, the act of understanding these multiple references to a common referent is called co-reference resolution. On one hand, such multimodal explanations enhance comprehension, because the visual and verbal components support both visualizers and verbalizers, and the informational redundancy of such representations reinforce learning. On the other hand, when the common referents of multiple representations (such as verbal descriptions, labels on diagrams, visual components of animation and video, etc.) are not clear to the reader, co-reference resolution can become difficult. To facilitate co-reference resolution in such instances, multimedia explanations should present different representations with a common referent close together in space (i.e. adjacent to each other on the screen). It is also important to provide such representations close to each other in the temporal dimension. Identical text, such as labels and phrases, appearing in multiple representations will support co-reference resolution. For instance, if labels or descriptive phrases appear in a diagram, use exactly the same labels and phrases in textual explanations, animations, and narrated explanations that may accompany animation or video. All these aid the viewer in quickly building accurate referential connections in his or her mental model. Referential connections may also be facilitated by linking multiple representations with the same referents through clickable hyperlinks, especially if these appear in different screens.

Understanding the spatial and temporal sequence of events (some of which may be simultaneous) that together result in the natural or designed operation or behavior of the entire system is a critical aspect of comprehension. Understanding the event chains of complex causal systems can be quite a challenge for a novice. As Baggett and Graesser (1995) discovered, longer event chains lead to more reasoning errors. This difficulty increases for systems with both sequential and simultaneous events. This is because learners tend to reason about events in an incremental fashion (Hegarty, 1992), so they tend to serialize even simultaneous events for ease of reasoning (Narayanan et al., 1995a). This serialization can lead to errors. The comprehension difficulty involving event chains is further exacerbated if the chains branch and merge in the dimensions of space and time.

Recent research (Hegarty, Kriz, & Cate, 2003) shows that comprehension of dynamic information about a system is improved if students are given an opportunity to mentally animate or simulate the system after they are given sufficient information to construct a static mental model. Mental animation or simulation is an instance of active processing, which, in the context of text understanding, has been shown to aid model construction better than passive acquisition of information (McNamara et al., 1996). One way of encouraging mental animation is to show snapshots of the system's operation at various points in a causal or logical chain of events, and encourage the viewer to mentally animate or simulate events that occur between the snapshots. Another way is to present "what-if" questions after the user has constructed a static mental model, but before he or she views an animation or explanation of how the system works. Again, for maximum effect, such mental animation should precede the viewing of an external animation.

Various kinds of visualizations can help with correctly communicating the flow of causality or logic in the operation of the system being explained, and transforming the static mental model into a dynamic one. For simple systems, an animation may be sufficient to convey information about both causality and movement. For a more complex system, a separate visualization of the causal connections may have to be presented prior to showing the animation of the system's operation for deeper understanding.

Yet another source of comprehension difficulty predicted by the cognitive model is that of comprehending animations. Animations can be difficult to comprehend for several reasons (Narayanan & Hegarty, 1998, 2002; Tversky et al., 2002). One cause of difficulty is a speed mismatch between processes of comprehension and the external animation. An animation may run too fast to completion for comprehension processes to keep up. A second cause is the limitation of visual attention. Since one can visually focus on only a small area of the screen at a time, if multiple events are depicted simultaneously on different parts of the screen, it is likely that the viewer may miss some of those events. Third, just as in the case of reading, re-inspection of something already seen and comparison of what is being seen now with what was seen before are likely to be important for accurate comprehension of the dynamic processes that animations typically show. But animations are fleeting and transient, and do not permit re-inspection and comparison.

Therefore, in order for an animation or video to be effective in communicating dynamic behaviors of a system, the viewer should be able to match the speed of animation or video with the speed of his or her comprehension of the events being presented. The viewer should always have control over the rate of information presentation through videos and animations. One way to achieve this is to provide VCR-like controls (i.e. play, pause, stop, repeat, reverse, etc.). Another approach is to segment a complex video or animation into causally or logically coherent "chunks", and present these segments in sequence. This provides the reader with an opportunity to pause, reflect on, and replay any segment before viewing the next one. We have found that segmented animations lead to better comprehension in the domain of algorithms (Hansen, Narayanan, & Hegarty, 2002).

The final source of comprehension difficulty predicted by the cognitive model is an inability to understand a certain event or behavior due to a lack of knowledge about an underlying law or principle of the domain. When the correct operation of an engineered system (such as a flushing cistern) or the behavior of a natural system (such as the weather) depends on basic principles that might not be understood by novices (e.g., the siphon principle or the Coriolis principle), a corresponding design guideline is to provide, in a separate section of the multimedia document, descriptions and illustrations of these principles in the context of the system being explained. This allows novices to gain knowledge of the law or principle while at the same time also understanding how it is instantiated within the system they are trying to understand. The knowledgeable viewers, on the other hand, are able to skip this section and proceed without the extraneous (to them) material becoming a distraction.

6.2 Design Principles

There is a growing body of recent work addressing cognitive constraints on multimedia comprehension. The essence of such research, both theoretical and empirical, is often articulated as concise design principles. For example, our research on the development of a cognitive process model of comprehension, its application to the design of interactive and explanatory multimedia, and several experiments to validate the model and evaluate the multimedia designs, have led to the following six design principles for expository multimedia. (1) *The design principle of decomposition:* provide cues, such as color coding, labels, exploded views, etc. in verbal and visual representations to help readers hierarchically analyze the system being explained in terms of its subsystems and components. (2) *The design principle of prior knowledge:* use descriptions and depictions that help readers identify and recognize system components, access any prior knowledge they might have about the components, and make mental connections to this prior knowledge in their mental models. (3) *The design principle of co-reference:* use spatial adjacency, temporal adjacency, interactivity (e.g. hyperlinking multiple representations with a common referent), and deictic features (e.g. simultaneous highlighting of different representations of the same object) to relate multiple verbal and visual representations with a common referent. (4) *The design principle of lines-of-action:* encourage a reader to infer the chains of events that occur in the system's operation or natural behavior, and then explain the physical, causal, and logical connections among system components that determine how the behavior of each influences that of others, creating these chains of events. (5) *The design principle of mental simulation:* encourage viewers to predict, or mentally simulate, the system that is being explained before providing an external animation or video; then provide accurate animation or video of the system's operation or behavior in meaningful segments and with full control over speed and direction. (6) *The design principle of basic laws:* when the operation of a system depends on basic principles that might not be understood by all readers, describe and illustrate these principles explicitly in the context of the system being explained in separate sections that novices can access and experts can skip.

These design principles are consistent with, and complement, the learning principles proposed by Mayer in the book *Multimedia Learning* (Mayer, 2001). Mayer's principles are the following: (1) *Multimedia principle:* learning from words and pictures is more effective than learning solely from words. (2) *Spatial contiguity principle:* learning is more effective when words and corresponding pictures are presented close to each other on the page or screen than when these are presented separately or far apart. (3) *Temporal contiguity principle:* learning is more effective when words and corresponding pictures are presented at the same time rather than one after the other. (4) *Coherence principle:* learning is impeded by the inclusion of interesting but irrelevant words, pictures, sound, and music, and learning is improved by removing unnecessary material. (5) *Modality principle:* students learn better when words are presented through the auditory channel when animation is engaging the visual channel compared to when words are presented as on-screen text along with animation. (6) *Redundancy principle:* learning from animation and narration is more effective than learning from animation, narration as well as on-screen text. (7) *Individual differences principle:* the above principles are more applicable to novices than knowledgeable students, and for low-spatial ability students than high-spatial ability students.

Tversky and colleagues (Tversky et al., 2002), based on an extensive review of literature on animations for learning, proposed two principles specifying conditions for successful animations. (1) *Congruence principle*: the structure and content of animated representations should match the structure and content of internal representations. For example, since observers segment events while perceiving and remembering them (Zacks et al., 2001), it is reasonable to assume that animations that are segmented based upon the event structure they portray will be more comprehensible than continuous animations. (2) *Apprehension principle*: the structure and content of animated representations should be of a grain size that can be readily and accurately perceived and comprehended. For example, fine metric distinctions made in an animation may not be accurately apprehended since people represent items such as distances and angles in gross categories. Similarly, multiple simultaneous events being depicted in an animation may not all be apprehended due to limitations of visual attention. The six design principles described earlier may be seen as providing specific guidance in designing multimedia consistent with these two more generally stated principles. The design principles of decomposition, prior knowledge, co-reference, and basic laws emphasize designing for apprehension. The design principles of decomposition, lines-of-action, and mental simulation support designing for congruence.

6.3 A Design Example

What might an expository multimedia document, designed in accordance with the aforementioned guidelines and principles in order to explain causal and dynamic systems to novices, look like? We answer this question by describing and illustrating the structure of an educational multimedia document that was designed in accordance with the cognitive model. Figure 3 shows the structure of this interactive multimedia document, which was built to explain the flushing cistern. Explaining this device presents interesting challenges for the

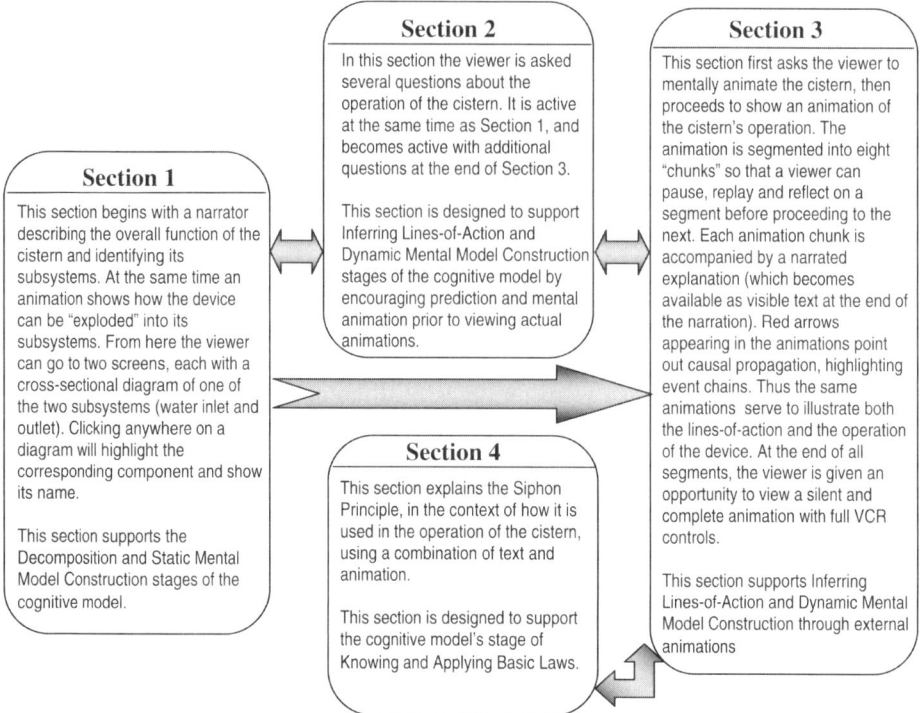

Figure 3: Structure of a multimedia document explaining the flushing cistern.

theory of comprehension outlined in this chapter because its operation involves causal chains of events that occur in tandem but are dependent on (interact with) each other. It also contains a siphon, raising the interesting question of how to explain a basic physics principle in the context of explaining how a specific machine works.

This document is divided into four sections, with the content and presentation in each section specifically designed to support various stages of the comprehension model. The first section is designed to assist (1) the decomposition of the device into its subsystems and components, (2) making internal connections in the viewer's mental model to prior knowledge about components such as rods and levers, (3) making internal connections in the mental model that encode the spatial structure of the device (i.e. spatial relations among components), and (4) co-reference resolution. It contains a cross-sectional diagram in which each component gets labeled and highlighted with a mouse click. Help for building referential connections is provided by the simultaneous labeling and highlighting of components. Since the flushing cistern is a planar device (all mechanical interactions occur in one plane), orthogonal and isometric views were not necessary to show the spatial relations for this machine.

To encourage mental animation, the document asks viewers to predict various behaviors of the system while they are viewing Section 1, before showing them any animation of the

Designing Expository Multimedia 257

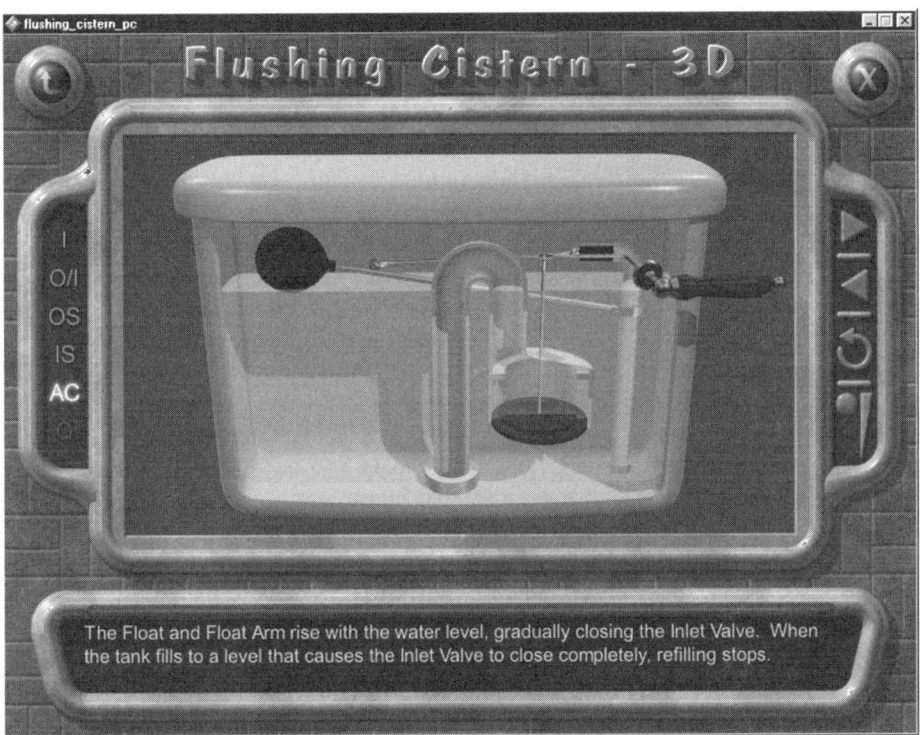

Figure 4: One screen of the multimedia document explaining the flushing cistern.

device's operation. Subsequently, a segmented animation shows the movements of various components and water during the operation of the cistern. A prominent red arrow is used in the animation to draw the viewer's attention to events in the causal chains in the order that they occur. These animation segments include narrations, and the narrated text becomes visible only after the animation and narration comes to a stop. At this point, the viewer can replay the segment, view an earlier segment, or play the next segment. Figure 4 shows a screen capture of an animation segment. There is also a section describing how a siphon works. This basic physics principle is essential to understanding how the flushing cistern flushes water out of the tank.

The design recommendations provided earlier in this chapter are based on the assumption that the best way of enhancing a reader's understanding is to guide the person through the stages of comprehension that facilitate the construction of a mental model of the system being explained. A series of empirical studies demonstrated the advantages of interactive multimedia documents designed in accordance with the cognitive model. For instance, we compared the multimedia cistern document of Figure 4 to a commercially available interactive CD-ROM (Macaulay, 1998) that described the same type of flushing cistern. This experiment indicated that learning from an interactive multimedia document designed according to the cognitive model was superior to learning from a document that was designed by a professional designer who was not informed by the cognitive model. Students who studied cognitively designed printed documents on the cistern spent about the same time as those who studied conventional printed materials, yet the former group of students performed significantly better than the latter. This indicates that cognitively designed documents can be effective without requiring more time for comprehension. These experiments, described in detail elsewhere (Hegarty et al., 1999, 2002; Narayanan & Hegarty, 2002), showed that documents that were designed according to the cognitive model were superior to conventionally designed documents, suggesting that cognitively based design is a significant improvement over conventional design of technical documents.

7 Conclusion

Causal and dynamic systems are often the subjects of technical documents such as textbooks and manuals. A reader of such documents should be able to develop accurate mental models of the systems described therein. Accurate mental models, with explanatory and predictive power, are critical to subsequent development of a more sophisticated understanding of these systems, so that one can analyze, design, explain, predict, and troubleshoot such systems. Technical documents produced at work are at the core of design, engineering, and operation of complex systems. However, understanding causal systems is difficult because many aspects of such systems are dynamic, invisible, and interdependent. Erroneous preconceptions and naïve beliefs can interfere with comprehension, and need to be countered with the acquisition of correct mental models. Therefore, designing expository documents, whether on paper or on the computer by employing interactive multimedia, which aid the cognitive processes of mental model construction is critical. Unfortunately, there is very little theoretically grounded and empirically validated design guidance available to a designer interested in developing multimedia expository documents about causal and dynamic systems. This chapter attempts to partially fill this void.

We began by pointing out that causal and dynamic systems can be characterized in terms of their hierarchical structure and the occurrence and propagation of events (component behaviors) mediated by governing laws of the domain. Properties of complex causal systems make understanding and solving problems involving such systems difficult for novices. Subsequent to enumerating these difficulties, a cognitive process model was articulated. This model explains the process by which a reader develops an accurate and "runnable" mental model of a causal and dynamic system from visual and verbal representations present in a technical document, in terms of five stages of processing: decomposition, constructing a static mental model, knowing and applying basic laws, inferring lines-of-action, and constructing a dynamic mental model. Several design guidelines and design principles for expository multimedia, derived from this model and extracted from extant literature, were then presented. Subsequently, an example illustrated the cognitive design of a multimedia document, i.e. designing multimedia in accordance with the cognitive model, design guidelines, and principles. Our hope is that the information in this chapter will serve different kinds of readers: document designers looking for practical guidance and researchers interested in cognitive theories of multimedia comprehension, and how document design may be guided by such theories.

Acknowledgments

This chapter developed from a keynote address titled "Cognitive Principles for Comprehensible Multimedia" that the author presented at the EARLI SIG Meeting on Multimedia Comprehension at the University of Poitiers in August 2002. It is based on the author's collaborative research with Mary Hegarty and several graduate students: Pam Freitas, Sarah Kriz, Roxanna Moreno, Jill Quilici, Naomi Shimozawa, and Steven Hansen. Our research was supported by the National Science Foundation under contracts CDA-9616513 and REC-9815016, and by the Office of Naval Research under contracts N00014-96-11187, N00014-03-10324, and N00014-96-10525. Thanks are due to Ashok Goel, Cindy Hmelo-Silver, and Sadhana Puntambekar for discussions on difficulties of learning about complex causal systems.

References

Adam, J. -M. (2000). L'hyperstructure: un mode privilégié de présentation des événements scientifiques [Hyperstructure: An advantageous way to present scientific events]? *Rencontres discursives entre sciences et politique dans les médias [Discursive encounters between science and politics in the media], Les carnets du Cediscor, 6* (pp. 133–150). Paris: Presses de la Sorbonne Nouvelle.

Adam, J. -M. (2001). Types de textes ou genres de discours? Comment classer les textes qui disent de et comment faire [Text types or discourse genres? How to classify texts that tell what to do and how to do it]. *Langages, 141*, 10–27.

Adam, J. -M., & Revaz, F. (1989). Aspects de la structuration du texte descriptif: Les marqueurs d'énumération et de reformulation [Aspects of the structuring of descriptive text: Markers of enumeration and reformulation]. *Langue Française, 81*, 59–98.

Agrifoglio, M. (2004). Sight translation and interpreting: A comparative analysis of constraints and failures. *Interpreting, 6*, 43–67.

Alamargot, D., & Chanquoy, L. (2001). Planning process. In G. Rijlaarsdam, D. Alamargot, & L. Chanquoy (Eds), *Through the models of writing* (9th ed., Vol. 9, pp. 33–64). Dordrecht: Kluwer Academic Publishers.

Alamargot, D., Chanquoy, L., & Chuy, M. (2005). L'élaboration du contenu du texte: de la mémoire à long terme à l'environnement de la tâche. *Psychologie Française, 50*(3), 287–304.

Alamargot, D., Chesnet, D., Dansac, C., & Ros, C. (2006). Eye and Pen: A new device to study reading during writing. *Behavior Research Methods, Instruments and Computers, 38*(2), 287–299.

Alamargot, D., Terrier, P., & Cellier, J. -M., (coord.). (2005). *Production, compréhension et usages des écrits techniques au travail [Production, comprehension and usage of technical texts in the workplace]*. Toulouse: Octares Editions.

Albers, M. J. (2005). The future of technical communication: Introduction to this special issue. *Technical Communication, 52*(3), 267–272.

Allal, L., Chanquoy, L., & Largy, P. (Eds). (2004). *Revision. Cognitive and instructional processes*. Boston/Dordrecht/New York/London: Kluwer Academic Publishers.

Allen, T. M., Lunenfeld, H., & Alexander, G. J. (1971). Driver information needs. *Highway Research Record, 366*, 102–115.

Allwood, C. M., & Kalen, T. (1997). Evaluating and improving the usability of user manual. *Behavior and Information Technology, 16*(1), 43–57.

Al-Madani, H., & Al-Janahi, A. (2002). Assessment of drivers' comprehension of traffic signs based on their traffic, personal and social characteristics. *Transportation Research, Part F: Traffic Psychology and Behaviour, 5*, 63–76.

Amerine, R., & Bilmes, J. (1988). Following instructions. *Human Studies, 11*, 327–339.

Ammer, J. J. (1998). Peer evaluation model for enhancing writing performance of students with learning disabilities. *Reading and Writing Quarterly: Overcoming Learning Difficulties, 14*, 263–282.

Anderson, A., Garrod, S. C., & Sanford, A. J. (1983). The accessibility of pronominal antecedents as a function of episode shifts in narrative. *Quarterly Journal of Experimental Psychology, 35A*, 427–440.

Anderson, J. R. (1982). Acquisition of cognitive skill. *Psychological Review, 89*, 369–406.

Anderson, J. R. (1983). *The architecture of cognition*. Cambridge, MA: Harvard University Press.

Anderson, J. R. (1996). ACT: A simple theory of complex cognition. *American Psychologist, 51*, 355–365.

Anderson, J. R., Boyle, C. F., Farrell, R., & Reiser, B. (1984). Cognitive principles in the design of computer tutors. *Proceedings of the sixth annual conference of the cognitive science society*. Boulder, CO: Institute of Cognitive Science, University of Colorado (June).

Anderson, P. V. (1991). *Technical writing: A reader-centered approach* (2nd ed.). New York: Harcourt Brace Jovanovich College Publishers.

Andersson, B., Dahl, J., Holmkvist, K., Holsanova, J., Johansson, V., Karlsson, H., Stromqvist, S., Tufvesson, S., & Wengelin, A. (2006). Combining keystroke-logging with eye-tracking. In L. Van Waes, M. Leijten, & C. Neuwirth (Eds), *Writing and digital media* (pp. 166–172). Amsterdam: Elsevier.

Anglin, G. J., Towers, R. L., & Levie, W. H. (1996). Visual message design and learning: The role of static and dynamic illustrations. In D. H. Jonassen (Ed.), *Handbook of research for educational communications and technology* (pp. 755–794). New York: MacMillan.

Anis, J. (1997). Lire des visuo-textes. In M. Marquilló (Ed.), *"Écritures et textes d'aujourd'hui"*, *Cahiers du Français contemporain*, no. 4 (pp. 29–45). Fontenay-St Cloud: Crédif, ENS Éditions.

ANSI (American National Standards Institute) Z535. (1987). *Criteria for safety symbols. American National Standards Institute*. New York: National Electrical Manufacturers Association.

ANSI (American National Standards Institute). (1991). *American National Standard for Safety Warnings, Z535.1 to .5*. Arlington, VA: National Electrical Manufacturers Association.

Arcand, R., & Bourbeau, N. (1995). *La communication efficace [Effective communication]*. Montréal: CEC.

Arend, U., Muthig, K. -P., & Wandmacher, J. (1987). Evidence for global feature superiority in menu selection by icons. *Behavior and Information Technology*, 6, 411–426.

Ariel, M. (2001). Accessibility theory: An overview. In T. Sanders, J. Schilperoord, & W. Spooren (Eds), *Text representation: Linguistic and psycholinguistic aspects* (pp. 29–87). Amsterdam: John Benjamins.

Armour, S. (2005, June 14). Warning: Your clever little blog could get you fired. *USA Today*. Retrieved April 6, 2006 from http://www.usatoday.com/money/workplace/2005-06-14-worker-blogs-usat_x.htm.

Averous, B. (1975). Connaissance de la signalisation routière [The knowledge of road signs]. Arcueil, France: *Cahiers d'étude de l'ONSER*.

Babcock, R. A., & Salthouse, T. A. (1990). Effects of increased processing demands on age differences in working memory. *Psychology and Aging*, 5, 421–428.

Baddeley, A. (1986). *Working memory*. Oxford, England: Clarendon Press/Oxford University Press.

Baddeley, A., Gathercole, S., & Papagno, C. (1998). The phonological loop as a language learning device. *Psychological Review*, 105(1), 158–173.

Baddeley, A., & Hitch, G. J. (1974). Working memory. In G. H. Bower (Ed.), *The psychology of learning and motivation* (Vol. 8, pp. 47–89). New York: Academic Press.

Baecker, R., Small, I., & Mander, R. (1991). Bringing icons to life. *Proceedings of the CHI'91 conference on human factors in computing systems*, 1–6. New York: ACM.

Baggett, W. B., & Graesser, A. C. (1995). Question answering in the context of illustrated expository text. *Proceedings of the 17th annual conference of the cognitive science society* (pp. 334–339). Hillsdale, N.J: Lawrence Erlbaum Associates.

Bahtia, V. K. (1993). *Analysing genre: Language use in professional settings*. London: Longman.

Bajo, M. T., Padilla, F., & Padilla, P. (2000). Comprehension processes in simultaneous interpreting. In A. Chesterman, N. Gallardo San Salvador, & Y. Gambier (Eds), *Translation in context* (pp. 127–142). Amsterdam: John Benjamins Publishing.

Balcytiene, A. (1999). Exploring individual processes of knowledge construction with hypertext. *Instructional Science*, 27(3), 303–328.

Balota, D. A., & Chumbley, J. I. (1984). Are lexical decisions a good measure of lexical access? The role of word frequency in the neglected decision stage. *Journal of Experimental Psychology: Human Perception and Performance*, 10, 340–357.

Bamberg, M. (1997). *Narrative development: Six approaches*. Mahwah, NJ: Lawrence Erlbaum Associates.

Barbaro, M. (2006, March 7). Wal-Mart enlists bloggers in P. R. campaign. *NYTimes Online*. Retrieved April 6, 2006 from www.nytimes.com/2006/03/07/technology/07blog.html.
Barcenilla, J. (1993). *Etude sur la compréhension et le suivi d'instructions lors de l'apprentissage de dispositifs techniques* [A study of understanding and applying instructions when learning technical devices]. Doctoral dissertation, Université de Paris 8.
Barcenilla, J. (2005). Les déterminants de l'utilisabilité des aides opératoires [Some factors influencing the usability of written instructions]. In D. Alamargot, P. Terrier, & J. -M. Cellier (Eds), *Production, compréhension et usages des écrits techniques au travail* (pp. 181–198). Toulouse: Octarès.
Barcenilla, J., & Brangier, E. (1998). Les mots pour travailler. Analyse de la compréhension des aides au travail par des opérateurs de bas niveau de qualification travaillant dans des entreprises lorraines [The words for work: An analysis of understanding of aids at work by operators with a low level of instruction in ten factorys of Lorraine]. *Rapport au Groupe Permanent de Lutte contre l'Illettrisme (GPLI), 138*. Paris: Ministère de l'Emploi et de la Solidarité.
Barcenilla, J., & Brangier, E. (2000). Propositions pour une intervention en ergonomie des aides textuelles au travail [Ergonomics guidelines for written texts at work]. In C. El-Hayek (Dir.), *Illettrisme et monde du travail*. Paris: La Documentation Française.
Barcenilla, J., & Tijus, C. (2002). Compréhension et Evaluation de Pictogrammes: Effets du Contexte. [Understanding and assessing road signs: Contextual effects]. *Psychologie Française, 47*(1), 55–64.
Barik, H. C. (1969). *A study of simultaneous interpretation*. Unpublished doctoral dissertation. University of North Carolina, Chapel Hill, NC.
Barsalou, L. W. (1993). Flexibility, structure, and linguistic vagary in concepts: Manifestations of a compositional system of perceptual symbols. In A. C. Collins, S. E. Gathercole, & M. A. Conway (Eds), *Theories of memories* (pp. 29–101). Hillsdale, NJ: Lawrence Erlbaum Associates.
Barsalou, L. W. (1999). Perceptual symbol systems. *Behavioral and Brain Sciences, 22*, 577–660.
Barsalou, L. W., & Wiemer-Hastings, K. (2005). Situating abstract concepts. In D. Pecher & R. Zwaan (Eds), *Grounding cognition: The role of perception and action in memory, language, and thought* (pp. 129–163). New York: Cambridge University Press.
Bartlett, E. J. (1981). *Learning to write: Some cognitive and linguistic components*. Washington, DC: Center for Applied Linguistics.
Bateman, J., & Rondhuis, K. J. (1997). "Coherence relations": Towards a general specification. *Discourse Processes, 24*(1), 3–50.
Baudet, S. (1990). Représentation d'état, d'événement, d'action et de causation. [State, event, action and causation representations] In J. François & G. Denhière, (Eds), *Cognition et language* [Cognition and Language]. *Langages, 100*, 45–64.
Bazerman, C. (1985). Physicists reading physics: Schema-laden purposes and purpose-laden schemas. *Written Communication, 2*(1), 3–23.
Beaudet, C. (1998). Littératie et rédaction: vers la définition d'une pratique professionnelle. In G. A. Legault (Ed.), *L'intervention: usages et méthodes* (pp. 69–88). Sherbrooke, Quebec, Canada. (Éditions GGC, collection Analyse des pratiques professionnelles.)
Beaudet, C. (2000). Clarté, lisibilité, intelligibilité des textes: un état de la question et une proposition pédagogique [Clarity, readability, and intelligibility of texts: An overview of the issue and a pedagogical proposal]. *Recherches en rédaction professionnelle [Research in professional writing], 1*(1). http://pages.usherbrooke.ca/rrp-cb/
Beaudet, C. (2005). *Stratégies d'argumentation et impact social: le cas des textes utilitaires [Argumentation strategies and social impact: The case of pragmatic texts]*. Québec: Nota bene.
Beltran, F. S., & Auque, Y. (1993). Processing typical objects in scenes: Effects of photographs versus line drawings. *Perceptuals and motor skills, 76*, 307–312.
Bereiter, C., & Scardamalia, M. (1987). *The psychology of written composition*. Hillsdale, NJ: Lawrence Erlbaum Associates.

Berkenkotter, C. (1983). Decisions and revisions: The planning strategies of a publishing writer. *College Composition and Communication, 34*(2), 156–169.

Bernardini, C., Ambrogi, V., Peroli, L. C., Tiraltri, M., & Fardella, G. (2000). Comprehensibility of the package leaflets of all medicinal products for human use: A questionnaire survey about the use of symbols and pictograms. *Pharmacological Research, 41*(6), 679–688.

Berners-Lee, T. (2000). *Weaving the web: The original design and ultimate destiny of the World Wide Web.* New York: Harper Business.

Bestgen, Y., & Vonk, W. (1995). The role of temporal segmentation markers in discourse processing. *Discourse Processes, 19*, 385–406.

Bieger, G. R., & Glock, M. D. (1986). Comprehending spatial and contextual information in picture-text instructions. *Journal of Experimental Education, 54*, 181–188.

Bilhaut, F., Charnois, T., Enjalbert, P., & Mathet, Y. (2003). Passage extraction in geographical documents. In M. A. Klopotek, S. T. Wierzchon, & K. Trojanowski (Eds), *Intelligent information processing and web mining, Proceedings of the International IIS: IIPWM'03 conference*, Zakopane, Poland (pp. 121–130). Berlin, Heidelberg, New York: Springer-Verlag.

Billingham, J. (2002). *Editing and revising text.* New York: Oxford University Press. (One Step Ahead Series.)

Bisaillon, J. (1991). Le plaisir d'écrire en langue seconde par un enseignement axé sur la révision. *La revue québécoise de linguistique, 21*(1), 57–78.

Bisaillon, J. (1992). La révision de texte, un processus à enseigner pour l'amélioration des productions écrites. *The Canadian Modern Language Review/La Revue canadienne des langues vivantes, 48*(2), 276–291.

Bisaillon, J. (1997). Interrelations entre la mise en texte, la révision et le traitement de texte chez quatre scripteurs en langue seconde. *The Canadian Modern Language Review/La Revue canadienne des langues vivantes, 53*(3), 530–565.

Bisaillon, J. (1999). Effects of the teaching of revision strategies in a computer-based environment. In M. C. Pennington (Ed.), *Writing in an electronic medium: Research with language learners* (pp. 131–157). Houston, TX: Athelstan.

Bisaillon, J. (in press). Au-delá des modifications que les reviseurs professionnels apportent au texte: une visée normative ou une visée communicationnelle de la révision? In I. Clerc and C. Beaudet (Eds), *Langue, médiation culturelle et efficacité communicationnelle.* Québec: Nota bene.

Bjork, R. A. (1975). Short-term storage: The ordered output of a central processor. In F. Restle, R. M. Shiffrin, N. J. Castellan, H. R. Lindman, & D. B. Pisoni (Eds), *Cognitive theory* (Vol. 1). Hillsdale, NJ: Erlbaum & Associates.

Black, J. B., & Bower, G. H. (1980). Story understanding and problem solving. *Poetics, 9*, 223–250.

Blanchard, J., & Mikkelson, V. (1987). Underlining performance outcomes in expository text. *Journal of Educational Research, 80*(4), 197–201.

Blood, R. (2002). *The weblog handbook: Practical advice on creating and maintaining your weblog.* Cambridge, MA: Perseus.

Bodner, R. (1994). A comparison of identification rates of static and animated buttons. *Proceedings of CASCON'94, CD-ROM.* Toronto: IBM Canada Ltd.

Boechler, P. M. (2001). How spatial is hyperspace? Interacting with hypertext documents: Cognitive processes and concepts. *Cyberpsychology and Behavior, 4*(1), 23–46.

Bolger, F., & Karmiloff-Smith, A. (1990). The development of communicative competence. *Archives de Psychologie, 58*, 257–273.

Borowsky, A., Shinar, D., & Parmet, Y. (2005). Recognition of road signs relative to their location and driver expectation. *Proceedings of road safety on four continents.* Warsaw, CDRom.

Boswell, J. (1948). *The life of Samuel Johnson.* Garden City, NY: Garden City Publishing Co., Inc.

Bouayad-Agha, N., Scott, D., & Power, R. (2001). The influence of layout on the interpretation of referring expressions. *Proceedings of 4th international multidisciplinary approaches to discourse (MAD)* (pp. 133–141). Ittre, Belgium: Workshop.

Boucheix, J. -M. (2003). Simulation et compréhension de documents techniques: le cas de la formation des grutiers. (Simulation and technical documents understanding: Crane driver training). *Le Travail Humain*, 66(3), 253–282.

Boucheix, J. -M., & Coiron, M. (2005). L'usage des écrits techniques: le cas de l'activité de transmission écrite au cours des relèves de postes des infirmières. In D. Alamargot, P. Terrier, & J-M. Cellier (Eds), *Production, Compréhension et Usages des Ecrits Techniques au Travail* (pp.199–223). Toulouse: Octarès Editions.

Boutet, J., & Gardin, B. (2001). Une linguistique du travail. In A. Borzeix & B. Fraenkel (Eds), *Langage et Travail, Communication, Cognition, Action* (pp. 89–111). Paris: CNRS Edition.

Bovair, S., & Kieras, D. E. (1991). Toward a model of acquiring procedures from text. In B. Barr, M. L. Kamil, P. Mosenthal, & D. Pearboy (Eds), *Handbook of reading research* (Vol. II, pp. 206–221). New York: Longman.

Brangier, E., Barcenilla, J., & Eberhart, I. (2000). Evaluation des modalités de communication des consignes (sécurité et prévention) sur le port des équipements de protections individuelles. *Pratiques Psychologiques*, 2, 49–58.

Brangier, E., & Barcenilla, J. (2001, Octobre). La mise en place de documents professionnels en entreprise: la psychologie ergonomique à la croisée de l'ergonomie cognitive et de la psychologie sociale? (The setting up of written documentation at work: The ergonomics at the crossing of cognitive ergonomics and social psychology?) In *EPIQUE 2001, Actes des Journées d'études en psychologie ergonomique* (pp. 179–187). Nantes: IRCCyN.

Bransford, J. D., Barclay, J. R., & Franks, J. J. (1972). Sentence memory: A constructive versus interpretive approach. *Cognitive Psychology*, 3, 193–209.

Brant, D. (1992). The cognitive as the social, an ethnomethodological approach to writing process research. *Written Communication*, 9(3), 315–355.

Breetvelt, I., Van den Bergh, H., & Rijlaarsdam, G. (1996). Rereading and generating and their relation to text quality. An application of multilevel analysis on writing process data. In G. Rijlaarsdam, H. Van den Bergh, & M. Couzijn (Eds), *Theories, models, and methodology in writing research* (pp. 10–20). Amsterdam: Amsterdam University Press.

Brinkerhoff, J. D., Klein, J. D., & Koroghlanian, C. M. (2001). Effects of overviews and computer experience on learning from hypertext. *Journal of Educational Computing Research*, 25(4), 427–440.

Britton, B. K., Dusen, L., Gulgöz, S., & Glynn, S. M. (1989). Instructional texts rewritten by five expert teams: Revisions and retention improvements. *Journal of Educational Psychology*, 81(2), 226–239.

Britton, J. (1982). Shaping at the point of utterance. In G. M. Pradl (Ed.), *Prospect and retrospect: Selected essays of James Britton*. London: Boynton/Cook Publishers, Inc.

Bromberg, M., Tijus, C., Georget, P., Jadot, F., Leproux, C., & Poitrenaud, S. (2002). *L'Interopérabilité et la sécurité des trains à grande vitesse*. [Interoperability and safety for high speed railways]. Research report. Paris: International Union of Railways.

Bronckart, J. P. (1996). *Activité langagière, textes et discours [Language activity, texts, and discourse]*. Lausanne: Delachaux et Niestlé.

Brown, A. L., & Day, J. D. (1983). Macrorules for summarizing texts: The development of expertise. *Journal of Verbal Learning & Verbal Behavior*, 22(1), 1–14.

Brown, A. L., Day, J. D., & Jones, R. S. (1983). The development of plans for summarizing texts. *Child Development*, 54(4), 968–979.

Brown, J. S., Collins, A., & Duguid, P. (1989). Situated cognition and the culture of learning. *Educational Researcher, 33*, 32–42.

Brun, J. -P. (1992). *Les hommes de lignes: analyse des phénomènes sociaux et subjectifs dans l'activité de travail des monteurs de lignes électriques*. PhD thesis. Paris: École Pratique des Hautes Études, Laboratoire d'ergonomie physiologique et cognitive (CMAN).

Brusilovsky, P. (2001). Adaptive hypermedia. *User modeling and user adapted interaction, 11*(1–2), 87–110.

Buehler, M. F. (2003). Situational editing: A rhetorical approach for the technical editor. *Technical Communication, 50*(4), 458–465.

Bush, V. (1945). As we may think. *The Atlantic Monthly, 176*(1), 101–108.

Byrne, M. D. (1993). Using icons to find documents: Simplicity is critical. *Proceedings of INTERCHI '93*, 446–453. Amsterdam: ACM.

Cabré, M. -T. (1999). *Terminology: Theory, methods and applications*. Amsterdam: John Benjamins.

Cabré, M. -T., Estopa, R., & Vivaldi, J. (2000). Automatic term detection: A review of current systems. In D. Bourigault, C. Jacquemin, & M. -Cl. L'homme (Eds), *Recent advances in computational terminology* (pp. 53–87). Amsterdam: John Benjamins.

Caccamise, D. J. (Ed.). (1987). *Idea generation in writing*. Westport, CT: Ablex Publishing.

CACP report. (2000). The role of pictograms in the conveying of consumer safety information, URN 97/751, http://www.dti.gov.uk/homesafetynetwork/pdf/picto.pdf

Cailliès, S., Denhière, G., & Kintsch, W. (2002). The effect of prior knowledge on understanding from text: Evidence from primed recognition. *European Journal of Cognitive Psychology, 14*(2), 267–286.

Cailliès, S., & Tapiero, I. (1997). Structures textuelles et connaissances initiales. *L'Année Psychologique, 97*, 611–639.

Calcaterra, A., Antonietti, A., & Underwood, J. (2005). Cognitive style, hypermedia navigation and learning. *Computers and Education, 44*, 441–457.

Cañas, J. J., Salmerón, L., & Fajardo, I. (2004). Toward the analysis of the interaction in the joint cognitive system. In A. Pirhonen, H. Isomäki, C. Roast, & P. Saariluoma (Eds), *Future interaction design*. London: Springer-Verlag.

Cariglia-Bull, T., & Pressley, M. (1990). Short-term memory differences between children predict imagery effects when sentences are read. *Journal of Experimental Child Psychology, 49*, 394–398.

Carreiras, M., Carriedo, N., Alonso, M. A., & Fernandez, A. (1997). The role of verbal tense and verbal aspect in the foregrounding of information in reading. *Memory and Cognition, 23*, 438–446.

Carroll, J. M. (Ed.) (1998). *Minimalism beyond the Nurnberg funnel*. Cambridge, MA: The MIT Press.

Carroll, J. M., & Mack, R. L. (1984). Learning to use a word processor by doing, by thinking, and by knowing. In J. C. Thomas & M. L. Schneider (Eds), *Human factors in computer systems* (pp. 13–51). Norwood, NJ: Ablex.

Catrambone, R. (1990). Specific versus general procedures in instructions. *Human Computer Interaction, 5*, 49–93.

Catrambone, R. (1995). Following instructions: Effects of principles and examples. *Journal of Experimental Psychology: Applied, 1*, 227–244.

Cellier, J. -M. (2005). Caractéristiques et fonctions des textes procéduraux. In D. Alamargot, P. Terrier, & J-M. Cellier (Eds), *Production, compréhension et usages des ecrits techniques au travail* (pp. 161–180). Toulouse: Octarès Editions.

Cellier, J. -M., & Terrier, P. (2001). Le rôle de la mise en forme matérielle dans le traitement cognitif de consignes. *Langages, 141*, 79–91.

Celuch, K. G., Lust, J. A., & Showers, L. S. (1992). Product owner manuals: An explanatory study of nonreaders versus readers. *Journal of Applied Social Psychology, 22*, 492–507.

Chafe, W. L. (1976). Givenness, contrastiveness, definiteness, subjects, topics and point of view. In C. N. Li (Ed.), *Subject and topic*, (pp. 25–56). New York: Academic Press.

Chapman, M. L. (1995). The sociocognitive construction of written genres in first grade. *Research in the Teaching of English, 29*, 164–192.

Charolles, M. (1988). Les plans d'organisation textuelle. Périodes, chaînes, portées et séquences [Frameworks of textual organization: Periods, chains, ranges and sequences]. *Pratiques, 57,* 3–13.

Charolles, M. (1994). Cohésion, cohérence et pertinence du discours [Cohesion, coherence, and relevance in discourse]. *Revue internationale de linguistique française, 29,* 125–151.

Charolles, M. (1997). L'encadrement du discours: Univers, champs, domaines et espaces. *Cahier de Recherche Linguistique,* 6, Landisco, URA-CNRS 1035 Université Nancy 2, pp. 1–73.

Charolles, M., Le Draoulec, A., Péry-Woodley, M. -P., & Sarda, L. (2005). Temporal and spatial dimensions of discourse organisation. *Journal of French Language Studies, 15*(2), 203–218.

Chen, C., & Rada, R. (1996). Interacting with hypertext: A meta-analysis of experimental studies. *Human–Computer Interaction, 11,* 125–156.

Chen, S., & MacRedie, R. (2002). Cognitive styles and hypermedia navigation: Development of a learning model. *Journal of the American Society for Information Science and Technology, 53*(1), 3–15.

Chesnet, D., & Alamargot, D. (2005). Analyses en temps réel des activités oculaires et graphomotrices de scripteur: Intérêt du dispotif 'eye and pen'. *L'Année Psychologique, 105*(3), 477–520.

Chi, M. T. H., DeLeeuw, N., Chiu, M., & LaVancher, C. (1994). Eliciting self-explanations improves understanding. *Cognitive Science, 18,* 439–477.

Christ, R. E., & Corso, G. (1982). The effects of extended practice on the evaluation of visual display codes. *Human Factors, 25,* 71–84.

Cirilo, R., & Foss, D. (1980). Text structure and reading time for sentences. *Journal of Verbal Learning and Verbal Behavior, 19,* 96–109.

Clancey, W. (1993). The knowledge level reinterpreted: Modelling socio-technical systems. In K. Ford & J. Bradshaw (Eds), *International Journal of Intelligent Systems*: Special Issue on Knowledge Acquisition as Modelling, *8*(1), 33–50.

Clark, H. H., & Haviland, S. E. (1977). Comprehension and the given-new contract. In R. O. Freedle (Ed.), *Discourse production and comprehension* (pp. 1–40). Norwood, NJ: Ablex.

Clerc, I. (2000). *La démarche de rédaction [The writing process].* Québec: Éditions *Nota Bene.*

Coirier, P., Gaonac'h, D., & Passerault, J. -M. (1996). *Psycholinguistique textuelle. Approche cognitive de la compréhension et de la production des textes [Textual psycholinguistics. A cognitive approach to comprehension and production of texts].* Paris: Armand Colin.

Collins, A., Brown, J. S., & Newman, S. E. (1989). Cognitive apprenticeship: Teaching the craft of reading, writing, and mathematics. In L. B. Resnick (Ed.), *Knowing, learning, and instruction: Essays in honor of Robert Glaser.* Hillsdale: Lawrence Erlbaum Associates.

Collins, A. M., & Loftus, E. F. (1975). A spreading activation theory of semantic processing. *Psychological Review, 82,* 407–428.

Collins, B. L., & Lerner, N. D. (1982). Assessment of fire-safety symbols. *Human Factors, 24*(1), 75–84.

Condamines, A. (2002). Corpus analysis and conceptual relation patterns. *Terminology, 8*(1), 141–162.

Condamines, A., & Rebeyrolle, J. (2001). Searching for and identifying conceptual relationships via a corpus-based approach to a terminological knowledge base (CTKB): Method and results. In D. Bourigault, M. -C. L'homme, & C. Jacquemin (Eds), *Recent advances in computational terminology* (pp. 127–148). Amsterdam: John Benjamins.

Conger, J. A., & Kanungo, R. N. (1988). The empowerment process: Integrating theory and practice. *Academy of Management Review, 13*(3), 471–482.

Conklin, J. (1987). Hypertext: An introduction and survey. *IEEE Computer, 20*(9), 17–41.

Converse, S. A. (1994). *Operating procedures: Do they reduce operator errors?* Paper presented at the Human Factors and Ergonomics Society 38th Annual Meeting.

Cornish, F. (1986). *Anaphoric relations in English and French, a discourse perspective.* London: Croom Helm.

Cottereau, A., Daviet, J. -P., & Thévenot, L. (1989). Les imprimés d'entreprises à la Bibliothèque nationale. Une mine à découvrir pour la recherche scientifique. In *Industrie Textile, Industrie Mécanique: Inventaire d'un Fond d'Imprimés d'Entreprises*. Paris: Imprimerie Nationale.

Cross, R. T. (1994). Iconicity and associative meaning: What are we looking for? *Proceedings from the 6th biennial conferences of ISAAC* (pp. 126–127). Hoensbroek: IRV.

Cruse, D. A. (1986). *Lexical semantics*. Cambridge: Cambridge University Press.

Dahlbäck, N., Höök, K., & Sjölinder, M. (1996, July). *Spatial cognition in the mind and in the world: The case of hypermedia navigation*. Paper presented at the 18th Annual Meeting of the Cognitive Science Society. University of California, San Diego.

Dale, E., & O'Rourke, J. (1981). *The living word vocabulary: A national vocabulary inventory*. Chicago: World Book-Childcraft International.

Damasio, A. R. (1989). Time-locked multiregional retroactivation: A systems-level proposal for the neural substrates of recall and recognition. *Cognition, 33*, 25–62.

Danks, J. H., & Griffin, J. (1997). Reading and translation. In H. J. Danks, G. M. Shreve, S. B. Fountain, & M. K. McBeath (Eds), *Cognitive processes in translation and interpreting* (pp. 161–175). Thousand Oak, CA: Sage.

Dansac, C., & Alamargot, D. (1999). Accessing referential information during text composition. In M. Torrance & D. Galbraith (Eds), *Knowing what to write: Conceptual processes in text production* (pp. 79–97). Amsterdam: Amsterdam University Press.

Davies, S., Haines, H., Norris, B., & Wilson, J. R. (1998). Safety pictograms: Are they getting the message across? *Applied Ergonomics, 29*, 15–23.

Davison, A. (1984). Syntactic markedness and the definition of sentence topic. *Language, 60*(4), 797–846.

De Brito, G. (2000). Analyse ergonomique du Suivi des Procédures Ecrites dans les Environnements Dynamiques (SPEED) appliquée à l'Aéronautique [Ergonomic Analysis of a Cognitive Modeling of Procedure-Following in Aeronautics (SPEED)]. Thèse de doctorat. Université de Paris V, Paris, France.

De Groot, A. M. B. (1997). The cognitive study of translation and interpretation: Three approaches. In H. J. Danks, G. M. Shreve, S. B. Fountain, & M. K. McBeath (Eds), *Cognitive processes in translation and interpreting* (pp. 25–56). Thousand Oak, CA: Sage.

De Groot, A. M. B. (2000). A complex skill approach to translation and interpreting. In S. Tirkkonen-Condit & R. Jääkeltäinen (Eds), *Tapping and mapping the processes of translation and interpreting* (pp. 53–68). Amsterdam: John Benjamins.

De Groot, A. M. B., & Nas, G. L. J. (1991). Lexical representation of cognates and noncognates in compound bilinguals. *Journal of Memory and Language, 30*, 90–123.

De Jong, T., & Van der Hulst, A. (2002). The effects of graphical overviews on knowledge acquisition in hypertext. *Journal of Computer Assisted Learning, 18*(2), 219–231.

De Montmollin, M. (Ed.) (1995). *Vocabulaire de l'ergonomie*. Toulouse: Octares Éditions, collection Travail.

De Villers, M.-É. (2003). Le Multidictionnaire de la langue française (4th ed.), Montereal: Éditions Québec-Amérique.

Dean, A. L., Scherzer, E., & Chabaud, S. (1986). Sequential ordering in children's representations of rotation movements. *Journal of Experimental Child Psychology, 42*, 99–114.

deBrito, G. (1999). *Human error in procedure following: A first classification*. Paper presented at the Human Error, Safety and Systems Development, Liege, Belgium.

Degand, L., Lefèvre, N., & Bestgen, Y. (1999). The impact of connectives and anaphoric expressions on expository discourse comprehension. *Document Design, 1*, 39–51.

Degani, A., & Wiener, E. L. (1994). *On the design of flight-deck procedures. NASA-Ames Research Center 177642*. Moffett Field, CA: NASA Ames Research Center.

Degani, A., & Wiener, E. L. (1997). Procedures in complex systems: The airline cockpit. *IEEE Transactions on Systems, Man, and Cybernetics — Part A: Systems and Humans, 27*(3), 302–312.

DeGroff, L. J. C. (1987). The influence of prior knowledge on writing, conferencing, and revising. *Elementary School Journal, 88*(2), 105–118.

Delany, P., & Gilbert, J. K. (1991). Hypercard stacks for Fielding's Joseph Andrews: Issues of design and content. In P. Delany & G. P. Landow (Eds), *Hypermedia and literary studies* (pp. 287–298). Cambridge, MA: The MIT Press.

Delin, J., Bateman, J., & Allen, P. (2002). A model of genre in document layout. *Information Design Journal, 11*(1), 54–66.

Delin, J., Hartley, A., & Scott, D. (1996). Towards a contrastive pragmatics: Syntactic choice in English and French instructions. *Language Sciences, 18*(3–4), 897–931.

Denis, C., & Veyrac, H. (2002). Incidence du format de présentation d'un texte procédural sur sa mémorisation et la représentation de sa structure causale. *Psychologie Française, 47*, 75–80.

Denis, M. (1996). Imagery and the description of spatial configurations. In M. De Vega, M. J. Intons-Peterson, P. N. Johnson-Laird, M. Denis, & M. Marschark (Eds), *Models of visuo-spatial cognition* (pp. 128–197). New York: Oxford University Press.

Denis, M., & Cocude, M. (1992). Structural properties of visual images constructed from poorly or well-structured descriptions. *Memory and Cognition, 20*(5), 497–506.

Deutsch, C. (2005, February 20). Live by the blog, die by the blog. *NYTimes Online*. Retrieved February 10, 2006, from www.nytimes.com/2005/02/20/business/yourmoney/20suits.html

Di Eugenio, B. (1998). An action representation formalism to interpret natural language instructions. *Computational Intelligence, 14*(1), 89–133.

Diaz, P., & Souza, A. P. (1997). Understanding navigation and disorientation in hypermedia learning environments. *Journal of Multimedia and Hypermedia, 6*(2), 173–185.

Diehl, M., Willis, S. L., & Schaie, K. W. (1995). Everyday problem solving in older adults: Observational assessment and cognitive correlates. *Psychology and Aging, 10*, 478–491.

Diehl, V. A. (2004). Access to affordances, development of situation models, and identification of procedural texts problems. *IEEE Transactions on Professional Communication, 47*(1), 54–64.

Diehl, V. A., & Mills, C. B. (1995). The effects of interaction with the device described by procedural text on text measures and task performance. *Memory and Cognition, 23*, 675–688.

Diehl, V. A., & Mills, C. B. (2002). Procedural text structure and reader perceptions and performance. *Journal of General Psychology, 129*(1), 18–35.

Dijkstra, A., & Van Heuven, W. J. B. (1998). The BIA model and bilingual word recognition. In J. Grainger & A. Jacobs (Eds), *Localist connectionists approaches to human cognition* (pp. 189–225). Mahwah, NJ: Lawrence Erlbaum Associates.

Dillinger, M. (1994). Comprehension during interpreting: What do interpreters know that bilinguals don't? In S. Lambert & B. Moser-Mercer (Eds), *Bridging the gap: Empirical research in simultaneous interpretation* (pp. 155–189). Amsterdam: John Benjamins.

Dillon, A., & Gabbard, R. (1998). Hypermedia as an educational technology: A review of the quantitative research literature on learner comprehension, control, and style. *Review of Educational Research, 68*, 322–349.

Doane, S. M., Sohn, Y. W., McNamara, D. S., & Adams, D. (2000). Comprehension-based skill acquisition. *Cognitive Science, 24*(1), 1–52.

Doheny-Farina, S. (1986). Writing in an emerging organization, an ethnographic study. *Written Communication, 3*(2), 158–185.

Donovan, C. A. (2001). Children's development and control of written story and informational genres: Insights from one elementary school. *Research in the Teaching of English, 35*, 452–497.

Dowse, R., & Ehlers, M. S. (1998). Pictograms in pharmacy. *The International Journal of Pharmacy Practice, 6,* 109–118.

Dowse, R., & Ehlers, M. S. (2003). The influence of education on the interpretation of pharmaceutical pictograms for communicating medicine instruction. *International Journal of Pharmacy Practice*, *11*, 11–18.

Droste, F. G. (1976). The grammar of traffic signs. *Semiotica*, *5*, 256–262.

Drury, C. G., & Prabhu, P. (1996). Information requirements of aircraft inspection: Framework and analysis. *International Journal of Human-Computer Studies*, *45*, 679–695.

Drury, C. G., & Sarac, A. (1997). *A design aid for improved documentation in aircraft maintenance: A precursor to training*. In Human Factors and Egonomics Society 41st Annual Meeting Proceedings (pp. 1158–1162). Santa Monica, CA: HFES.

Dubois, D., Fleury, D., & Mazet, C. (1987). Catégorisation et interprétation de scènes visuelles: le cas de l'environnement urbain et routier [Categorization and interpretation of visual scenes: The case of urban and road environment]. *Psychologie Française*, *32*, 85–96.

Duggan, G. B., & Payne, S. J. (2001). Interleaving reading and acting while following procedural instructions. *Journal of Experimental Psychology: Applied*, *7*(4), 297–307.

Dunn, J. C., & Kirsner, K. (1988). Discovering functionally independent mental processes: The principle of reversed association. *Psychological Review*, *95*, 91–101.

Easterby, R. S., & Hakiel, S. R. (1981). Field testing of consumer safety signs: The comprehension of pictorially presented messages. *Applied Ergonomics*, *12*, 143–152.

Editors' Association of Canada/Association canadienne des réviseurs (2005). Retrieved July 22, 2005, from http://www.reviseurs.ca/publications/profession.htm

Edworthy, J., & Adams, A. (1996). *Warning design. A research prospective*. London: Taylor & Francis.

Einstein, G. O., & Hunt, R. R. (1980). Levels of processing and organization: Additive effects of individual item and relational processing. *Journal of Experimental Psychology: Human Learning and Memory*, *6*(5), 588–598.

Einstein, G. O., McDaniel, M. A., Owen, P. D., & Coté, N. C. (1990). Encoding and recall of texts: The importance of material appropriate processing. *Journal of Memory and Language*, *29*(5), 566–581.

Eklundh, K. S., & Kollberg, P. (1996). A computer tool and framework for analyzing online revisions. In C. M. Levy & S. Ransdell (Eds), *The science of writing. Theories, methods, individual differences, and applications* (pp. 163–188). Mahwah, NJ: Erbaum Associates.

Eklundh, K. S., & Kollberg, P. (2003). Emerging discourse: Computer-assisted episode analysis as a window to global revision in university student's writing. *Journal of Pragmatics*, *35*, 869–891.

Elbow, P. (1973). *Writing without teachers*. New York: Oxford University Press.

Elbow, P. (1981). *Writing with power*. Oxford, MS: Oxford University Press.

Ells, J. G., & Dewar, R. E. (1979). Rapid comprehension of verbal and symbolic traffic sign messages. *Human Factors*, *21*, 161–168.

Elm, W. C., & Woods, D. D. (1985). *Getting lost: A case study in interface design*. Paper presented at the Human Factors Society 29th Annual Meeting.

Engelkamp, J. (1998). *Memory for actions*. Hove: Psychology Press.

Engle, R. W., Carullo, J. J., & Collins, K. W. (1991). Individual differences in working memory for comprehension and following directions. *Journal of Educational Research*, *84*(5), 253–262.

Ericsson, K. A., & Kintsch, W. (1995). Long-term working memory. *Psychological Review*, *102*(2), 211–245.

Evans, S. (2005, May 24). Why bosses blog-and why it's cheesy. *BBC News Online*. Retrieved January 15, 2006, from http://news.bbc.co.uk/2/hi/business/4576737.stm.

FAA. (1995). *7100.65j air traffic control* (No. 7110.65J): Federal Aviation Administration.

Fabbro, F. (Ed.) (1999). *The neurolinguistics of bilingualism. An introduction*. Hove, UK: Psychology Press.

Falzon, P., & Lapeyrière, S. (1998). L'usager et l'opérateur: Ergonomie et relations de service. *Le Travail Humain*, *61*(1), 167–178.

Farnham-Diggory, S. (1992). *Cognitive Processes in Education.* New York: Harper Collins.

Fayol, M. (1992). Comprendre ce qu'on lit: De l'automatisme au contrôle. [Understanding what we read: From automatism to control]. In M. Fayol, J. -E. Gombert, P. Lecocq, L. Sprenger-Charolles, & D. Zagar (Eds), *Psychologie cognitive de la lecture* (pp. 73–105). Paris: PUF.

Fayol, M. (2002a). Les documents techniques: Bilan et perspectives. *Psychologie Française, 47*(1), 9–18.

Fayol, M. (Dir.). (2002b). *Production du langage [Production of language].* Paris: Hermes Science.

Feltovich, P. J., Coulsen, R. L., Spiro, R. J., & Dawson-Saunders, B. K. (1992). Knowledge application and transfer for complex tasks in ill-structured domains: Implications for instruction and testing in biomedicine. In D. Evans & V. L. Patel (Eds), *Advanced models of cognition for medical training and practice* (pp. 213–244). Berlin: Springer-Verlag.

Fernbach, N. (1990). *La lisibilité dans la rédaction juridique au Québec [Readability in legal writing in Quebec].* Ottawa: Le Centre de production de la lisibilité, Centre canadien d'information juridique.

Ferrari, M., & Chi, M. T. H. (1998). The nature of naive explanations of natural selection. *International Journal of Science Education, 20*(10), 1231–1256.

Fillietaz, L. (2002). *La parole en action; Éléments de pragmatique psycho-sociale.* Québec: Éditions Nota bene; Collection Langue et pratiques discursives.

Firth, J. R. (1969). *Papers in linguistics 1934–1951* (5th ed.: 1957). Oxford: Oxford University Press.

Fischer, S., Lowe, R. K., & Schwan, S. (2006). Effects of presentation speed of a dynamic visualization on the understanding of a mechanical system. In R. Sun & N. Miyake (Eds), *Proceedings of the 28th annual conference of the cognitive science society* (pp.1305–1310). Mahwah, NJ: Lawrence Erlbaum Associates.

Fitzgerald, J., & Markham, L. (1987). Teaching children about revision in writing. *Cognition and Instruction, 4*(1), 3–24.

Fletcher, C. R., & Chrysler, S. T. (1990). Surface forms, textbases, and situation models: Recognition memory for three types of textual information. *Discourse Processes, 13,* 175–1991.

Flower, L. S. (1979). Writer-based prose: A cognitive basis for problems in writing. *College English, 41*(1), 19–37.

Flower, L. S., & Hayes, J. R. (1980). The dynamics of composing: Making plans and juggling constraints. In L. W. Gregg & E. R. Steinberg (Eds), *Cognitive processes in writing.* Hillsdale, NJ: Lawrence Erlbaum Associates.

Flower, L. S., Hayes, J. R., Carey, L., Schriver, K. A., & Stratman, J. F. (1986). Detection, diagnosis, and the strategic of revision. *College Composition and Communication, 37*(1), 16–55.

Foley, W. A., & Van Valin Jr., R. D. (1985). Information packaging in the clause. In T. Shopen (Ed.), *Syntactic typology and linguistic description 1* (pp. 282–364). Cambridge: Cambridge University Press.

Foltz, P. W. (1996). Comprehension, coherence and strategies in hypertext and linear text. In J. -F. Rouet, J. J. Levonen, A. Dillon, & R. J. Spiro (Eds), *Hypertext and cognition.* Mahwah, NJ: Lawrence Erlbaum Associates.

Foltz, P. W., Kintsch, W., & Landauer, T. K. (1998). The measurement of textual coherence with latent semantic analysis. *Discourse Processes, 25,* 285–307.

Ford, N., & Chen, S. Y. (2000). Individual differences, hypermedia navigation and learning: An empirical study. *Journal of Educational Multimedia and Hypermedia, 9*(4), 281–312.

Fraenkel, B. (2001). La résistible ascension de l'écrit au travail. In A. Borzeix & B. Fraenkel (Eds), *Langage et travail: Communication, cognition, action* (pp. 113–142). Paris: CNRS Éditions, collection CNRS Communication.

François, J. (1991). La pertinence linguistique des représentations propositionnelles de la sémantique cognitive [The linguistic relevance of propositional representations from cognitive semantic]. *Sémiotiques* (Institut National de la Langue Française, Paris), pp. 69–80.

Franklin, N., & Tversky, B. (1990). Searching imagined environments. *Journal of Experimental Psychology: General, 119*(1), 63–76.

Frantz, J. P. (1993). Effect of location and presentation format on attention to and compliance with product warnings and instructions. *Journal of Safety Research, 24*, 131–154.

Frase, L. T. (1981). Writing, text and the reader. In C. H. Frederiksen & J. F. Dominic (Eds), *Writing: The nature, development and teaching of written communication. Process, development and communication* (Vol. 2, pp. 209–221). Hillsdale, NJ: Lawrence Erlbaum Associates.

Freedman, A. (1993). Show and tell? The role of explicit teaching in the learning of new genres. *Research in the Teaching of English, 22*, 222–251.

Fries, P. H. (1995). Patterns of information in initial position in English. In P. H. Fries & M. Gregory (Eds), *Discourse in society: Systemic functional perspectives. Meaning and choice in language: Studies for Michael Halliday* (pp. 47–66). Norwood: Ablex.

Gagne, R., & Briggs, L. J. (1974). *Principles of instructional design*. New York: Holt, Rinehart and Winston.

Galbraith, D. (1999). Writing as a knowledge-constituting process. In M. Torrance & D. Galbraith (Eds), *Knowing what to write: Conceptual processes in text production* (pp. 139–160). Amsterdam: Amsterdam University Press.

Galbraith, D., & Torrance, M. (1999). Conceptual processes in writing: From problem solving to text production. In M. Torrance & D. Galbraith (Eds), *Knowing what to write: Conceptual processes in text production* (pp. 1–12). Amsterdam: Amsterdam University Press.

Ganier, F. (2002a). L'analyse des fonctionnements cognitifs: un support à l'amélioration de la conception des documents procéduraux. [Cognitive processing analysis: An aid to the improvement of the design of procedural documents]. *Psychologie Française, 47*(1), 41–52.

Ganier, F. (2002b). Évaluer l'efficacité des documents techniques procéduraux: Un panorama des méthodes. [Evaluating the efficiency of technical documents: A panoramic view]. *Le Travail Humain, 65*(1), 1–27.

Ganier, F. (2004). Factors affecting the processing of procedural instructions: Implications for document design. *IEEE Transactions on Professional Communication, 47*(1), 15–26.

Ganier, F., Gombert, J. -E., & Fayol, M. (2000). Effets du format de présentation des instructions sur l'apprentissage de procédures à l'aide de documents techniques. [The effects of instructional formats on procedural learning when using technical documents]. *Le Travail Humain, 63*(2), 121–152.

Ganier, F., & Heurley, L. (2003). La compréhension de consignes. [Understanding written instructions]. In D. Gaonac'h & M. Fayol (Eds), *Aider les élèves à comprendre: du texte au multimédia* (pp. 114–136). Paris: Hachette.

Ganier, F., & Heurley, L. (2005). La prise en compte de l'utilisateur et de son utilisation des documents procéduraux: une précondition nécessaire à la conception de documents adaptés. In D. Alamargot, P. Terrier, & J. -M. Cellier (Eds), *Production, compréhension et usages des écrits techniques au travail*. Toulouse: Octarès Éditions.

Gaonac'h, D., & Passerault, J. -M. (1990). Importance markers and treatment of textual elements: Immediate and delayed effects. *European Journal of Psychology of Education, 5*(1), 59–68.

Garcia-Debanc, C. (Ed.) (2001). Les discours procéduraux, *Langages, 141* (mars 2001).

Garcia-Debanc, C., & Grandaty, M. (2001). Incidence des variations de la mise en forme textuelle sur la compréhension et la mémorisation de textes procéduraux (règles de jeux) par des enfants de 8 à 12 ans. *Langages, 141*, 92–104.

Garcia-Mila, M., Rojo, N., & Andersen, C. (2005). Prise de notes, élaboration d'un rapport scientifique et raisonnement scientifique: Étude de cas basée sur une analyse microgénétique. *Lettre d'AIRDIF, 37*(2), 15–19.

Geiger, J. F., & Millis, K. K. (2004). Assessing the impact of reading goals and text structures on comprehension. *Reading Psychology, 25*, 93–110.

Gellert, E. (1962). Children's conception of the structure and function of the human body. *Genetic Psychology Monographs, 65*, 193–405.

Gentner, D., & Stevens, A. (Eds). (1983). *Mental models*. Hillsdale, NJ: Lawrence Erlbaum Associates.

Gerloff, P. (1986). Second language learner's reports on the interpretive process: Talk-aloud protocols of translation. In J. House & S. Blum-Kulka (Eds), *Interlingual and intercultural communication: Discourse and cognition in translation* (pp. 245–262). Tübingen: Narr.

Gernsbacher, M. A. (1990). *Language comprehension as structure building*. Hillsdale, NJ: Lawrence Erlbaum Associates.

Gerver, D. (1976). Empirical studies of simultaneous interpretation: A review and a model. In R. W. Brislin (Ed.), *Translation: Applications and research* (pp. 165–207). New York: Gardiner.

Gibson, E. J. (1969). *Principles of perceptual learning and development*. New York: Appleton-Century-Crofts.

Gibson, J. J. (1966). *The senses considered as perceptual systems*. Boston: Houghton-Mifflin.

Gile, D. (1994). The process-oriented approach in translation training. In C. Dollerup & A. Lindegaard (Eds), *Teaching translation and interpreting* (Vol. 2, pp. 197–102). Amsterdam: John Benjamins.

Gile, D. (1995). *Regards sur la recherche en interprétation de conférence*. Lille: Presses Universitaires de Lille.

Gile, D. (1997). Conference interpreting as a cognitive management problem. In H. J. Danks, G. M. Shreve, S. B. Fountain, & M. K. McBeath (Eds), *Cognitive processes in translation and interpreting* (pp. 196–214). Thousand Oak, CA: Sage.

Glenberg, A. M. (1997). What memory is for. *Behavioral and Brain Sciences*, 20(1), 1–19.

Glenberg, A. M., Kruley, P., & Langston, W. E. (1994). Analogical processes in comprehension: Simulation of a mental model. In M. A. Gernsbacher (Ed.), *Handbook of psycholinguistics* (pp. 609–640). San Diego, CA: Academic Press.

Glenberg, A. M., & Langston, W. E. (1992). Comprehension of illustrated text: Pictures help to build mental models. *Journal of Memory and Language*, 31, 129–151.

Glenberg, A. M., & Robertson, D. A. (1999). Indexical understanding of instructions. *Discourse Processes*, 28, 1–26.

Glenberg, A. M., & Robertson, D. A. (2000). Symbol grounding and meaning: A comparison of high-dimensional and embodied theories of meaning. *Journal of Memory and Language*, 43(3), 379–401.

Glynn, S. M., & DiVesta, F. J. (1979). Control of prose processing via instructional and typographical cues. *Journal of Educational Psychology*, 71, 595–603.

Goldman, A. I. (1970). *A theory of human action*. Englewood Cliffs, N.J.: Prentice Hall.

Goldman-Eisler, F. (1972). Segmentation of input in simultaneous translation. *Journal of Psycholinguistic Research*, 1, 127–140.

Gomez-Gonzàlez, M. -A. (2001). *The theme-topic interface: Evidence from English*. Amsterdam: John Benjamins.

Goodman, P. C., & DiPalo, C. A. (1991). *Human factors information systems: A tool to assess error related to human performance in US nuclear power plants*. In Human Factors and Ergonomics Society 35th Annual Meeting Proceedings (Vol. 1, pp. 662–665). Santa Monica, CA: HFES.

Gordon, P. C., & Hendrick, R. (1998). The representation and processing of co-reference in discourse. *Cognitive Science*, 22(4), 389–424.

Gowers, G. (1973). *The complete plain words*. London: Her Majesty's Stationery Office.

Graesser, A. C. (1981). *Prose comprehension beyond the word*. New York: Springer-Verlag.

Graesser, A. C. (1999). *How do adults comprehend the mechanisms of everyday devices: Texts, illustrations and breakdown scenarios*. Paper presented at the Annual Meeting of the American Educational Research Association, Montréal, Canada.

Graesser, A. C., & Clark, L. F. (1985). *Structures and procedures of implicit knowledge*. Norwood, NJ: Ablex.

Graesser, A. C., & Riha, J. R. (1984). An application of multiple regression techniques to sentence reading times. In D. E. Kieras & M. A. Just (Eds), *New methods in reading comprehension research* (pp. 183–218). Hillsdale, NJ: Lawrence Erlbaum Associates.

Graesser, A. C., Robertson, S. P., Lovelace, E. R., & Swinehart, D. M. (1980). Answers to why questions of story plot and predict recall of actions. *Journal of Verbal Learning and Verbal Behaviour, 19*, 110–119.

Graesser, A. C., & Zwaan, R. A. (1995). Inference generation and the construction of situation models. In C. A. Weaver, S. Mannes, & C. R. Fletcher (Eds), *Discourse comprehension: Strategies and processing revisited* (pp. 117–139). Hillsdale, NJ: Lawrence Erlbaum Associates.

Graff, M. G. (2005). Individual differences in hypertext browsing strategies. *Behaviour and Information Technology, 24*(2), 93–100.

Graves, D. H. (1994). *A fresh look at writing*. Portsmouth, NH: Heinemann.

Gray-Wilson, S., Rinck, M., McNamara, T. P., Bower, G. H., & Morrow, D. G. (1993). Mental models and narrative comprehension: Some qualifications. *Journal of Memory and Language, 32*, 141–154.

Green, D. W. (1998). Mental control of the bilingual lexico-semantic system. *Bilingualism: Language and Cognition, 1*, 67–81.

Griffin, J. A., Keller, D., Pandey, I., Pedersen, A., & Skinner, C. (2006). Local practices, institutional positions: Results from the 2003–2004 WCRP national survey of writing centers. Retrieved September 29, 2006 from University of Louisville, The Writing Centers Research Project web site: http://coldfusion.louisville.edu/webs/as/wcrp/reports/analysis/WCRPSurvey03-04.html.

Grosjean, F. (1997). Processing mixed languages: Issues, findings, and models. In A. M. B. de Groot & J. F. Kroll (Eds), *Tutorials in bilingualism: Psycholinguistic perspectives* (pp. 225–254). Mahwah, NJ: Lawrence Erlbaum Associates.

Grosjean, F. (1998). Studying bilinguals: Methodological and conceptual issues. *Bilingualism: Language and Cognition, 1*, 131–149.

Grosjean, M., & Lacoste, M. (1999). *Communication et Intelligence Collective. Le Travail à l'Hôpital*. Paris: PUF, Collection "Le Travail Humain".

Grosz, B. J., & Sidner, C. L. (1986). Attention, intentions, and the structure of discourse. *Computational Linguistics, 12*(3), 175–204.

Grote, B. (1999). Decomposing discourse relations for instructional texts. *Proceedings of Levels of Representation in Discourse Workshop*. University of Edinburgh (http://www.hcrc.ed.ac.uk/~lorid99).

Gruber, T. R. (1991). The role of common ontology in achieving sharable, reusable knowledge bases. In J. A. Allen, R. Fikes, & E. Sandewell (Eds), *Principles of knowledge representation and reasoning — proceedings of the second international conference* (pp. 601–602). Amsterdam: Morgan Kaufmann.

Gruber, T. R. (1993). A translation approach to portable ontologies. *Knowledge Acquisition, 5*(2), 199–220.

Guérin, F., Laville, A., Daniellou, F., Duraffourg, J., & Kerguelen, A. (2006). *Comprendre le travail pour le transformer* (2nd ed.). Lyon: Anact.

Gundel, J. K., Hedberg, N., & Zacharski, R. (1993). Cognitive status and the form of referring expressions. *Language, 69*, 274–307.

Gurak, L. (2001). *Cyberliteracy: Navigating the internet with awareness*. New Haven, CT: Yale University Press.

Guthrie, J. T., Bennett, S., & Weber, S. (1991). Processing procedural documents: A cognitive model for following written directions. *Educational Psychology Review, 3*, 249–265.

Guthrie, J. T., & Mosenthal, P. (1987). Literacy as multidimensional: Locating information on reading comprehension. *Educational Psychologist, 22*(3, 4), 279–297.

Haber, R. N., & Myers, B. L (1982). Memory for pictograms, pictures, and words separately and all mixed. *Perception, 11,* 57–64.

Haberlandt, K. F., & Graesser, A. C. (1985). Component processes in text comprehension and some of their interactions. *Journal of Experimental Psychology: General, 114*(3), 357–374.

Hacker, D. J. (1994). Comprehension monitoring as a writing process. In E. C. Butterfield (Ed.), *Children's writing: Toward a process theory of the development of writing skill* (Vol. 2, pp. 143–172). London: JAI Press Inc.

Hacker, D. J., Plumb, C., Butterfield, E. C., Quathamer, D., & Heineken, E. (1994). Text revision: Detection and correction of errors. *Journal of Educational Psychology, 86,* 1–15.

Haenggi, D., Kintsch, W., & Gernsbacher, M. A. (1995). Spatial situation models and text comprehension. *Discourse Processes, 19,* 173–199.

Haigh, R. (1993). The ageing process: A challenge for design. *Applied Ergonomics, 24,* 9–14.

Hameen-Anttila, K., Kemppainen, K., Enlund, H., Bush, P. J., & Marja, A. (2004). Do pictograms improve children's understanding of medicine leaflet information? *Patient Education and Counseling, 55,* 371–378.

Hansen, S. R., Narayanan, N. H., & Hegarty, M. (2002). Designing educationally effective algorithm visualizations: Embedding analogies and animations in hypermedia. *Journal of Visual Languages and Computing, 13*(3), 291–317.

Harmon, L. D., & Julesz, B. (1973). Masking in visual recognition: Effects of two-dimensional filtered noise. *Science, 180,* 1194–1197.

Harris, B. (1977). The importance of natural translation. *Working Papers on Bilingualism, 12,* 96–114.

Hartley, J. (1995). Is this chapter any use? Methods for evaluating text. In J. R. Wilson & E. Nigel Corlett (Eds), *Evaluation of human work* (pp. 285–309). London: Taylor & Francis.

Hasse, D. (1992). *Alpa ground proximity warning system survey.* Paper presented at the Flight Safety Foundation 45th Annual International Air Safety Seminar, Long Beach, CA.

Hayes, J. R. (1989). Writing research: The analysis of a very complex problem. In D. Klahr & K. Kotovsky (Eds), *Complex information processing: The impact of Herbert A. Simon.* Hillsdale, NJ: Lawrence Erlbaum Associates.

Hayes, J. R. (1995). Un nouveau modèle du processus d'écriture. In J-Y. Boyer, J-P. Dionne, & P. Raymond (Eds), *La production de textes; Vers un modèle d'enseignement de l'écriture* (pp. 49–72). Montréal: Les éditions logiques.

Hayes, J. R. (1996). A new framework for understanding cognition and affect in writing. In C. M. Levy & S. Ransdell (Eds), *The science of writing: Theories, methods, individual differences and applications* (pp. 1–27). Mahwaw, NJ: Lawrence Erlbaum Associates.

Hayes, J. R. (1998). Un nouveau cadre pour intégrer cognition et affect dans la rédaction. [A new framework for understanding cognition and affect in writing, 1996]. In A. Piolat & A. Pélissier (Eds), *La rédaction de textes. Approche cognitive* (pp. 51–101). Lausanne/Paris: Delachaux and Niestlé. (Also published in 1996 as: A new framework for understanding cognition and affect in writing. In C. M. Levy & S. Ransdell (Eds), *The science of writing: Theories, methods, individual differences, and applications.* Mahwah, NJ: Lawrence Erlbaum Associates.).

Hayes, J. R. (2004). What triggers revision? In G. Rijlaarsdam (Series Ed.), L. Allal, L. Chanquoy, & P. Largy (Vol. Eds), *Studies in writing,* (Vol. 13), *Revision: Cognitive and instructional processes* (pp. 9–20). Dordrecht: Kluwer Academic Publishers.

Hayes, J. R., & Flower, L. S. (1980). Identifying the organization of writing processes. In L. Gregg, & E. R. Steinberg (Eds), *Cognitive processes in writing* (pp. 3–30). Hillsdale, NJ: Lawrence Erlbaum Associates.

Hayes, J. R., & Flower, L. S. (1983). Uncovering cognitive processes in writing. In P. Mosenthal, L. Tamor, & S. A. Walmsley (Eds), *Research in writing: Principles and methods* (pp. 207–220). New York: Longman.

Hayes, J. R., Flower, L. S., Schriver, K. A., Stratman, J. F., & Carey, L. (1987). Cognitive processes in revision. In S. Rosenberg (Ed.), *Advances in applied psycholinguistics,* (Vol. II), *Reading, writing, and language learning* (pp. 176–240). Cambridge, MA: Cambridge University Press.

Hearst, M. A. (1992). Automatic acquisition of hyponyms from large text corpora. *Proceedings of the 14th international conference on computational linguistics*, Nantes, France. (pp. 539–545).

Hegarty, M. (1992). Mental animation: Inferring motion from static displays of mechanical systems. *Journal of Experimental Psychology: Learning, Memory, and Cognition, 18*(5), 1084–1102.

Hegarty, M., & Just, M. A. (1993). Constructing mental models of machines from texts and diagrams. *Journal of Memory and Language, 32,* 717–742.

Hegarty, M., Kriz, S., & Cate, C. (2003). The roles of mental animations and external animations in understanding mechanical systems. *Cognition and Instruction, 21*(4), 325–360.

Hegarty, M., Narayanan, N. H., & Freitas, P. (2002). Understanding machines from multimedia and hypermedia presentations. In J. Otero, J. A. Leon, & A. Graesser, (Eds), *The psychology of science text comprehension* (pp. 357–384). Hillsdale, NJ: Lawrence Erlbaum Associates.

Hegarty, M., Quilici, J., Narayanan, N. H., Holmquist, S., & Moreno, R. (1999). Multimedia instruction: Lessons from evaluation of a theory based design. *Journal of Educational Multimedia and Hypermedia, 8,* 119–150.

Hegarty, M., & Sims, V. K. (1994). Individual differences in mental animation during mechanical reasoning. *Memory and Cognition, 22*(4), 411–430.

Helyar, P. S. (1992). Products liability: Meeting legal standards for adequate instructions. *Journal of Technical Writing and Communication, 22,* 125–147.

Henry, A., & Monkam-Daverat, I. (1998). *Rédiger les procédures de l'entreprise, guide pratique*. Paris, Éditions d'Organisation (2e éd.).

Herring, S. C., Scheidt, L. A., Bonus, S., & Wright, E. (2005). Weblogs as a bridging genre. *Information, Technology, & People, 18*(2), 142–171.

Heurley, L. (1994). Traitement de textes procéduraux: Etude de psycholinguistique cognitive des processus de production et de compréhension chez des adultes non experts. [The processing of procedural texts: A Psycholinguistics study of production and comprehension processes in non-experts adults]. *Doctoral Dissertation*. Université de Bourgogne, Dijon.

Heurley, L. (2001). Cinq approches differentes du texte procédural. *Pratiques, Les textes de consignes, 111–112,* 39–64.

Heurley, L., & Ganier, F. (2002). La production de textes techniques écrits. [Producing written technical texts]. In M. Fayol (Ed.), *Traité des sciences cognitives: Production du langage* (pp. 229–249). Paris: Hermès.

Hidalgo, A. J., & Otero, J. (2004). An analysis of the understanding of geological time by students at secondary and post-secondary level. *International Journal of Science Education, 26,* 845–847.

Hidi, S. E., & Anderson, V. (1986). Producing written summaries: Task demands, cognitive operations, and implications for instruction. *Review of Educational Research, 56*(4), 473–493.

Higelé, P. (1992). Evaluation des effets de transfert des ateliers de raisonnement logique. In F. Ginsbourger, V. Merle, & G. Vergnaud (Eds), *Formation et apprentissage des adultes peu qualifiés* (pp. 122–124). Paris: La Documentation Française.

Hillocks, G. (1986). *Research in written composition: New directions for teaching*. Urbana, IL: ERIC Clearinghouse on Reading and Communication Skills and National Conference on Research in English.

Hinton, G. E., McClelland, J. L., & Rumelhart, D. E. (1990). Distributed representations. In M. A. Boden (Ed.), *The philosophy of artificial intelligence* (pp. 248–280). New York: Oxford University Press.

Hmelo, C. E., Holton, D. L., & Kolodner, J. L. (2000). Designing to learn about complex systems. *Journal of the Learning Sciences, 9,* 247–298.

Hmelo-Silver, C. E., & Pfeffer, M. G. (2004). Comparing expert and novice understanding of a complex system from the perspective of structures, behaviors, and functions. *Cognitive Science, 28*(1), 127–138.

Hoecker, D. G., Corker, K. M., Roth, E. M., Lipner, M. H., & Bunzo, M. S. (1994). *Man-machine design and analysis system (midas) applied to a computer-based procedure-aiding system.* In Human Factors and Ergonomics Society 38th Annual Meeting Proceedings (Vol. 1, pp. 195–199). Santa Monica, CA: HFES.

Hofman, R., & Van Oostendorp, H. (1999). Cognitive effects of a structural overview in a hypertext. *British Journal of Educational Technology, 30,* 129–140.

Honold, L. (1997). A review of the literature on employee empowerment. *Empowerment in Organizations, 5*(4), 202–212.

Horton, W. (1994). *The icon book.* New York: Wiley.

Hudson, J. A., & Shapiro, L. R. (1991). From knowing to telling: The development of children's scripts, stories, and personal narratives. In A. McCabe & C. Peterson (Eds), *Developing narrative structure* (pp. 89–136). Hillsdale, NJ: Lawrence Erlbaum Associates.

Hunt, R. R. (2003). Two contributions of distinctive processing to accurate memory. *Journal of Memory and Language, 48,* 811–825.

Hunt, R. R., & Einstein, G. O. (1981). Relational and item-specific information in memory. *Journal of Verbal Learning and Verbal Behavior, 20,* 497–514.

Hutchins, E. (1995). *Cognition in the wild.* Cambridge, MA: The MIT Press.

Hyland, K. (2005). *Metadiscourse. Exploring interaction in writing.* London: Continuum.

Hyona, J., Lorch, R. F., Jr., & Kaakinen, J. K. (2002). Individual differences in reading to summarize expository text: Evidence from eye fixation patterns. *Journal of Educational Psychology, 94*(1), 44–55.

INPO. (1986). *A maintenance analysis of safety significant events.* Atlanta, GA: Institute of Nuclear Power Operations.

International Organization for Standardization/International Electrotechnical Commission, ISO/IEC. (1995). *Guide 37: Instructions for use of products of consumer interest.* Genève: Organisation Internationale de Normalisation.

International Organization for Standardization (ISO), ISO 9186. (2001). *Graphical symbols — Test methods for judged comprehensibility and for comprehension.* Geneva: International Organization for Standardization.

International Organization for Standardization (ISO), ISO TR10013. (2001). *Guidelines for quality management system documentation.* Geneva: ISO: International Organization for Standardization, ISO/TC 176, SC 3.

International Organization for Standardization (ISO), ISO 9000. (2005). *Quality management systems—Fundamentals and vocabulary.* Geneva: ISO: International Organization for Standardization, ISO/TC 176, SC 1.

Irwin, J. W., & Pulver, C. J. (1984). Effects of explicitness, clause order, and reversibility on children's comprehension of causal relationships. *Journal of Educational Psychology, 76,* 399–407.

Jacobson, M. J. (2001). Problem solving, cognition, and complex systems: Differences between experts and novices. *Complexity, 6*(2), 1–9.

Janssen, D., Van Waes, L., & Van den Bergh, H. (1996). Effects of thinking aloud on writing processes. In C. M. Levy & S. Ransdell (Eds), *The science of writing: Theories, methods, individual differences, and applications* (pp. 233–250). Mahwah, NJ: Lawrence Erlbaum Associates.

Jeffroy, F., & Charron, S. (1997). *From safety assessment to research in the domain of human factors: The case of operation with computerised procedures.* Paper presented at the IEEE Sixth Annual Human Factors Meeting, Orlando, FL.

Johnson-Laird, P. N. (1983). *Mental models: Toward a cognitive science of language, inference, and consciousness.* Cambridge, MA: Harvard University Press.

Jonassen, D. H. (1990). Semantic network elicitation: Tools for structuring of hypertext. In R. McAleese & C. Green (Eds), *Hypertext: The state of the art.* London: Intellect.

Jordan, M. P. (2001). *Paragraphing in legislative writing: Linguistic and pragmatic foundations.* Research report commissioned by the English Legislative Language Commission, Department of Justice, Ottawa, pp. 75, March.

Just, M. A., & Carpenter, P. A. (1987). *The psychology of reading and language comprehension.* Newton, MA: Allyn and Bacon.

Just, M. A., & Carpenter, P. A. (1992). A capacity theory of comprehension: Individual differences in working memory. *Psychological Review, 99*(1), 122–149.

Juvina, I., & Van Oostendorp, H. (2004). Individual differences and behavioural aspects involved in modelling web navigation. In C. Stary & C. Stephanidis (Eds) *User-Centered Interaction Paradigms for Universal Access in the Information Society, UI4ALL, 8th ERCIM Workshop on user interfaces for all, Vienna, Austria* (pp. 77–95). Berlin, Heidelberg, New York: Springer-Verlag.

Kaestle, C. F., Campbell, A., Finn, J. D., Johnson, S. T., & Mikulecky, L. J. (2001). Adult literacy and education in America. *Education Statistics Quarterly, 3*(4), 67–72.

Kallman, D. A., Plato, C. C., & Tobin, J. D. (1991). The role of muscle loss in age-related decline of grip strength: Cross-sectional and longitudinal perspectives. *Journal of Gerontology: Medical Sciences, 45*, 82–86.

Kamberelis, G. (1999). Genre development and learning: Children writing stories, science reports, and poems. *Research in the Teaching of English, 33*, 403–460.

Karmiloff-Smith, A. (1992). *Beyond modularity: A developmental perspective on cognitive science.* Cambridge, MA: The MIT Press.

Kaufer, D. S., & Carley, K. M. (1993). *Communication at a distance: The influence of print on sociocultural organization and change.* Hillsdale, NJ: Lawrence Erlbaum Associates.

Kaufer, D. S., Hayes, J. R., & Flower, L. S. (1986). Composing written sentences. *Research in the Teaching of English, 20*, 121–140.

Kellogg, R. T. (1987). Effects of topic knowledge on the allocation of processing time and cognitive effort to writing processes. *Memory and Cognition, 15*(3), 256–266.

Kellogg, R. T. (1996). A model of working memory in writing. In C. M. Levy & S. Ransdell (Eds), *The science of writing: Theories, methods, individual differences, and applications* (pp. 57–71). Mahwah, NJ: Lawrence Erlbaum Associates.

Kellogg, R. T. (2001). Long-term working memory in text production. *Memory and Cognition, 29*(1), 43–52.

Kern, R. P. (1985). Modeling users and their use of technical manuals. In T. M. Duffy & R. Waller (Eds), *Designing usable texts* (pp. 341, 375). London: Academic Press Inc.

Kieras, D. E., & Bovair, S. (1984). The role of a mental model in learning to operate a device. *Cognitive Science, 8*, 255–273.

Kim, H., & Hirtle, S. C. (1995). Spatial metaphors and disorientation in hypertext browsing. *Behavior and Information Technology, 14*(4), 239–250.

King, J., & Just, M. A. (1991). Individual differences in syntactic processing: The role of working memory. *Journal of Memory and Language, 30*, 580–602.

King, L. E. (1975). Recognition of symbols and word traffic signs. *Journal of Safety Research, 7*, 80–84.

Kintsch, W. (1988). The role of knowledge in discourse comprehension: A construction-integration model. *Psychological Review, 95*(2), 163–182.

Kintsch, W. (1991). A theory of discourse comprehension: Implications for a tutor for word algebra problems. In M. Carretero, M. Pope, R.-J. Simons, & J. I. Pozo (Eds), *Learning Instruction* (pp. 235–245). Oxford: Pergamon Press.

Kintsch, W. (1998). *Comprehension: A paradigm for cognition.* Cambridge, New York: Cambridge University Press.

Kintsch, W., Mandel, T. S., & Kozminsky, E. (1977). Summarizing scrambled stories. *Memory and Cognition, 5*, 547–552.

Kintsch, W., & Van Dijk, T. A. (1978). Toward a model of text comprehension and production. *Psychological Review, 85*, 363–394.

Kintsch, W., Patel, V. L., & Ericsson, K. A. (1999). The role of long-term working memory in text comprehension. *Psychologia, 42*, 186–198.

Kintsch, W., Welsch, D. M., Schmalhofer, F., & Zimny, S. (1990). Sentence memory: A theoretical analysis. *Journal of Memory and Language, 29*, 133–159.

Kirlik, A. (1993). Modeling strategic behavior in human-automation interaction: Why an "aid" can (and should) go unused. *Human factors, 35*(2), 221–242.

Kline, D. W., & Scialfa, C. T. (1997). Sensory and perceptual functionning: Basic research and human factors implications. In A. D. Fisk & W. A. Rogers (Eds), *Handbook of human factors and the older adult* (pp. 27–54). New York: Academic Press.

Klusewitz, M., & Lorch, R. F. (2000). Effects of headings and familiarity with a text on strategies for searching a text. *Memory and Cognition, 28*(4), 667–676.

Knapp, P., Raynor, D. K., Jebar, A. H., & Price, S. J. (2005). Interpretation of medication pictograms by adults in the UK. *The Annals of Pharmacotherapy, 39*, 1227–1233.

Knott, A., & Sanders, T. J. M. (1998). The classification of coherence relations and their linguistic markers: An exploration of two languages. *Journal of Pragmatics, 30*, 135–175.

Kobayashi, K. (2005). What limits the encoding effect of note-taking? A meta-analytic examination. *Contemporary Educational Psychology, 30*(2), 242–262.

Kolers, P. A. (1969). Some formal characteristics of pictograms. *American Scientist, 57*, 348–363.

Kosslyn, S. M., Cave, C. B., Provost, D. A., & Von Gierke, S. M. (1988). Sequential processes in image generation. *Cognitive Psychology, 20*, 319–343.

Kroll, B. M. (1986). Explaining how to play a game. The development of informative writing skills. *Written Communication, 3*(2), 195–218.

Kroll, B. M., & Lempers, J. D. (1981). Effect of mode of communication on the informational adequacy of children's explanations. *The Journal of Genetic Psychology, 138*, 27–35.

Kroll, J. F., & Stewart, E. (1994). Category interference in translation and picture naming: Evidence for asymmetric connections between bilingual memory representations. *Journal of Memory and Language, 33*, 149–174.

La Heij, W., De Bruyn, E., Elens, E., Hartsuiker, R., & Helaha, D. (1990). Ortographic facilitation and categorical interference in a word-translation variant of the stroop task. *Canadian Journal of Psychology, 44*, 76–83.

Labasse, B. (1999). La lisibilité rédactionnelle: Fondements et perspectives [Readability in writing: Foundations and perspectives]. *Communication et Langages, 121*, 86–103.

Lachance, G. (2006). *La révision linguistique en français. Le métier d'une passion, la passion d'un métier*. Québec: Éditions du Septentrion.

Lacoste, M. (2001). Quand communiquer c'est coordonner. Communication à l'hôpital et coordination des équipes. In A. Borzeix & B. Fraenkel (Eds), *Langage et Travail, Communication, Cognition, Action* (pp. 323–349). Paris: CNRS Edition.

Laflamme, C. (2007). L'autorévision et la révision professionnelle: Regard sur les contextes de l'activité révisionnelle. In J. Bisaillon (Ed.), *La révision professionnelle: Processus, stratégies et pratiques* (pp. 21–47). Québec: Nota bene.

Lambrecht, K. (1994). *Information structure and sentence form. Topic, focus and the mental representations of discourse referents*. Cambridge: Cambridge University Press.

Lamonde, F., & Montreuil, S. (1995). Work, ergonomics and industrial relations. *Relations Industrielles-Industrial Relations, 50*(4), 695–718.

Landry, S. J., & Jacko, J. A. (2006). Improving pilot procedure following using displays of procedure context. *International Journal of Applied Aviation Studies, 6*(1), 47–70.

Langston, W. E., Kramer, D. C., & Glenberg. A. M. (1998). The representation of space in mental models derived from text. *Memory and Cognition, 26,* 247–262.

Lankshear, C., & Knobel, M. (2001, January). Do we have your attention? New literacies, digital technologies and the education of adolescents. Paper presented at the State of the Art Conference, University of Georgia, Athens, GA. Retrieved March 5, 2006, from http://www.geocities.com/c.lankshear/attention.html?20065

Lankshear, C., & Knobel, M. (2003). *New literacies: Changing knowledge and classroom learning.* Buckingham, UK: Open University Press.

Largy, P. (2001). Nominal and verbal agreement revision in children. *L'Année Psychologique, 101*(2), 221–245.

Larkin, J. H., & Simon, H. A. (1987). Why a diagram is (sometimes) worth ten thousand words. *Cognitive Science, 11,* 65–99.

Laughery, R., & Persensky, J. (1994). *Network modeling of nuclear operator procedures.* In Human Factors and Ergonomics Society 38th Annual Meeting Proceedings (Vol. 1, pp. 210–214). Santa Monica, CA: HFES.

Lawless, K. A., & Kulikowich, J. M. (1998). Domain knowledge, interest, and hypertext navigation: A study of individual differences. *Journal of Educational Multimedia and Hypermedia, 7*(1), 51–70.

Lee, J. D., & Moray, N. (1994). Trust, self-confidence, and operators' adaptation to automation. *International Journal of Human-Computer Studies, 40,* 153–184.

Lee, K., & Karmiloff-Smith, A. (1996). The development of cognitive constraints on notations. *Archives de Psychologie, 64*(248), 3–26.

Lee, K., Karmiloff-Smith, A., Cameron, C. A., & Dodsworth, P. (1998). Notation adaptation in children. *Canadian Journal of Behavioural Science, 30*(3), 159–171.

Lee, L. (2005). Dell: In the bloghouse. *BusinessWeek Online.* Retrieved April 14, 2006 from http://www.businessweek.com/technology/content/aug2005/tc20050825_2021.htm. August 25.

LeFevre, J. -A., & Dixon, P. (1986). Do written instructions need examples? *Cognition & Instruction, 3*(1), 1–30.

Lehto, M. R. (1992). Designing warning signs and warning labels: Scientific basis for initial guidelines. *Ergonomics, 10,* 115–138.

Leplat, J. (1998). À propos des procédures. *Performances humaines et techniques, 94,* 6–15.

Leplat, J. (2004). Procédures d'objectivation dans un entretien de recherche, *@ctivités, 1*(2), 195–216. http://www.activites.org/v1n2/Leplat.pdf

Levelt, J. M. W. (1982). Linearization in describing spatial networks. In S. Peters & E. Saarinen (Eds), *Processes, beliefs, and questions* (pp. 119–220). Dordrecht: Reidel.

Levy, B. A., Newell, S., Snyder, J., & Timmins, K. (1986). Processing changes across reading encounters. *Journal of Experimental Psychology: Learning, Memory, and Cognition, 12*(4), 467–478.

Levy, C. M., & Ransdell, S. (1996). *The science of writing. Theories, methods, individual differences, and applications.* Mahwah, NJ: Lawrence Erbaum Associates.

Liben, L. (1981). Spatial representation and behavior: Multiple perspectives. In L. S. Liben, A. M. Patterson, & N. Newcombe (Eds), *Spatial representation and behavior across the life span* (pp. 16–37). New York: Academic Press.

Lin, H. X., & Salvendy, G. (1999). Instruction effect on human error reduction. *International Journal of Cognitive Ergonomics, 3*(2), 115–129.

Lindgren, E., & Sullivan, K. P. H. (2006). Writing and the analysis of revision: An overview. In K. P. H. Sullivan & E. Lindgren (Eds), *Computer keystroke logging and writing: Methods and applications.* Amsterdam: Elsevier.

Loman, N. L., & Mayer, R. E. (1983). Signaling techniques that increase the understandability of expository prose. *Journal of Educational Psychology, 75,* 402–412.

Lorch, R. F. (1989). Text signaling devices and their effects on reading and memory processes. *Educational Psychology Review, 1*, 209–234.

Lorch, R. F. Jr., & Lorch, E. P. (1985). Topic structure representation and text recall. *Journal of Educational Psychology, 77*(2), 137–148.

Lorch, R. F., & Lorch, E. P. (1995). Effects of organizational signals on text processing strategies. *Journal of Educational Psychology, 87*, 537–544.

Lorch, R. F., & Lorch, E. P. (1996). Effects of organizational signals on free recall of expository text. *Journal of Educational Psychology, 88*, 38–48.

Lorch, R. F., Lorch, E. P., & Inman, W. E. (1993). Effects on signaling topic structure in text recall. *Journal of Educational Psychology, 85*, 281–290.

Lowe, R. K. (1993). Constructing a mental representation from an abstract technical diagram. *Learning and Instruction, 3*, 157–179.

Lowe, R. K. (1994). Selectivity in diagrams: Reading beyond the lines. *Educational Psychology, 14*, 467–491.

Lowe, R. K. (1999). Extracting information from an animation during complex visual learning. *European Journal of Psychology of Education, 14*(2), 225–244.

Lowe, R. K. (2001). Understanding information presented by complex animated diagrams. In J-F. Rouet, J. J. Levonen, & A. Biardeau (Eds), *Multimedia learning: Cognitive and instructional issues* (pp. 65–74). London: Pergamon.

Lowe, R. K. (2003). Animation and learning: Selective processing of information in dynamic graphics. *Learning and Instruction, 13*, 157–176.

Lowe, R. K. (2004). Interrogation of a dynamic visualization during learning. *Learning and Instruction, 14*, 257–274.

Lowe, R. K., & Munt, R. (1999). *Learning to draw house sections from building plans.* Paper presented at the 9th Biennial Conference of the European Association for Research on Learning and Instruction. Fribourg, Switzerland.

Lowe, R. K., & Pramono, H. (2006). Using graphics to support comprehension of dynamic information in texts. *Information Design Journal, 14*, 22–34.

Lowe, R. K., & Schnotz, W. (in press). *Learning with animation: Research and implications for design.* New York: Cambridge University Press.

Luc, C., Mojahid, M., Péry-Woodley, M. -P., & Virbel, J. (2000). Les énumérations: structures visuelles, syntaxiques et rhétoriques. In M. Gaio & E. Trupin (Eds), *Proceedings of CIDE 2000 (Colloque International sur le Document Électronique)* (pp. 21–40). Lyon, France: Europia Productions.

Luc, C., Mojahid, M., Virbel, J., Garcia-Debanc, C., & Péry-Woodley, M. -P. (1999). A linguistic approach to some parameters of layout: A study of enumerations. In R. Power & D. Scott (Eds), *AAAI 1999 Fall Symposia: Using Layout for the Generation, Understanding or Retrieval of Documents* (pp. 20–29). Menlo Park, CA: AAAI Press.

Luc, C., & Virbel, J. (2001). Le modèle d'architecture textuelle: Fondements et expérimentation. *Verbum, 23*(1), 103–123.

Lumbelli, L., Paoletti, G., & Frausin, T. (1999). Improving the ability to detect comprehension problems: From revising to writing. *Learning and Instruction, 9*(2), 143–166.

Lyons, J. (1977). *Semantics.* Cambridge: Cambridge University Press.

Macaulay, D. (1998). *The new way things work, CD-ROM.* New York: DK Interactive Learning.

Machamer, P., Darden, D., & Carver, C. (2000). Thinking about mechanisms. *Philosophy of Science, 67*, 1–25.

Macizo, P. (2003). *Procesos cognitivos en la traducción: Comprensión y memoria de trabajo* [Cognitive processes in translation: Comprehension and working memory]. Unpublished doctoral dissertation, University of Granada, Granada, Spain.

Macizo, P., & Bajo, M. T. (2004a). *Working memory and comprehension in within-language and between-language tasks.* Paper presented at the V meeting of the Spanish Society of Experimental Psychology, Madrid, Spain.

Macizo, P., & Bajo, M. T. (2004b). When translation makes the difference: Sentence processing in reading and translation. *Psicológica, 25,* 181–205.

Macizo, P., & Bajo, M. T. (2005). Working Memory and translation. *Cognitiva, 17,* 29–54.

Macizo, P., & Bajo, M. T. (2006). Reading for understanding and reading for translation: Do they involve the same processes? *Cognition, 99,* 1–34.

Mackie, J. L. (1980). *The cement of the universe: A study of causation.* Oxford: Clarendon Press.

Madrid, R. I., Salmeron, L., Cañas, J. J., & Fajardo, I. (2005). Cognitive factors related to text comprehension with hypertext overviews. In G. Chiazzese, M. Allegra, A. Chifari, & S. Ottaviano (Eds), *Methods and technologies for learning* (pp. 597–598). Southampton: WIT Press.

Magee, J. M. (1995). *Grace under pressure: A qualitative and quantitative case study of the revision process of a corporation president.* Unpublished doctoral dissertation, University of Indiana, Pennsylvania.

Magliano, J. P., Trabasso, T., & Graesser, A. C. (1999). Strategic processing during comprehension. *Journal of Educational Psychology, 91,* 615–629.

Maingueneau, D. (1991). *L'analyse du discours [Discourse analysis].* Paris: Hachette.

Mani, I., & Maybury, M. (Eds), (1999). *Advances in automatic text summarization.* Cambridge, MA: MIT Press.

Mani, I. (2001). *Automatic summarization.* Amsterdam: John Benjamins.

Mann, W. C., & Thompson, S. A. (1988). Rhetorical structure theory: Toward a functional theory of text organization. *Text, 8*(3), 243–281.

Mann, W. C., & Thompson, S. A. (Eds). (1992). *Discourse description. Diverse linguistic analyses of a fund-raising text.* Amsterdam: John Benjamins.

Mannes, S. M., & Kintsch, W. (1987). Knowledge organization and text organization. *Cognition and Instruction, 4*(2), 91–115.

Marcu, D. (2001). *The theory and practice of discourse parsing and summarization.* Cambridge, MA: The MIT Press.

Marcus, N., Cooper, M., & Sweller, J. (1996). Understanding instructions. *Journal of Educational Psychology, 88,* 1, 49–63.

Mariné, C. (1992). Maîtrise des opérations logiques par des stagiaires en préformation. In F. Ginsbourger, V. Merle, & G. Vergnaud (Eds), *Formation et apprentissage des adultes peu qualifiés* (pp. 125–128). Paris: La Documentation Française.

Market Sentinel, Onalytica, & immediate future, Inc. (2005). *Measuring the influence of bloggers on corporate reputation.* Retrieved April 14, 2006, from http://www.publicrelationsonline.com/files/MeasuringBloggerInfluence61205.pdf.

Markman, E. M. (1979). Realizing that you don't understand: Elementary school children's awareness of inconsistencies. *Child Development, 50*(3), 643–655.

Marsden, P. (1996). Procedures in the nuclear industry. In N. Stanton (Ed.), *Human factors in nuclear safety* (pp. 99–116). London: Taylor & Francis.

Martí, E., & Tantaros, S. (2005). From action to notation. The production of procedural text by seven- to ten-year old children. In L. Allal & J. Dolz (Eds), *Proceeding Writing2004 [CD].* Adcom Productions.

Matsuhashi, A. (1981). Pausing and planning: The tempo of written discourse production. *Research in the Teaching of English, 15*(2), 113–134.

Matsuhashi, A. (1987). Revising the plan and altering the text. In A. Matsuhashi (Ed.), *Writing in real time: Modelling production processes* (pp. 197–223). Norwood, NJ: Ablex.

Mayer, R. E. (1993). Comprehension of graphics in text. An overview. In E. De Corte & W. Schnotz (Eds), *Comprehension of graphics in texts. Special issue of learning and instruction* (pp. 239–245). Oxford: Pergamon Press.

Mayer, R. E. (2001). *Multi-media learning*. New York: Cambridge University Press.

Mayer, R. E., & Anderson, R. B. (1991). Animations need narrations: An experimental test of a dual-coding hypothesis. *Journal of Educational Psychology, 83*, 484–490.

Mayer, R. E., & Moreno, R. (1998). A split-attention effect in multimedia learning: Evidence for dual processing systems in working memory. *Journal of Educational Psychology, 90*, 312–320.

Mazeau, M. (1998). Procédures: recommandations minimales de réalisation et d'utilisation. *Performances humaines et techniques, 95*, 8–13.

McCarthy, J. C., Wright, P. C., Monk, A. F., & Watts, L. A. (1998). Concerns at work: Designing useful procedures. *Human-Computer Interaction, 13*(4), 433–457.

McCutchen, D. (1986). Domain knowledge and linguistic knowledge in the development of writing ability. *Journal of Memory and Language, 25*(4), 431–444.

McCutchen, D. (1996). A capacity theory of writing: Working memory in composition. *Educational Psychology Review, 8*(3), 299–325.

McCutchen, D. (2000). Knowledge, processing, and working memory: Implications for a theory of writing. *Educational Psychologist, 35*(1), 13–23.

McCutchen, D., Covill, A., Hoyne, S. H., & Mildes, K. (1994). Individual differences in writing: Implications of translating fluency. *Journal of Educational Psychology, 86*(2), 256–266.

McCutchen, D., & Kerr, S. (1997). Revising for meaning: Effects of knowledge and strategy. *Journal of Educational Psychology, 89*, 667–676.

McDaniel, M. A., & Einstein, G. O. (1989). Material-appropriate processing: A contextualist approach to reading and studying strategies. *Educational Psychology Review, 1*, 113–145.

McDonald, J., & Carpenter, P. A. (1981). Simultaneous translation: Idiom interpretation and parsing heuristics. *Journal of Verbal Learning and Verbal Behavior, 20*, 231–247.

McDonald, S., & Stevenson, R. J. (1996). Disorientation in hypertext: The effects of three text structures on navigation performance. *Applied Ergonomics. Special Issue: Shiftwork, 27*(1), 61–68.

McDougall, S. J. (2001). The effects of visual information on users' mental models: An evaluation of pathfinder analysis as a measure of icon usability. *International Journal of Cognitive Ergonomics, 5*, 59–84.

McGinley, W. (1992). The role of reading and writing while composing from sources. *Reading Research Quarterly, 27*(3), 226–248.

McNamara, D. S. (2004). SERT: Self-explanation reading training. *Discourse Processes, 38*, 1–30.

McNamara, D. S., & Kintsch, W. (1996). Learning from text: Effect of prior knowledge and text coherence. *Discourse Processes, 22*, 247–288.

McNamara, D. S., Kintsch, E., Songer, N. B., & Kintsch, W. (1996). Are good texts always better? Interactions of text coherence, background knowledge, and levels of understanding in learning from text. *Cognition & Instruction, 14*(1), 1–43.

McNamara, D. S., & Scott, J. L. (1999). Training reading strategies. *Proceedings of the twenty-first annual meeting of the cognitive science society* (pp. 387–392). Hillsdale, NJ: Lawrence Erlbaum Associates.

Meunier, J. G. (1998). Categorial structure of iconic languages. *Theory and Psychology, 8*, 805–827.

Meyer, B. J. F. (1975). *The organization of prose and its effects in memory*. Amsterdam: North Holland.

Meyer, B. J. F., & Poon, L. W. (2001). Effects of structure strategy training and signaling on recall of text. *Journal of Educational Psychology, 93*, 141–159.

Meyer, B. J. F., & Rice, G. E. (1982). The interaction of reader strategies and the organization of text. *Text, Interdisciplinary Journal for the Study of Discourse, 2*, 155–192.

Meyer, I. (2001). Extracting Knowledge-rich contexts for terminography: A conceptual and methodological framework. In D. Bourigault, C. Jacquemin, & M. -Cl. L'homme (Eds), *Recent advances in computational terminology* (pp. 279–302). Amsterdam: John Benjamins.

Miller, A. N., & Kroll, J. F. (2002). Stroop effects in bilingual translation. *Memory and Cognition, 30*, 614–628.

Miller, C., & Shepherd, D. (2004). Blogging as social action: A genre analysis of the weblog. In L. J. Gurak, S. Antonijevic, L. Johnson, C. Ratliff, & J. Reyman (Eds), *Into the blogosphere: Rhetoric, community, and culture of weblogs*. Retrieved August 13, 2004, from http://blog.lib.umn.edu/blogosphere/blogging_as_social_action_a_genre_analysis_of_the_weblog.html

Miller, G. A., & Johnson-Laird, P. N. (1976). *Language and perception*. Cambridge, MA: Harvard University Press.

Mills, C. B., Diehl, V. A., Birkmire, D. P., & Mou, L. C. (1993). Procedural text: Predictions of importance ratings and recall by models of reading comprehension. *Discourse Processes, 16*, 279–316.

Mills, C. B., Diehl, V. A., Birkmire, D. P., & Mou, L. C. (1995). Reading procedural text: Effects of purpose and predictions of reading comprehension models. *Discourse Processes, 20*, 79–107.

Minel, J. -L. (2003). *Filtrage sémantique. Du résumé automatique à la fouille de textes*. Paris: Hermès-Lavoisier.

Minzoni-Déroche, A. (1998). Culture de sûreté et procédures de conduite accidentelle. *Performances humaines et techniques, 95*, 14–23.

Mitchell, D. C. (1994). Sentence parsing. In M. A. Gernsbacher (Ed.), *Handbook of psycholinguistics* (pp.375–409). San Diego, CA: Academic Press.

Mitchell, R. (1979). *Less than words can say*. Boston: Little, Brown and Company.

Miyake, A., & Shah, P. (1999). Toward unified theories of working memory: Emerging general consensus, unresolved theoretical issues, and future research directions. In A. Miyake & P. Shah (Eds), *Models of working memory: Mechanisms of active maintenance and executive control* (pp. 442–481). New York: Cambridge University Press.

Molinari, G., & Tapiero, I. (2000, July 19–21). *Integration of domain knowledge from an outline and a target text: Effects of expertise, and semantic information*. Paper presented at the Tenth Annual Meeting of the Society for Text and Discourse, Lyon (France).

Moltzen, E. F. (2006, January 9). Michael Dell and the bloggers. *CRN*. Retrieved April 14, 2006 from http://www.crn.com/sections/hardware/hardware.jhtml?articleId = 175802571

Moran, M. H. (1997). Connections between reading and successful revision. *Journal of Basic Writing, 16*(2), 76–89.

Morrell, R. W., Park, D. C., & Poon, L. W. (1990). Effects of labelling techniques on memory and comprehension of prescription information in young and old adults. *Journal of Gerontology, 45*(4), 166–172.

Morris, C. D., Bransford, J. D., & Franks, J. J. (1977). Levels of processing versus transfer appropriate processing. *Journal of Verbal Learning and Verbal Behavior, 16*, 519–533.

Morrow, D. G., Greenspan, S., & Bower, G. H. (1987). Accessibility and situation models in narrative comprehension. *Journal of Memory and Language, 26*, 165–187.

Morrow, D. G., & Leirer, V. O. (1999). Designing medication instructions for older adults. In D. C. Park, R. W. Morrell, & K. Shiffren (Eds), *Processing of medical information in aging patients* (pp. 249–265). Mahwah, NJ: Lawrence Erlbaum Associates.

Mosier, K. L., Palmer, E. A., & Degani, A. (1992). *Electronic checklists: Implications for decision making*. In Human Factors and Ergonomics Society 36th Annual Meeting Proceedings (Vol. 1, pp. 7–11). Santa Monica, CA: HFES.

Muir, B. M. (1987). Trust between humans and machines, and the design of decision aids. *International Journal of Man-Machine Studies, 27*, 527–539.

Murray, D. M. (1978). Internal revision: A process of discovery. In C. R. Cooper & L. Odell (Eds), *Research on composing: Points of departure*. Urbana, IL: National Council of Teachers of English.

Myers, J. L., O'Brien, E. J., Balota, D. A., & Toyofuku, M. (1984). Memory search without inference: The role of integration. *Cognitive Psychology, 16,* 217–242.

Narayanan, N. H., & Chandrasekaran, B. (1991). Reasoning visually about spatial interactions. *Proceedings of international joint conference on artificial intelligence (IJCAI'91)* (pp. 360–365). San Mateo, CA: Morgan Kaufmann Publishers.

Narayanan, N. H., & Hegarty, M. (1998). On designing comprehensible interactive hypermedia manuals. *International Journal of Human-Computer Studies, 48*(2), 267–301.

Narayanan, N. H., & Hegarty, M. (2002). Multimedia design for communication of dynamic information. *International Journal of Human-Computer Studies, 57*(4), 279–315.

Narayanan, N. H., Suwa, M., & Motoda, H. (1994a). A study of diagrammatic reasoning from verbal and gestural data. *Proceedings of the sixteenth annual conference of the cognitive science society* (pp. 652–657). Hillsdale, NJ: Lawrence Erlbaum Associates.

Narayanan, N. H., Suwa, M., & Motoda, H. (1994b). How things appear to work: Predicting behaviors from device diagrams. *Proceedings of the 12th national conference on artificial intelligence* (pp. 1161–1167). Menlo Park, CA: AAAI Press.

Narayanan, N. H., Suwa, M., & Motoda, H. (1995a). Diagram-based problem solving: The case of an impossible problem. *Proceedings of the seventeenth annual conference of the cognitive science society* (pp. 206–211). Hillsdale, NJ: Lawrence Erlbaum Associates.

Narayanan, N. H., Suwa, M., & Motoda, H. (1995b). Behavior hypothesis from schematic diagrams. In J. I. Glasgow, N. H. Narayanan, & B. Chandrasekaran, (Eds), *Diagrammatic reasoning: Cognitive and computational perspectives.* Boston, MA: MIT Press and Menlo Park, CA: AAAI Press.

Nash, J. G., Schumacher, G. M., & Carlson, B. W. (1993). Writing from sources: A structure-mapping model. *Journal of Educational Psychology, 85*(1), 159–170.

Naumann, A., Waniek, J., Brunstein, A., & Krems, J. F. (2003). Text comprehension processes and hypertext design. In D. Harris, V. Duffy, M. Smith, & C. Stephanidis (Eds), *Human-centred computing: Cognitive, social and ergonomic aspects* (pp. 1303–1307). Mahwah, NJ: Lawrence Erlbaum Associates.

Naumann, A., Waniek, J., & Krems, J. F. (2001). Knowledge acquisition, navigation and eye movements from text and hypertext. In U. -D. Reips & M. Bosnjak (Eds), *Dimensions of internet science* (pp. 293–304). Lengerich: Pabst.

Newell, A. F., & Gregor, P. (2001, July, 4–6). User sensitive inclusive design. *Actes du Colloque Interaction Homme/Machine et Assistance* (pp. 18–20). JIM'2001, Metz.

Nist, S. L., & Simpson, M. L. (1988). The effectiveness and efficiency of training college students to annotate and underline text. *National Reading Conference Yearbook, 37,* 251–257.

Norman, D. A. (1990). *The design of everyday things.* New York: Doubleday.

Norman, D. A., & Shallice, T. (1986). Attention to action: Willed and automatic control of behaviour. In R. J. Davidson, G. E. Schwarts, & D. Shapiro (Eds), *Consciousness and self-regulation: Advances in research and theory* (Vol. 4, pp. 1–18). New York: Plenum.

Nunberg, G. (1990). *The linguistics of punctuation.* Menlo Park, CA: Center for the Study of Language and Information.

Ockerman, J. J., Najjar, L. J., & Thompson, J. C. (1999). Fast: Future technology for today's industry. *Computers in Industry, 38*(1), 53–64.

Ockerman, J. J., & Pritchett, A. R. (1998). *Preliminary study of wearable computers for aviation inspection.* Paper presented at the 1998 International Conference on Human-Computer Interaction in Aeronautics, Montreal, Canada.

Ockerman, J. J., & Pritchett, A. R. (2000). A review and reappriasal of task guidance: Aiding workers in procedure following. *International Journal of Cognitive Ergonomics, 4*(3), 191–212.

Ockerman, J. J., & Pritchett, A. R. (2004). Improving performance on procedural tasks through presentation of locational procedure context: An empirical evaluation. *Behaviour and Information Technology, 23*(1), 11–20.

Ockerman, J. J., & Pritchett, A. R. (submitted). Impact of procedure context on pilot judgments of the accuracy of automatically-generated emergency descent trajectories.

Ockerman, J. J., Thompson, J. C., & Najjar, L. J. (1997). Wearable computer performance support: Initial feasibility study. *Personal Technology, Selected Papers from the First International Symposium on Wearable Computers, 1*(4), 251–259.

O'Donnell, R. D., & Eggemeier, F. T. (1986). Workload assessment methodology. In K. Boff, L. Kaufman, & J. Thomas (Eds), *Handbook of perception and performance* (Vol. II). New York: Wiley.

Office québécois de la langue française. [n.d.]. *Le grand dictionnaire terminologique*, at http://www.granddictionnaire.com

Olive, T., & Piolat, A. (2002). Suppressing visual feedback in written composition: Effects on processing demands and coordination of the writing process. *International Journal of Psychology, 37*(4), 209–218.

Olivesi, S. (2002). *La communication au travail: une critique des nouvelles formes de pouvoir dans les entreprises*. Collection La communication en plus. Saint-Martin-d'Hères, Isère: Presses Universitaires de Grenoble.

Olson, D. R. (1970). Language and thought: Aspects of a cognitive theory of semantics. *Psychological Review, 77*, 257–273.

Omanson, R. C. (1982). The relation between centrality and story category variation. *Journal of Verbal Learning and Verbal Behavior, 21*, 326–337.

O'Reilly, T. (2005). What is Web 2.0: Design patterns and business models for the next generation of software. Retrieved March 5, 2006, from http://www.oreillynet.com/lpt/a/6228.

Otsubo, S. M. (1988). A behavioral study of warning labels for consumer products: Perceived danger and use of pictographs. *Proceedings of the 32nd annual meeting of human factors* (pp. 536–540). Santa Monica, CA: Human Factor Society.

Oulasvirta, A. (2004). Task-processing demands and memory in web interaction: A levels-of processing approach. *Interacting with Computers, 16*(2), 217–241.

Padilla, F., Bajo, M. T., & Macizo, P. (2005). Articulatory suppression in language interpretation: Working Memory capacity, dual tasking and word knowledge. *Bilingualism: Language and Cognition, 8*, 207–219.

Paivio, A. (1986). *Mental representations*. New York: Oxford University Press.

Palinscar, A. S., & Brown, D. A. (1984). Reciprocal teaching of comprehension-fostering and comprehension-monitoring activities. *Cognition and Instruction, 1*, 117–175.

Palmer, E. A., & Degani, A. (1991). *Electronic checklists: Evaluation of two levels of automation*. Paper presented at the Sixth International Symposium on Aviation Psychology. Columbus, OH: Ohio State University.

Pappas, C. C. (1993). Is narrative "primary"? Some insights from kindergartners' pretend readings, stories and information books. *Journal of Reading Behavior, 24*, 97–129.

Parasuraman, R., & Riley, V. (1997). Humans and automation: Use, misuse, disuse, abuse. *Human Factors, 39*(2), 230–253.

Park, J., Jeong, K., & Jung, W. (2005). Identifying cognitive complexity factors affecting the complexity of procedural steps in emergency operating procedures of a nuclear power plant. *Reliability Engineering & System Safety, 89*(2), 121–136.

Park, J., & Jung, W. (2003). The operators' non-compliance behavior to conduct emergency operating procedures — comparing with the work experience and the complexity of procedural steps. *Reliability Engineering & System Safety, 82*(2), 115–131.

Park, O. (1994). Dynamic visual displays in media-based instruction. *Educational Technology, 34*(4), 21–25.

Pascual, E. (1991). *Représentation de l'architecture textuelle et génération de texte* [*Representation of textual architecture and generation of text*]. Doctorat, Université Paul-Sabatier, Toulouse.

Patel, S., Drury, C. G., & Lofgren, J. (1994). Design of workcards for aircraft inspection. *Applied Ergonomics, 25*(5), 283–293.

Patel, V. L., Branch, T., & Arocha, J. A. (2002). Errors in interpreting quantities as procedures: The case of pharmaceutical labels. *International Journal of Medical Informatics, 65,* 193–211.

Pearl, A., & Drury, C. G. (1995). *Improving the reliabilty of maintenance checklists* (No. DOT/FAA/AM-95/xx). Washington, DC: Federal Aviation Administration, Biomedical and Behavior Sciences Division, Office of Aviation Medicine, Department of Transportation.

Pearson, J. (1998). *Terms in context.* Amsterdam: John Benjamins.

Pelegrina, M., & Gallifa, J. (1994). Typical and atypical information as structural categories in the instructional process. *Perceptual and Motor Skills, 79,* 1319–1334.

Pemberton, M. (1995). Rethinking the WAC/writing center connection. *The Writing Center Journal, 15*(2), 116–133.

Perkins, D. N., & Grotzer, T. A. (2000). *Models and moves: Focusing on dimensions of causal complexity to achieve deeper scientific understanding.* Paper presented at the Annual Meeting of the American Educational Research Association, New Orleans, LA.

Péry-Woodley, M. P. (2001). Mode d'organisation et de signalisation dans des textes procéduraux (Organisation and signalling in procedural texts). *Langages, 141,* 28–46.

Péry-Woodley, M. P. (2005). Organisation discursive des textes procéduraux: caractériser des segments naturels pour un accès sélectif. In D. Alamargot, P. Terrier, & J.-M. Cellier (Eds), *Production, compréhension et usage des écrits techniques au travail* (pp. 31–47). Toulouse: Octarès Éditions.

Peskin, J. (1998). Constructing meaning when reading poetry: An expert-novice study. *Cognition and Instruction, 16*(3), 235–263.

Pfister, F. R., & Petrik, J. E. (1980). A heuristic model for creating a writer's audience. *College Composition and Communication, 31,* 213–220.

Piaget, J. (1974a). *La prise de conscience.* Paris: Presses Universitaires de France.

Piaget, J. (1974b). *Réussir et comprendre.* Paris: Presses Universitaires de France.

Piaget, J., & Inhelder, B. (1948). *La représentation de l'espace chez l'enfant.* Paris: Presses Universitaires de France.

Pillet, M. (2004). *Six Sigma: comment l'appliquer.* Paris: Éditions d'organisation.

Piolat, A. (2007). Les avantages et les inconvénients de l'usage d'un traitement de texte pour réviser. In J. Bisaillon (Ed.), *La révision professionnelle: processus, stratégies et pratiques.* Marseille: (pp. 189–211). Québec: Nota bene.

Piolat, A., Roussey, J.-Y., Olive, T., & Farioli, F. (1996). Charge mentale et mobilisation des processus rédactionnels: examen de la procédure de Kellogg. *Psychologie Française, 41*(4), 339–354.

Piolat, A., Roussey, J.-Y., & Thunin, O. (1997). Effect of screen presentation on text reading and revising. *International Journal of Human-Computer Studies, 47,* 565–589.

Poitrenaud, S. (1995). The procope semantic network: An alternative to action grammars. *International Journal of Human-Computer Studies, 42,* 31–69.

Poitrenaud, S., Richard, J.-F., Tijus, C., & Leproux, C. (1992). Analyse de systèmes et aides à l'utilisation [An analysis of technical devices and instructions for their use]. In D. Boullier & M. Legrand (Eds), *Les mots pour le faire* (pp. 97–147). Paris: Editions Descartes.

Pope, A. (1758). *An essay on criticism.* London: Printed for T. Daniel, W. Thompson, and J. Steele, and A. Todd.

Potelle, H., & Rouet, J.-F. (2003). Effects of content representation and readers' prior knowledge on the comprehension of hypertext. *International Journal of Human-Computer Studies, 58,* 327–345.

Power, R., Scott, D., & Bouayad-Agha, N. (2003). Document structure. *Computational Linguistics, 29*(2), 211–260.

Préfontaine, C., & Lecavalier, J. (1996). Analyse de l'intelligibilité de textes prescriptifs [Analysis of the intelligibility of prescriptive texts]. *Revue québécoise de linguistique, 25*(1), 99–144.

Pressley, M., & McCormick, C. B. (1995). *Advanced educational psychology for educators, researchers and policymakers.* New York: Harper Collins College Publishers.

Prince, E. F. (1981). Toward a taxonomy of given-new information. In P. Cole (Ed.), *Radical pragmatics* (pp. 223–255). New York: Academic Press.

Pritchett, A. R. (1999). Pilot performance at collision avoidance during closely spaced parallel approaches. *Air Traffic Control Quarterly, 7*(1), 47–75.

Pritchett, A. R., & Yankosky, L. J. (2003). Pilot-performed in-trail spacing and merging: An experimental study. *Journal of Guidance, Control, and Dynamics, 26*(1), 143–150.

Psoinos, A., & Smithson, S. (2002). Employee empowerment in manufacturing: A study of organisations in the UK. *NewTechnology, Work and Employment, 17*(2), 132–148.

Quathamer, D., & Heineken, E. (2002). Kohärenzbildung beim Lesen Von Texten. Fisheye-Views als kognitive Werkzeuge. [Maintaining global coherence during reading: Fisheye views as cognitive tools] *Zeitschrift für Entwicklungspsychologie und Pädagogische Psychologie, 34*(2), 72–79.

Radvansky, G. A., Zwaan, R. A., Federico, T., & Franklin, N. (1998). Retrieval from temporally organized situation models. *Journal of Experimental Psychology: Learning, Memory and Cognition, 24*, 1224–1237.

Ransom, S., Wu, X., & Schmidt, H. (1997). Disorientation and cognitive overhead in hypertext systems. *International Journal of Artificial Intellligence Tools, 6*(2), 227–253.

Rapp, D. N., & Taylor, H. A. (2004). Interactive dimensions in the construction of mental representations for text. *Journal of Experimental Psychology: Learning, Memory, and Cognition, 30*, 988–1001.

Rasmussen, J. (1985). The role of hierarchical knowledge representation in decision making and system management. *IEEE Transactions on Systems, Man and Cybernetics, 15*, 234–243.

Rayner, K. (1998). Eye movements in reading and information processing: 20 years of research. *Psychological Bulletin, 124*, 372–422.

Read, C. (1981). Writing is not the inverse of reading for young children. In C. H. Frederiksen & J. F. Dominic (Eds), *Writing: The nature, development, and teaching of written communication.* Hillsdale, NJ: Lawrence Erlbaum Associates.

Redcker, G. (1991). Linguistic markers of discourse structure. *Linguistics, 29*, 1139–1172.

Resnick, M., & Wilensky, U. (1998). Diving into complexity: Developing probabilistic decentralized thinking through role-playing activities. *Journal of the Learning Sciences, 7*(2), 153–172.

Rey, A. (1995). *Essays on terminology.* Amsterdam: John Benjamins.

Richard, J. -F. (1990). Compréhension de textes à visée pragmatique. [Understanding procedural texts]. In J. -F. Richard, C. Bonnet, & R. Ghiglione (Eds), *Traité de Psychologie Cognitive 2: Le traitement de l'information symbolique* (pp. 80–92). Paris: Dunod.

Richard, J. -F. (1994). Compréhension de textes de consignes d'action. [Understanding texts including instructions for use]. In R. Ghiglione & J. F. Richard (Eds), *Cours de psychologie, Vol. 3: Champs et théories* (pp. 23–33). Paris: Dunod.

Richard, J. -F. (2002). Compréhension de textes procéduraux et catégorisation. *Psychologie Française, 47*(1), 19–32.

Richard, J. -F., Barcenilla, J., Brie, B., Charmet, E., Clément, E., & Reynard, P. (1993). Le traitement de documents administratifs par des populations de bas niveau de formation. [The processing of administrative forms by poorly educated people]. *Le Travail Humain, 56*, 345–368.

Riondet, O. (1992). L'organisation des connaissances de personnes peu scolarisées lors de l'interrogation de l'annuaire électronique [The organisation of knowledge of people with a low level of instruction when interrogating an electronqiue directory]. In F. Ginsbourger, V. Merle, & G. Vergnaud (Eds), *Formation et apprentissage des adultes peu qualifiés* (pp. 190–192). Paris: La Documentation Française.

Robert, P. (1993). *Le Nouveau Petit Robert, Dictionnaire alphabétique et analogique de la langue française*. Paris: Éditions Le Robert.

Rogers, Y. (1989). Icon design for the user interface. In D. J. Oborne (Ed.), *International Reviews of Ergonomics* (Vol. 2, pp. 129–154). New York: Taylor & Francis.

Roy, R. (2000). Les outils d'aide à la rédaction: une solution aux besoins francophones en matière de rédaction? *Actes du séminaires de Bruxelles des 24 et 25 novembre 1997: La rédaction technique*. Bruxelles: Éditions Duculot (Collection: Champs linguistiques).

Rubin, A. D. (1980). A theoretical taxonomy of the differences between oral and written language. In R. J. Spiro, B. C. Bruce, & W. F. Brewer (Eds), *Theoretical issues in reading comprehension*. Hillsdale, NJ: Lawrence Erlbaum Associates.

Ruiz, C., Paredes, N., Macizo, P., & Bajo, M. T. (2004). *The activation of the target language during reading for translation*. Poster presented at the Vth meeting of the Spanish Society of Experimental Psychology, Madrid, Spain.

Rumelhart, D. E., & Norman, D. A. (1988). Representation in memory. In R. C. Atkinson, R. J. Herrnstein, G. Lindzey, & R. Duncan Luce (Eds), *Steven's handbook of experimental psychology*. New York: Wiley.

Russell, D. R. (1991). *Writing in the academic disciplines, 1870–1990*. Carbondale, IL: Southern Illinois University Press.

Ryle, G. (1949). *The concept of mind*. New York: Barnes & Noble.

Sager, C. (1973). *Improving the quality of written composition through pupil use of rating scale*. Unpublished doctoral dissertation, Boston University School of Education, Boston MA.

Sager, J. C. (1990). *A practical course in terminology processing*. Amsterdam: John Benjamins.

Salmerón, L., Cañas, J. J., Kintsch, W., & Fajardo, I. (2005). Reading strategies and hypertext comprehension. *Discourse Processes, 40*(3), 171–191.

Salmerón, L., Kintsch, W., & Cañas, J. J. (2006). Reading strategies and prior knowledge in learning from hypertext. *Memory & Cognition, 34*(5), 1157–1171.

Salthouse, T. A. (1991). Mediation of adult age differences in cognition by reductions in working memory and speed of processing. *Psychological Science, 2*, 179–183.

Sánchez-Casas, R. M., Davis, C. W., & García-Albea, J. E. (1992). Bilingual lexical processing: Exploring the cognate-noncognate distinction. *European Journal of Cognitive Psychology, 4*, 293–310.

Sanders, T. J. M., & Noordman, L. (2000). The role of coherence relations and their linguistic markers in text processing. *Discourse Processes, 29*(1), 37–60.

Sanders, T. J. M., & Spooren, W. (2001). Text representation as an interface between language and its users. In T. Sanders, J. Schilperoord, & W. Spooren (Eds), *Text representation: Linguistic and psycholinguistic aspects* (pp. 1–28). Amsterdam: John Benjamins.

Sanford, A. J. (1987). *The mind of man: Models of human understanding*. Brighton, England: Yale University Press.

Sanford, A. J., & Garrod, S. C. (1981). *Understanding written language: Explorations in comprehension beyond the sentence*. New York: Wiley.

Santa, J. L. (1977). Spatial transformation of words and pictures. *Journal of Experimental Psychology: Human Learning and Memory, 3*, 418–427.

Scaife, M., & Rogers, Y. (1996). External cognition: How do graphical representations work? *International Journal of Human-Computer Studies, 45*, 185–213.

Scardamalia, M., & Bereiter, C. (1991). Literate expertise. In K. A. Ericsson (Ed.), *Toward a general theory of expertise: Prospects and limits* (pp. 172–194). New York: Cambridge University Press.

Schaeken, W., Johnson-Laird, P. N., & d'Ydewalle, G. (1996). Mental models and temporal reasoning. *Cognition, 60*, 205–234.

Schaie, K. W. (1994). The course of adult intellectual development. *American Psychologist, 49*, 304–313.

Schank, R. C., & Abelson, R. (1977). *Scripts, plans, goals and understanding: An inquiry into human knowledge structures*. Hillsdale, NJ: Lawrence Erlbaum Associates.

Schilperoord, J. (1996). The distribution of pause time in written text production. In G. Rijlaarsdam, H. Van den Bergh, & M. Couzijn (Eds), *Theories, models and methodology in writing research* (pp. 21–35). Amsterdam: Amsterdam University Press.

Schmalhofer, F., & Glavanov, D. (1986). Three components of understanding programmer's manual: Verbatim, propositionnal, and situationnal representations. *Journal of Memory and Language, 25*, 279–294.

Schmidt, R. A., & Bjork, R. A. (1992). New conceptualizations of practice: Common principles in three paradigms suggest new concepts for training. *Psychological Science, 3*, 207–217.

Schneider, B. (2002). Theorizing structure and agency in workplace writing, an ethnomethodological approach. *Journal of Business and Technical Communication, 16*(2), 170–195.

Schneider, W. (1985). Training high-performance skills: Fallacies and guidelines. *Human Factors, 27*(3), 28–300.

Schnotz, W. (2001). Sign systems, technologies, and the acquisition of knowledge. In J-F. Rouet, J. J. Levonen, & A. Biardeau (Eds), *Multimedia learning: Cognitive and instructional issues* (pp. 9–29). London: Pergamon.

Schnotz, W., & Bannert, M. (2003). Construction and interference in learning from multiple representation. *Learning and Instruction, 13*, 141–156.

Schnotz, W., & Lowe, R. K. (2003). External and internal representations in multimedia learning. *Learning and Instruction, 13*, 117–123.

Schriver, K. A. (1992a). Plain language through protocol-aided revision. In E. R. Steinberg (Ed.), *Plain language: Principles and practice* (pp. 148–172). Detroit: Wayne State University Press.

Schriver, K. A. (1992b). Teaching writers to anticipate readers' needs: A classroom-evaluated pedagogy. *Written Communication, 9*(2), 179–208.

Schriver, K. A. (1997). *Dynamics in document design*. New York: Wiley.

Schutte, P. C., & Trujillo, A. C. (1996). *Flight crew task management in non-normal situations*. In Human Factors and Ergonomics Society 40th Annual Meeting Proceedings (pp. 244–248). Santa Monica, CA: HFES.

Schwan, S., & Riempp, R. (2004). The cognitive benefits of interactive videos: Learning to tie nautical knots. *Learning and Instruction, 14*, 293–357.

Schwartz, D. L., & Black, J. B. (1996). Analog imagery in mental model reasoning: Depictive models. *Cognitive Psychology, 30*, 154–219.

Schwartz, D. L., & Hegarty, M. (1996). Coordinating multiple representations for reasoning about mechanical devices. In P. Olivier (Ed.), *Cognitive and computational models of spatial representation*, Technical Report SS-96-03. Menlo Park, CA: AAAI Press.

Scott, D., Delin, J., & Hartley, A. (1998). Identifying congruent pragmatic relations in procedural texts. *Languages in Contrast, 1*(1), 45–82.

Searle, J. R. (1969). *Speech acts: An essay in the philosophy of language*. Cambridge: Cambridge University Press.

Seleskovitch, D. (1976). Interpretation: A psychological approach to translating. In R. W. Brislin (Ed.), *Translation: Applications and research* (pp. 92–116). New York: Gardner.

Shanahan, T. (1984). Nature of the reading-writing relation: An exploratory multivariate analysis. *Journal of Educational Psychology, 76*, 466–477.

Shanahan, T., & Lomax, R. G. (1986). An analysis and comparison of theoretical models of the reading-writing relationship. *Journal of Educational Psychology, 78*, 116–123.

Shanahan, T., & Lomax, R. G. (1988). A developmental comparison of three theoretical models of the reading-writing relationship. *Research in the Teaching of English, 22*(2), 196–212.

Shapiro, A. M. (1998). Promoting active learning: The role of system structure in learning from hypertext. *Human-Computer Interaction, 13*, 1–35.

Shapiro, A. M. (2000). The effect of interactive overviews on the development of conceptual structure in novices learning from hypermedia. *Journal of Educational Multimedia and Hypermedia, 9*, 57–78.

Shapiro, A. M., & Niederhauser, D. (2004). Learning from hypertext. Research issues and findings. In D. H. Jonassen (Ed.), *Handbook of research on educational communications and technology* (2nd ed., pp. 605–620). Mahwah, NJ: Lawrence Erlbaum Associates.

Shreve, G. M., & Diamond, B. J. (1997). Cognitive processes in translation and interpreting: Critical issues. In H. J. Danks, G. M. Shreve, S. B. Fountain, & M. K. McBeath (Eds), *Cognitive processes in translation and interpreting* (pp. 120–136). Thousand Oak, CA: Sage.

Silver, N. C. L., & Wogalter, M. S. (1991). Pest-control products: Hazards perception, product type and label characteristics. *Proceedings of the human factors society 35th annual meeting* (pp. 106–110). Santa Monica, CA: Human Factors Society.

Sims, V. K., & Hegarty, M. (1997). Mental animation in the visual-spatial sketchpad: Evidence from dual-task studies. *Memory and Cognition, 25*, 321–333.

Skuce, D., & Meyer, I. (1991). Terminology and knowledge engineering: Exploring a symbiotic relationship. *In proceedings of the 6th international workshop on knowledge acquisition for knowledge-based systems* (pp. 29-1–29-21). University of Calgary, Canada: SRDG Publications.

Smeltzer, L. R., & Thomas, G. F. (1994). Managers as writers, a meta-analysis of research in context. *Journal of Business and Technical Communication, 8*(2), 186–211.

Smillie, R. J. (1985). Design strategies for job performance aids. In T. M. Duffy & R. Waller (Eds), *Designing usable texts* (pp. 213, 243). London: Academic Press Inc.

Smith, E. E., & Goodman, L. (1984). Understanding written instructions: The role of an explanatory schema. *Cognition and Instruction, 1*(4), 359–396.

Sommers, N. (1980). Revision strategies of student writers and experienced adult writers. *College Composition and Communication, 31*(4), 378–388.

Speer, N., & Zacks, J. M. (2005). Temporal changes as event boundaries: Processing and memory consequences of narrative time shifts. *Journal of Memory and Language, 53*, 125–140.

Sperber, D., & Wilson, D. (1989). *La pertinence*. Paris: Éditions de minuit (Published in English as *Relevance: Communication and Cognition*. Cambridge, MA: Harvard University Press).

Spilich, G. J., Vesonder, G. T., Chiesi, H. L., & Voss, J. F. (1979). Text processing of domain-related information for individuals with high and low domain knowledge. *Journal of Verbal Learning and Verbal Behavior, 18*(3), 275–290.

Spinuzzi, C. (2002). Documentation, participatory citizenship, and the web: The potential of open systems. *ACM SIGDOC 2002 Conference Proceedings* (pp. 194–199). New York: ACM.

Spinuzzi, C., Bowie, J. L., Rodgers, I., & Li, X. (2003). Open systems and citizenship: Designing a departmental web site as an open system. *Computers and Composition, 20*(2), 168–193.

Spinuzzi, C., & Zachry, M. (2000). Genre ecologies: An open-system approach to understanding and constructing documentation. *ACM Journal of Computer Documentation, 24*, 169–181.

Spiro, R. J., Coulson, R., Feltovich, P. J., & Anderson, D. (1988). Cognitive flexibility theory: Advanced knowledge acquisition in ill-structured domains. *Proceedings of the 10th annual conference of the cognitive science society*. Hillsdale, NJ: Lawrence Erlbaum Associates.

Spivey, N. N., & King, J. R. (1989). Readers as writers composing from sources. *Reading Research Quarterly, 24*(1), 7–26.

Spyridakis, J. H. (1989a). Signaling effects: A review of the research–Part I. *Journal of Technical Writing and Communication, 19*(3), 227–240.

Spyridakis, J. H. (1989b). Signaling effects: Increased content retention and new answers–Part II. *Journal of Technical Writing and Communication, 19*(4), 395–415.

Stanfield, R. A., & Zwaan, R. A. (2001). The effect of implied orientation derived from verbal context on picture recognition. *Psychological Science, 12,* 153–156.

Stanovich, K. E. (1990). Concepts in developmental theories of reading skill: Cognitive resources, automaticity, and modularity. *Developmental Review, 10*(1), 72–100.

Starke-Meyerring, D. (2005). Meeting the challenges of globalization: A framework for global literacies in professional communication programs. *Journal of Business and Technical Communication, 19,* 468–499.

Sticht, T. G. (1977). Comprehending reading at work. In M. A. Just & P. A. Carpenter (Eds), *Cognitive processes in comprehension*. Hillsdale, NJ: Lawrence Erlbaum Associates.

Sticht, T. G. (1985). Understanding readers and their uses of texts. In T. M. Duffy & R. Waller (Eds), *Designing usable texts* (pp. 315, 340). London: Academic Press Inc.

Storrer, A. (2002). Coherence in text and hypertext. *Document Design, 3*(2), 157–168.

Strunk, W. (2000). *The elements of style*. Boston, MS: Allyn & Bacon.

Swales, J. M. (1990). *Genre analysis, English in academic and research settings*. Cambridge: Cambridge University Press.

Swaney, J. H., Janik, C. J., Bond, S. J., & Hayes, J. R. (1991). Editing for comprehension: Improving the process through reading protocols. In E. R. Steinberg (Ed.), *Plain language: Principles and practice* (pp. 173–186). Detroit, MI: Wayne State University Press.

Swezey, R. W. (1987). Design of job aids and procedure writing. In G. Salvendy (Ed.), *Handbook of human factors* (pp. 1039–1057). New York: Wiley.

Szlichcinski, K. P. (1980). The syntax of pictorial instructions. In P. A. Kolers, M. E. Wrolstad, & H. Bouma (Eds), *Processing of visible language* (Vol. 2, pp. 113–124). New York: Plenum Press.

Tapiero, I., & Otero, J. (1999). Distinguishing between textbase and situation model in the processing of inconsistent information: Elaboration versus tagging. In H. Van Oostendorp & S. R. Goldman (Eds), *The construction of mental representation during reading* (pp. 341–365). Hillsdale, NJ: Lawrence Erlbaum Associates.

Tapiero, I., Van den Broek, P., & Quintana, M. -P. (2002). The mental representation of narrative texts as networks: The role of necessity and sufficiency on the detection of four types of causal textual relations. *Discourse Processes, 34*(3), 237–258.

Tapscott, D., & Ticoll, D. (2003). *The naked corporation: How the age of transparency will revolutionize business*. New York: Free Press.

Tardieu, H., & Gyselinck, V. (2002). Working memory constraints in the integration and comprehension of information in a multimedia context. In H. Van Oostendorp (Ed.), *Cognition in a digital world*. Mahwah, NJ: Lawrence Erlbaum Associates.

Taylor, H. A., & Tversky, B. (1992). Spatial mental models derived from survey and route descriptions. *Journal of Memory and Language, 31,* 262–292.

Technorati (2006, April 17). *The state of the blogosphere*. Retrieved April 17, 2006, from http://technorati.com/weblog/2006/04/96.html.

Terrier, P., Lemercier, C., Cellier, J. -M., & Mojahid, M. (2004). Text format and the enactment effect in an assembly task. (Poster presentation at the 28th International Congress of Psychology. Beijing, 8–13th Aug.)

Teufel, S., & Moens, M. (1999). Argumentative classification of extracted sentences as a first step towards flexible abstracting. In I. Mani & M. Maybury (Eds), *Advances in automatic text summarization*. Cambridge, MA: MIT Press.

Thatcher, A., Mahlangu, S., & Zimmerman, C. (2006). Accessibility of ATMS for the functionally illiterate through icon-based interfaces. *Behaviour & Information Technology, 25,* 65–81.

The College Board College Handbook (44th ed.). (2006). Plano, TX: College Board Publications.

Therriault, D. J., & Raney, G. E. (2002). The representation and comprehension of place-on-the-page and text-sequence memory. *Scientific Studies of Reading, 6*(2), 117–134.

Thomas, D. L. (1995). *Integrated maintenance information system (imis): User field demonstration and test.* Technical Report No. AL/TR-1995-0034. Dayton, OH: Armstrong Laboratories, Wright-Patterson Air Force Base.

Thompson, S. A. (1985). Grammar and written discourse: Initial vs. final purpose clauses in English. *Text, 5*(1–2), 55–84.

Tierney, R. J., Carter, M. A., & Desai, L. E. (1991). *Portfolio assessment in the reading-writing classroom.* Norwood, MA: Christopher-Gordon.

Tijus, C. (2001). Contextual categorization and cognitive phenomena. In V. Akman, P. Bouquet, R. Thomason, & R. A. Young (Eds), *Modeling and using context* (pp. 316–329). Berlin: Springer-Verlag.

Tijus, C., Barcenilla, J., Cambon de Lavalette, B., Lambinet, L., & Lacaste, A. (2005). Conception, compréhension et usages de l'information iconique véhiculée par les pictogrammes [Conception, understanding and the use of iconic information in pictograms]. In D. Alamargot, P. Terrier, & J. -M. Cellier (Eds), *Production, compréhension et usages des écrits techniques au travail*. Toulouse: Octares.

Tijus, C., Chêne, D., Jadot, F., Leproux, C., Poitrenaud, S., & Richard, J. -F. (2001). Taxonomies pour la signalétique: de la signalisation routière aux I.H.M [Taxonomies for signaletics: From road signs to HMI]. In B. Cambon de Lavalette, J. Doré, & C. Tijus (Eds), *La signalétique: Conception, validation, usages* (pp. 79–92). Paris: Collections de l'INRETS.

Tijus, C., Poitrenaud, S., & Richard, J. -F. (1996). Propriétés, objets, procédures: les réseaux sémantiques d'action appliqués à la représentation des dispositifs techniques. [Properties, objects, procedures: The PROCOPE semantic network model applied to the representation of technical devices]. *Le Travail Humain, 59,* 209–229.

Todorov, T. (1984). *Mikhail Bakhtin: The dialogical principle* (translated by Wlad Godzich). Minneapolis: University of Minnesota Press.

Torrance, M., & Bouayad-Agha, N. (2001). Rhetorical structure analysis as a method for understanding writing processes. In L. Degand, Y. Bestgen, W. Spooren, & L. V. Waves (Eds), *Multidisciplinary Approaches to Discourse* (pp. 51–59). Amsterdam: Amsterdam & Nodus Publications.

Torrance, M., & Galbraith, D. (2006). The processing demands of writing. In C. MacArthur, S. Graham, & J. Fitzgerald (Eds), *Handbook of writing research* (pp. 67–82). New York: Guilford Publishers.

Tower, C. (2003). Genre development and elementary student's informational writing: A review of the literature. *Reading Research and Instruction, 42*(4), 14–39.

Townsend, D. J. (1997). Processing clauses and their relationships during comprehension. In J. Costermans & M. Fayol (Eds), *Processing interclausal relationships — studies in the production and comprehension of text* (pp. 265–282). London: Lawrence Erlbaum Associates.

Trabasso, T., & Magliano, J. P. (1996). Conscious understanding during text comprehension. *Discourse Processes, 21,* 255–288.

Trabasso, T., Secco, T., & Van den Broek, P. W. (1984). Causal cohesion and story coherence. In H. Mandl, N. L. Stein, & T. Trabasso (Eds), *Learning and comprehension of text.* Hillsdale, NJ: Lawrence Erlbaum Associates.

Trabasso, T., & Van den Broek, P. W. (1985). Causal thinking and the representation of narrative events. *Journal of Memory and Language, 24*(5), 612–630.

Trabasso, T., Van den Broek, P. W., & Sue, S. Y. (1989). Logical necessity and transitivity of causal relations in stories. *Discourse Processes, 12,* 1–25.

Tremblay, M., & Simard, G. (2005). La mobilisation du personnel: l'art d'établir un climat d'échanges favorable basé sur la réciprocité. *Gestion, 30*(2), 60–68.

Triggs, T., & Harris, W. (1982). Reaction time of drivers to road stimuli. *Human Factors Report No. HFR-12,* ISBN 0 86746 147 0.

Trosborg, A. (2000). *Analysing professional genres.* Amsterdam: John Benjamins.

Turcot, G., & Coltier, D. (1988). Des agents doubles de l'organisation textuelle, les marqueurs d'intégration linéaire [Double agents of textual organisation, markers of linear integration]. *Pratiques, 57*, 57–79.

Turkle, S. (1997). *Life on the screen: Identity in the age of the internet*. New York: Touchstone.

Turner, M. L., & Engle, R. W. (1989). Is working memory capacity task dependent? *Journal of Memory and Language, 28*(2), 127–154.

Tversky, B. (1991). Spatial mental models. In G. H. Bower (Ed.), *The psychology of learning and motivation: Advances in research and theory* (Vol. 27, pp. 109–145). N.Y.: Academic Press.

Tversky, B., Bauer Morrison, J., & Bétrancourt, M. (2002). Animation: Can it facilitate? *International Journal of Human-Computer Studies, 57*(4), 247–262.

Unz, D. C., & Hesse, F. W. (1999). The use of hypertext for learning. *Journal of Educational Computing Research, 20*(3), 279–295.

Van den Broek, P. W. (1990). Causal inferences and the comprehension of narrative text. In A. C. Graesser & G. H. Bower (Eds), *Inferences and text comprehension* (pp. 175–196). San Diego, CA: Academic Press.

Van den Broek, P. W., & Lorch, R. F. (1993). Network representations of causal relations in memory for narrative texts: Evidence from primed recognition. *Discourse Processes, 16*, 75–98.

Van der Geest, T. (2006). Conducting usability studies with users who are elderly or have disabilities. *Technical Communication, 53*, 14–22.

Van Dijk, T. A., & Kintsch, W. (1983). *Strategies of discourse comprehension*. New York: Academic Press.

Van Hees, M. M. W. (1996). User instructions for the elderly: What the literature tells us. *Journal of Technical Writing and Communication, 26*(4), 521–536.

Van Oostendorp, H. (1996). Updating situation models derived from newspaper articles. *Medienpsychologie, 8*, 21–33.

Vander Linden, K., & Martin, J. H. (1995). Expressing rhetorical relations in instructional text: A case study of the purpose relation. *Computational Linguistics, 21*(1), 29–58.

Vanderdorpe, C. (1999). *Du papyrus à l'hypertexte. Essai sur les mutations du texte et de la lecture* [*From papyrus to hypertext. Essay on changes in text and reading*]. Montréal: Boréal.

Vanderheiden, G. C. (2000). Fundamental principles and priority setting for universal usability. *Proceedings ACM conference on universal usability*. Washington (DC), November 2000.

Vermersch, P. (1985). Données d'observation sur l'utilisation d'une consigne écrite: L'atomisation de l'action. [Observed data about the use of written instructions: The action atomization]. *Le Travail Humain, 48*, 161–172.

Veyrac, H. (2001). Aperçu de la variété des fonctions des consignes dans le monde du travail. *Pratiques, Les textes de consignes, 111–112*, 65–92.

Veyrac, H., Cellier, J.-M., & Bertrand, A. (1997). Modèle de l'opérateur et modèle du prescripteur. Le cas des consignes de résolution de situations incidentelles pour les conducteurs de trains. [Operator's model and instruction writer's model: The example of train drivers' instructions for dealing with incident situations]. *Le Travail Humain, 60*(4), 387–407.

Vezin, J. F. (1984). Apport informationnel des schémas dans l'apprentissage [Informational support of schematas in learning]. *Le Travail Humain, 47*(1), 61–74.

Virbel, J. (1985). Langage et métalangage dans le texte du point de vue de l'édition en informatique textuelle [Language and metalanguage in text, from the perspective of text-based computing]. *Cahiers de Grammaire, 10*, 5–72.

Virbel, J. (1989). The contribution of linguistic knowledge to the interpretation of text structures. In J. André, V. Quint, & R. K. Furuta (Eds), *Structured documents* (pp. 161–181). Cambridge: Cambridge University Press.

Virbel, J. (1999). Contributions de la théorie des actes du langage à une taxonomie des consignes. In J. Virbel, J.-M. Cellier, & J.-L. Nespoulous (Eds), *Cognition, Discours procédural, Action* (pp. 1–44). Toulouse: PRESCOT.

Virtanen, T. (1992a). *Discourse functions of adverbial placement in English*. Åbo: Åbo Akademi University Press.

Virtanen, T. (1992b). Given and new information in adverbials: Clause initial adverbials of time and place. *Journal of Pragmatics, 17*(2), 99–117.

Voss, J. F., Vesonder, G. T., & Spilich, G. J. (1980). Text generation and recall by high-knowledge and low-knowledge individuals. *Journal of Verbal Learning and Verbal Behavior, 19*(6), 651–667.

Walker, C. H., & Meyer, B. J. F. (1980). Integrating different types of information in text. *Journal of Verbal Learning and Verbal Behavior, 19*, 263–275.

Walker, J. (2003, August, 22). Final version of weblog definition. Retrieved February 10, 2006, from http://huminf.uib.no/~jill/archives/blog_theorising/final_version_of_weblog_definition.html.

Walker, M., Joshi, A., & Prince, E. F. (Eds). (1998). *Centering theory in discourse*. Oxford: Clarendon Press.

Wallace, D. L., & Hayes, J. R. (1991). Redefining revision for freshmen. *Research in the Teaching of English, 25*, 54–66.

Wallace, D. L., Hayes, J. R., Hatch, J. A., Miller, W., Moser, G., & Silk, C. M. (1996). Better revision in eight minutes? Prompting first-year college writers to revise globally. *Journal of Educational Psychology, 88*(4), 682–688.

Waniek, J., Brunstein, A., Naumann, A., & Krems, J. F. (2003). Interaction between text structure representation and situation model in hypertext reading. *Swiss Journal of Psychology. Special Issue: Studying the Internet: A Challenge for Modern Psychology, 62*, 103–111.

Warren, T. L. (1993). Three approaches to reader analysis. *Technical Communication, 40*(1), 81–88.

Waters, G. S., & Caplan, D. (1996). Processing resource capacity and the comprehension of garden path sentences. *Memory and Cognition, 24*, 342–355.

Weaver, C. A., & Kintsch, W. (1991). Expository text. In R. Barr, M. Kamil, P. Mosenthal, & P. Pearson (Eds), *The handbook of reading research* (Vol. 2, pp. 230–245). White Plains, NY: Longman.

Wenger, M. J., & Payne, D. G. (1996). Comprehension and retention of nonlinear text: Considerations of working memory and material-appropriate processing. *American Journal of Psychology, 109*(1), 93–130.

Wikipedia. (2006, April 19). *Blog*. Retrieved 25 April, 2006, from http://en.wikipedia.org/wiki/Blog.

Wilensky, U., & Resnick, M. (1999). Thinking in levels: A dynamic systems approach to making sense of the world. *Journal of Science Education and Technology, 8*, 3–19.

Wilkinson, A., Barnsley, G., Hanna, P., & Swan, M. (1980). *Assessing language development*. Oxford: Oxford University Press.

Wilkinson, R., Cary, J., Barr, N., & Reynolds, J. (1997). Comprehension of pesticide safety information: Effects of pictorial and textual warnings. *International Journal of Pest Management, 43*, 239–245.

Wils, T., Labelle, C., Guérin, G., & Tremblay, M. (1998). Qu'est-ce que la mobilisation des employés? *Gestion, 23*(2), 30–39.

Winn, W. D. (1993). An account of how readers search for information in diagrams. *Contemporary Educational Psychology, 18*, 162–185.

Wogalter, M. S., Allison, S., & McKenna, N. A. (1989). Effects of cost and social influence on warning compliance. *Human Factors, 31*(2), 133–140.

Wogalter, M. S., Wolff, J. S., Magurno, A. M., & Kohake, J. R. (1994). Iterative test and development of pharmaceutical pictorials. *Ergonomics and Design, IEA '94, 4*, 360–362.

Wolff, J. S., & Wogalter, M. S. (1998). Comprehension of pictorial symbols: Effects of context and test method. *Human Factors, 40*(2), 173–186.

Wood, S. (1996). High commitment management and unionization in the UK. *International Journal of Human Resource Management, 7*(1), 41–58.

Wright, P. (1977). Presenting technical information: A survey of research findings. *Instructional Science, 6*, 93–134.

Wright, P. (1981). The instructions clearly state...Can't people read? *Applied Ergonomics, 12*(3), 131–141.

Wright, P. (1999). Printed Instructions: Can research make difference? In H. Zwaga, T. Boersema, & H. Hoonout (Eds), *Visual information for everyday use* (pp. 45–66). London: Taylor & Francis.

Wright, P., Creighton, P., & Threllfall, S. M. (1982). Some factors determining when instructions will be read. *Ergonomics, 25*(3), 225–237.

Wright, P., Pocock, S., & Fields, B. (1998). *The prescription and practice of work on the flight deck.* Paper presented at the Ninth European Conference on Cognitive Ergonomics, Rocquencourt, France.

Young, R. E., & Gordon, J. (1995). Mellon College of Science Faculty Survey of Student Writing Abilities. March, 10. Unpublished Manuscript.

Zach, S. E. (1980). *Control room operating procedures: Content and format.* In Human Factors and Ergonomics Society 41st Annual Meeting Proceedings (pp. 444–447). Santa Monica, CA: HFES.

Zacks, J. M., & Tversky, B. (2003). Structuring information interfaces for procedural learning. *Journal of Experimental Psychology: Applied, 9*, 88–100.

Zacks, J. M., Tversky, B., & Iyer, G. (2001). Perceiving, remembering, and communicating structure in events. *Journal of Experimental Psychology: General, 130*(1), 29–58.

Zeitz, C. M., & Spoher, K. T. (1989). Knowledge organization and the acquisition of procedural expertise. *Applied Cognitive Psychology, 3*, 313–336.

Zwaan, R. A. (1999). Situation models: The mental leap into imagined worlds. *Current Directions in Psychological Science, 8*(1), 15–18.

Zwaan, R. A. (2004). The immersed experiencer: Toward an embodied theory of language comprehension. In B. H. Ross (Ed.), *The psychology of learning and motivation* (Vol. 44, pp. 35–62). New York: Academic Press.

Zwaan, R. A., Langston, M. C., & Graesser, A. C. (1995). The construction of situation models in narrative comprehension: An event-indexing model. *Psychological Science, 6*(5), 292–297.

Zwaan, R. A., Magliano, J. P., & Graesser, A. C. (1995). Dimensions of situation model construction in narrative comprehension. *Journal of Experimental Psychology: Learning, Memory and Cognition, 21*(2), 386–397.

Zwaan, R. A., & Radvansky, G. A. (1998). Situation models in language comprehension and memory. *Psychological Bulletin, 123*(2), 162–185.

Zwaan, R. A., & Van Oostendorp, H. (1993). Do readers construct spatial representations in naturalistic story comprehension? *Discourse Processes, 16*, 125–143.

Zwaga, H., & Easterby, R. S. (1984). Developing effective symbols for public information. In R. Easterby & H. Zwaga (Eds), *Information design: The design and evaluation of signs and printed material* (pp. 277–297). New York: Wiley.

Author Index

Abelson, R., 161, 165
Adam, J. -M., 34–35, 46
Adams, A., 27
Adams, D., 59
Agrifoglio, M., 204
Alamargot, D., 62, 64, 66, 70, 74
Albers, M. J., 108
Alexander, G. J., 21
Al-Janahi, A., 21
Allal, L., 71, 75, 109
Allen, P., 14
Allen, T. M., 21
Allison, S., 56–57
Allwood, C. M., 60
Al-Madani, H., 21
Alonso, M. A., 171
Ambrogi, V., 20
Amerine, R., 52, 56
Ammer, J. J., 108
Andersen, C., 104
Anderson, A., 171
Anderson, D., 212
Anderson, J. R., 22, 60, 66, 97–98, 112
Anderson, P. V., 78, 239
Anderson, R. B., 239
Anderson, V., 69
Andersson, B., 74
Anglin, G. J., 236
Anis, J., 38
Antonietti, A., 213
Arcand, R., 39
Arend, U., 19
Ariel, M., 11
Armour, S., 135
Arocha, J. A., 53

Auque, Y., 31
Averous, B., 21

Babcock, R. A., 52
Baddeley, A., 65, 67
Baecker, R., 22
Baggett, W. B., 251, 253
Bahtia, V. K., 8
Bajo, M. T., 196–200, 202–204
Balcytiene, A., 211, 213
Balota, D. A., 173, 200
Bamberg, M., 100
Bannert, M., 233
Barbaro, M., 137
Barcenilla, J., 21–22, 24, 27, 29,
    51, 53, 56–57, 59
Barclay, J. R., 181
Barik, H. C., 194
Barnsley, G., 100–101
Barr, N., 22
Barsalou, L. W., 164, 167, 168, 181
Bartlett, E. J., 121
Bateman, J., 13–14
Baudet, S., 164
Bauer Morrison, J., 235, 253, 255
Bazerman, C., 69
Beaudet, C., 35, 141
Beltran, F. S., 31
Bennett, S., 50
Bereiter, C., 62, 63, 64, 66, 67, 68, 74
Berkenkotter, C., 75
Bernardini, C., 20
Berners-Lee, T., 128, 132
Bertrand, A., 54, 56, 146
Bestgen, Y., 13, 171
Bétrancourt, M., 235, 253, 255

Bieger, G. R., 232
Bilhaut, F., 16
Billingham, J., 76, 78
Bilmes, J., 52, 56
Birkmire, D. P., 178, 188–189
Bisaillon, J., 89–91
Bjork, R. A., 69, 183, 190
Black, J. B., 173, 251
Blanchard, J., 70
Blood, R., 126, 129, 130, 131, 132, 133
Bodner, R., 22
Bolger, F., 100–102
Bond, S. J., 60
Bonus, S., 126, 133
Borowsky, A., 21
Boswell, J., 69
Bouayad-Agha, N., 13–14
Boucheix, J. -M., 53
Bourbeau, N., 39
Boutet, J., xiv
Bovair, S., 97, 232
Bower, G. H., 169, 173
Bowie, J. L., 131
Boyle, C. F., 112
Branch, T., 53
Brangier, E., 53, 57, 59
Bransford, J. D., 177, 181, 190–191
Brant, D., 140
Breetvelt, I., 67
Brie, B., 53
Briggs, L. J., 111
Brinkerhoff, J. D., 208
Britton, B. K., 75
Britton, J., 73
Bromberg, M., 29
Bronckart, J. P., 37
Brown, A. L., 69–70
Brown, D. A., 72
Brown, J. S., 111–112
Brun, J. -P., 144
Brunstein, A., 208, 211, 214
Brusilovsky, P., 215
Buehler, M. F., 80
Bunzo, M. S., 227–228
Bush, P. J., 24

Bush, V., 213
Butterfield, E. C., 77
Byrne, M. D., 19

Cabré, M. -T., 5
Caccamise, D. J., 67
Cailliès, S., 187
Calcaterra, A., 213
Cambon de Lavalette, B., 22, 24, 29
Cameron, C. A., 100–102
Campbell, A., 62
Cañas, J. J., 191, 214
Caplan, D., 199
Carey, L., 63, 71, 76–78, 82, 84, 108
Cariglia-Bull, T., 98
Carley, K. M., 129
Carlson, B. W., 70
Carpenter, P. A., 65, 161, 194
Carriedo, N., 171
Carroll, J. M., 57, 227
Carter, M. A., 108
Carullo, J. J., 52, 56
Carver, C., 244
Cary, J., 22
Cate, C., 253
Catrambone, R., 53, 220
Cave, C. B., 98
Cellier, J. -M., 38, 54, 56, 146, 186, 188
Celuch, K. G., 52, 56
Chabaud, S., 98
Chafe, W. L., 10
Chandrasekaran, B., 251
Chanquoy, L., 62, 66, 70, 71, 75, 109
Chapman, M. L., 96
Charmet, E., 53
Charnois, T., 16
Charolles, M., 12, 34, 37
Charron, S., 223, 227–228
Chen, C., 205, 214
Chen, S. Y., 213
Chêne, D., 17, 28
Chesnet, D., 74
Chi, M. T. H., 247, 249
Chiesi, H. L., 67
Chiu, M., 249

Christ, R. E., 19
Chrysler, S. T., 181
Chumbley, J. I., 200
Chuy, M., 62, 70
Cirilo, R., 187
Clancey, W., 4
Clark, H. H., 11
Clark, L. F., 173
Clément, E., 53
Clerc, I., 38
Cocude, M., 169
Coirier, P., 38
Coiron, M., xv
Collins, A. M., 66
Collins, A., 111–112
Collins, B. L., 23
Collins, K. W., 52, 56
Coltier, D., 34
Condamines, A., 6–7
Conger, J. A., 156
Conklin, J., 214
Converse, S. A., 220, 227–228
Cooper, M., 50
Corker, K. M., 227–228
Cornish, F., 8
Corso, G., 19
Coté, N. C., 190
Cottereau, A., xiv
Coulsen, R. L., 244, 248
Coulson, R., 212
Covill, A., 65
Creighton, P., 52
Cross, R. T., 19
Cruse, D. A., 6

d'Ydewalle, G., 172
Dahl, J., 74
Dahlbäck, N., 214
Dale, E., 119
Damasio, A. R., 167
Daniellou, F., 143, 145, 156
Danks, J. H., 195, 199
Dansac, C., 64, 74
Darden, D., 244
Davies, S., 19

Daviet, J. -P., xiv
Davis, C. W., 195
Davison, A., 11
Dawson-Saunders, B. K., 244, 248
Day, J. D., 69–70
De Brito, G., xiii
De Bruyn, E., 197
De Groot, A. M. B., 194, 197, 200
De Jong, T., 208
De Montmollin, M., 143
Dean, A. L., 98
deBrito, G., 222, 225
Degand, L., 13
Degani, A., 54, 217–218, 222
DeGroff, L. J. C., 67
Delany, P., 213
DeLeeuw, N., 249
Delin, J., 11–14
Denhière, G., 187
Denis, C., 186
Denis, M., 169, 235
Desai, L. E., 108
Deutsch, C., 135
Dewar, R. E., 23
Di Eugenio, B., 12
Diamond, B. J., 193
Diaz, P., 213
Diehl, M., 53
Diehl, V. A., 178–180, 182, 187–189
Dijkstra, A., 197
Dillinger, M., 201
Dillon, A., 205, 209
DiPalo, C. A., 219
DiVesta, F. J., 186
Dixon, P., 53
Doane, S. M., 59
Dodsworth, P., 100–102
Doheny-Farina, S., 140
Donovan, C. A., 96, 100
Dowse, R., 20
Droste, F. G., 26
Drury, C. G., 217–218, 221–222
Dubois, D., 21
Duggan, G. B., 52, 180–183, 190
Duguid, P., 111

Dunn, J. C., 181
Duraffourg, J., 143, 145, 156
Dusen, L., 75

Easterby, R. S., 19–20, 28
Eberhart, I., xiii
Edworthy, J., 27
Eggemeier, F. T., 208
Ehlers, M. S., 20
Einstein, G. O., 177, 182, 190–191
Eklundh, K. S., 80, 86
Elbow, P., 65, 73
Elens, E., 197
Ells, J. G., 23
Elm, W. C., 220, 227
Engelkamp, J., 182
Engle, R. W., 52, 56, 65
Enjalbert, P., 16
Enlund, H., 24
Ericsson, K. A., 67, 214
Estopa, R., 5
Evans, S., 134

Fabbro, F., 195
Fajardo, I., 191, 214
Falzon, P., 144
Fardella, G., 20
Farioli, F., 65
Farnham-Diggory, S., 112
Farrell, R., 112
Fayol, M., 50, 56, 105–106, 183–184
Federico, T., 171
Feltovich, P. J., 212, 244, 248
Fernandez, A., 171
Fernbach, N., 39
Ferrari, M., 247
Fields, B., 225–226
Fillietaz, L., 143–144
Finn, J. D., 62
Firth, J. R., 8
Fischer, S., 241
Fitzgerald, J., 71
Fletcher, C. R., 181
Fleury, D., 21

Flower, L. S., 62–67, 71, 73–74, 76–78, 82, 84, 108, 140
Foley, W. A., 11
Foltz, P. W., 207, 208, 209, 210, 211, 213
Ford, N., 213
Foss, D., 187
Fraenkel, B., 156
François, J., 161
Franklin, N., 170–171
Franks, J. J., 177, 181, 190–191
Frantz, J. P., xiii
Frase, L. T., 52
Frausin, T., 92
Freedman, A., 96, 100
Freitas, P., 239
Fries, P. H., 11

Gabbard, R., 205, 209
Gagne, R., 111
Galbraith, D., 66, 73
Gallifa, J., 31
Ganier, F., 50, 52, 58–60, 78, 105–106, 140, 183
Gaonac'h, D., 38, 70
García-Albea, J. E., 195
Garcia-Debanc, C., 14
Garcia-Mila, M., 104
Garrod, S. C., 161, 165, 171
Gathercole, S., 67
Geiger, J. F., 179, 181, 189–190
Gellert, E., 248
Gentner, D., 249
Georget, P., 29
Gerloff, P., 193
Gernsbacher, M. A., 161, 163, 166, 168, 171
Gerver, D., 195, 197
Gibson, J. J., 25
Gilbert, J. K., 213
Gile, D., 194, 196–197, 199, 204
Glavanov, D., 59, 181, 189
Glenberg, A. M., 164–167, 171–172, 179, 181–182
Glock, M. D., 232
Glynn, S. M., 75

Goldman, A. I., 12
Goldman-Eisler, F., 198, 200
Gombert, J. -E., 50, 105
Gomez-Gonzàlez, M. -A., 10, 11
Goodman, L., 225
Goodman, P. C., 219
Gordon, J., 107–108
Gordon, P. C., 250
Gowers, G., 45
Graesser, A. C., 164–165, 169, 171, 173–174, 201–202, 210, 248, 251, 253
Graff, M. G., 213
Grandaty, M., 14
Graves, D. H., 108
Gray-Wilson, S., 170
Green, D. W., 203
Greenspan, S., 169
Gregor, P., 55
Griffin, J. A., 108
Griffin, J., 195, 199
Grosjean, F., 203
Grosjean, M., xv
Grosz, B. J., 11
Grote, B., 13
Grotzer, T. A., 248
Gruber, T. R., 5
Guérin, F., 143, 145, 156
Guérin, G., 139
Gulgöz, S., 75
Gundel, J. K., 11
Gurak, L., 128–130, 132
Guthrie, J. T., 50, 182, 186
Gyselinck, V., 214

Haber, R. N., 23
Haberlandt, K. F., 202
Hacker, D. J., 64, 72, 77
Haenggi, D., 163
Haigh, R., 52
Haines, H., 19
Hakiel, S. R., 28
Hameen-Anttila, K., 24
Hanna, P., 100–101
Hansen, S. R., 254

Harmon, L. D., 26
Harris, B., 193
Harris, W., 21
Hartley, A., 11–13
Hartley, J., 60
Hartsuiker, R., 197
Hasse, D., 223
Hatch, J. A., 63, 72, 90, 114, 121
Haviland, S. E., 11
Hayes, J. R., 60, 62–67, 71–74, 76–78, 82, 84, 90, 108–109, 114, 118, 121, 140, 185
Hearst, M. A., 6
Hedberg, N., 11
Hegarty, M., 52, 56, 105, 232, 236, 239, 248–251, 253–254, 258
Heineken, E., 77, 208
Helaha, D., 197
Helyar, P. S., 58
Hendrick, R., 250
Henry, A., 155
Herring, S. C., 126, 133
Hesse, F. W., 206, 209–210
Heurley, L., 50, 58–60, 78, 140
Hidalgo, A. J., 173
Hidi, S. E., 69
Higelé, P., 53
Hillocks, G., 109–110, 112
Hinton, G. E., 66
Hirtle, S. C., 206
Hitch, G. J., 65, 67
Hmelo, C. E., 248
Hmelo-Silver, C. E., 248
Hoecker, D. G., 227–228
Hofman, R., 207, 209
Holmkvist, K., 74
Holmquist, S., 250, 258
Holsanova, J., 74
Holton, D. L., 248
Honold, L., 156
Höök, K., 214
Horton, W., 23
Hoyne, S. H., 65
Hudson, J. A., 96, 101
Hunt, R. R., 177, 182, 184, 190–191

Hutchins, E., 225
Hyland, K., 46
Hyona, J., 70

Inhelder, B., 98
Inman, W. E., 186
Irwin, J. W., 186
Iyer, G., 187, 255

Jacko, J. A., 229
Jacobson, M. J., 248
Jadot, F., 17, 28–29
Janik, C. J., 60
Janssen, D., 63, 74
Jebar, A. H., 20
Jeffroy, F., 223, 227–228
Jeong, K., 221
Johansson, V., 74
Johnson, S. T., 62
Johnson-Laird, P. N., 161, 163–164, 166–170, 172–173, 232
Jonassen, D. H., 213
Jones, R. S., 69–70
Jordan, M. P., 41
Joshi, A., 11
Julesz, B., 26
Jung, W., 221–222
Just, M. A., 52, 56, 65, 105, 161, 199
Juvina, I., 214

Kaakinen, J. K., 70
Kaestle, C. F., 62
Kalen, T., 60
Kallman, D. A., 52
Kamberelis, G., 96, 100
Kanungo, R. N., 156
Karlsson, H., 74
Karmiloff-Smith, A., 95, 98–102
Kaufer, D. S., 62–63, 67, 71, 73, 129
Keller, D., 108
Kellogg, R. T., 67, 72, 74
Kemppainen, K., 24
Kerguelen, A., 143, 145, 156
Kern, R. P., 56, 58–59
Kerr, S., 78

Kieras, D. E., 97, 232
Kim, H., 206
King, J. R., 70
King, J., 199
King, L. E., 23
Kintsch, E., 179, 190, 207, 210, 253
Kintsch, W., 64, 67, 97, 161–164, 166, 168, 171, 177–179, 181, 183, 187–191, 201, 207, 209–211, 214, 249, 253
Kirlik, A., 222
Kirsner, K., 181
Klein, J. D., 208
Kline, D. W., 51
Klusewitz, M., 186
Knapp, P., 20
Knobel, M., 132, 136, 138
Knott, A., 13
Kobayashi, K., 70
Kohake, J. R., 20, 31
Kolers, P. A., 23
Kollberg, P., 80, 86
Kolodner, J. L., 248
Koroghlanian, C. M., 208
Kosslyn, S. M., 98
Kozminsky, E., 162
Kramer, D. C., 162
Krems, J. F., 208, 211, 214
Kriz, S., 253
Kroll, B. M., 100–101
Kroll, J. F., 195, 197
Kruley, P., 171
Kulikowich, J. M., 210–211

La Heij, W., 197
Labasse, B., 35
Labelle, C., 139
Lacaste, A., 22, 24, 29
Lachance, G., 78
Lacoste, M., xv
Laflamme, C., 76
Lambinet, L., 22, 24, 29
Lambrecht, K., 11
Lamonde, F., 143
Landauer, T. K., 207, 209

Landry, S. J., 229
Langston, M. C., 164–165, 171, 174
Langston, W. E., 162, 171
Lankshear, C., 132, 136, 138
Lapeyrière, S., 144
Largy, P., 65, 71, 75, 109
Larkin, J. H., 235
Laughery, R., 228
LaVancher, C., 249
Laville, A., 143, 145, 156
Lawless, K. A., 210–211
Le Draoulec, A., 12
Lecavalier, J., 36
Lee, J. D., 223
Lee, K., 100–102
Lee, L., 125
LeFevre, J. -A., 53
Lefèvre, N., 13
Lehto, M. R., 23
Leirer, V. O., 54
Lemercier, C., 188
Lempers, J. D., 100
Leplat, J., 140, 145
Leproux, C., 17, 28–29, 60
Lerner, N. D., 23
Levelt, J. M. W., 235
Levie, W. H., 236
Levy, B. A., 71
Levy, C. M., 38
Li, X., 131
Liben, L., 214
Lin, H. X., 145
Lindgren, E., 71
Lipner, M. H., 227–228
Lofgren, J., 218, 221
Loftus, E. F., 66
Loman, N. L., 185–186
Lomax, R. G., 64
Lorch, E. P., 185–186, 234
Lorch, R. F., 70, 173, 183, 185–186, 234
Lovelace, E. R., 164
Lowe, R. K., 233, 235–239, 241–242, 248
Luc, C., 13–14
Lumbelli, L., 92
Lunenfeld, H., 21

Lust, J. A., 52, 56
Lyons, J., 6

Macaulay, D., 257
Machamer, P., 244
Macizo, P., 196–204
Mack, R. L., 57
Mackie, J. L., 173
MacRedie, R., 213
Madrid, R. I., 214
Magee, J. M., 75
Magliano, J. P., 165, 169, 210
Magurno, A. M., 20, 31
Mahlangu, S., 20
Maingueneau, D., 37
Mandel, T. S., 162
Mander, R., 22
Mani, I., 16
Mann, W. C., 13
Mannes, S. M., 162, 178
Marcu, D., 13, 16
Marcus, N., 50
Mariné, C., 53
Marja, A., 24
Market Sentinel, 126
Markham, L., 71
Markman, E. M., 72
Marsden, P., 217, 219, 222, 228
Martí, E., 102
Martin, J. H., 13
Mathet, Y., 16
Matsuhashi, A., 68, 73
Maybury, M., 16
Mayer, R. E., 105, 185–186, 239, 255
Mazeau, M., 146, 155
Mazet, C., 21
McCarthy, J. C., 221–222, 225
McClelland, J. L., 66
McCormick, C. B., 97
McCutchen, D., 65, 67–68, 78
McDaniel, M. A., 177, 190–191
McDonald, J., 194
McDonald, S., 213
McDougall, S. J., 22, 24
McGinley, W., 70

McKenna, N. A., 56–57
McNamara, D. S., 59, 179, 190, 207, 210, 253
McNamara, T. P., 170
Meunier, J. G., 25–26
Meyer, B. J. F., 183, 185–186, 188
Meyer, I., 5–7
Mikkelson, V., 70
Mikulecky, L. J., 62
Mildes, K., 65
Miller, A. N., 197
Miller, C., 126, 132–133
Miller, G. A., 164
Miller, W., 63, 72, 90, 114, 121
Millis, K. K., 179, 181, 189–190
Mills, C. B., 178–180, 182, 187–189
Minel, J. -L., 16
Minzoni-Déroche, A., 156
Mitchell, D. C., 199
Mitchell, R., 39
Miyake, A., 196
Moens, M., 16
Mojahid, M., 14, 188
Molinari, G., 164
Moltzen, E. F., 136
Monk, A. F., 221–222, 225
Monkam-Daverat, I., 155
Montreuil, S., 143
Moran, M. H., 91
Moray, N., 223
Moreno, R., 239, 250, 258
Morrell, R. W., 54
Morris, C. D., 177, 190–191
Morrow, D. G., 54, 169–170
Mosenthal, P., 182, 186
Moser, G., 63, 72, 90, 114, 121
Mosier, K. L., 217
Motoda, H., 250–251, 253
Mou, L. C., 178, 189
Muir, B. M., 223
Munt, R., 236
Murray, D. M., 73
Muthig, K. -P., 19
Myers, B. L 23
Myers, J. L., 173

Najjar, L. J., 219–220, 228
Narayanan, N. H., 232, 239, 248–251, 253–254, 258
Nas, G. L. J., 200
Nash, J. G., 70
Naumann, A., 208, 211, 214
Newell, A. F., 55
Newell, S., 71
Newman, S. E., 112
Niederhauser, D., 208–209, 212
Nist, S. L., 70
Noordman, L., 13
Norman, D. A., 17, 29, 55, 97, 163, 172, 196
Norris, B., 19
Nunberg, G., 13–14

O'Brien, E. J., 173
O'Donnell, R. D., 208
O'Reilly, T., 127, 130
O'Rourke, J., 119
Ockerman, J. J., 183, 191, 217, 219–220, 228–229
Olive, T., 65, 71
Olivesi, S., 140
Olson, D. R., 23
Omanson, R. C., 173
Onalytica, 126
Otero, J., 163, 173
Otsubo, S. M., 18, 20
Oulasvirta, A., 206
Owen, P. D., 190

Padilla, F., 198, 203–204
Padilla, P., 198
Paivio, A., 23
Palinscar, A. S., 72
Palmer, E. A., 217–218
Pandey, I., 108
Paoletti, G., 92
Papagno, C., 67
Pappas, C. C., 100
Parasuraman, R., 223
Paredes, N., 197, 200
Park, D. C., 54

Park, J., 221–222
Park, O., 235
Parmet, Y., 21
Pascual, E., 34
Passerault, J. -M., 38, 70
Patel, S., 218, 221
Patel, V. L., 53, 214
Payne, D. G., 206, 214
Payne, S. J., 52, 180–183, 190
Pearl, A., 217, 221–222
Pearson, J., 5
Pedersen, A., 108
Pelegrina, M., 31
Pemberton, M., 108
Perkins, D. N., 248
Peroli, L. C., 20
Persensky, J., 228
Péry-Woodley, M. -P., xvii, 3, 12, 14, 34, 37
Peskin, J., 67
Petrik, J. E., 90
Pfeffer, M. G., 248
Pfister, F. R., 90
Piaget, J., 98
Pillet, M., 145
Piolat, A., 65, 71, 85–86, 89, 93
Plato, C. C., 52
Plumb, C., 77
Pocock, S., 225–226
Poitrenaud, S., 17, 28–29, 57, 60
Poon, L. W., 54, 185
Pope, A., 68
Potelle, H., 207
Power, R., 14
Prabhu, P., 218, 221
Pramono, H., 235, 242
Préfontaine, C., 36, 77
Pressley, M., 97–98
Price, S. J., 20
Prince, E. F., 11
Pritchett, A. R., 183, 191, 217, 220, 223–224, 229
Provost, D. A., 98
Psoinos, A., 156
Pulver, C. J., 186

Quathamer, D., 77, 208
Quilici, J., 250, 258
Quintana, M. -P., 173

Rada, R., 205, 214
Radvansky, G. A., 165, 169–171, 182
Raney, G. E., 185
Ransdell, S., 38, 213
Rapp, D. N., 169
Rasmussen, J., 244
Rayner, K., 74
Raynor, D. K., 20
Read, C., 64
Rebeyrolle, J., 7
Redeker, G., 13
Reiser, B., 112
Resnick, M., 247–248
Revaz, F., 34
Rey, A., 5
Reynard, P., 53
Reynolds, J., 22
Rice, G. E., 186
Richard, J. -F., 17, 28, 52–53, 56–57, 60, 183–184
Riempp, R., 239
Riha, J. R., 201
Rijlaarsdam, G., 67
Riley, V., 223
Rinck, M., 170
Riondet, O., 53
Robert, P. (1993)
Robertson, D. A., 167, 179, 182
Robertson, S. P., 164
Rodgers, I., 131
Rogers, Y., 27, 233
Rojo, N., 104
Rondhuis, K. J., 13
Ros, C., 74
Roth, E. M., 227–228
Rouet, J. -F., 207
Roussey, J. -Y., 65, 86, 89
Roy, R., 140
Rubin, A. D., 64
Ruiz, C., 197, 200
Rumelhart, D. E., 66, 97, 163, 172

Russell, D. R., 108
Ryle, G., 97

Sager, C., 109
Sager, J. C., 5
Salmerón, L., 191, 214
Salthouse, T. A., 51–52
Salvendy, G., 145
Sánchez-Casas, R. M., 195
Sanders, T. J. M., 9, 13
Sanford, A. J., 161, 165, 171
Santa, J. L., 23
Sarac, A., 221
Sarda, L., 12
Scaife, M., 233
Scardamalia, M., 62–64, 64, 66–68, 74
Schaeken, W., 172
Schaie, K. W., 51, 53
Schank, R. C., 161, 165
Scheidt, L. A., 126, 133
Scherzer, E., 98
Schilperoord, J., 68
Schmalhofer, F., 59, 181, 189
Schmidt, H., 213
Schmidt, R. A., 183, 190
Schneider, B., 140
Schneider, W., 111–112
Schnotz, W., 233–234
Schriver, K. A., 54, 63, 71, 76–78, 82, 84, 108, 110, 112, 114
Schumacher, G. M., 70
Schutte, P. C., 223
Schwan, S., 239, 241
Schwartz, D. L., 251
Scialfa, C. T., 51
Scott, D., 11–14
Scott, J. L., 210
Searle, J. R., 36
Secco, T., 173
Seleskovitch, D., 195
Shah, P., 196
Shallice, T., 196
Shanahan, T., 64
Shapiro, A. M., 208–209, 212
Shapiro, L. R., 96, 101

Shepherd, D., 126, 132–133
Shinar, D., 21
Showers, L. S., 52, 56
Shreve, G. M., 193
Sidner, C. L., 11
Silk, C. M., 63, 72, 90, 114, 121
Silver, N. C. L., 54
Simard, G., 139
Simon, H. A., 235
Simpson, M. L., 70
Sims, V. K., 251
Sjölinder, M., 214
Skinner, C., 108
Skuce, D., 5
Small, I., 22
Smeltzer, L. R., 140
Smillie, R. J., 59
Smith, E. E., 225
Smithson, S., 156
Snyder, J., 71
Sohn, Y. W., 59
Sommers, N., 71, 85
Songer, N. B., 179, 190, 207, 210, 253
Souza, A. P., 213
Speer, N., 171
Sperber, D., 78, 83
Spilich, G. J., 67
Spinuzzi, C., 131
Spiro, R. J., 212, 244, 248
Spivey, N. N., 70
Spoher, K. T., 98
Spooren, W., 9
Spyridakis, J. H., 183–185
Stanfield, R. A., 167
Stanovich, K. E., 65
Starke-Meyerring, D., 130
Stevens, A., 249
Stevenson, R. J., 213
Stewart, E., 195
Sticht, T. G., 54
Storrer, A., 207–208
Stratman, J. F., 63, 71, 76–78, 82, 84, 108
Stromqvist, S., 74
Strunk, W., 71
Sue, S. Y., 173–174

Sullivan, K. P. H., 71
Suwa, M., 250–251, 253
Swales, J. M., 8, 35
Swan, M., 100–101
Swaney, J. H., 60
Sweller, J., 50
Swezey, R. W., 224
Swinehart, D. M., 164
Szlichcinski, K. P., 26

Tantaros, S., 102
Tapiero, I., 163–164, 173, 187
Tapscott, D., 125, 133, 137
Tardieu, H., 214
Taylor, H. A., 169
Terrier, P., 186, 188
Teufel, S., 16
Thatcher, A., 20
Therriault, D. J., 185
Thévenot, L., xiv
Thomas, D. L., 221
Thomas, G. F., 140
Thompson, J. C., 219–220, 228
Thompson, S. A., 10, 13
Threllfall, S. M., 52
Thunin, O., 86, 89
Ticoll, D., 125, 133, 137
Tierney, R. J., 108
Tijus, C., 17, 21–22, 24–25, 27–29, 57, 60
Timmins, K., 71
Tiraltri, M., 20
Tobin, J. D., 52
Todorov, T., 8
Torrance, M., 13, 66
Tower, C., 96, 100
Towers, R. L., 236
Townsend, D. J., 13
Toyofuku, M., 173
Trabasso, T., 161, 173–174, 187, 210
Tremblay, M., 139
Triggs, T., 21
Trosborg, A., 9
Trujillo, A. C., 223
Tufvesson, S., 74
Turcot, G., 34

Turkle, S., 132
Turner, M. L., 65
Tversky, B., 169–170, 186–187, 232, 235, 253, 255

Underwood, J., 213
Unz, D. C., 206, 209–210

Van den Bergh, H., 63, 67, 74
Van den Broek, P. W., 161, 173–174, 187
Van der Geest, T., 52
Van der Hulst, A., 208
Van Dijk, T. A., 64, 161–162, 164, 166, 168, 177–178, 183, 188–189, 207, 214
Van Hees, M. M. W., 51–52, 54
Van Heuven, W. J. B., 197
Van Oostendorp, H., 162, 170, 207, 209, 214
Van Valin Jr., R. D., 11
Van Waes, L., 63, 74
Vander Linden, K., 13
Vanderdorpe, C., 40
Vanderheiden, G. C., 55
Vermersch, P., 52, 182–183
Vesonder, G. T., 67
Veyrac, H., 54, 56, 146, 186
Vezin, J. F., 23
Virbel, J., 13–14, 34, 185
Virtanen, T., 11–12
Vivaldi, J., 5
Von Gierke, S. M., 98
Vonk, W., 171
Voss, J. F., 67

Walker, C. H., 188
Walker, J., 126
Walker, M., 11, 126, 188
Wallace, D. L., 63, 72, 90, 114, 121
Wandmacher, J., 19
Waniek, J., 208, 211, 214
Warren, T. L., 91
Waters, G. S., 199
Watts, L. A., 221–222, 225
Weaver, C. A., 201

Weber, S., 50
Welsch, D. M., 181
Wengelin, A., 74
Wenger, M. J., 206, 214
Wiemer-Hastings, K., 181
Wiener, E. L., 54, 222
Wilensky, U., 247–248
Wilkinson, A., 100–101
Wilkinson, R., 22
Willis, S. L., 53
Wils, T., 139
Wilson, D., 78, 83
Wilson, J. R., 19
Winn, W. D., 236
Wogalter, M. S., 20, 24, 31, 54, 56–57
Wolff, J. S., 20, 24, 31
Wood, S., 139
Woods, D. D., 220, 227

Wright, E., 126, 133
Wright, P. C., 221–222, 225
Wright, P., 50, 52, 183, 225–226
Wu, X., 213

Yankosky, L. J., 224
Young, R. E., 107–108

Zach, S. E., 222
Zacharski, R., 11
Zachry, M., 131
Zacks, J. M., 171, 186–187, 232, 255
Zeitz, C. M., 98
Zimmerman, C., 20
Zimny, S., 181
Zwaan, R. A., 164–165, 167, 169–171, 174, 181–182
Zwaga, H., 19–20

Subject Index

Acquisition, 96–100, 207, 210, 211, 212, 214, 239
Action, 227–228, 246, 247, 250, 255
Adult, 53, 70, 95, 96, 101, 102, 103, 104
Affordant, 49, 51, 55, 57, 164, 167, 175, 179
Analogy, 43, 57, 161, 166, 238
Animation, 22–23, 231–232, 235, 236–242, 248, 251–257
Argument-, 25, 37
Assessment, 116–123, 184–185, 218
Attention-, 11–12, 18, 38, 39, 51, 65, 72, 75, 77, 80, 83, 90, 91, 98, 99, 100, 106, 111, 125, 127, 132, 133, 141, 151, 156, 166, 170, 171, 174, 178, 179, 180, 181, 196, 199, 208, 213, 236, 237, 238, 239, 240, 241, 242, 253, 255, 257
Audience, 46, 64, 66, 69, 71, 95, 100, 102, 106, 111, 113, 114–115, 116, 117, 118, 119, 131, 136, 185
Authoring, 4, 130

Bilingual-, 81, 193, 195, 197, 198, 203
Blog-, 125–137
Businesses, 126, 127, 128, 133–137, 140

Categorization, 18, 19, 24–25
Child-, 24, 51, 52, 59, 95–105, 178
Chunking, 180, 190
Clarity, 33, 35, 42, 44, 45, 46, 78, 79, 80, 83, 88, 110, 113, 114
Client, 61, 76, 77, 78, 80, 82, 84, 85, 86, 114, 144, 145, 148, 149, 150, 154
Cognition, 164, 167, 181, 187, 214, 251
Coherence, 3, 9, 10, 12, 16, 34, 37–40, 41–43, 44, 46, 58, 64, 80, 162, 166, 168, 169, 171, 187, 189, 191, 205, 207, 209, 210, 211, 212, 213, 255
Communicat-, 5, 11, 26, 35, 36, 46, 75, 76, 77, 78, 79, 80, 83, 86, 90, 91, 93, 95, 107, 123, 125, 126, 128–129, 130, 131, 132, 133, 134–135, 136, 139, 156, 184, 205, 220, 225, 231
Company, 4, 125, 127, 134, 135, 136, 137, 139, 140, 141, 143, 144, 145, 148, 149, 151, 152, 153, 222
Competence, 13, 99, 101, 102, 193
Compos-, 8, 61–73, 100, 109, 110
Comprehen-, 9, 11, 13, 14–15, 17, 18, 19, 20, 22, 24, 29, 31, 34, 36, 38, 45, 52, 53, 56, 57, 62, 63, 64, 65, 68, 69, 70, 71, 72, 75, 76, 77, 78, 81, 82, 88, 89, 92, 126, 140, 151–152, 153, 156, 157, 161–174, 177, 181, 182, 183, 184, 185, 187, 189, 190, 191, 193–202, 205–215, 231, 233, 237, 241, 242, 243, 244, 247–251, 252, 253, 254, 255, 256, 257, 258
Computational, 8, 13, 250–251
Computer, 7, 16, 17, 22, 27, 29, 54, 60, 65, 80, 81, 86, 87, 88, 89, 90, 112, 128, 150, 231, 243, 249, 251
Concept-, 6, 7, 15, 27, 40, 43, 44, 53, 66, 71, 98, 106, 108, 128, 132, 141, 142–144, 156, 164, 166, 167, 168, 179, 180, 181, 183, 195, 219, 224, 239, 251, 252
Consciousness, 10, 98, 100, 106
Constraint, 97, 98, 100, 101, 163, 229, 235
Context, 11, 14, 15, 19, 20, 21, 22, 23, 24, 25, 26, 31, 35, 36, 50, 54, 55–56, 58, 67, 73, 75, 78, 82, 125, 126, 127–133, 139–154, 184, 185, 186,

Context (*Contd.*) 187, 188, 191, 205, 217–229, 242, 250, 253, 254, 255, 256
Control, 20, 51, 55, 72, 97, 98, 101, 110, 135, 198, 200, 206, 211, 212, 221, 222, 225, 226, 237, 238, 239, 240, 242, 248, 249, 253, 254
Corrections, 77, 80, 86, 87, 88, 89, 90, 92
Culture, 140, 141, 156
Curriculum, 108, 110
Customer, 126, 127, 130, 134, 135, 136

Demand-, 43, 65, 97, 100, 134, 145, 173, 201, 202, 236, 237
Depiction, 236, 237, 238, 240, 241, 242
Description, 13, 23, 34, 37, 40–41, 98, 96–100, 101, 147, 169, 172, 189, 224, 233, 244, 252, 254
Designer, 31, 127, 135, 152, 207, 224, 225, 232, 233, 234, 241, 242, 243, 244, 249, 251, 258
Development-, 4, 5–6, 11, 15, 16, 39, 43, 51, 58–59, 95, 96–100, 107, 108, 126, 128, 135, 140, 148, 149, 156, 178, 186, 217, 231, 237, 244, 251, 254
Device, 10, 11, 14, 46, 51, 55, 56, 59, 60, 95, 97, 98, 103, 104, 126, 177–191
Diagram, 52, 56, 97, 98, 100, 153, 240–241, 249, 250, 251, 252, 256
Difficult-, 4, 6, 18, 19, 21, 23, 24, 49, 50, 52, 53, 54, 56, 57, 71, 72, 73, 74, 75, 78, 89, 95, 96, 97, 98, 100, 101, 102, 103, 140, 141, 143, 152, 153, 162, 164, 179, 183, 184, 185, 187, 190, 202, 218, 222, 225, 243, 244, 247–249, 251, 252, 253, 254
Discourse, 3, 9, 10, 11, 12, 13, 14, 16, 33, 34, 35, 36, 37, 38, 39, 40, 45, 57, 64, 101, 125, 131, 132, 133, 135, 142, 161, 162, 163, 165, 166, 168, 173, 181, 193, 194, 195, 197, 201–202, 207, 249, 250
Documentation, 4–6, 9, 59, 153, 218, 231–242
 administrative documents, xi

 digitised documents, 15
 drafting documents, xiii, 149
 electronic documents, xiv, 54, 55, 89, 231
 house documents, xii
 internal documents, xii
 legal documents, xiii, xiv
 multimedia documents, xviii, 243, 244, 249, 251, 252, 254, 255, 256, 257
 private documents, xii
 procedural documents, xiii, xv, xvi, 49, 50–58, 95, 191
 professional documents, xi, xv, 11, 95, 96, 102, 105, 106
 source documents, 61, 69, 70
 technical documents, xi, xii, xv, xviii, 3–16, 56, 59, 60, 95, 145, 243, 244, 258
 written documents, xi–xviii, 16, 95, 96, 186, 218, 235
Drafts, xi, xii, xiii, xiv, 33, 34, 35, 36, 42, 44, 45, 73, 95, 109, 110, 149, 150, 152, 153
Drawings, 23, 27, 53, 97, 98, 100, 102, 147, 148, 152
Dynamics, 134, 225, 231, 233, 235, 236, 239, 241

Edit-, xvi, 22, 60, 62, 65, 75–92, 109
Educational, 20, 123, 249, 255
Electronic-, xiv, 54, 55, 80, 89, 208, 217, 219, 224, 231, 232
Email, 73, 129, 149
Employee, 127, 134–135, 143, 146, 147, 148, 150, 151, 152, 153
Employer, 43, 137
Enactment effect, 181, 182, 188, 189
Engineer-, 3, 4, 5, 9, 14–16, 107–123, 127, 221, 243, 258
Environment, 24, 25, 31, 54, 62, 81, 90, 92, 97, 105, 133, 138, 139, 141, 169, 170, 209, 218, 219, 222, 225, 226, 234, 247
Ergonomics, 17, 143, 144, 145, 156, 206

Errors, 31, 62, 65, 71, 72, 76, 78, 80, 82, 86, 88, 89, 90, 91, 112, 145, 180, 183, 195, 218, 221, 227, 229, 231
Evaluat-, 18, 27–29, 61, 62, 63, 64, 65, 71, 72, 73, 82, 93, 109, 111, 121, 229
Events, 23, 39, 53, 65, 96, 133, 161, 162, 164–165, 167, 168, 169, 171, 172, 173, 226, 235, 245, 246, 248, 250, 253, 254, 255, 256, 257
Examining, 33, 35, 84, 197, 210, 211, 218
Exercise, 91, 114, 115, 116, 120
Experiment, 22, 52, 57, 81, 106, 149, 172, 180, 188, 189, 198, 208, 209, 210, 211, 212, 214, 229, 257
Expert-, xi, xvi, 7, 22, 53, 59, 61, 62, 63, 64, 66, 67, 68, 73, 75, 78, 81, 96, 98, 100, 101, 114, 117, 118, 128, 145, 151, 156, 183, 190, 204, 218, 220–221, 224, 225, 228, 248, 252
Explanation, xvii, 35, 52, 68, 99, 100, 167, 182, 185, 187, 217, 235, 237, 241, 251, 253
Eye fixations, 70
Eye-tracking, 74

Feedback, xvi, 51, 57, 59–60, 107, 109, 110, 111, 112, 113, 114, 116, 117, 121, 152, 154, 218
Figurative, 18, 27, 103, 170
Formats, 98, 100, 103, 104, 129, 175, 231, 232
Formulation, 35, 58, 161, 194, 195, 196, 197, 199, 204, 224
Functional, xiii, xvi, 11, 20, 25, 28, 34, 55, 81, 98, 103, 128, 139–154, 162, 241, 242, 249

Generating, 61, 66, 67, 68, 73, 156, 168, 236
Genre, 3, 7–9, 15, 16, 38, 44–45, 69, 78, 83, 93, 96, 100, 126, 130, 131, 132
Goal, xi, xv, 4, 5, 7, 15, 29, 39, 56, 58, 59, 62, 63, 64, 65, 66, 67, 68, 69, 72, 73, 77, 80, 82, 96, 101, 109, 162, 166, 170, 173, 174, 178, 187, 189, 190, 191, 200, 204, 208, 209, 210, 214, 221, 223, 224, 225, 228, 241
Government, 81, 123, 134, 140, 153
Grammar-, 6, 10, 14, 15, 16, 25, 37, 76, 77, 78, 80, 88, 107, 179, 204
Graphic-, xviii, 13, 14, 15, 21, 37, 46, 65, 71, 91, 104, 214, 235, 236, 237, 240, 241, 242, 252
Guide-, xvi, 4, 9, 12, 13, 36, 45, 57, 58, 64, 69, 90, 96, 183, 186, 191, 208, 217–229, 234, 240, 242, 243, 257

Hypermedia, xvi, 214, 251
Hypertext, xvii, 127, 171, 191, 205–215, 232

Iconic, 17, 18, 19, 23, 25, 26, 167
Illustration, xii, 55, 139, 222, 235, 236
Image, 17, 18, 23, 24, 27, 28, 29, 50, 58, 155, 163, 167, 213, 214
Industr-, 55, 61, 123, 127, 134, 139–154, 218, 219, 221
Institutions, xvi, 123, 133, 134, 155
Instruction-, xi, xvi, 11, 12, 13, 14, 21, 34, 35, 44, 55, 56, 72, 96, 97, 103, 104, 105, 107, 108, 111, 112, 113, 114, 116, 117, 122, 123, 125, 138, 139, 146, 147, 149, 150, 152, 155, 170, 182, 226, 227, 239
Intelligibility, 33–45
Intentions, 11, 14, 20, 185
Interest, 4, 14, 36, 39, 44, 126, 127, 140, 211, 212, 218, 244
Interference, 23, 74, 91, 196, 197, 198, 199, 208
Internet, 17, 45, 61, 81, 125, 127, 128, 129, 130, 131, 132, 136

Keystroke, 74, 129

Learner, 97, 98, 209, 249, 250
Legal, xi, xiii, xiv, 18, 33–45
Legislative, 33, 36
Lexical, 3–16, 34, 181, 193, 194, 195, 196, 197, 198, 199, 200, 201, 214

Linguist-, 5, 6, 8, 9, 11, 13, 15, 17, 26
Literacy, 18, 19, 20, 62, 64, 73

Machine, 28, 55, 129, 148, 251, 252, 256
Macroplanning, 64, 68
Macrostructure-, 36, 64, 68, 69, 70, 178, 184, 191
Manage-, 3, 4–9, 61, 76, 108, 134–135, 139, 140, 141, 144, 145, 146, 148, 149, 152, 154, 155, 156, 206, 208–209, 222
Manuals, 71, 131, 147, 222
Manufacturing, 139, 140, 141, 144, 148, 149, 150, 153
Mark-, 3–16, 33, 34, 35, 37, 38, 40, 42, 44, 46, 101, 103, 104, 105, 106, 122, 171, 182, 188, 191
Meaning, xi, 10, 12, 18, 19, 21, 22, 23, 24, 25, 26, 28, 31, 34, 35, 36, 37, 39, 40, 46, 62, 63, 81, 82, 83, 88, 89, 91, 161, 163, 196, 197, 198, 224
Measuring, 53, 105, 140, 210, 211
Media-, 55, 57, 69, 82, 102, 103, 125, 126, 127, 128, 129, 130, 133, 135, 136, 137, 152, 155, 166, 171, 172, 214
Memory-, 23, 38, 50, 51, 52, 53, 54, 56, 61, 62, 63, 64, 65–69, 97, 98, 100, 146, 156, 161, 164, 165, 166, 168, 170, 173, 177, 178, 181, 182, 183, 184, 185, 186, 187, 188, 190, 191, 193, 194, 197, 204, 206, 213, 214, 217, 218, 219, 220, 227, 237, 248, 250
Metadiscourse, 46
Metatextual, 33, 35, 39
Microstructure-, 64, 68
Model
   cognitive model, 243, 244, 251, 253, 254, 255, 257, 258
   conceptual model, 167
   Construction-Integration model, 249
   Event Indexing model, 164, 165, 171
   mental model, 98, 161, 162, 163, 172, 213, 232, 233, 234, 236, 238, 243, 244, 248, 249, 250–251, 252, 253, 256, 257
   physical model, 167
   referential model, 188
   situation model, xvii, 64, 161, 162, 163, 164, 165, 166, 168, 169, 170, 171, 172, 173, 175, 177, 178, 179, 180, 181, 182, 183, 189, 190, 203, 207, 209, 210, 211
   spatial model, 170
   temporal model, 173
Monitoring, 58, 72, 152, 154
Multidisciplinary, 114, 157
Multimedia, 214, 243–258

Narrat-, 25, 96, 100, 101, 164, 165, 173, 177, 178, 184, 187, 188, 189, 190, 201, 202, 239, 252, 255, 257

Ontologies, 5, 18, 29, 31
Operators, 143, 144, 221, 222, 224
Organization, 19, 29, 33, 34, 35, 37, 39, 44, 80, 83, 89, 90, 91, 95, 98, 101, 103, 106, 109, 110, 112, 123, 137, 140, 141, 144, 145, 148, 155, 166, 177, 186, 187, 201, 222, 224, 247
Orthographic, 71, 198, 252

Paragraph, 37, 39, 68, 80, 82, 83, 84, 93, 186, 201, 202
Percept-, 21, 25, 51, 143, 164, 167, 168, 173, 181, 182, 194, 198, 199, 203, 213, 222, 223, 236, 238, 239, 240, 241, 242
Perform-, 21, 22, 24, 25, 29, 55, 57, 58, 59, 60, 67, 77, 83, 95, 97, 98, 99, 100, 101, 123, 134, 143, 144, 145, 146, 154, 177, 178, 179, 180, 181, 182, 185, 189, 190, 197, 198, 202, 208, 209, 211, 214, 217–229, 232, 236
Phonolog-, 71, 196, 198, 200
Phrase, 63, 68, 83, 152, 182, 186, 194, 195, 252
Physiological, 51, 53, 143, 247
Pictogram, 17–32
Picture, 19, 25, 26, 135, 141, 172, 239, 240, 255

Subject Index 313

Planning, 58, 61, 62, 64, 65, 66, 67, 68, 70, 71, 72, 73, 74, 93, 144, 148, 149, 150, 208
Policies, 125, 131, 135, 155, 222
Practic-, 10, 42, 51, 54–55, 67, 74, 78, 81, 89, 91, 96, 97, 98, 107, 109, 110, 111, 112–113, 114, 116, 121, 123, 126, 127, 133, 134, 135, 136, 137, 140, 143, 145, 150–151, 152, 178, 181, 183, 190, 198, 218, 232, 235, 240, 241, 242, 243, 244, 258
Procedu-, 11, 22, 33–45, 49–59, 78, 91, 95–105, 177–190, 217–229, 231–242
Processing, 85–89, 152–154, 188–190, 197–202, 237–238
  cognitive processes, 23–25, 61–73
  comprehension processes, xi–xiv, 161–174, 193–202
  discourse processes, 201–202
  encoding processes, 23, 65, 67, 68, 182
  mental processes, 60, 65, 233, 234
  production processes, 140, 151, 199
  reading processes, 53, 64, 65, 74, 93, 213
  writing processes, 63, 64, 65, 66, 71, 73, 74, 140, 152, 155
Production
  discourse production, 64, 207
  text production, 13, 62, 64, 96, 100, 101, 110, 140, 141, 153
  written production, 139, 142
Professional, 11, 36, 55, 61–73, 75, 76–92, 95, 96, 100, 102, 113, 114, 123, 125–137, 147, 155, 193, 194, 195, 197, 198, 199, 200, 201, 204, 218, 258
Psycholinguistic, 11, 13, 14, 197
Psycholog-, 17, 18, 38, 93, 122
Punctuation, 6, 14, 16, 34, 77, 78, 82, 88, 106, 111, 123

Quality, 10, 23, 36, 56, 62, 72, 75–92, 95, 108, 109, 110, 111, 116, 133, 135, 140, 145, 152, 155, 233, 234

Readability, 18, 33–45, 79, 80
Read-, 53, 61–73, 77–78, 82–84, 90–91, 110, 113, 151–152, 205–215
Reasoning, 4, 5, 59, 60, 162, 193, 199, 220, 225, 227, 228, 229, 248, 251, 253
Recall, 20, 24, 31, 60, 67, 69, 70, 91, 98, 162, 173, 177, 178, 179, 180, 181, 182, 184, 185–186, 187, 188, 189, 190, 201, 252
Recogniz-, 17, 21, 23, 25, 29, 60, 63, 69, 70, 72, 74, 93, 109, 171, 181, 187, 188, 193, 197, 223, 232, 236, 246, 248, 254
Recommendations, 18, 29–31, 50, 53, 58, 60, 78, 152, 257
Referential, 40, 97, 100, 161, 188, 250, 252, 256
Reformulation, 194, 195, 196, 197, 199, 204
Representation, 151, 233–234
Resources, 15, 16, 49, 52, 65, 67, 72, 107, 108, 133, 141, 148, 155, 156, 181, 194, 197, 199, 202, 203, 208, 214, 236, 238, 242
Retrieval, 15, 65, 66, 67, 68, 69, 70, 171, 182, 197, 213
Review, 43, 45, 49, 50, 60, 61, 62, 63, 65, 68, 71–73, 75, 76, 77, 78, 80, 82, 84, 85, 86, 88, 89, 90, 114, 117, 118, 121, 132, 150, 208, 224
Rhetorical, 3, 10, 12–13, 14, 16, 63, 66, 69, 72, 126, 132, 133

Safety, 17, 18, 19, 20, 22, 29, 57, 58, 144, 148, 152, 217, 218, 220
Scale, 9, 110, 116, 118, 119, 172, 228
Scenario, 21, 65, 165, 166
Schema, 22, 31, 72, 73, 90, 100, 161, 163–164, 203–204, 214
Semantic-, 3, 5, 6, 7, 12, 13, 14, 15, 16, 24, 25, 28, 29, 64, 66, 71, 97, 100, 162, 164, 166, 181, 183, 184, 185, 187, 195, 197, 198, 200, 201, 207, 209, 211

Semiotic, 18, 23, 25–27
Sentence, 198–200
Sign, 20, 21–22, 24, 26, 27, 29, 98, 168, 218
Signaletic, 17, 18, 23, 29
Signals, 10, 11, 21, 37, 42, 177, 178, 182, 183, 184–186, 190, 191, 213, 234
Source, 21, 41, 61, 62, 68, 69, 70, 81, 86, 96, 106, 108, 128, 134, 156, 181, 193, 196, 198, 199, 204, 220, 247, 248, 251, 252, 253, 254
Specify-, 7, 43, 57, 64, 141, 148, 156, 165, 208, 235, 236
Speech, 7, 74, 81, 132, 194–195, 198, 240, 252
Spelling, 77, 82, 85
Storage, 23, 56, 67
Stories, 129, 164, 173, 174
Strategic, 45, 66, 211, 212, 240
Summarize, 15, 16, 17, 40, 43, 62, 69, 70, 95, 112, 189, 219
Superstructure, 37
Symbol, 18, 19, 20, 21, 23, 24, 25, 26, 27, 31, 53, 163, 166–168, 250, 252
Syntax-, 6, 10, 11, 12, 13, 25, 34–35, 37, 53, 59, 71, 77, 85, 89, 193, 195, 196, 197, 198, 199

Teach-, 73, 77, 89–92, 93, 108, 109–110, 111, 112, 121, 122, 138, 204
Technic-, 3–16, 46, 55, 107–123, 126, 128, 138, 205, 217, 219, 231, 232, 235, 240, 241, 249
Terminology, 4, 5, 6, 7, 53, 152, 221
Text, 7–14, 35–36, 40–44, 75–92, 95–105, 177–190, 234–235
  descriptive texts, 147, 189
  electronic texts, 208
  explanatory texts, 13
  expository texts, 177, 178, 184, 185, 186, 188, 190, 191, 201, 205
  informational texts, 96
  instructional texts, 13, 14, 96
  legal texts, 33–45
  narrative texts, 96, 100, 147, 165, 187, 188, 189, 201, 202
  prescriptive texts, 35, 39, 44
  procedural texts, 33–45, 49–60, 95–105, 183–184
  scientific texts, 164
  specialized texts, 38
  source texts, 70
  written texts, 14, 46, 62, 65, 90, 97, 100, 194, 239
Textbase, 161, 162, 163, 169, 171, 177, 178, 179, 180, 181, 182, 184, 185, 188, 189, 190, 207, 209, 210, 211
Topic, 66, 68, 70, 73, 74, 88, 92, 96, 113, 114, 118, 164, 177, 184, 186, 191, 197, 203, 205, 207, 211, 234
Training, 29, 57, 60, 81, 95, 106, 108–110, 113, 144, 146, 147, 148, 149, 150, 151, 154, 180, 181, 193, 197, 204, 226
Translat-, 61, 62, 63, 65, 67, 68, 152, 172, 193–202, 203, 204
Tutor, 107–123

Understanding, 17–29
User, 18, 49–60, 238–239

Verbalization, 77
Visuospatial, 234, 235, 236, 238, 240, 241, 242

Web-, 76, 122, 125–137, 153
Work-, xi–xiv, 14–16, 22–23, 78–81, 84, 85–89, 90, 139–154, 217–229
Working memory, 52, 65–66
Write-, 61–73, 139–154
Writing, 62–63, 65–73, 84–85, 107–123, 125–137

List of Volumes

Volume 1: Theories, Models and Methodology in Writing Research
Gert Rijlaarsdam, Huub van den Bergh, Michel Couzijn (Eds.) 1996
pages 558; Paperback, ISBN 90-5356-197-8

Volume 2: Effective Teaching and Learning of Writing. Current Trends in Research
Gert Rijlaarsdam, Huub van den Bergh, Michel Couzijn (Eds.) 1996
pages 388; Paperback, ISBN 90-5356-198-6

Volume 3: The Cognitive Demands of Writing. Processing Capacity and Working Memory Effects in Text Production
Mark Torrance, Gaynor Jeffery (Eds.) 1999
pages 113: Paperback, ISBN 90-5356-308-3

Volume 4: Knowing What to Write. Conceptual Processes in Text Production
Mark Torrance, David Galbraith (Eds.) 1999
pages 190; Paperback, ISBN 90-5356-307-5

Volume 5: Foundations of Argumentative Text Processing
Pierre Coirier, Jerry Andriessen (Eds.) 2000
Pages 273; Paperback, ISBN 90-5356-340-7

Volume 6: Metalinguistic Activity in Learning to Write
Anna Camps, kMarta Milian (Eds.) 2000
pages 228: Paperback, ISBN 90-5356-341-5

Volume 7: Writing as a Learning Tool
Päivi Tynjälä, Lucia Mason, Kirsti Lonka (Eds.) 2001
Hardbound, ISBN 0-7923-6877-0; Paperback, ISBN 0-7923-6914-9

Volume 8: Developmental Aspects in Learning to Write
Liliana Tolchinsky (Ed.) 2001
Paperback, ISBN 0-7923-7063-5; Hardbound, ISBN 0-7923-6979-3

Volume 9: Through the Models of Writing:
Denis Alamargot, Lucile Chanquoy (2001)
Paperback, ISBN 0-7923-7159-3; Hardbound, ISBN 0-7923-6980-7

Volume 10: Contemporary Tools and Techniques for Studying Writing
Thierry Olive, C. Michael Levy (Eds.) 2001
Hardbound, ISBN 1-4020-0035-9; Paperback, ISBN 1-4020-0106-1

Volume 11: New Directions for Research in L2 Writing:
Sarah Ransdell, Marie-Laure Barbier (Eds.) 2002
281 p. Paperback, ISBN 1-4020-0539-3; Hardbound, ISBN 1-4020-0538-5

Volume 12: Teaching Academic Writing in European Higher Education
Lennart Björk, Gerd Bräuer. Lotte Rienecker, Peter Stray Jörgensen (Eds.) 2003
240 p. Hardbound, ISBN 1-4020-1208-X; Paperback, ISBN 1-4020-1209-8

Volume 13: Revision: Cognitive and Instructional Processes
Linda Allal, Lucile Chanquoy, Pierre Largy (Eds.) 2004
248 p. Hardbound, ISBN 1-4020-7729-7

Volume 14: Effective Learning and Teaching of Writing. A Handbook of Writing in Education
Gert Rijlaarsdam, Huub van den Bergh & Michel Couzijn, M. (Eds.)
2nd ed., 2004, X, 670 p. 21 illus., Hardcover, ISBN: 1-4020-2724-9; Softcover, ISBN: 1-4020-2725-7

Volume 15: Writing in Context(s). Textual Practices and Learning Processes in Sociocultural Settings
Triantafillia Kostouli (Ed.) 2005
280 p., Hardcover, ISBN: 0-387-24237-6; Softcover, ISBN: 0-387-24238-4

Volume 16: Teaching Writing in Chinese Speaking Areas
Mark Shiu Kee Shum; De Lu Zhang (Eds.) 2005
276 p., Hardcover, ISBN: 0-387-26392-6

Volume 17: Writing and Digital Media
van Waes, Leijten & Neuwirth (Eds.) 2006
380 pp., Hardcover, ISBN: 0-08-044863-1

Volume 18: Computer Key-Stroke Logging and Writing
Sullivan & Lindgren (Eds.) 2006
248 pp., Hardcover, ISBN: 0-08-044934-4

Volume 19: Writing and Motivation
Hidi & Boscolo (Eds.) 2007
332 pp., Hardcover, ISBN: 978-0-08-045325-5

Volume 20: Writing and Cognition
Torrance, van Waes & Galbraith (Eds.) 2007
392 pp., Hardcover, ISBN: 978-0-08-045094-0